Analytics in Practice

Analytics in Practice

Soumendra Mohanty
Partner
Information Management Practice
Accenture India

Tata McGraw Hill Education Private Limited
NEW DELHI

McGraw-Hill Offices
New Delhi New York St Louis San Francisco Auckland Bogotá Caracas
Kuala Lumpur Lisbon London Madrid Mexico City Milan Montreal
San Juan Santiago Singapore Sydney Tokyo Toronto

Tata McGraw Hill

Published by Tata McGraw Hill Education Private Limited,
7 West Patel Nagar, New Delhi 110 008

ISBN-13 : 978-1-25-900576-3
ISBN-10 : 1-25-900576-3

Vice President and Managing Director—Asia-Pacific Region: *Ajay Shukla*
Executive Publisher—Professional: *R Chandra Sekhar*
Assistant Sponsoring Editor—Science, Technology and Computing: *Simanta Borah*
Manager—Production: *Sohan Gaur*
AGM—Sales and Business Development: *S Girish*
Deputy Marketing Manager—Science, Technology and Computing: *Rekha Dhyani*
General Manager—Production: *Rajender P Ghansela*
Assistant General Manager—Production: *B L Dogra*

Typeset at Print-O-World, 2579, Mandir Lane, Shadipur, New Delhi 110 008, and printed at Adarsh Printers, C-50-51, Mohan Park, Navin Shahdara, Delhi 110 032

Cover Design: Kapil Gupta

Cover Printer : A.P. Offset

RZCCRRCCDRACQ

The McGraw·Hill Companies

Advance Praise for Analytics in Practice

The book collates a lot of learning and research on analytics, targeting a mix of audiences. It is a source of summary knowledge for the enthusiast as well as a repository of information for solution architects and practitioners to jumpstart an actual implementation. Starting with the theory on quantitative techniques, the book effectively correlates it with real-life examples across multiple industry domains. It provides a detailed understanding of the actual implementations, which can be effectively leveraged for gaining a detailed understanding of analytics. It also acts as a ready reckoner during both the solution outline and design phases of an analytics project. The book is well structured and precisely written to enable use as a handy ready reckoner during analytics implementations. Should I ever get into the difficult role of helping my clients move towards analytics, I will re-read this book first and refer to it during the work.

Ahijit Chatterjee
Program Manager —Business Analytics and Optimization
IBM GBS

Analytics is a popular term, being used by many companies today. However, it is not always clear what these companies mean by analytics and whether they truly understand the potential analytics can bring in. In this book, Mr. Mohanty clarifies analytics by articulating a simple, straightforward approach coupled with examples and case studies to illustrate his points in a way that is meaningful to the novice reader as well as experts.

Mary Ohara
Senior Manager
Accenture

It has always been a struggle to make oneself familiar with Analytics and how to implement Analytics solutions. This book provides the right depth and breadth of information about Analytics for practitioners and is certainly a well-written book.

Shagufta Kohli
Analytics Practitioner

Very well-written; after reading the book I find myself immensely knowledgeable in Analytics.

Sudha Sahasrabudhe
BI Thought Leader

I wish this book was there when I was venturing into Analytics; it is a very valuable handbook for practitioners like us.

Anand Rawat
Analytics Practitioner

Analytics is the next management discipline, and this book is very timely for practitioners as well as managers.

Uttama Mukherjee
BI Thought Leader

Very insightful; I particularly liked the Business Analytics chapter. For years we have struggled to articulate the value of Analytics and its contribution to a company's performance. This book is of immense value for my day-to-day interactions with clients and practitioners.

Smita Deshpande
Analytics Practitioner

Foreword

During each transformational journey, many new ideas and concepts that must be culled for the nugget that can become the defining template of the next big thing, come forward. Analytics, around in theory for a long time but rather limited in practice, is one such concept that is full of promises to change the way we do business. There are few truly authoritative views around really executing an Analytics agenda from a practitioner's perspective—What is it? Where do you start? How do you design such solutions? This book is a work of scholarship that delves into the depths of the what, why and how's of Analytics, and it is very aptly titled *Analytics in Practice.* It is a work that explains the realms of Analytics from a practitioner's point of view.

In this new decade, when advancements in technology lead to such amazing new possibilities, there has been massive innovation in mobile and social technologies which, when correctly leveraged, will create more value for users, customers, vendors, and businesses. The best companies—from established global enterprises to pioneering start-ups—are creating incredible value by succeeding in a new way—leveraging distinct strands of technology and innovations to create new products, services, and offerings, all powered by Analytics. In what we can expect from someone as knowledgeable, prescient, and committed to innovations as Soumendra, the most critical knowledge bytes a practitioner needs to master are brought to life in this book.

Soumendra examines the founding principles of Information Management and very clearly links it to Analytics as the business optimization state. The value of this book is in that it not only reveals the heretofore unrecognized forces that have created the need for Analytics, but it goes beyond that to provide a clear and concise set of guidelines and methods to implement such concepts in practice. In a world where we are told that there is competition for anything and everything, and therefore insightfulness is a killer differentiating skill, Soumendra provides elaborate examples, by industry, to help the practitioners further appreciate the finer aspects of Business Analytics. At a time when we, technology professionals, inhale the astounding achievements in technology, industry relevance is extremely critical. In this book, Soumendra has done a tremendous job in illustrating the industry applications for Analytics, covering how to develop analytic solutions for a wide variety of industries, business models, and channels, including capital markets, insurance, telecom, travel and tourism, and e-commerce.

All practitioners who read this book will understand that Analytics is that 'next big thing', and there are well defined approaches, methods, tools, and solutions.

Soumendra's varied and successful career as a technology advisor, outsourcing executive, and implementation consultant makes him one of the industry's most provocative thought leaders. Most importantly, his fresh insights and wise counsel prepares us for deciding how to best navigate, compete, and excel in the realm of Analytics. The well-researched examples in this book will inspire you.

Practitioners always ask me: What is in store for the future? Where is technology going? What skills do we need to focus on? Predicting the future is simple. The future is whatever we imagine. What is ahead of us is whatever we innovate, and I am convinced that Analytics is that future.

Sajid Usman
Accenture Executive Partner and
Global Lead, Process and Information Management

Preface

Data Mining and Analytics is the buzzword of today, and not to forget, a whole lot of vendor literature in this area is fueling the momentum. Most often I am told, "Learn SAS—you will know what Analytics is all about!" I also keep hearing a lot about churn management, fraud detection, segmentation, clustering, predictive analytics, text mining, and web analytics—and all these are mindboggling and mindnumbing for someone learning the trade of doing analytics. Hence the following all-important questions—How do I learn these things? How do I develop analytical modules? What are the dos and don'ts?

These are typical of the questions I often faced while growing up as a practitioner. Some questions were easily answered by someone experienced in Data Mining and Analytics guiding me, but a whole lot of other questions sent me digging into a veritable library of books and articles on wide-ranging subjects, to get a simple answer. Much fundamental information that I thought should be at my fingertips, lay deeply buried in voluminous handbooks or obscure references.

This was the idea that chartered the course for this book. I have endeavored to collect here, in one convenient place, the type of information often called for by practitioners, developers, and specialists working in the Data Mining and Analytics area. Hence the reader will find topics ranging from "Foundations of Analytics" to "Business Analytics" and further to "Sentiment Analysis and Opinion Mining", useful case studies, tips as well as techniques, and best practices.

This book has evolved from a mere handbook to a well-endowed reference, which I hope will help fill a major gap between those who take a fancy to Data Mining and Analytics and those whose job is to develop Data Mining and Analytics modules as deliverables for their clients. Frequently, the resources assigned to develop Data Mining and Analytics models are ill prepared for the unique challenges of setting up a scalable repeatable process and applying the right methodologies. Therefore, I have included suggestions for following a detailed Data Mining and Analytics Life Cycle that can be more easily understood from theory to practice, including lists of dos and donts, as well as advice for improving across the development life cycle.

I have also included many sections in an effort to keep up with the rapid pace of change in the industry. While Data Mining, for long years, had stayed as a theory, analytics has seen widespread adoption across many industry verticals. I have included numerous examples of case studies and illustrations to explain in simple yet detailed terms how analytics is applied to industry verticals like banking, insurance, retail, and telecom, all in an attempt to make the book even more useful to my fellow practitioners.

When asked by a colleague who my intended audience were, I had to confess that I wrote the book for myself and for practitioners like me, whose responsibilities straddle the fence between learning what is new and delivering to the client relevant business deliverables. Data Mining and Analytics is a highly interdisciplinary effort, and the most successful analytical models are developed through close collaboration between experts in various areas of technology and business. Business, for example, would do well to understand what they need to do to capture larger percentages of the customers' wallet. On the other hand, technologists would take an implementation view and would look at the same problem by trying to understand what is the meaning of *share of wallet*, what are the levers influencing the customer, what are his/her preferences, etc.

It is often an educational and sometimes surprising experience for a Data Mining and Analytics practitioner to drown with mountains of data without understanding the business problem well. At the same time, it is also true that Data Mining and Analytics is not a silver bullet answer and certainly not a magic lamp that would give all sorts of solutions. Things do not always turn out as expected. The potential hazards are great, as are the economic consequences of an incorrect inference from past data. And this works both ways. However, a broad knowledge base is the common denominator that can bridge the gap and facilitate what can sometimes be a very rewarding process.

Although this book is specifically designed for practitioners, there is enough material here of general technical interest to make the book useful to anyone interested in Data Mining and Analytics.

The Table of Contents will help familiarize readers with the overall content of the book. Bibliographic references and recommended reading list follow each chapter. I apologize in advance for liberal use of Techno-Functional English language which, unfortunately, is still a necessity to explain a complex and technology-oriented topic like Data Mining and Analytics. If you find any repetition of concepts, those are deliberate, since I feel that certain important concepts need repeating.

ORGANIZATION OF THE BOOK

The book is organized into eleven concise chapters.

There are several books on Analytics. Some focus on statistical algorithms, some on consumer analytics, and some others on vendor tool based best practices. This book, though not exhaustive, aims to be a handbook for practitioners—helping them on methodology, technical architecture, analytics techniques, and best practices. At the same time, this book intends to hold the interest of those new to analytics, by giving them a deep insight into the analytics world.

Chapter 1 – Analytics in Practice: What it Means?

In this chapter, the concept of analytics is introduced. The business reasons behind undertaking an analytics initiative are outlined. What challenges business users face today, what are the trends in analytics, and what factors are important to put analytics in practice are explained.

Chapter 2 – Overview of Statistics, Data Mining, and Analytics

In this chapter, the basics of statistics, data mining, and analytics are touched upon. The foundational techniques of analytics are explained at length. This chapter also covers the scope of analytics, classical statistical techniques, and next generation analytics techniques with examples and case studies.

Chapter 3 – Effective Decision Making and Analytics

This chapter aims at establishing the role of analytics in effective decision making. Various approaches to analytics are also explained with a realistic point of view on how to identify analytics opportunities through inside-out and outside-in concepts.

Chapter 4 – Choosing the Right Analytics Technique and Tools

This chapter continues the discussion on analytics techniques as applicable to different business problem types, with a detailed discussion on opaque modeling versus transparent modeling.

Chapter 5 – Technical Architecture for Analytics Solutions

Vendor products and off-the-shelf analytics tools have considerably simplified the various architecture components that constitute the analytics technical architecture. However, it is essential for practitioners and architects to understand the various components of an analytics solution, how they are interlinked, how they perform, and what design considerations must be taken into account to develop a scalable and optimally functioning analytics solution. This chapter covers the technical architecture components including detailed points of view about development architecture and operational architecture.

Chapter 6 – Implementing Analytic Solutions

Implementing analytics solutions is very different from any of the other application implementations, including data warehousing solutions, and hence the design considerations are diverse. This chapter provides an in-depth and step-by-step approach to implementation of analytic solutions. There are also several best practices discussed in this chapter, providing invaluable tips and tricks to the practitioners.

Chapter 7 - Business Analytics and Applications

This chapter provides an industry perspective of analytics. It covers the data management, banking, insurance, stock exchanges, retail, and travel industries; the business problem is unique and diverse in nature. This chapter engages the readers with various applications of analytics relevant to business challenges with case studies.

Chapter 8 - Putting It together—Integrated View of Customers

At the very center of any business is the "customer". This chapter provides a unique perspective of the customer life-cycle value chain, how it influences and impacts business performance, and how we bring in analytics to understand the customer better and then formulate strategies to improve business performance. To enable customer analytics, it is essential to have an integrated view of the customer across business functions. This chapter serves as the definitive ground to design and develop a "single view of the customer" and how to use the single view through analytics techniques like segmentation and decision tree.

Chapter 9 - Taming the Unstructured—Text Mining

Understanding and interpreting the unstructured text has always been a challenge. This chapter covers the various approaches to analyze unstructured text. Information retrieval, tokenization parts of speech, categorization, and summarization are emerging concepts in text mining that are covered.

Chapter 10 - Sentiment Analysis and Opinion Mining

With the increasing popularity of social media networks, today's consumers have turned prosumers—they are playing a significant role in defining what a product should be, and their opinions are defining the marketing and sales strategies. This chapter aims to provide a foundational platform for practitioners to understand the various approaches adopted for sentiment analysis and opinion mining.

Chapter 11 - Online Business Channel and Web Analytics

The ever-increasing influence of the Internet as a business channel is well-established. Payment gateways, catalog-based services, and eCommerce are active components of any business strategy. This chapter covers various aspects of web analytics, case studies, and best practices.

Feedback

As readers, you are welcome to report any errata or omissions and to make suggestions for future editions. Please contact me if you feel you have information that would make a useful addition.

Practitioners live and breath through real-world problem-solving scenarios; no amount of theoretical knowledge will help them implement the solutions that will work in production like efficiency and effectiveness; they need more of "how to's" and less of "what it is". I have attempted to bring in all those practical tools and kits that will put at your fingertips the information you need to perform your "analytics work" more efficiently.

Thanks for reading.

SOUMENDRA MOHANTY

Acknowledgements

I would like to send a grateful nod to the experts and colleagues in Accenture's AIMS practice at the India Delivery Center. They have time and again provided their support and incisive insights, which eventually helped me write this book.

A special appreciation to the trio—Goofy, Cindy, and Jaycy—for being faithful critic in everything I wrote!

I am grateful to numerous clients. There is nothing comparable to real-world experiences gained while working with them, and those experiences have helped me a lot to further refine my thoughts in this book.

On the personal front, I am grateful for the love and support of my wife Snigdha, and sons Pratik and Pratyush—both superb analysts in their own right.

SOUMENDRA MOHANTY

Contents

CHAPTER 1

ANALYTICS IN PRACTICE: WHAT IT MEANS

Analytics is defined as the extensive use of data, statistical and quantitative analyses, explanatory and predictive modeling, and fact-based management to drive decision making.

Analytics is all about providing business users with better insights, particularly from operational data stored in transactional systems. The key consumer of these analytics is the *business user*, a person whose job is not directly related to analytics *per se* (e.g., a merchandiser, marketer, sales person), but who typically must use analytical tools to improve the results of a business process along one or more dimensions (e.g., profit, improved time to market, reduced cost to delivery, etc.). Fortunately, data mining, analytic applications, and business intelligence systems are now being better integrated with transactional systems creating a closed loop between operations allowing data to be analyzed faster and the analysis results quickly reflected in business actions.

Note: The terms data mining and analytics are used interchangeably here to denote the general process of exploration and analysis of data to discover and identify new and meaningful patterns in data.

BUSINESS USERS AND THEIR CHALLENGES

Regardless of advances in analytic systems, it continues to be the case that a business user, while an expert in his/her area, is unlikely also to be an expert in data analysis and statistics. Business users are expected to better utilize the extracted information and improve performance along multiple metrics (also known as enterprise performance management). To make decisions analysis-based, the business user must either rely on a data analyst, who would extract the data from various source systems, analyze those and iterate back with business users, or employ analytic applications that blend data analysis technologies with task-specific knowledge without the overhead of underlying technology knowhow.

In the first case, the business user must impart domain knowledge to the analyst, then wait till the analyst organizes and analyzes the data, and then communicates back the results. These results typically may raise further questions to be asked and hence several iterations are necessary before the business user can start acting on the analysis.

In the second case, analytic applications must not only incorporate a variety of data mining and analytical techniques, but also provide recommendations to the business user of how to best analyze data and present the extracted information.

Unfortunately, the gap between the relevant analytics and the critical needs of the intended business users still remains significant. The following challenges highlight characteristics of this gap:

- *The time to perform the overall cycle of collecting, analyzing, and acting on enterprise data must be reduced.* While business constraints may impose limits on reducing the overall cycle time, business users want to be empowered and rely less on other people to help with these tasks. Within this cycle, the time and analytic expertise necessary to analyze data must be reduced.
- *Clear business goals and metrics must be defined.* Data collection efforts must have clear goals. Once metrics are identified, organizations must strive to collect the appropriate data and transform them. In many situations, data analysis is often an afterthought, restricting the possible value of any analysis.
- *Analysis results must be distributed to a wider audience.* Most analysis tools are designed for quantitative analysts – very rich in statistical algorithms, not for the broader base of business users who need the output to be translated into language and visualizations that are appropriate for the business needs.
- *Data must be integrated from multiple sources.* The extract-transform-load (ETL) process is typically complex and its cost and difficulty are usually underestimated. Data must be cleansed and quality assured to provide relevant and accurate outcomes.
- *Acceptance criteria of the analytics models must be clearly stated;* care should be taken not to define a wish list, rather what is practical and what is important for the organization to achieve should be kept at the forefront.

TRENDS IN BUSINESS ANALYTICS

Let us discuss how the recent advancements in technology and increasing maturity in processes are helping bridge the gaps discussed above.

Verticalization

In order to reduce discovery cycle time, the analytics solutions are more and more getting verticalized. In other words, analytics solutions are becoming increasingly focused on industry specific problem solving. For example, how to analyze customer data to determine the effectiveness of a marketing campaign; how to analyze click-stream data generated by a web site to reduce shopping cart abandonment and improve ad effectiveness; about how an investment bank consolidates its general ledger and is able to produce various types of forecasts; or how an insurance company is able to analyze data in order to provide an optimally priced policy to an existing customer. The use of industry-specific knowledge is not limited to the components of analytic applications, but also affects how the extracted information is presented and accessed in each industry. For example, in banking industry there will not be much need of information to be shared across mobile devices. However for telecommunications, energy and utility industries it will require a different framework for information delivery to field force personnel than C level executives seating in a board room analyzing the company performance.

Comprehensive Models and Transformations for Insight

With the need to let business users analyze data and provide insight quickly, and the goal of reducing the reliance on analytics experts, comprehensible models are more commonly used than opaque models.

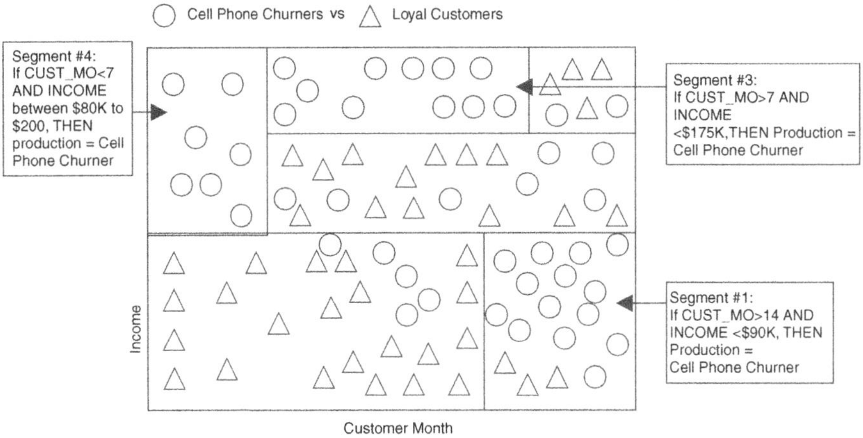

Figure 1.1 Segmentation of cell phone subscribers into churners vs. loyal customers.

Consider Fig. 1.1, which summarizes a segmentation technique to provide visually appealing, intuitive, relevant and precise information to the business users.

Figure 1.2 provides a very easy-to-understand visual representation of high life time value of customers using various attributes as decision points.

Business users prefer simple yet comprehensive models with rich visualization functionalities that show only a few and the most important attributes from a larger set of attributes that were determined by the analytics module. Business users do not want to deal with advanced statistical concepts. They want straightforward visualizations and task-relevant outputs.

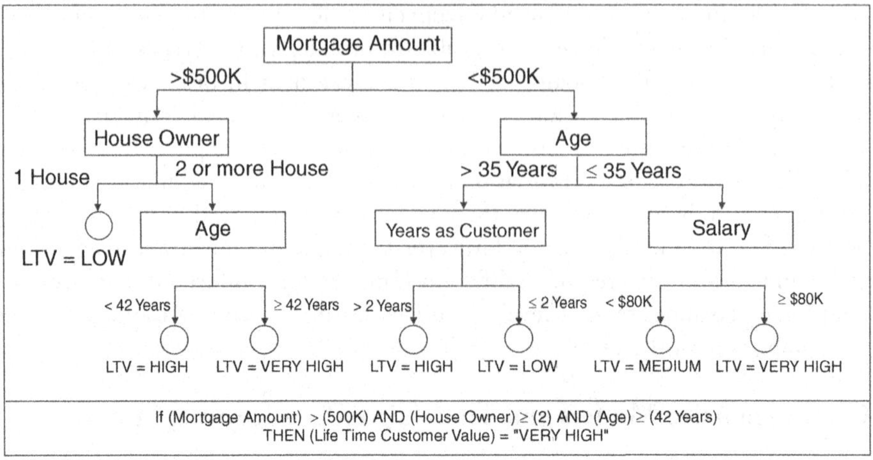

Figure 1.2 Decision tree technique of predicting life time value of customers based on certain characteristics.

ANALYTICS AS AN INTEGRAL PART OF THE DECISION MAKING ECOSYSTEM

Competitive forces and business dynamics have redefined the needs for data analysis capabilities. These are now being designed into processes, applications and systems, instead of being an afterthought.

Analysis of customer data has always attracted the most attention and has provided success in reducing customer attrition, improving customer profitability, increasing the value of e-commerce purchases, and increasing the response of direct mail and e-mail marketing campaigns. Advances in data integration technologies and data management have enabled collection of huge amount of data about customers, products, suppliers, and other third party data. Business has started demanding for sophisticated applications to analyze this data to provide insights about the performance of suppliers and partners, material expenditures, accuracy of sales forecasts to better control materials inventory, accuracy of production plans, the accuracy of plans for order delivery, etc.

The wide adoption of CRM and Supply Chain Management software has allowed enterprises to fully interface/integrate their demand and supply chains. Based on this integration, enterprises are now able to capture up-to-the-minute data about the demand for a particular product, as well as data of similar granularity about the corresponding supply situation. By analyzing these two data streams corporations are able to optimize the price of a particular product along several dimensions to ensure the available supply meets demand. For example, the price of a product may be different through one channel, e.g., the Web, than through another, e.g., in the retail store. Such price optimizations allow corporations to maximize the profit margin of each item sold while reducing their inventory.

Once corporations have been able to analyze data about their customers and their suppliers, it is only natural for them to begin analyzing data about their employees. A new generation of analytic applications allows enterprises to identify workforce trends, such as attrition rates, and perform tasks such as compensation and benefits analyses. Companies whose cost or revenue model is dependent on hourly models, e.g., contact centers or systems integrators, are able to use this new generation of workforce analytics to optimize staffing levels and skills requirements in order to minimize the number of employees that are not chargeable or utilized fully.

Specifically, the following key components are critical for a successful analytics solution:

- *Data collection* - You cannot analyze what you do not collect. So collecting rich data is critical.
- *Integration with multiple data sources* - Analysis is more effective when data is available from multiple sources. For example, in customer analytics it is important to merge data from multiple touch points, such as the web, call center, physical stores, and campaigns (both direct and online). Behavioral data can be more powerful when overlaid with demographic and socio-economic data from other sources.
- *Ability to create and manage single source of truth (unique identifiers)*- In order to help merge information from several sources and remove duplicate data, systems must generate unique keys to join data and store them. This is very critical from an analytics modeling perspective as well, since the model runs on a large de-normalized data set, it is important to resolve all sorts of data-related anomalies and ensure data consistency is maintained.
- *Hardware sizing, Performance Considerations and Scalability* - Data analysis requires significant hardware to deal with large amounts of data. Multiple iterations on trained data set is run before finalizing on the model. Often this process needs to re-look at the number of variables, types of models to be built, running against various samples of data, etc. Companies have traditionally underestimated the need for sophisticated IT infrastructure and powerful hardware to make analysis feasible in a timely manner.

ANALYTICS IN PRACTICE

Analytics has become an oft-quoted word in business. Whether in magazines, on television or on a sign posted at an airport, vendors are promoting the analytics message, often in very broad terms, to attract attention to their offerings. This buzzword continues to be popular as more businesses realize how the effective use of analytics can be a significant competitive advantage for their business. In today's tough economic environment, companies will need to secure customer loyalty by offering customers a more personalized experience. This increases the perceived value of their offerings so that customers' decisions are not driven solely on price. It presents an enormous challenge for organizations that are striving to defend and maintain their existing revenue base, let alone grow their revenues.

For many small and medium-sized companies, and even some large enterprises, it's not easy to derive benefits from analytics. In fact, many struggle to get started with analytics in their organization. In subsequent chapters of this book we will learn some key foundational aspects, so that you can get started with and, most importantly understand the life cycle of implementing an analytics solution. The four areas that will be discussed include:

- Defining the business problem
- Assessing and securing the data
- Selecting and using the right resources (human and software tools) including the right methodology
- Implementation—taking action, influencing change, and promoting a healthy culture.

Defining the Business Problem

In a broad sense, organizations are concerned with increasing revenue, decreasing costs, growing revenues faster than expenses, or some combination of increasing revenues and decreasing/managing costs.

Analytics can be used to develop a strategy to increase profitability by providing insights to the following questions: Does your organization understand/know the characteristics that differentiate your profitable customers from your unprofitable ones? Do you know which ones are leaving you to spend their money with one of your competitors? Could you grow revenues from the existing customer base by cross-selling and/or up-selling other products to them? Which types of customers (groups or segments) are likely to buy which products, when and in what order? Do you know which offer is best to send to your existing customers? These are all important questions that need to be thought-through if you want to develop a proactive strategy to retain or to acquire profitable customers.

As you embark on the analytics journey, it is advisable to start with a business objective that is critical to the success of your business and can be achieved in a short time frame—three to six months. This will ensure a measurable return on investment.

Accessing and Securing the Data

Once you have defined your business problem, the next step is to assess and secure the required data. *Data is at the core of any analytics project.*

Do you collect customer purchasing data, demographic data, customer loyalty information, and marketing and advertising response data? You may be able to perform better analytical investigations if you also gather more information such as pricing and marketing information on your competitors.

To get started with analytics, you don't need all the data. In fact, if you don't have any data as yet, don't despair. *Start collecting information about key business processes and then slowly in an iterative manner start collecting relevant data.* The data-collection process will be an iterative and interactive process. As you evaluate and understand the structure and format of the data and tie it to the business problem, you will gain a better understanding of what other data elements could be helpful. *It is also critical that your data strategy evolves over time, because your customers' preferences will change, as will your competitors'.* It is a continual learning and improvement process with analytics, because as your data gets better (more accurate and robust) over time, your analytical models will need to be refreshed and updated more often with the most current data to deliver improved forecasts and insights.

Selecting and Using the Right Resources

For an organization to benefit from analytics, it must have the "right" resources, which includes human resources, technology and methodology.

Harnessing Analytic Expertise

It is important to identify individuals who possess both an analytical mindset and strong business acumen along with some foundational statistics/mathematical training and background. Many companies underestimate the need to have individuals who can translate the applicability and benefits of the analysis to their business context. Organizations can choose to recruit internally, hire new employees, or engage consultants. The optimal decision for your organization will depend on several considerations including skills, capacity, and financial resources. It is essential that the individuals' primary responsibility is analytics.

As your need for analytic resources and expertise increases, you can hire specialists with extensive education in statistics or applied mathematics to supplement the team. Providing the right environment for your analytic staff is essential for their growth and development. It is like nurturing the growth of a plant—it will only blossom if it has the right growth elements: water, fertilizer and surrounding environment.

Analytics experts must also be open to learning and adapting to changes in technology and techniques. To nurture these qualities, internal activities (best-practices sharing, peer reviews and centers of excellence) and external activities (conferences, training and expert-to-expert workshops) are necessary to support growth and development. These can be crucial to unlocking innovation from your analytics team within your organization.

Choosing the Right Technology

Having the "right" technology in place is critical to a sustainable, long-term analytics foundation. Which technology and tool you will need largely depends on the size of your data, skills of the user base, complexities of business processes, etc. In addition, you will need to address the following areas:

- *Data preparation and cleansing* - Before any analysis can be done, data will need to be prepared and cleansed. Analytics experts along with line-of-business domain experts can provide guidance to the data stewards in your organization to prepare and cleanse the data for the type of analysis that will be performed.
- *Data analysis* - Your analytics experts will need a robust set of tools to perform the data analysis. While some initial progress can be accomplished with manual coding or tedious "back-of-the-envelope" assumptions, in the long run, the best benefits come from commercially available tools that allow you to build models quickly, assess results and modify the analysis based on feedback from domain experts. The tools should also facilitate self-documentation and automation of the analytical process for audit trails and manageability.
- *Tool/software selection* - Determine the range of expertise in your organization and therefore the broadness of the tool. Having a single tool that provides a graphical interface with easy point-and-click access—that also offers experts significant control (inside the black box) by tweaking defaults—will allow users at both ends of the spectrum to use the same tool. As your organization becomes more proficient with analytics, you'll find new challenges to address and be faced with bigger and more complex analysis needs. Over the years the size of the data required for analysis will grow exponentially. It is therefore important that you look for a tool that is scalable to handle large volumes of data—this will reduce the unnecessary costs associated with learning new tools in the future. In addition, look for tools that support a variety of techniques—this will enable you to compare multiple techniques and find the optimal combination to meet your business needs.
- *Reporting* - Visually appealing reports play a critical role in communicating results to the decision makers in your organization. Ideally, the way the results are demonstrated should be integrated in with your analysis software. This will ensure that the latest analysis and results are readily available, making it compelling for your company's decision makers to use analytics.

Analytics Methodology

Many IT managers and business analysts are so overwhelmed with the sheer volume of data that they do not know where to start. Given these massive amounts of data, many ask, how can we even begin to move from data to information? Is there a methodology that can guide us step by step? Are there best practices we can follow to do sampling, do visual representations for data exploration, do statistical analysis, modeling, and then assess the results.

While everybody wants to find out the illusive relationships and patterns that would otherwise be "hidden" in their transaction data, at the same time there are humungous challenges to overcome. Following are some of the common issues:

- Data are not properly aggregated
- Data are not prepared for analysis
- Relationships in the data are too complex to be seen readily via human observation
- Databases are too large to be processed economically as a whole.

All of these conditions are complex problems that present their own unique challenges. For example, organizing data by subject areas into data warehouses or data marts can solve problems associated with aggregation. Data that contain errors, missing values, or other problems can be cleaned in preparation for analysis. Relationships that are counter-intuitive or highly complex can be revealed by applying predictive modeling techniques such as neural networks, regression analysis, and decision trees as well as exploratory techniques like clustering, associations and sequencing. However, processing large databases en masse is another story—one that carries along with it its own unique set of problems.

Having a methodology and set of best practices to deal with such challenges is always a big plus. *Cross Industry Standard Process for Data Mining (CRISP-DM) and Sample, Explore, Modify, Model, Assess (SEMMA) are two most widely practiced Analytics/Data Mining methodologies.*

CRISP-DM

CRISP-DM was conceived in late 1996 by three "veterans" of the young and immature data mining forum. DaimlerChrysler (then Daimler–Benz) was already experienced, ahead of most industrial and commercial organizations, in applying data mining in its business operations. SPSS (then ISL) had been providing services based on data mining since 1990 and had launched the first commercial data mining workbench (Clementine, 1994). NCR, as part of its aim to deliver added value to its Teradata data warehouse customers, had established teams of data mining consultants and technology specialists to service its clients' requirements.

At that time, early market interest in data mining was showing signs of exploding into widespread uptake with numerous points of views around how to go about developing analytics/data mining applications. Key questions this group tried to address were:

- What is the standardized and right way of doing it?
- Is every new adopter of analytics/data mining going to have to learn by trial and error?
- How could we demonstrate to prospective customers that analytics/data mining is sufficiently mature to be adopted as a key part of their business initiatives?

The answer was a standard process model which is non-proprietary and freely available addressing the various phases of analytics/data mining application development for all practitioners.

The CRISP-DM data mining methodology is described in terms of a hierarchical process model, consisting of sets of tasks:

Business understanding: This initial phase focuses on understanding the project objectives and requirements from a business perspective; then converting this knowledge into a data mining problem definition, and a preliminary plan designed to achieve the objectives.

Data understanding: The data understanding phase starts with an initial data collection and proceeds with activities in order to get familiar with the data, to identify data quality problems, to discover first insights into the data or to detect interesting subsets to form hypotheses for hidden information.

Data preparation: The data preparation phase covers all activities to construct the final data set (data that will be fed into the modeling tool(s)) from the initial raw data. Data preparation tasks are likely to be performed multiple times and not in any prescribed order.

Modeling: In this phase, various modeling techniques are selected and applied and their parameters are calibrated to optimal values. Typically, there are several techniques for the same data mining problem type. Some techniques have specific requirements on the form of data. Therefore, stepping back to the data preparation phase is often necessary.

Evaluation: At this stage in the project you have built a model (or models) that appears (or appear) to have high quality from a data analysis perspective. Before proceeding to final deployment of the model, it is important to more thoroughly evaluate the model and review the steps executed to construct the model to be certain it properly achieves the business objectives.

A key objective is to determine if there is some important business issue that has not been sufficiently considered. At the end of this phase, a decision on the use of the data mining results should be reached.

Deployment: Creation of the model is generally not the end of the project. Even if the purpose of the model is to increase knowledge of the data, the knowledge gained will need to be organized and presented in a way that the customer can use it. It often involves applying "live" models within an organization's decision making processes, for example in real-time personalization of Web pages or repeated scoring of marketing databases. However, depending on the requirements, the deployment phase can be as simple as generating a report or as complex as implementing a repeatable data mining process across the enterprise. In many cases it is the customer, not the data analyst, who carries out the deployment steps. However, even if the analyst will not carry out the deployment effort it is important for the customer to understand up front what actions need to be carried out in order to actually make use of the created models.

SEMMA

SEMMA methodology is defined and popularized by SAS Institute and refers to the core process of developing analytics/data mining applications. Beginning with a statistically representative sample of data, SEMMA provides a framework to apply exploratory statistical and visualization techniques, select and transform the most significant predictive variables, model the variables to predict outcomes, and confirm a model's accuracy. Steps such as formulating a well defined business or research problem and assembling quality representative data sources are critical to the overall success of any data mining project. SEMMA is focused on the model development aspects of data mining:

Sample: Sample organization data by extracting a portion of a large data set big enough to contain the significant information, yet small enough to manipulate quickly. For optimal cost and performance, SAS Institute advocates a sampling strategy, which applies a reliable, statistically representative sample of large full detail data sources. Mining a representative sample instead of the whole volume reduces the processing time required to get crucial business information. If general patterns appear in the data as a whole, these will be traceable in a representative sample. If a niche is so tiny that it's not represented in a sample and yet so important that it influences the big picture, it can be discovered using summary methods. SAS Institute also advocates creating partitioned data sets as stated below:

- *Training* - used for model fitting.
- *Validation* - used for assessment and to prevent over fitting.
- *Test* - used to obtain an honest assessment of how well a model generalizes.

Explore: Explore organization data by searching for unanticipated trends and anomalies in order to gain understanding and ideas. Exploration helps refine the discovery process. If visual exploration doesn't reveal clear trends, you can explore the data through statistical techniques including factor analysis, correspondence analysis, and clustering. For example, in data mining for a direct mail campaign, clustering might reveal groups of customers with distinct ordering patterns. Knowing these patterns creates opportunities for personalized mailings or promotions.

Modify: Modify organization data by creating, selecting, and transforming the variables to focus the model selection process. Based on the discoveries in the exploration phase, you may need to manipulate the data to include information such as the grouping of customers and significant subgroups, or to introduce new variables. You may also need to look for outliers and reduce the number of variables, to narrow them down to the most significant ones.

Model: Model organization data by following techniques like un-supervised learning to search automatically for a combination of data that reliably predicts a desired outcome. Modeling techniques in data mining include neural networks, tree-based models, logistic models, and other statistical models, such as time series analysis, memory-based reasoning, and principal components. Each type of model has particular strengths, and is appropriate within specific data mining situations depending on the data. For example, neural networks are very good at fitting highly complex nonlinear relationships.

Assess: Assess the organization data by evaluating the usefulness and reliability of the findings from the data mining process and estimate how well it performs. A common means of assessing a model is to apply it to a portion of data set aside during the sampling stage. If the model is valid, it should work for this reserved sample as well as for the sample used to construct the model. Similarly, you can test the model against known data. For example, if you know which customers in a file had high retention rates and your model predicts retention, you can check to see whether the model selects these customers accurately. In addition, practical applications of the model, such as partial mailings in a direct mail campaign, help prove its validity.

By assessing the results gained from each stage of the SEMMA process, you can determine how to model new questions raised by the previous results, and thus proceed back to the exploration phase for additional refinement of the data.

Once you have developed the champion model, it then needs to be deployed to score new customer cases. Model deployment is the end result of data mining—the final phase in which the ROI from the mining process is realized.

Implementation: From Analysis to Action

In order to benefit, action must be taken based on the analysis! It is essential to continually adapt processes to accommodate new information and improved decision making. For instance, analytics may reveal that a major driver for products return is difficulty of usage and your customer service representatives are not aware of this problem in addition to them having not enough knowledge about the product to guide customers over phone. In this instance, the ACTIONS that might be driven by the analysis could be to provide additional training to staff to help customers over phone on "how to", quick tips, etc., and also to provide direct feedback to the product manufacturing company about the issues with their product. Imagine the amount of money spent on product launch campaigns. At one end while the increase in product sales figures are making the dealers and retailers happy, at the other end increase in product return numbers are showing a disturbing trend, which if not managed upfront, will spell doom for the product making company.

Monitoring the KPIs has become a standard practice for any business. If done regularly and diligently, these can flag alerts when it is time to take action and/or implement process changes so that the company continues to be successful. However, often it is seen that the insight is restricted to a core group of people within the company, whereas the real action and dying need for analytics is at the ground level. Thus, it is important to have an information management strategy that quickly disseminates relevant and actionable information to the shop floor users so that they can take actions quickly. *Often, organizations get started with analytics without giving enough consideration for how they will go from analysis to action.* As they mature, this becomes a restricting force hindering their ability to grow and gain exponential benefits from analytics.

BUILDING AN ANALYTICS CULTURE

Culture is the hardest piece to put into place in an organization. To understand if you are building an analytics-embracing culture, think about the responses from each person in the company to the following questions: Does everyone in the organization understand and appreciate how they use analytics to inform their decisions? Do individuals use gut instincts more than they rely on facts, numbers? While there is a role for intuition, analytics should substantiate the intuition. Also, to ensure that you are building an analytics-embracing culture, there needs to be focus and emphasis from the top. If this is constant and consistent, then everyone will adopt that culture. In other words, while the use of analytics needs to be bottom-up, the endorsement, emphasis and commitment must resonate from the highest levels of the organization.

You also need to critically evaluate whether you are fostering an environment that supports appropriate risk taking and does not penalize every failure. Build a culture where people are not afraid of change. If the organization is unwilling to embrace change, you may never see the benefits from analytics because of the lack of will to execute on the insights from the analysis.

A word of caution: *If the organization does not build the right culture, executives may become overtly focused on watching monthly KPIs and concerned solely with revenue growth. Alternatively, they could blindly implement the recommendations without appropriate consideration to business relevance. Both instances could prove to be fatal mistakes; there is no substitute for business acumen and relevance.*

INTEGRATION OF ANALYTICS WITH ACTION AND MEASUREMENT

Increasingly, analytics users are asking two key questions, "How do I turn discovered information into action?" and "How do I know the effect of each action?" While in the past, success stories of data mining ended with a novel analytical result, it is becoming increasingly necessary that analytic solutions use the results as a starting point towards the critical next steps—action and measurement. It is no longer enough for cluster-discovery algorithms, for example, to uncover interesting groups of customers. *The successful analytic solution must make it easier for the user to grasp the significance of these clusters in the context of the business action plan: "Here are people with a propensity to purchase new fashions."*

Integration with other business processes and systems within the organization is a key to both action and measurement. For example, the analytic application identifies customers likely to respond to a promotion, but if it takes a bunch of

IT specialists a good amount of time to incorporate the relevant data into the campaign management system to run and execute the promotion, then there is a critical dependency and may introduce latency in "insight to action" cycle. Similarly, if promotion targeting solutions enable distribution of catalogs with optimized promotions, but the order submission system isn't tied closely back into the analytics, the resulting lag in the ROI reports will prevent a timely adjustment in the next catalog mailing. These types of integration between operation and analytics systems have seen major initiatives in the last five years, including entire products whose value proposition is precisely the optimization of the collect-analyze-act-measure cycle.

END POINTS

Business value is measured as progress towards bridging the gap between the needs of the business user and the accessibility and usability of analytic tools. In an effort to make analytics more relevant and tangible to the business user, it is highly critical to put "analytics in practice". Lately, analytics solutions have started to focus more and more on specific vertical applications and tailoring the results and interfaces towards the business audience, so they are comprehensive and provide relevant insight. For ease of use, simpler and effective deployment, and optimum value, increasingly it is becoming a necessity to have analytics embedded within the business processes and applications/systems landscape of the organization. On the other hand, issues such as data collection, storage, and processing specific to analytics are equally important issues in overall system design and which must be carefully architected to reap the benefits.

In efforts to broaden the effectiveness of analytics in the business processes, solutions are emerging that go beyond the customer facing applications, reaching "behind the scenes" to applications in sales, marketing, supply chain visibility, price optimizations, and workforce analysis. Finally, in order to achieve full impact and value, an increasing number of analytic solutions are making results actionable and measurement of changes key components.

Analytics can be a powerful component of your company strategy in the recovering global economy, especially with increasing customer expectation, intensified competition and the necessity to secure customer loyalty and grow profitability. Recent advancements in computer processing power, massive data stores and analytics capabilities today offer the ability to glean insights like never before. Analytics has become an essential part of doing business. Think of analytics as a continual improvement process and not a onetime event. Companies that embrace and develop a deliberate strategy to incorporate analytics into their DNA will realize long-term benefits. It's not too late to get started, but failure to integrate fact-based decision making and analytical insights could be a grave mistake and one that, in the long term, will differentiate the winners from the losers.

REFERENCES

Davenport, Thomas H. and Harris, Jeanne G., *Competing on Analytics,* Harvard Business School Press, March 2007.

Pyle, D., *Business Modeling and Data Mining* (The Morgan Kaufmann Series in Data Management Systems), May 2003.

CRISP-DM: Cross Industry Standard Process for Data Mining.

SEMMA: SAS Institute Inc: SAS Enterprise Miner.

CHAPTER 2

OVERVIEW OF STATISTICS, DATA MINING, AND ANALYTICS

Leveraging business data can be a challenge for companies that need to respond to rapidly evolving markets and changing customer dynamics. Analyzing business conditions requires analytic horsepower beyond conventional query and reporting tools.

Data mining and Analytics is an iterative process of discovering hidden information from large databases and thus allowing businesses to make proactive, knowledge-driven decisions. Most companies already collect and refine massive quantities of data. There are a number of specialized statistical algorithms, data mining and analytics techniques, which run through massive databases to find answers to questions such as, "Which clients are most likely to respond to my next promotional mailing, and why?"

However, before we delve deep into the realms of analytics, we need to understand the foundational components and the basic techniques of statistics, data mining and analytics. Several examples of analytical techniques illustrating their relevance to business problems as well as a basic description of how to deliver the value of analytics to end-users have been discussed throughout this chapter.

THE FOUNDATIONS OF ANALYTICS

Analytics techniques are the result of a long process of research and product development. This evolution began when business data first started getting stored on computers, thereby enabling software programs and algorithms to be developed to analyze this data without spending too much of a manual effort. Continued improvements in data access and advances in statistical analysis techniques pushed the envelope even further allowing users to navigate through their data quickly, and most importantly helped them understand the facts buried within the data. Analytics took this evolutionary process beyond after the fact analysis to prospective- and proactive analysis. With the advances in technology, we can say now analytics is ready for widespread adoption in the business community because it is supported by technologies that are now sufficiently mature to handle:

- Exploding volume of data,
- Powerful multiprocessing architectures, and
- Increased sophistication in data mining algorithms

Commercial databases have grown at unprecedented rates. The obvious needs for improved computational engines are now being met in a cost-effective manner with parallel multiprocessor technologies like grid computing. Statistical and data mining algorithms embody techniques that have existed for at least 10 years, but have only recently been implemented as mature, reliable, understandable tools that consistently outperform older statistical methods.

In the evolution from business data to business information, each new step is built upon the previous one. For example, dynamic data access is critical for drill-through in data navigation applications, and the ability to store large databases is critical to analytics. From the user's point of view, the four phases listed in Table 2.1 were revolutionary because they allowed new business questions to be answered quickly and accurately.

Table 2.1 Evolution from business data to business transformations

Evolutionary Step	*Business Question*	*Enabling Technologies*	*Characteristics*
Data Collection	What was my total revenue in last five years?	Computers, Tapes, Disks	Retrospective static data delivery
Data Access	What were the unit sales in Seattle last March?	Relational DBMS, Structured Query Language (SQL), ODBC	Retrospective dynamic data delivery—selection based
Data Warehousing and Decision Support	What were the unit sales in Seattle last March? Drill down to Bellevue and Redmond and also give me a comparative analysis of February and April data	OLAP, multi-dimensional databases, data warehouses	Retrospective dynamic data delivery at multiple levels
Data Mining/Analytics	What is likely to happen to Bellevue unit sales in next 3 months?	Advanced algorithms, statistical analysis, what-if scenarios	Prospective proactive information delivery

The core components of data mining technology have been under development for decades, in research areas such as statistics, artificial intelligence, and machine learning. Today, the maturity of these techniques, coupled with high-performance relational database engines and broad data integration innovations, make these technologies practical to be put into wide spread usage across industry.

THE SCOPE OF DATA MINING AND ANALYTICS

Data mining derives its name from the similarities between searching for valuable business information in a large database, e.g., finding linked products in gigabytes of store scanner data, and mining a mountain for a vein of valuable ore. Both processes require either digging deep through an immense amount of raw material, or intelligently probing it to find exactly where the value resides. Below are some of the commonly quoted examples:

- *Automated prediction of trends and behaviors* - Analytics automates the process of finding predictive information in large databases. Questions that traditionally required extensive hands-on analysis can be answered directly from the data, quickly. A typical example of a predictive problem is targeted marketing. Analytics uses data on past promotional mailings to identify the targets most likely to maximize return on investment in future mailings. Other predictive problems include forecasting bankruptcy and other forms of default, and identifying segments of a population likely to respond similarly to given events.
- *Automated discovery of previously unknown patterns* - Data mining algorithms and analytics techniques can analyze very large databases and identify previously hidden patterns in one step. An example of pattern discovery is the analysis of retail sales data to identify seemingly unrelated products that are often purchased together. Other pattern discovery problems include detecting fraudulent credit card transactions and identifying anomalous data that could represent data entry keying errors.

So, how do the data mining and analytics capabilities find these answers? There are a host of specialized techniques and products which assist in analyzing voluminous data. Table 2.2 contains a glossary of data mining and analytics terms which will be often referred throughout this book.

Table 2.2 Glossary of analytics/data mining terms

Terminology	*Description*
Analytical Model	A structure and process for analyzing a data set. For example, a decision tree is a model for the classification of a data set.
Anomalous Data	Data that result from errors (for example, data entry keying errors) or that represent unusual events. Anomalous data should be examined carefully because it may carry important information.
Artificial Neural Networks	Non-linear predictive models that learn through training and resemble biological neural networks in structure.
CART	Classification and Regression Trees. A decision tree technique used for classification of a data set. Provides a set of rules that you can apply to a new (unclassified) data set to predict which records will have a given outcome. Segments a data set by creating 2-way splits. Requires less data preparation than CHAID.
CHAID	Chi Square Automatic Interaction Detection. A decision tree technique used for classification of a data set. Provides a set of rules that you can apply to a new (unclassified) data set to predict which records will have a given outcome. Segments a data set by

Table 2.2 *Contd.*

Terminology	*Description*
	using chi square tests to create multi-way splits. Preceded, and requires more data preparation than, CART.
Classification	The process of dividing a data set into mutually exclusive groups such that the members of each group are as "close" as possible to one another, and different groups are as "far" as possible from one another, where distance is measured with respect to specific variable(s) you are trying to predict. For example, a typical classification problem is to divide a database of companies into groups that are as homogeneous as possible with respect to a creditworthiness variable with values "Good" and "Bad."
Clustering	The process of dividing a data set into mutually exclusive groups such that the members of each group are as "close" as possible to one another, and different groups are as "far" as possible from one another, where distance is measured with respect to all available variables.
Data Cleansing	The process of ensuring that all values in a data set are consistent and correctly recorded.
Data Mining	The extraction of hidden predictive information from large databases.
Data Navigation	The process of viewing different dimensions, slices, and levels of detail of a multi-dimensional database. See OLAP.
Data Visualization	The visual interpretation of complex relationships in multi-dimensional data.
Data Warehouse	A system for storing transactional data in a subject oriented manner and delivering clean and consistent to the enterprise for consumption.
Decision Tree	A tree-shaped structure that represents a set of decisions. These decisions generate rules for the classification of a data set. See CART and CHAID.
Dimension	In a flat or relational database, each field in a record represents a dimension. In a multi-dimensional database, a dimension is a set of similar entities; for example, a multi-dimensional sales database might include the dimensions Product, Time, and City.
Exploratory data analysis	The use of graphical and descriptive statistical techniques to learn about the structure of a data set.
Genetic Algorithms	Optimization techniques that use processes such as genetic combination, mutation, and natural selection in a design based on the concepts of natural evolution.
Linear Model	An analytical model that assumes linear relationships in the coefficients of the variables being studied.
Linear Regression	A statistical technique used to find the best-fitting linear relationship between a target (dependent) variable and its predictors (independent variables).
Logistic Regression	A linear regression that predicts the proportions of a categorical target variable, such as type of customer, in a population.
Multi-dimensional Database	A database designed for on-line analytical processing. Structured as a multi-dimensional hypercube with one axis per dimension.

Table 2.2 *Contd.*

Terminology	*Description*
Multiprocessor Computer	A computer that includes multiple processors connected by a network. See parallel processing.
Nearest Neighbor	A technique that classifies each record in a data set based on a combination of the classes of the k record(s) most similar to it in a historical data set. Sometimes called a k-nearest neighbor technique.
Non-Linear Model	An analytical model that does not assume linear relationships in the coefficients of the variables being studied.
OLAP	On-line analytical processing. Refers to array-oriented database applications that allow users to view, navigate through, manipulate, and analyze multi-dimensional databases.
Outlier	A data item whose value falls outside the bounds enclosing most of the other corresponding values in the sample. May indicate anomalous data. Should be examined carefully; may carry important information.
Parallel Processing	The coordinated use of multiple processors to perform computational tasks. Parallel processing can occur on a multiprocessor computer or on a network of workstations or PCs.
Predictive Model	A structure and process for predicting the values of specified variables in a data set.
Prospective Data Analysis	Data analysis that predicts future trends, behaviors, or events based on historical data.
RAID	Redundant Array of Inexpensive Disks. A technology for the efficient parallel storage of data for high-performance computer systems.
Retrospective Data Analysis	Data analysis that provides insights into trends, behaviors, or events that have already occurred.
Rule Induction	The extraction of useful if-then rules from data based on statistical significance.
SMP	Symmetric multiprocessor. A type of multiprocessor computer in which memory is shared among the processors.
Terabyte	One trillion bytes.
Time Series Analysis	The analysis of a sequence of measurements made at specified time intervals. Time is usually the dominating dimension of the data.

HOW ANALYTICS WORKS?

How exactly analytics is able to tell us important things that we did not know, or how is it able to predict what is going to happen next? The technique that is used to perform these feats in analytics is called *modeling*.

Modeling is simply the act of building a model in one situation where you know the answer, and then applying it to another situation that you don't.

For instance, if you were looking for a sunken Spanish galleon on the high seas the first thing you might do is to research the times when Spanish treasure had been found by others in the past. You might note that these ships often tend to be found off the coast of Bermuda and that there are certain characteristics to the ocean currents, and certain routes that have likely been taken by the ship's captains in that era. You note these similarities and build a model that includes the characteristics that are common to the locations of these sunken treasures. With these models in hand you sail off looking for treasure where your model indicates that it might be the most likely one given a similar situation in the past. Hopefully, if you have got a good model, you find your treasure.

This act of model building is thus something that people have been doing for a long time, certainly before the advent of computers or data mining and analytics as established technology. What happens on computers, however, is not much different than the way people build models. Computers are loaded up with lots of information about a variety of situations where an answer is known and then the analytics applications on the computer must run through that data and distill the characteristics of the data that should go into the model. Once the model is built it can then be used in similar situations where we don't know the answer.

For example, let us say that you are the director of marketing for a telecommunications company and you'd like to acquire some new long distance phone customers. You could just randomly go out and mail coupons to the general population—just as you could randomly sail the seas looking for sunken treasure. In neither case would you achieve the results you desired and of course you have the opportunity to do much better than random—you could use your business experience stored in your database to build a model. As the marketing director you have access to a lot of information about all of your customers: their age, sex, credit history, where they stay, where their relatives stay and their long distance calling usage. The good news is that you also have a lot of information about your prospective customers as well: their age, sex, credit history, where they are staying, and do they have relatives not staying in the near vicinity, etc. Your problem is that you don't know the long distance calling usage of these prospects (since they are most likely now customers of your competition). You'd like to concentrate on those prospects who have large amounts of long distance usage. You can accomplish this by building a model. Table 2.3 illustrates the data used for building a model for new customer prospecting.

Table 2.3 Model for new customer prospecting based on known customer data

Type of Data	*Existing Customers*	*Prospects*
General information (e.g., demographic data)	Known	Known
Proprietary information (e.g., customer transactions)	Known	Unknown

The goal in prospecting is to make some calculated guesses about the information in the lower right hand quadrant based on the model that we build going from customer general information to customer proprietary information. For instance, a simple model for a telecommunications company might be:

- 98% of my existing customers who make more than $60,000/year spend more than $80/month on long distance.

- You also have found an interesting pattern in your data—your existing customers spent a lot of money in the first few months when they moved in to a new location.

This model could then be applied to the prospect data to try to tell something about the proprietary information that this telecommunications company does not currently have access to. With this model in hand, new customers can be selectively targeted—you can now send targeted mailers with attractive discount offers and other value-add services to the selected group of prospects who earn more than $60,000 and have recently moved from other location. The chances of success of your campaign have now gone from "random" to "predictive".

Table 2.4 shows another common scenario for building models—predict what is going to happen in the future.

Table 2.4 Approach to build and test models

Type of Data	*Yesterday*	*Today*	*Tomorrow*
Demographic data, Marketing plans	Known	Known	Known
Customer Transactions	Known	Known	Unknown

If someone told you that he had a model that could predict customer usage how would you know if he really had a good model? The first thing you might try would be to ask him to apply his model to your customer base, where you already knew the answer. With data mining, the best way to accomplish this is by setting aside some of your data (test data set) to isolate it from the mining process. Once the mining is complete, the results can be tested against the test data set to confirm the model's validity. If the model works, its observations should hold true for rest of the data.

DATA MINING AND ANALYTICS—ARE THEY SAME?

In reality, there is probably very little difference between data mining and analytics. However, from an applications and usage perspective, analytics has gained much wider acceptance in the industry, whereas the broader discipline of statistics and data mining are most widely used for research and development purpose.

A wide range of companies have deployed successful applications of data mining. While early adopters of this technology have tended to be in information-intensive industries, such as financial services, telecommunication, retail, and healthcare, the technology is applicable to any company looking to explore large amount of their transactional data and make informed decisions. Two critical factors for success with data mining are: a large, well-integrated data warehouse, and a well-defined understanding of the business process within which data mining is to be applied (such as customer prospecting, retention, fraud detection, price optimization, and so on).

Some examples of successful data mining and analytic applications are:

- A pharmaceutical company can analyze the recent activities of its sales force to improve targeting of high-value physicians and determine which marketing activities will have the greatest impact in the next few months. The data to be analyzed can include competitor market activity as well as information about the local healthcare systems. The results can then be distributed to the sales force.

- A credit card company can leverage its customer transaction data to identify customers most likely to be interested in a new credit product. Using a small test mailing, the attributes of customers with an affinity for the product can be identified. Having specific campaigns to reach these customers and converting them from prospects to customers could more or less result in a 20-fold decrease in costs for targeted mailing campaigns over conventional mass mailing approaches.
- A diversified transportation company with a large direct sales force can apply data mining to identify the best prospects for its services. Using data mining to analyze its own customer experience, this company can build a unique segmentation identifying the attributes of high-value prospects. Applying this segmentation to a general business database such as those provided by Dun & Bradstreet can yield a prioritized list of prospects by region.
- A large consumer package goods company can apply data mining to improve its sales process to retailers. Data from consumer panels, shipments, and competitor activity can be applied to understand the reasons for brand and store switching. Through this analysis, the manufacturer can select promotional strategies that best reach their target customer segments.

Analytics is the capability of harnessing business information from otherwise huge stockpile of enterprise transactional data. The term analytics refers to the applied use of statistical techniques and data mining to gain understanding and value from structured and unstructured data in enterprise, line of business, departmental and third-party databases and repositories.

The research firm Gartner Inc. has described - "Analytics leverage data in a particular functional process (or application) to enable context-specific insight that is actionable."

Analytics measure ratios and percentages, often employing complex statistical and mathematical algorithms to understand relationships within and among data sets. Statistical methods are applied to both historic and near real-time data for separate or combined purposes. One practical application of Analytics is the automatic sending of alerts or notifications when a business event needs your attention, such as decreasing inventory levels or a critical customer situation. Analytics helps by providing business analysts with the ability to investigate data relationships and discover new business factors previously hidden in the huge volume of data that exists in the business world today.

On the other hand, Data mining is, in some ways, an extension of statistics, with a few artificial intelligence and machine learning twists thrown in. Like statistics, data mining is not a business solution it is just an iterative process.

For example, consider a catalog retailer who needs to decide who should receive information about a new product. A historical database contains information of previous interactions with customers and their demographics, such as age, zip code, etc. The data mining software would use this historical information to build a model of customer behavior that could be used to predict which customers would be likely to respond to the new product. By using this information a marketing manager can select only the customers who are most likely to respond. The operational business software can then feed these recommendations to the appropriate touch point systems (call centers, direct mail, web sites, email systems, etc.) so that the right customers receive the right offers.

Statistical techniques are driven by the data and are used to discover patterns and build predictive models. And from the users perspective an easily explainable outcome is much desirable keeping away the algorithms and statistical formulae hidden somewhere else.

Analytics consists of two distinct approaches and application areas:

- Descriptive Modeling (who/where are our customers and what do they need?) and
- Predictive Modeling (what's the most profitable way of communicating with each customer?).

Descriptive models search for previously unknown patterns and associations in the data using some of the techniques like:

- *Cluster Analysis* - Cluster analysis encompasses a number of different classification algorithms to help organize customers into clusters when we do not have any hypotheses but are exploring our data.
- *Decision Trees* - Decision trees are used to classify customers into different groups by using a hierarchical system of sorting customers based on various partitioning rules (e.g., age over 40 vs. age under 40; income over $40k vs. income under $40k, presence of children vs. no children, etc.).
- *Affinity analysis of transactions ("market-basket analysis")* - To detect relationships or associates between consumer preferences (e.g., consumers who buy product A, often also buy product B).

Predictive Modeling is a class of models that predicts the likelihood that a customer will respond to marketing, sales and service actions, based upon historical data. In addition, predictive models are built to determine what customers might do of their own accord, e.g., propensity to close the account, propensity to move life stage segment, etc. Models can be based on positive and/or negative responses to previous actions:

- Positive response is typically used in a situation such as predicting the likelihood a customer will purchase a product or service. The data consist of customers who have exhibited the desired behavior previously compared with a group of people who did not.
- Negative response is usually applied to predict attrition or the likelihood a person will not exhibit the desired behavior, such as a drop in a membership.

Both the modeling approaches (Descriptive and Predictive) have widespread industry usage. Few more examples are given here:

- Customer/Consumer segmentation (base segmentation and market segmentation for several business objectives, e.g., loyalty, brand management, differentiated customer experience, etc.)
- Customer behavior analysis
- Propensity and churn risk (predictive) models
- Lead generation and prospect models
- Precision targeting for acquisition/retention/development
- Loyalty analytics (for loyalty management)
- Pricing analytics (for pricing management)
- Customer experience analytics (for experience optimization)
- Identify economically attractive customers to serve their requirements
- Prioritize customers in terms of customer value, likelihood to adopt new offers and probability of leaving or reducing spend
- Identify customer behavior and need patterns to better focus product/service development
- Quantify impact of different customer experience elements in terms of overall customer satisfaction, retention, and profitability

Before we proceed deeper into analytics, it is important to understand the basics of how to understand data, since at the core of analytics is grouping, counting, and summarizing the data, and a lot of other statistical techniques.

DATA, STATISTICS AND PROBABILITY

One thing that is always true about analytics is that there is always some form of statistics applied to data to find patterns and trends. At the very basic level we use counting, summarization, grouping, etc. to analyze data and represent the findings through standard bar charts, pie charts, etc. There is also a complex side of statistics but the idea of collecting data and counting it is often at the base of even those more sophisticated techniques. The first step then in understanding statistics is to understand how the data is collected into a higher level form—one of the most notable ways of doing this is by following some of the classical statistics techniques.

CLASSICAL STATISTICS TECHNIQUES

Histograms

One of the best ways to summarize data is to provide a histogram of the data. In the simple example database shown in Table 2.5, we can create a histogram of eye color by counting the number of occurrences of different colors of eyes in our database. For this example, a database consisting of 10 records is fairly easy to do, and the results are only slightly more interesting than the database itself. However, for a database of many more records this is a very useful way of getting a high level understanding of the database.

Table 2.5 Sample database of customers

ID	*Name*	*Age*	*Balance ($)*	*Income*	*Eyes*	*Gender*
1	Amy	62	0	Medium	Brown	F
2	Al	53	1,800	Medium	Green	M
3	Betty	47	16,543	High	Brown	F
4	Bob	32	45	Medium	Green	M
5	Carla	21	2,300	High	Blue	F
6	Carl	27	5,400	High	Brown	M
7	Donna	50	165	Low	Blue	F
8	Don	46	0	High	Blue	M
9	Edna	27	500	Low	Blue	F
10	Ed	68	1,200	Low	Blue	M

In the above histogram eye color can serve as a very effective predictor, no matter if there are 100 customer records in the database or 100 million. There are, however, other predictors that have many more distinct values and can create a much more complex histogram. Consider, for instance, the histogram of ages of the customers in the population. In this case the histogram can be more complex but can also be enlightening. Try finding the histogram of your customer data as it does in Fig. 2.1.

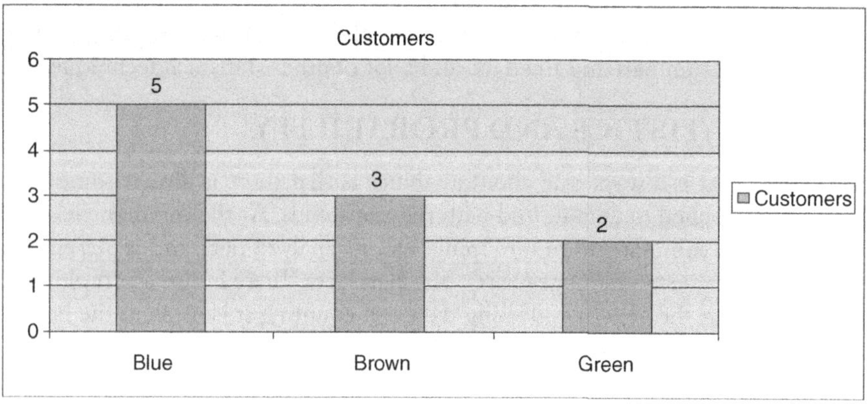

Figure 2.1 Histogram of customers with eye color as determinant.

Figure 2.1 shows the number of customers with various eye colors. This summary can quickly show important information about the database such as, that blue eyes are the most frequent.

The histogram in Fig. 2.2 shows the number of customers of different ages and quickly tells the viewer that the majority of customers are over the age of 50.

In fact, it is also possible to build an intuition about other important factors. Such as; the average age of the population and the maximum and minimum age. All of which are important. These values are called summary statistics. Some of the most frequently used summary statistics include:

- Max—the maximum value for a given predictor.

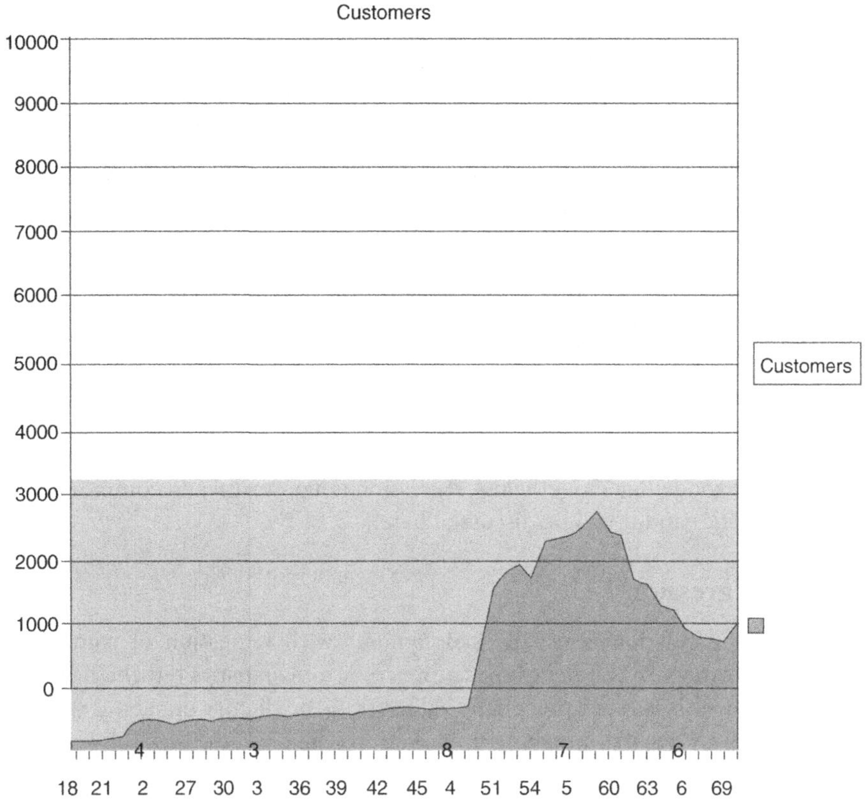

Figure 2.2 Histogram of number of customers of different ages.

- Min—the minimum value for a given predictor.
- Mean—the average value for a given predictor.
- Median—the value for a given predictor that divides the database as nearly as possible into two databases of equal numbers of records.
- Mode—the most common value for the predictor.
- Variance—the measure of how spread-out the values are from the average value.

Sometimes the shape of the distribution of data can be calculated by an equation rather than just represented by the histogram. This is called data distribution. Like a histogram a data distribution can be described by a variety of statistics. Many data distributions are well described by just two numbers, the mean and the variance.

The mean is something most people are familiar with. The variance, however, can be problematic. The easiest way to think about it is that it measures the average distance of each predictor value from the mean value over all the records in the database. If the variance is high it implies that the values are all over the place and are very different. If the variance is low most of the data values are fairly close to the mean. To be precise the actual definition of the variance uses the square of the distance rather than the actual distance from the mean and the average is taken by dividing the squared sum by one less than the total number of records. In terms of prediction a user could make some guess at the value of a predictor without knowing anything else but just by knowing the mean and also gain some basic sense of how variable the guess might be based on the variance.

Statistics for Prediction

In this book the term "prediction" is used for a variety of types of analysis that may elsewhere be more precisely called regression. It is done so in order to simplify some of the concepts and to emphasize the common and most important aspects of predictive modeling. Nonetheless, regression is a powerful and commonly used tool in statistics and it will be discussed here.

Linear Regression

In statistics prediction is usually synonymous with regression of some form. There are a variety of different types of regression in statistics but the basic idea is that a model is created that maps values from predictors in such a way that the lowest error occurs in making a prediction. The simplest form of regression is simple linear regression that just contains one predictor and a prediction. The relationship between the two can be mapped on a two dimensional space and the records plotted for the prediction values along the Y axis and the predictor values along the X axis. The simple linear regression model then could be viewed as the line that minimized the error rate between the actual prediction value and the point on the line (the prediction from the model).

Graphically this would look like Fig. 2.3. The simplest form of regression seeks to build a predictive model that is a line that maps between each predictor value to a prediction value. Of the many possible lines that could be drawn through the data the one that minimizes the distance between the line and the data points is the one that is chosen for the predictive model.

On average, if you guess the value on the line it should represent an acceptable compromise amongst all the data at that point giving conflicting answers. Likewise if there is no data available for a particular input value the line will provide the best guess at a reasonable answer based on similar data.

Linear regression is similar to the task of finding the line that minimizes the total distance to a set of data. The predictive model is the line shown in Fig. 2.3. The line will take a given value for a predictor and map it into a given value for a prediction. The actual equation would look something like: Prediction = a + b * Predictor. As an example for a bank the predicted average consumer bank balance

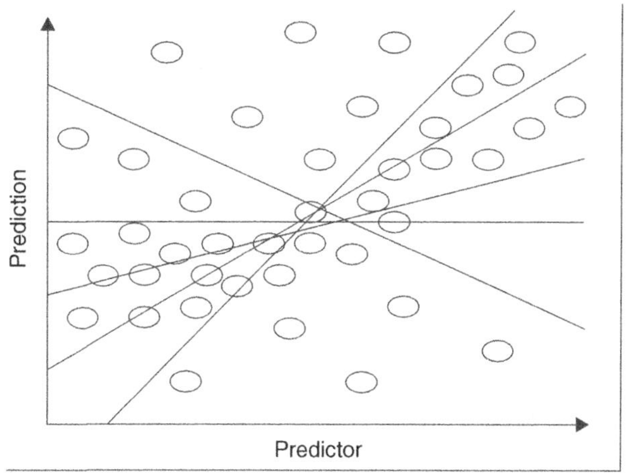

Figure 2.3 Linear regression example.

might equal $1,000 + 0.01 * customer's annual income. The trick, as always with predictive modeling, is to find the model that best minimizes the error. The commonest way to calculate the error is the square of the difference between the predicted value and the actual value.

What if the pattern in my data doesn't look like a straight line?

Regression can become more complicated than the simple linear regression we've discussed so far. There could be several variations:

- More predictors than just one.
- Transformations applied to the predictors.
- Predictors multiplied together and used as terms in the equation.

Modifications can be made to accommodate response predictions that just have yes/no or 0/1 values.

Adding more predictors to the linear equation can produce more complicated lines that take more information into account and hence make a better prediction. This is called multiple linear regression and might have an equation like the following if five predictors were used (X1, X2, X3, X4, X5):

Y = a + b1(X1) + b2(X2) + b3(X3) + b4(X4) + b5(X5)

This equation still describes a line but it is now a line in a 6 dimensional space rather than the two dimensional space.

Transforming the predictors by squaring, cubing, or taking their square root, it is possible to use the same general regression methodology and now create much more complex models that are no longer simple shaped like lines. This is called non-linear regression. In many real world cases analysts perform a wide variety of transformations on their data just to try them out. If the predictors do not contribute to a useful model, their coefficients in the equation will tend toward zero, and then they can be removed. The other transformation of predictor values that is often performed is multiplying them together. For instance a new predictor created by dividing hourly wage by the minimum wage might be a much more effective predictor than hourly wage by itself.

When trying to predict a customer response that is just yes or no (e.g., they bought the product or they did not, or they defaulted or they did not, etc.) the standard form of a line doesn't work. Since there are only two possible values to be predicted it is relatively easy to fit a line through them. However, that model would be the same, no matter what predictors were being used or what particular data was being used. Typically in these situations a transformation of the prediction values is made in order to provide a better predictive model. This type of regression is called logistic regression and because so many business problems are response problems, logistic regression is one of the most widely used statistical techniques for creating predictive models.

Nearest Neighbor

Clustering and the Nearest Neighbor prediction technique are among the oldest techniques used in analytics. Most people have an intuition that they understand what clustering is—namely that like records are grouped or clustered together. Nearest neighbor is a prediction technique that is quite similar to clustering—in order to predict what a prediction value is in one record, looks for records with similar predictor values in the historical database and uses the prediction value from the record that is "nearest" to the unclassified record.

A simple example of clustering would be the clustering that most people perform when they do the laundry—grouping the permanent press, dry cleaning, whites and brightly colored clothes is important because they have similar characteristics. And it turns out they have important attributes in common about the way they behave (and can be ruined) in the wash. To "cluster" your laundry most of your decisions are relatively straightforward. There are of course difficult decisions to be made about which cluster your white shirt with red stripes goes into (since it is mostly white but has some color and is permanent press). When clustering is used in business the clusters are often much more dynamic—even changing weekly to monthly and many more of the decisions concerning which cluster a record falls into can be difficult.

A simple example of the nearest neighbor prediction algorithm is that if you look at the people in your neighborhood (in this case those people that are in fact geographically near to you). You may notice that, in general, you all have somewhat similar incomes. Thus, if your neighbor has an income greater than \$100,000 chances are good that you too have a high income. Certainly the chances that you have a high income are greater when all of your neighbors have incomes over \$100,000 than if all of your neighbors have incomes of \$20,000. Within your neighborhood there may still be a wide variety of incomes possible among even your "closest" neighbors but if you had to predict someone's income based on only knowing their neighbors your best chance of being right would be to predict the incomes of the neighbors who live closest to the unknown person.

The nearest neighbor prediction algorithm works in very much the same way except that "nearness" in a database may consist of a variety of factors not just where the person lives. It may, for instance, be far more important to know which school someone attended and what degree they graduated with when predicting income. The better definition of "near" might in fact be other people that you graduated from college with rather than the people that you live next to.

Nearest Neighbor techniques are among the easiest to use and understand because they work in a way similar to the way that people think—by detecting closely matching examples. They also perform quite well in terms of automation, as many of the algorithms are robust with respect to dirty data and missing data. In the Fig. 2.4 the nearest neighbors are shown graphically for three unclassified records: A, B, and C.

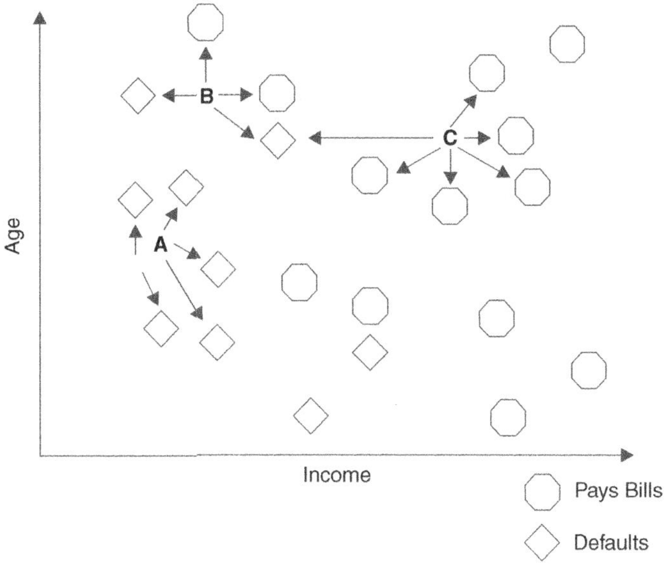

Figure 2.4 Nearest neighbor example.

How to use Nearest Neighbor for Prediction?

One of the essential elements underlying the concept of clustering is that one particular object (whether they be cars, food, or customers) can be closer to another object than some third object. It is interesting that most people have an innate sense of ordering placed on a variety of different objects. Most people would agree that an apple is closer to an orange than it is to a tomato and that a Toyota Corolla is closer to a Honda Civic than to a Porsche. This sense of ordering on many different objects helps us place them in time and space, and to make sense of the world. It is what allows us to build clusters—both in databases on computers as well as in our daily lives. This definition of nearness that seems to be ubiquitous, also allows us to make predictions.

The nearest neighbor prediction algorithm simply stated is: Objects that are "near" to each other will have similar prediction values as well. Thus, if you know the prediction value of one of the objects you can predict it for its nearest neighbors.

Where has the Nearest Neighbor Technique been used in Business?

One commonly found area where nearest neighbor has been used for prediction has been in text retrieval. The problem to be solved in text retrieval is one where the end user defines a document (e.g., Wall Street Journal article, technical conference paper, etc.) that is interesting to them and they solicit the system to "find more documents like this one". In essence, it is defining a target like, "this is an interesting document" or "this is not interesting". The prediction problem is that only a very few of the documents in the database actually have values for this prediction field (namely only the documents that the reader has had a chance to look at so far). The nearest neighbor technique is used to find other documents that share important characteristics with those documents that have been marked as interesting.

Using Nearest Neighbor for Stock Market Data

As with almost all prediction algorithms, nearest neighbor can be used in a variety of places. Its successful use is mostly dependent on the pre-formatting of the data so that nearness can be calculated and where individual records can be defined. In the text retrieval example this was not too difficult—the objects were documents. Consider what it might be like in a time series problem, say, for predicting the stock market. In this case the input data is just a long series of stock prices over time without any particular record that could be considered to be an object. The value to be predicted is just the next value of the stock price.

The way that this problem is solved for both nearest neighbor techniques and for some other types of prediction algorithms is to create training records by taking, for instance, 10 consecutive stock prices and using the first 9 as predictor values and the 10th as the prediction value. Doing things this way, if you had 100 data points in your time series you could create 10 different training records.

You could create even more training records than 10 by creating a new record starting at every data point. For instance you could take the first 10 data points and create a record. Then you could take the 10 consecutive data points starting at the second data point, then the 10 consecutive data point starting at the third data point. Even though some of the data points would overlap from one record to the next the prediction value would always be different. In our example of 100 initial data points 90 different training records could be created this way as opposed to the 10 training records created via the other method.

Clustering

Clustering is the method by which like records are grouped together. Usually this is done to give the end user a high level view of data distribution and relationships. Clustering is sometimes used to mean segmentation. For example, grouping the population by demographic information into segments that are useful for direct marketing and sales. To build these groupings information such as income, age, occupation, housing, and race are collected from census data and then assigned tag names to the clusters.

Some examples of clustering are shown in Table 2.6.

Table 2.6 Clustering example

Name	*Income*	*Age*	*Education*
Blue blood estates	Wealthy	35-54	College
Shotguns and Pickups	Middle income	35-64	High school
Southside City	Poor income	Mix	Grade school
Living off the land	Middle–poor Income	School age families	Primary education
University USA	Very low income	Young–mix	Medium to high
Sunset Years	Medium income	Seniors	Medium

This clustering information is then used by the end user to identify the customers in their database. Once this is done the business user can get a quick high level view of what is happening within the cluster. Once the business user has worked with these codes for some time they also begin to build intuitions about how these different customer clusters will react to the marketing offers particular to their business.

Sometimes clustering is performed not so much to keep records together as to make it easier to see when one record sticks out from the rest.

For instance, a sale on men's suits is being held in all branches of a department store for southern California. All stores with these characteristics have seen at least a 100% jump in revenue since the start of the sale except one. It turns out that this store had, unlike the others, advertised via radio rather than television.

Note: The nearest neighbor algorithm is basically a refinement of clustering in the sense that they both use distance in some feature space to create either structure in the data or predictions. The nearest neighbor algorithm is a refinement since part of the algorithm usually is a way of automatically determining the weighting of the importance of the predictors and how the distance will be measured within the feature space. Clustering is one special case of this where the importance of each predictor is considered to be equivalent.

How to Put Clustering and Nearest Neighbor to Work for Prediction?

To see clustering and nearest neighbor prediction in use, let's go back to our example database and now look at it in two ways. First let's try to create our own clusters—which if useful we could use internally to simplify and clarify large quantities of data (and maybe if we did a very good job sell these new codes to other business users). Secondly let us try to create predictions based on the nearest neighbor.

First take a look at the data. How would you cluster the data in Table 2.7?

Table 2.7 Customer database example

ID	*Name*	*Age*	*Balance ($)*	*Income*	*Eyes*	*Gender*
1	Amy	62	0	Medium	Brown	F
2	Al	53	1800	Medium	Green	M
3	Betty	47	16543	High	Brown	F
4	Bob	32	45	Medium	Green	M
5	Carla	21	2300	High	Blue	F
6	Carl	27	5400	High	Brown	M
7	Donna	50	165	Low	Blue	F
8	Don	46	0	High	Blue	M
9	Edna	27	500	Low	Blue	F
10	Ed	68	1200	Low	Blue	M

If these were your friends rather than your customers (hopefully they could be both) and they were single, you might cluster them based on their compatibility with each other. If you were a pragmatic person you might cluster your database as follows because you think that marital happiness is mostly dependent on financial compatibility and create three clusters as shown in Table 2.8.

Table 2.8 Clustering example

ID	*Name*	*Age*	*Balance ($)*	*Income*	*Eyes*	*Gender*
3	Betty	47	16,543	High	Brown	F
5	Carla	21	2,300	High	Blue	F
6	Carl	27	5,400	High	Brown	M
8	Don	46	0	High	Blue	M
1	Amy	62	0	Medium	Brown	F
2	Al	53	1,800	Medium	Green	M
4	Bob	32	45	Medium	Green	M
7	Donna	50	165	Low	Blue	F
9	Edna	27	500	Low	Blue	F
10	Ed	68	1,200	Low	Blue	M

Is There a Right Way to Cluster?

If on the other hand you are more of a romantic you might note some incompatibilities between 46 year old Don and 21 year old Carla (even though they both make very good incomes). You might instead consider age and some physical characteristics to be most important in creating clusters of friends. Another way you could cluster your friends would be based on their ages and on the color of their eyes. This is shown in Table 2.9. Here three clusters are created where each person in the cluster is about the same age and some attempt has been made to keep people of like eye color together in the same cluster.

Table 2.9 Clustering example

ID	*Name*	*Age*	*Balance ($)*	*Income*	*Eyes*	*Gender*
5	Carla	21	2,300	High	Blue	F
9	Edna	27	500	Low	Blue	F
6	Carl	27	5,400	High	Brown	M
4	Bob	32	45	Medium	Green	M
8	Don	46	0	High	Blue	M
7	Donna	50	165	Low	Blue	F
10	Ed	68	1,200	Low	Blue	M
3	Betty	47	16,543	High	Brown	F
2	Al	53	1,800	Medium	Green	M
1	Amy	62	0	Medium	Brown	F

Looks like a more "Romantic" Clustering of the example database to optimize for Your Dating Service. This example, though simple, brings out some important questions about clustering. For instance: Is it possible to say whether the first clustering that was performed above (by financial status) was better or worse than the second clustering (by age and eye color)? Probably not, since the clusters were constructed for no particular purpose except to note similarities between some of the records, and that the view of the database could be somewhat simplified by using clusters. But even the differences that were created by the two different clustering were driven by slightly different motivations (financial vs. romantic). In general, the reasons for clustering are just this ill-defined because clusters are used more often than not for exploration and summarization as much as they are used for prediction.

What is the Difference between Clustering and Nearest Neighbor Prediction?

The main distinction between clustering and the nearest neighbor technique is that clustering falls under unsupervised learning technique and nearest neighbor is generally used for prediction or a supervised learning technique.

Unsupervised learning techniques are unsupervised in the sense that when they are run there is no predefined intent to arrive at. For example, in clustering there is no particular sense of why certain records are near to each other, or why they all fall into the same cluster. In prediction, the patterns that are found in the database and presented in the model are always the most important patterns and to a larger extent the intent is established at the beginning of the modeling process. Some of the differences between clustering and nearest neighbor prediction are summarized in Table 2.10.

Table 2.10 Difference between clustering and nearest neighbor techniques

Nearest Neighbor	*Clustering*
Used for prediction as well as consolidation.	Used mostly for consolidating data into a high-level view and general grouping of records into like behaviors.
Space is defined by the problem to be solved (supervised learning).	Space is defined as default n-dimensional space, or is defined by the user, or is a predefined space driven by past experience (unsupervised learning).
Generally only uses distance metrics to determine nearness.	Can use other metrics besides distance to determine nearness of two records—for example linking two points together.

Hierarchical and Non-Hierarchical Clustering

There are two main types of clustering techniques—those that create a hierarchy of clusters and those that do not. The hierarchical clustering techniques create a hierarchy of clusters from small to big. Since clustering is an unsupervised learning technique, and as such, there is no absolutely correct answer, depending on the particular application of the clustering, fewer or greater numbers of clusters may be desired. With a hierarchy of clusters it is possible to choose the number of clusters that are desired. At the extreme it may have as many clusters as there are records in the database. In that case the records within the cluster are optimally similar to each other (since there is only one) and certainly different from the other clusters. But of course such a clustering technique is not immensely helpful as the main objective of clustering is to find useful patters in the database that summarizes data and makes it easier to understand.

Any clustering algorithm that ends up with as many clusters as there are records has not helped the user understand the data any better. Thus one of the main points about clustering is that the number of clusters should be fewer than the number of original records. Exactly how many clusters should be formed is a matter of interpretation. The advantage of hierarchical clustering methods is that they allow the end user to choose from either many clusters or only a few.

The hierarchy of clusters is usually viewed as a tree where the smallest clusters merge together to create the next highest level of clusters and those at that level merge together to create the next highest level of clusters. Figure 2.5 shows how several clusters might form a hierarchy. When a hierarchy of clusters like this is created the user can determine what is the right number of clusters that could adequately summarize the data while still providing useful information (at the other extreme a single cluster containing all the records is a great summarization but does not contain enough specific information to be useful).

There are two main types of hierarchical clustering algorithms:

- *Agglomerative* - Agglomerative clustering technique starts with as many clusters as there are records where each cluster contains just one record. The clusters that are nearest to each other are merged together to form the next largest cluster. This merging is continued until a hierarchy of clusters is built with just a single cluster containing all the records at the top of the hierarchy.

- *Divisive* - Divisive clustering techniques take the opposite approach from agglomerative techniques. These techniques start with all the records in one cluster and then try to split that cluster into smaller pieces and then in turn try to split those smaller pieces.

Of the two, the agglomerative techniques are the most commonly used for clustering and have more algorithms developed for them. The non-hierarchical technique in general are faster to create from the historical database but requires the user to make some decision about the number of clusters desired or the minimum "nearness" required for two records to be within the same cluster.

These non-hierarchical techniques often times are run multiple times starting off with some random clustering and then iteratively improving the clustering by shuffling records around.

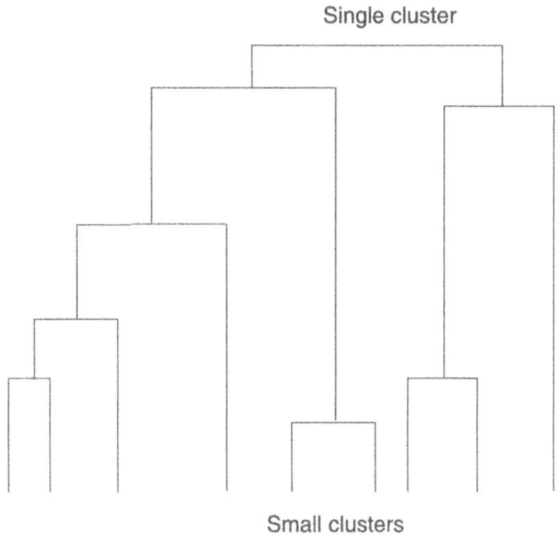

Figure 2.5 Several clusters forming a hierarchy of clusters.

Non-Hierarchical Clustering

There are two main non-hierarchical clustering techniques. The first ones are the single pass methods. They derive their name from the fact that the database must only be passed through once in order to create the clusters (i.e., each record is only read from the database once). The other class of techniques are called reallocation methods. They get their name from the movement or "reallocation" of records from one cluster to another in order to create better clusters. The reallocation techniques do use multiple passes through the database but are relatively fast in comparison to the hierarchical techniques.

Some techniques allow the user to request the number of clusters that they would like to be pulled out of the data. Pre-defining the number of clusters rather than having them driven by the data might seem to be a bad idea as there might be some very distinct and observable clustering of the data into a certain number of clusters which the user might not be aware of.

For instance the user may wish to see their data broken up into 10 clusters but the data itself partitions very cleanly into 13 clusters. These non-hierarchical techniques will try to force fit these extra three clusters into the existing 10 rather than creating 13 which best fit the data.

Hierarchical Clustering

Hierarchical clustering has the advantage over non-hierarchical techniques in that the clusters are defined solely by the data (not by the users pre-determining the number of clusters) and that the number of clusters can be increased or decreased by simply moving up and down the hierarchy.

The hierarchy is created by starting either at the top (one cluster that includes all records) and subdividing (divisive clustering), or by starting at the bottom with as many clusters as there are records and merging (agglomerative clustering). Usually the merging and subdividing are done with two clusters at a time.

The main distinction between the techniques is their ability to favor long, compact clusters that are linked together record by record. It may seem strange, when the underlying space looks quite different from the spherical clusters, and the clusters that should be formed are not based on the distance from the center of the cluster but instead based on the records being "linked" together. Consider the examples shown in Figs. 2.6 and 2.7. In these cases there are two clusters that are not very spherical in shape but could be detected by the single link technique.

When looking at the layout of the data in Fig. 2.6, there appears to be two relatively flat clusters running parallel to each along the income axis. These techniques rely on creating a "center" for each cluster and picking these centers so that they average distance of each record from this center is minimized. Points that are very distant from these centers would necessarily fall into a different cluster.

What makes these clusters "visible" in this simple two dimensional space is the fact that each point in a cluster is tightly linked to some other point in the cluster. For the two clusters we see the maximum distance between the nearest two points within a cluster is less than the minimum distance of the nearest two points in different clusters. That is to say that for any point in this space, the nearest point to it is always going to be another point in the same cluster. Now the center of gravity of a cluster could be quite distant from a given point but that every point is linked to every other point by a series of small distances.

There is no particular rule that would tell you when to choose a particular technique over another. Sometimes those decisions are made relatively arbitrarily

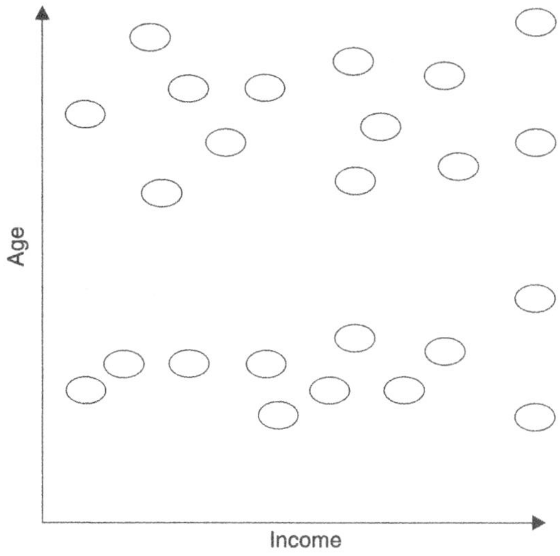

Figure 2.6 Clustering example.

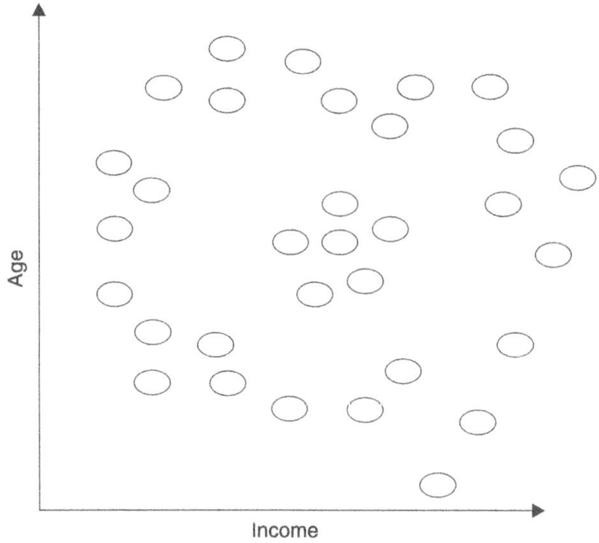

Figure 2.7 Clustering example.

based on the availability of data analysts who are most experienced in one technique over another. And even choosing one technique over some of the other newer techniques is more dependent on the availability of good tools and good analysts.

NEXT GENERATION TECHNIQUES: TREES, NETWORKS, AND INDUCTION RULES

The analytics techniques discussed in this section represent the most often used approaches that have been developed over the last two decades of research.

They also represent the vast majority of the much-discussed techniques in data mining and analytics. These techniques can be used for either discovering new information within large databases, or for building predictive models. Though the older decision tree techniques such as CHAID are currently highly used, the new techniques such as CART are gaining wider acceptance.

What is a Decision Tree?

A decision tree is a predictive model that, as its name implies, can be viewed as a tree. Specifically each branch of the tree is a classification question and the leaves of the tree are partitions of the data set with their classification. For instance if we were going to classify customers who churn (don't renew their phone contracts) in the cellular telephone industry a decision tree might look something like Fig. 2.8.

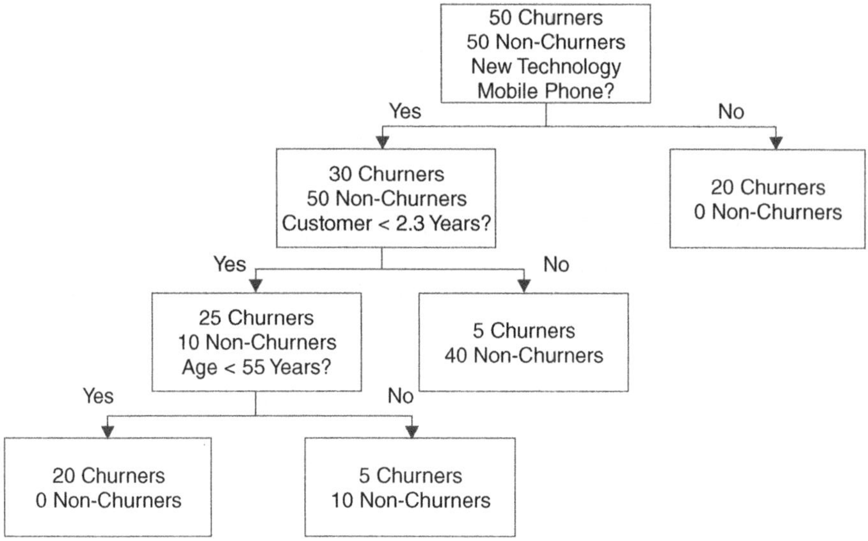

Figure 2.8 Decision tree for cell phone users.

You may notice some interesting things about the tree:

- It divides up the data on each branch point without losing any of the data (the number of total records in a given parent node is equal to the sum of the records contained in its two children).
- The number of churners and non-churners is conserved as you move up or down the tree
- It is pretty easy to understand how the model is being built (in contrast to the models from neural networks or from standard statistics).
- It would also be pretty easy to use this model if you actually had to target those customers that are likely to churn with a targeted marketing offer.

- You may also build some intuitions about your customer base. For example, customers who have been with you for a couple of years and have up-to-date cellular phones are pretty loyal.

From a business perspective decision trees can be viewed as creating a segmentation of the original data set (each segment would be one of the leaves of the tree). Segmentation of customers, products, and sales regions is something that marketing managers have been doing for many years. In the past this segmentation has been performed in order to get a high level view of a large amount of data—with no particular reason for creating the segmentation except that the records within each segmentation were somewhat similar to each other.

In this case the segmentation is done for a particular reason, namely, for the prediction of some important piece of information. The records that fall within each segment fall there because they have similarity with respect to the information being predicted—not just that they are similar—without similarity being well defined. These predictive segments that are derived from the decision tree also come with a description of the characteristics that define the predictive segment. Thus even if the decision trees and the algorithms that create them may be complex, the results can be presented in an easy-to-understand way that can be quite useful to the business user.

The first step in developing the tree is to grow the tree. Specifically the algorithm seeks to create a tree that works as perfectly as possible on all the data that is available. There is always noise in the database to some degree (there are variables that are not being collected that have an impact on the target you are trying to predict).

The key in growing the tree is in finding the best possible question to ask at each branch point of the tree. At the bottom of the tree you will come up with nodes that you would like to be all of one type or the other. Thus, the question: "Are you over 40?" probably does not sufficiently distinguish between those who are churners and those who are not—let us say it is 40%/60%. On the other hand there may be a series of questions that do quite a nice job in distinguishing those cellular phone customers who will churn and those who won't. Maybe the series of questions would be something like: "Have you been a customer for less than a year, do you have a telephone that is more than two years old and were you originally landed as a customer via telesales rather than direct sales?" This series of questions defines a segment of the customer population in which 90% churn. These are then relevant questions to ask in relation to predicting churn.

The difference between a good question and a bad question has to do with how much the question can organize the data, or in this case, change the likelihood of a churner appearing in the customer segment. If we started off with our population being half churners and half non-churners then we would expect that a question that didn't organize the data to some degree into one segment that was more likely to churn than the other, then it would not be a very useful question to ask. On the other hand if we asked a question that was very good at distinguishing between churners and non-churners, say, that split 100 customers into one segment of 50 churners and another segment of 50 non-churners then this would be considered to be a good question. In fact it had decreased the "disorder" of the original segment as much as was possible.

The decision tree algorithm looks at all possible distinguishing questions that could possibly break up the data set into segments that are nearly homogeneous with respect to the different classes being predicted. Some decision tree algorithms may use heuristics in order to pick the questions or even pick them at random.

If the decision tree algorithm just continued growing it could conceivably create more and more questions and branches in the tree so that eventually there is only one record in the segment. To let the tree grow to this size is both computationally expensive but also unnecessary. Most decision tree algorithms stop growing the tree when one of three criteria are met:

- The segment contains only one record. (There is no further question that you could ask which could further refine a segment of just one.)
- All the records in the segment have identical characteristics. (There is no reason to continue asking further questions segmentation since all the remaining records are the same.)
- The improvement is not substantial enough to warrant making the split.

Consider the example shown in Table 2.11 of a segment that we might want to split further which has just two examples. It has been created out of a much larger customer database by selecting only those customers aged 27 with blue eyes and salaries between $80,000 and $81,000.

Table 2.11 Segmentation example

Name	*Age*	*Eyes*	*Salary*	*Churned?*
Steve	27	Blue	$80,000	Yes
Alex	27	Blue	$80,000	No

In this case all of the possible questions that could be asked about the two customers turn out to have the same value (age, eyes, salary) except for name. It would then be possible to ask a question like: "Is the customer's name Steve?" and create the segments which would be very good at breaking apart those who churned from those who did not.

The problem is that we all have an intuition that the name of the customer is not going to be a very good indicator of whether that customer churns or not. It might work well for this particular 2 record segment but it is unlikely that it will work for other customer databases or even the same customer database at a different time. This particular example has to do with overfitting the model— in this case fitting the model too closely to the idiosyncrasies of the sample data. This can be fixed later on but clearly stopping the building of the tree short of either one record segment or very small segments in general is a good idea.

Applying Decision Tree to Business Problems

Because of their tree structure and ability to easily generate rules, decision trees are the favored technique for building understandable models. Because of this clarity they also allow for more complex profit and ROI models to be added easily on top of the predictive model. For instance once a customer population is found with high predicted likelihood to attrite, a variety of cost models can be used to see if an expensive marketing intervention should be used because the customers are highly valuable or a less expensive intervention should be used because the revenue from this sub-population of customers is marginal.

These techniques were originally developed for statisticians to automate the process of determining which fields in their database were actually useful or correlated with the particular problem that they were trying to understand. Partially because of this history, decision tree algorithms tend to automate the entire process of hypothesis generation and then validation much more completely and in a much more integrated way than any other data mining techniques. They are also particularly apt at handling raw data with little or no pre-processing. Perhaps also because they were originally developed to mimic the way an analyst interactively performs data mining they provide a simple-to-understand, predictive model based on rules (such as "90% of the time credit card customers of less than 3 months who max out their credit limit are going to default on their credit card loan.").

Because decision trees score so highly on so many of the critical features of data mining they can be used in a wide variety of business problems for both exploration and for prediction. They have been used for problems ranging from credit card attrition prediction to time series prediction of the exchange rate of different international currencies.

There are also some problems where decision trees will not do as well. Some very simple problems where the prediction is just a simple multiple of the predictor can be solved much more quickly and easily by linear regression. Usually the models to be built and the interactions to be detected are much more complex in real world problems and this is where decision trees excel.

Using Decision Trees for Exploration

The decision tree technique can be used for exploration of the data set and business problem. This is often done by looking at the predictors and values that are chosen for each split of the tree. Oftentimes these predictors provide usable insights or propose questions that need to be answered. For instance if you ran across the following in your database for cellular phone churn you might seriously wonder about the way your telesales operators were making their calls and maybe change the way that they are compensated: "IF customer lifetime < 1.1 years AND sales channel = telesales THEN chance of churn is 65%.

Using Decision Trees for Data Pre-Processing

Another way that the decision tree technique has been used is for pre-processing of data for other prediction algorithms. Because the algorithm is fairly robust with respect to a variety of predictor types (e.g., number, categorical etc.) and because it can be run relatively quickly, decision trees can be used on the first pass of an analytics process to create a subset of possibly useful predictors that can then be fed into neural networks, nearest neighbor, and normal statistical routines, which can take a considerable amount of time to run if there are large numbers of possible predictors to be used in the model.

ID3 and C4.5

In the late 1970s J. Ross Quinlan introduced a decision tree algorithm named ID3. It was one of the first decision tree algorithms, yet at the same time built solidly on work that had been done on inference systems and concept learning systems in that decade as well as from the preceding decade. Initially ID3 was used for tasks such as learning good game playing strategies for chess end games. Since then ID3 has been applied to a wide variety of problems in both academia and industry and has been modified, improved and borrowed from many times over.

ID3 picks predictors and their splitting values based on the gain in information that the split or splits provide. Gain represents the difference between the amount of information that is needed to correctly make a prediction before a split is made and after the split has been made. If the amount of information required is much lower after the split is made, then that split has decreased the disorder of the original single segment. Gain is defined as the difference between the entropy of the original segment and the accumulated entropies of the resulting split segments.

ID3 was later enhanced in the version called C4.5. C4.5 improves on ID3 in several important areas:

- Predictors with missing values can still be used
- Predictors with continuous values can be used
- Pruning is introduced
- Rule derivation

Many of these techniques appear in the CART and CHAID algorithms plus some others.

CART—Growing a Forest and Picking the Best Tree

CART stands for Classification and Regression Trees—a data exploration and prediction algorithm developed by Leo Breiman, Jerome Friedman, Richard Olshen, and Charles Stone. The algorithm is nicely detailed in their 1984 book "Classification and Regression Trees" (Breiman et al., 1984). These researchers from Stanford University and the University of California at Berkeley showed how this new algorithm could be used on a variety of different problems from to the detection of Chlorine from the data contained in a mass spectrum.

In building the CART tree each predictor is picked based on how well it singles out the records with different predictions. For instance one measure that is used to determine whether a given split point for a give predictor is better than another, is the entropy metric. The measure originated from the work done by Claude Shannon and Warren Weaver on information theory in 1949. They were concerned with how information could be efficiently communicated over telephone lines. Interestingly, their results also proved useful in creating decision trees. Predictors are picked as they decrease the disorder of the data.

One of the great advantages of CART is that the algorithm has the discovery as well as validation phases built deeply into the algorithm. CART accomplishes this by building a very complex tree and then pruning it back to the optimally general tree based on the results of cross validation or test set validation. The CART algorithm is relatively robust with respect to missing data. If the value is missing for a particular predictor in a record that record is not used in making the determination of the optimal split when the tree is being built. In effect CART utilizes as much information as it has on hand in order to make the decision for picking the best possible split. When CART is used to predict on new data, missing values are handled via surrogates. Surrogates are split values and predictors that mimic the actual split in the tree and can be used when the data for the preferred predictor is missing. For instance though shoe size is not a perfect predictor of height it could be used as a surrogate to try to mimic a split based on height when that information was missing from the particular record being predicted with the CART model.

CHAID

Another equally popular decision tree technology to CART is CHAID or Chi-Square Automatic Interaction Detector. CHAID is similar to CART in that, it builds a decision tree but it differs in the way that it chooses its splits. Instead of the entropy metrics for choosing optimal splits the technique relies on the chi square test used in contingency tables to determine which categorical predictor is furthest from independence with the prediction values.

Because CHAID relies on the contingency tables to form its test of significance for each predictor, all predictors must either be categorical or be coerced into a categorical form via binning (e.g., break up possible people ages into 10 bins from 0-9, 10-19, 20-29, etc.). Though this binning can have consequences, the actual accuracy performances of CART and CHAID have been shown to be comparable in real world direct marketing response models.

Neural Networks

Insofar as the choice of data mining algorithms is concerned, currently it is either decision trees or neural networks. Of the two, neural networks have probably been of greater interest through the formative stages of data mining technology. As we will see, neural networks do have disadvantages that can be limiting in their ease of use and ease of deployment, but they do also have some significant advantages. Foremost among these advantages is their highly accurate predictive models that can be applied across a large number of different types of problems.

To be more precise with the term "neural network" one might better speak of an "artificial neural network". True neural networks are biological systems (aka brains) that detect patterns, make predictions and learn. The artificial ones are computer programs implementing sophisticated pattern detection and machine learning algorithms on a computer to build predictive models from large historical databases. Artificial neural networks derive their name from historical development which started off with the premise that machines could be made to "think" if scientists found ways to mimic the structure and functioning of the human brain on the computer. Thus historically neural networks grew out of the community of Artificial Intelligence rather than from the discipline of statistics. Despite the fact that scientists are still far from understanding the human brain let alone mimicking it, neural networks that run on computers can do some of the things that people can do.

It is difficult to say exactly when the first "neural network" on a computer was built. During the World War II a seminal paper was published by McCulloch and Pitts which first outlined the idea that simple processing units (like the individual neurons in the human brain) could be connected together in large networks to create a system that could solve difficult problems and display behavior that was much more complex than the simple pieces that made it up. Since that time much progress has been made in finding ways to apply artificial neural networks to real world prediction problems and in improving the performance of the algorithm in general. In many aspects the greatest breakthroughs in neural networks in recent years have been in their application to more mundane real world problems like customer response prediction or fraud detection rather than the loftier goals that were originally set out for the techniques such as overall human learning and computer speech and image understanding.

How Does a Neural Network Look Like?

A neural network is loosely based on how some people believe that the human brain is organized and how it learns. Given that there are two main structures of consequence in the neural network:

- The node—which corresponds to the neuron in the human brain
- The link—which corresponds to the connections between neurons (axons, dendrites and synapses) in the human brain.

Figure 2.9 is a drawing of a simple neural network. The round circles represent the nodes and the connecting lines represent the links. The neural network functions by accepting predictor values at the left and performing calculations on those values to produce new values in the node at the far right. The value at this node represents the prediction from the neural network model. In this case the network takes in values for predictors for age and income and predicts whether the person will default on a bank loan.

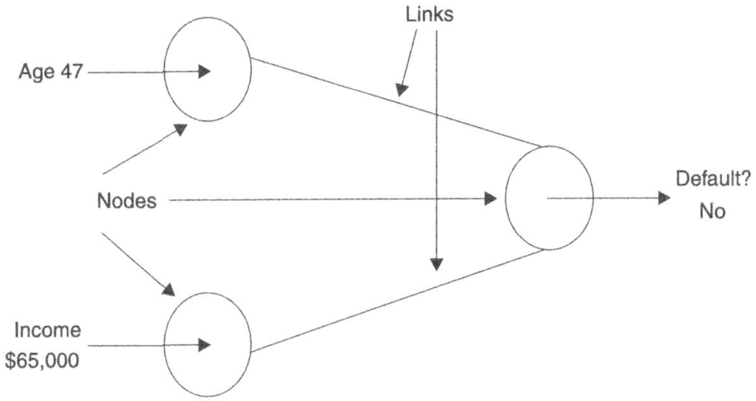

Figure 2.9 Neural network.

In order to make a prediction the neural network accepts the values for the predictors on what are called the input nodes. These become the values for those nodes, the values are then multiplied by values that are stored in the links (sometimes called links and in some ways similar to the weights that were applied to predictors in the nearest neighbor method). These values are then added together at the node at the far right (the output node), a special threshold function is applied and the resulting number is the prediction.

In our example, if the resulting number is 0 the record is considered to be a good credit risk (no default); if the number is 1 the record is considered to be a bad credit risk (likely default). Figure 2.10 below shows a simplified version of the calculations done as applicable to neural network modeling. Here the value age of 47 is normalized to fall between 0.0 and 1.0 and has the value 0.47 and the income is normalized to the value 0.65. This simplified neural network makes the prediction of no default for a 47 year old making $65,000. The links are weighted at 0.7 and 0.1 and the resulting value after multiplying the node values by the link weights is 0.39. The network has been trained to learn that an output value of 1.0 indicates default and that 0.0 indicates non-default. The output value calculated here (0.39) is closer to 0.0 than to 1.0; so, the record is assigned a non-default prediction.

The neural network model is created by presenting it with predictor values from records in the training set (examples are age and income) and the prediction value from those same records. By comparing the correct answer obtained from the training record and the predicted answer from the neural network it is possible to slowly change the behavior of the neural network by changing the values of the link weights. For the actual neural network it is the weights of the links that actually control the prediction value for a given record. Thus, the particular

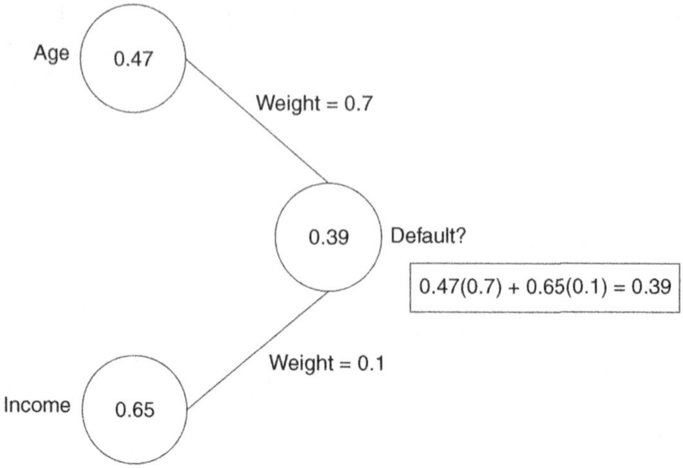

Figure 2.10 Neural network prediction calculation.

model that is being built by the neural network is in fact fully determined by the weights and the architectural structure of the network. For this reason, it is the link weights that are modified each time an error is made.

To understand how neural networks can detect patterns in a database an analogy is often made that they "learn" to detect these patterns and make better predictions in a way similar to how human beings do. This view is encouraged by the way the historical training data is often supplied to the network—one record (example) at a time. Neural networks do "learn" in a very real sense but under the hood the algorithms and techniques that are being deployed are not truly different from the techniques found in statistics or other data mining algorithms. It is for instance, unfair to assume that neural networks could outperform other techniques because they "learn" and improve over time while the other techniques are static. The other techniques in fact "learn" from historical examples in exactly the same way but often the examples (historical records) to learn from, are processed all at once in a more efficient manner than neural networks which often modify their model one record at a time.

A common claim for neural networks is that they are automated to a degree where the user does not need to know much about how they work, or predictive modeling, or even the database in order to use them. The implicit claim is also that most neural networks can be unleashed on your data straight out of the box without having to rearrange or modify the data very much to begin with.

Just the opposite is often true. There are many important design decisions that need to be made in order to effectively use a neural network such as:

- How should the nodes in the network be connected?
- How many neuron-like processing units should be used?
- When should "training" be stopped in order to avoid overfitting?

There are also several important steps required for pre-processing the data that goes into a neural network—most often there is a requirement to normalize numeric data between 0.0 and 1.0. Categorical predictors may need to be broken up into virtual predictors that are 0 or 1 for each value of the original categorical predictor. Also, as always, understanding what the data in your database means and a clear definition of the business problem to be solved are essential to ensuring eventual success. The bottom line is that neural networks provide no shortcuts.

Neural networks are very powerful predictive modeling techniques but some of the power comes at the expense of ease of use and ease of deployment. Neural networks create very complex models that are almost always impossible to fully understand even by experts. The model itself is represented by numeric values in a complex calculation that requires all of the predictor values to be in the form of a number. The output of the neural network is also numeric and needs to be translated if the actual prediction value is categorical (e.g., to predict the demand for blue, white, or black jeans for a clothing manufacturer requires that the predictor values blue, black, and white for the predictor color to be converted to numbers).

There are two ways that these shortcomings in understanding the meaning of the neural network model have been successfully addressed:

- The neural network is packaged into a complete solution such as fraud prediction. This allows the neural network to be carefully crafted for one particular application and once it has been proven successful it can be used over and over again without requiring a deep understanding of how it works.
- The neural network is packaged with expert consulting services. Here the neural network is deployed by trusted experts who have a track record of success. Either the experts are able to explain the models or they are trusted that the models do work.

The first tactic seems to work quite well because, when the technique is used for a well-defined problem many of the difficulties in pre-processing the data can be automated (because the data structures have been seen before), and interpretation of the model is less of an issue since entire industries begin to use the technology successfully and a level of trust is created.

Packaging neural networks with expert consultants is also a viable strategy that avoids many of the pitfalls of using neural networks, but it can be quite expensive. One of the great promises of data mining is, after all, the automation of the predictive modeling process. These neural network consulting teams are little different from the analytical departments many companies already have in-house. Since there is not a great difference in the overall predictive accuracy of neural networks over standard statistical techniques the main difference becomes the replacement of the statistical expert with the neural network expert. Either with statistics or neural network experts the value of putting easy to use tools into the hands of the business end user is still not achieved.

Rule Induction

Rule induction is one of the major forms of data mining technique, and is perhaps the most common form of knowledge discovery in unsupervised learning systems. It is also perhaps the form of data mining that most closely resembles the process that most people think about when they think about data mining, namely "mining" for gold through a vast database. The gold in this case would be a rule that is interesting—that tells you something about your database that you did not already know and probably were not able to explicitly articulate (aside from saying "show me things that are interesting").

Rule induction on a database can be a massive undertaking where all possible patterns are systematically pulled out of the data, and then an accuracy and significance are added to them that tells the user how strong the pattern is, and how likely it is to occur again. In general these rules are relatively simple such as for a market basket database of items scanned in a consumer market basket you might find interesting correlations in your database such as:

- If bagels are purchased then cream cheese is purchased 90% of the time and this pattern occurs in 3% of all shopping baskets.
- If live plants are purchased from a hardware store then plant fertilizer is purchased 60% of the time and these two items are bought together in 6% of the shopping baskets.

The rules that are pulled from the database are extracted and ordered to be presented to the user, based on the percentage of times that they are correct and how often they apply.

Rule induction systems are highly automated and are probably the best of data mining techniques for exposing all possible predictive patterns in a database. They can be modified to for use in prediction problems but the algorithms for combining evidence from a variety of rules comes more from rules of thumbs and practical experience.

The business value of rule induction techniques reflects the highly automated way in which the rules are created which makes it easy to use the system but also that this approach can suffer from an overabundance of interesting patterns which can make it complicated in order to make a prediction that is directly tied to return on investment (ROI).

In rule induction systems the rule itself is of a simple form of "if this and this and this then this". For example a rule that a supermarket might find in their data collected from scanners would be: "if pickles are purchased then ketchup is purchased', or

- if paper plates then plastic forks
- if dip then potato chips
- if salsa then tortilla chips

In order for the rules to be useful there are two pieces of information that must be supplied as well as the actual rule:

- *Accuracy* - How often is the rule correct?
- *Coverage* - How often does the rule apply?

Just because the pattern in the database is expressed as rule does not mean that it is true all the time. Thus just like in other data mining algorithms, it is important to recognize and make explicit the uncertainty in the rule. This is what the accuracy of the rule means. The coverage of the rule has to do with how much of the database the rule "covers" or applies to. Examples of these two measure for a variety of rules is shown in Table 2.12. In some cases accuracy is called the confidence of the rule and coverage is called the support.

Table 2.12 Rules examples

Rule	*Accuracy (%)*	*Coverage (%)*
If breakfast cereal purchased then milk purchased	85	20
If bread purchased then swiss cheese purchased	15	6
If 42 years old and purchased pretzels and purchased dry roasted peanuts then beer will be purchased	95	0.01

The rules themselves consist of two halves. *The left hand side is called the antecedent and the right hand side is called the consequent. The antecedent can consist of just one condition or multiple conditions which must all be true in order for the consequent to be true at the given accuracy.* Generally, the consequent is just a single condition (prediction of purchasing just one grocery store item) rather than multiple conditions. Thus, rules such as: "if x and y then a and b, and c".

When the rules are mined out of the database the rules can be used either for understanding the business problems that the data reflects or for performing actual predictions against some predefined prediction target. Since there is both a left side and a right side to a rule (antecedent and consequent), they can be used in several ways for business.

- *Target the antecedent* - In this case all rules that have a certain value for the antecedent are gathered and displayed to the user. For instance a grocery store may request all rules that have nails, bolts or screws as the antecedent in order to try to understand whether discontinuing the sale of these low margin items will have any effect on other higher margin. For instance maybe people who buy nails also buy expensive hammers but wouldn't do so at the store if the nails were not available.
- *Target the consequent* - In this case all rules that have a certain value for the consequent can be used to understand what is associated with the consequent and perhaps what affects the consequent. For instance it might be useful to know all of the interesting rules that have "coffee" in their consequent. These may well be the rules that affect the purchases of coffee and that a store owner may want to put close to the coffee in

order to increase the sale of both items. Or it might be the rule that the coffee manufacturer uses to determine in which magazine to place their next coupons.

- *Target based on accuracy* - Sometimes the most important thing for a user is the accuracy of the rules that are being generated. Highly accurate rules of 80% or 90% imply strong relationships that can be exploited even if they have low coverage of the database and only occur a limited number of times. For instance a rule that only has 0.1% coverage but if applied, 95% time it will very likely to be correct. If this turns out to be highly profitable then it can be worthwhile. This, for instance, is how some of the most successful data mining applications work in the financial markets—looking for that limited amount of time where a very confident prediction can be made.
- *Target based on coverage* - Sometimes user wants to know what the most ubiquitous rules are, or those rules that are most readily applicable. By looking at rules ranked by coverage they can quickly get a high-level view of what is happening within their database most of the time.
- *Target based on "interestingness"* - Rules are interesting when they have high coverage and high accuracy and deviate from the norm. There have been many ways that rules have been ranked by some measure of interestingness so that the trade-off between coverage and accuracy can be made.

Since rule induction systems are so often used for pattern discovery and unsupervised learning it is less easy to compare them. For example it is very easy for just about any rule induction system to generate all possible rules; it is, however, much more difficult to devise a way to present those rules (which could easily be in the hundreds of thousands) in a way that is most useful to the end user. When interesting rules are found they usually have been created to find relationships between many different predictor values in the database not just one well defined target of the prediction. For this reason, it is often much more difficult to assign a measure of value to the rule, aside from its interestingness. For instance it would be difficult to determine the monetary value of knowing that if people buy breakfast sausage they also buy eggs 60% of the time. For data mining systems which are more focused on prediction for things like customer attrition, targeted marketing response or risk, it is much easier to measure the value of the system and compare it to other systems and other methods for solving the problem.

Note: *Rules do not imply causality* - It is important to recognize that even though the patterns produced from rule induction systems are delivered as "if then rules" they do not necessarily mean that the left hand side of the rule (the "if" part) causes the right hand side of the rule (the "then" part) to happen. Purchasing cheese does not cause the purchase of wine even though the rule if cheese then wine may be very strong. This is particularly important to remember for rule induction systems because the results are presented as "if this then that" as many causal relationships are presented.

What Kind of Data Demographics Are Most Suitable for Rule Induction?

Typically rule induction is used on data with either fields of high cardinality (many different values) or many columns of binary fields. The classical case of this is, the super market basket data from store scanners that contains individual product names and quantities and may contain tens of thousands of different items with different packaging that create hundreds of thousands of SKU identifiers (Stock Keeping Units).

Sometimes in these databases the concept of a record is not easily defined within the database—consider the typical Star Schema for many data warehouses that store the supermarket transactions as separate entries in the fact table. Where the columns in the fact table are some unique identifier of the shopping basket (so all items can be noted as being in the same shopping basket), the quantity, the time of purchase, whether the item was purchased with a special promotion (sale or coupon). Thus each item in the shopping basket has a different row in the fact table. This layout of the data is not typically the best for most data mining algorithms which would prefer to have the data structured as one row per shopping basket and each column to represent the presence or absence of a given item.

This can be an expensive way to store the data, however, since the typical grocery store contains 60,000 SKUs or different items that could come across the checkout counter. This structure of the records can also create a very high dimensional space (60,000 binary dimensions) which would be unwieldy for many classical data mining algorithms like neural networks and decision trees.

The rules could immensely help in exploration or discover activities:

- *Macro level* - Patterns that cover many situations are provided to the user that can be used very often and with great confidence and can also be used to summarize the database.
- *Micro level* - Strong rules that cover only a very few situations can still be retrieved by the system and proposed to the end user. These may be valuable if the situations that are covered are highly valuable (maybe they only apply to the most profitable customers) or represent a small but growing subpopulation which may indicate a market shift or the emergence of a new competitor (e.g., customers are only being lost in one particular area of the country where a new competitor is emerging).

After the rules are created and their interestingness is measured, there is also a need for performing prediction with the rules. Each rule by itself can perform prediction—the consequent is the target and the accuracy of the rule is the accuracy of the prediction. But because rule induction systems produce many rules for a given antecedent or consequent and there could be conflicting predictions with different accuracies. This is an opportunity for improving the overall performance of the systems by combining the rules. This can be done in a variety of ways by summing the accuracies as if they were weights or just by taking the prediction of the rule with the maximum accuracy.

Table 2.13 shows how a given consequent or antecedent can be part of many rules with different accuracies and coverages. From this example consider the problem of predicting whether milk was purchased, based solely on the other items that were in the shopping basket. If the shopping basket contained only bread then from the table we would guess that there was a 35% chance that milk was also purchased. If, however, bread and butter and eggs and cheese were purchased what would be the prediction for milk then? 65% chance of milk because the relationship between butter and milk is the greatest at 65%? Or would all of the other items in the basket increase even further the chance of milk being purchased to well beyond 65%? Determining how to combine evidence from multiple rules is a key part of the algorithms for using rules for prediction.

Table 2.13 Rule induction example showing antecedent and consequent

Antecedent	*Consequent*	*Accuracy (%)*	*Coverage (%)*
Bagels	Cream Cheese	80	5
Bagels	Orange Juice	40	3
Bagels	Coffee	40	2
Bagels	Eggs	25	2
Bread	Milk	35	30
Butter	Milk	65	20
Eggs	Milk	35	15
Cheese	Milk	40	8

The general idea of a rule classification system is that rules are created that show the relationship between events captured in your database. These rules can be simple with just one element in the antecedent or they might be more complicated with many column value pairs in the antecedent all joined together by a conjunction (item1 and item2 and item3 … must all occur for the antecedent to be true).

The rules are used to find interesting patterns in the database but they are also used at times for prediction. There are two main things that are important to understanding a rule:

- *Accuracy* - Accuracy refers to the probability that if the antecedent is true that the precedent will be true. High accuracy means that this is a rule that is highly dependable.
- *Coverage* - Coverage refers to the number of records in the database that the rule applies to. High coverage means that the rule can be used very often and also that it is less likely to be a spurious artifact of the sampling technique or idiosyncrasies of the database.

How Important Is Accuracy and Coverage?

From a business perspective accurate rules are important because they imply that there is useful predictive information in the database that can be exploited, namely there is something far from independent between the antecedent and the consequent. The lower the accuracy the closer the rule comes to just random guessing. If the accuracy is significantly below that of what would be expected from random guessing then the negation of the antecedent may well in fact be useful (for instance people who buy denture adhesive are much less likely to buy fresh corn on the cob than normal).

From a business perspective coverage implies how often you can use a useful rule. For instance you may have a rule that is 100% accurate but is only applicable in 1 out of every 100,000 shopping baskets. You can rearrange your shelf space to take advantage of this fact but it will not make you much money since the event is not very likely to happen. Table 2.14 displays the trade-off between coverage and accuracy.

Table 2.14 Coverage and accuracy matrix

	Low Accuracy	*High Accuracy*
High coverage	Rule is rarely correct but can be used often	Rule is often correct and can be used often
Low coverage	Rule is rarely correct and can be only rarely used	Rule is often correct but can be only rarely used

An analogy between coverage and accuracy and making money may be drawn from betting on horses. Having a high accuracy rule with low coverage would be like owning a race horse that always won when he raced but could only race once a year. In betting, you could probably still make a lot of money on such a horse. In rule induction for retail stores it is unlikely that finding that one rule between mayonnaise, ice cream and sardines that seems to always be true will have much of an impact on your bottom line.

How to Evaluate the Rule?

One way to look at accuracy and coverage is to see how they relate so some simple statistics and how they can be represented graphically. From statistics coverage is simply the a priori probability of the antecedent and the consequent occurring at the same time. The accuracy is just the probability of the consequent conditional on the precedent. For instance if we were looking at the following super market basket scanner data, we would need the following information in order to calculate the accuracy and coverage for a simple rule (let's say milk purchase implies eggs purchased).

T = 100 = Total number of shopping baskets in the database.

E = 30 = Number of baskets with eggs in them.

M = 40 = Number of baskets with milk in them.

B = 20 = Number of baskets with both eggs and milk in them.

Accuracy is then just the number of baskets with eggs and milk in them divided by the number of baskets with milk in them. In this case that would be

20/40 = 50%. The coverage would be the number of baskets with milk in them divided by the total number of baskets. This would be 40/100 = 40%. This can be seen graphically in Fig. 2.11.

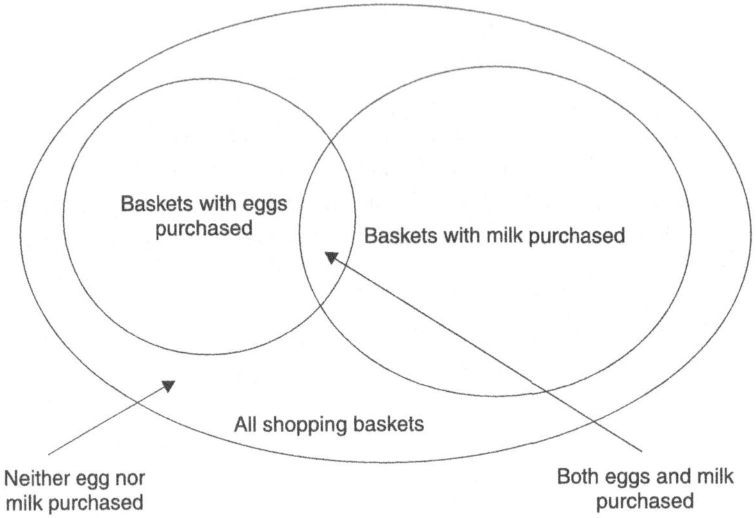

Figure 2.11 Rule induction example.

The coverage of the rule "If Milk then Eggs" is just the relative size of the circle corresponding to milk. The accuracy is the relative size of the overlap between the two to the circle representing milk purchased.

Notice that we haven't used "E" the number of baskets with eggs in these calculations. One way that eggs could be used is to calculate the expected number of baskets with eggs and milk in them based on the independence of the events. This would give us some sense of how unlikely and how special the event is that 20% of the baskets have both eggs and milk in them.

If the purchase of eggs and milk was independent of each other one would expect that $0.3 \times 0.4 = 0.12$ or 12% of the time we would see shopping baskets with both eggs and milk in them. The fact that this combination of products occurs 20% of the time is out of the ordinary if these events were independent. That is to say, there is a good chance that the purchase of one affects the other and the degree to which this is the case could be calculated through statistical tests and hypothesis testing.

One of the biggest problems with rule induction systems is the sometimes overwhelming number of rules that are produced. Most of which have no practical value or interest. Some of the rules are so inaccurate that they cannot be used some have so little coverage that though they are interesting they have little applicability, and finally many of the rules capture patterns and information that the user is already familiar with. To address such scenarios, following are some best practices to measure the usefulness or interestingness of rules.

Certainly any measure of interestingness would have something to do with accuracy and coverage. We might also expect it to have at least the following four basic behaviors:

- Interestingness = 0, if the accuracy of the rule is equal to the background accuracy (a priori probability of the consequent). The example in Table 2.15 shows this, where a rule for attrition is no better than just guessing the overall rate of attrition.
- Interestingness increases as accuracy increases (or decreases with decreasing accuracy) if the coverage is fixed.
- Interestingness increases or decreases with coverage if accuracy stays fixed.
- Interestingness decreases with coverage for a fixed number of correct responses (remember accuracy equals the number of correct responses divided by the coverage).

Table 2.15 Example of interestingness and accuracy

Antecedent	*Consequent*	*Accuracy (%)*	*Coverage (%)*
<No Constraints>	Then Customer will churn	10	100
If Customer Balance > $3000	Then Customer will churn	10	60
If Customer Eyes = Blue	Then Customer will churn	10	30
If Customer SSN = 144 30 8217	Then Customer will churn	100	0.000001

There are a variety of measures of interestingness that are used that have these general characteristics. They are used for pruning back the total possible number of rules that might be generated and then presented to the user.

Another important measure is that of simplicity of the rule. This is important solely for the end user. Complex rules, as powerful and interesting as they might be, may be difficult to understand or to confirm via intuition. Thus the user has a desire to see simpler rules and consequently this desire can be manifest directly in the rules that are chosen and supplied automatically to the user.

Finally, a measure of novelty is also required both during the creation of the rules—so that rules that are redundant but strong are less favored to be searched than rules that may not be as strong but cover important examples that are not covered by other strong rules. For instance there may be few historical records to provide rules on a little sold grocery item (e.g., mint jelly) and they may have low accuracy but since there are so few possible rules even though they are not interesting they will be "novel" and should be retained and presented to the user for that reason alone.

Rules vs. Decision Trees

Decision trees also produce rules but in a very different way than rule induction systems. The main difference between the rules that are produced by decision trees and rule induction systems is as follows:

Decision trees produce rules that are mutually exclusive and collectively exhaustive with respect to the training database while rule induction systems produce rules that are not mutually exclusive and might be collectively exhaustive.

In essence this means that for any given record there will be a rule to cover it and there will only be one rule for rules that come from decision trees. There may be many rules that match a given record from a rule induction system and for many systems it is not guaranteed that a rule will exist for each and every possible record that might be encountered (though most systems do create very general default rules to capture these records).

The reason for this difference is the way in which the two algorithms operate. Rule induction seeks to go from the bottom up and collect all possible patterns that are interesting. Use those patterns later on for some prediction target. Decisions trees, on the other hand, work from a prediction target downward in what is known as a "greedy" search—looking for the best possible split on the next step (i.e., greedily picking the best one without looking any further than the next step). Though the greedy algorithm can make choices at the higher levels of the tree which are less than optimal at the lower levels of the tree it is very good at effectively squeezing out any correlations between predictors and the prediction. Rule induction systems on the other hand retain all possible patterns even if they are redundant or do not aid in predictive accuracy.

For instance, consider that in a rule induction system that if there were two columns of data that were highly correlated (or in fact just simple transformations of each other) they would result in two rules whereas in a decision tree one predictor would be chosen and then since the second one was redundant it would not be chosen again. An example might be the two predictors annual charges and average monthly charges (average monthly charges being the annual charges divided by 12). If the amount charged was predictive then the decision tree would choose one of the predictors and use it for a split point somewhere in the tree. The decision tree effectively "squeezed" the predictive value out of the predictor and then moved onto the next. A rule induction system would on the other hand create two rules.

Perhaps something like:

- If annual charges > 12,000 then default = true 90% accuracy
- If average monthly charges > 1,000 the default = true 90% accuracy.

In this case we've shown an extreme case where two predictors were exactly the same, but there can also be less extreme cases. For instance height might be used rather than shoe size in the decision tree whereas in a rule induction system both would be presented as rules.

Neither one technique nor the other is necessarily better though having a variety of rules and predictors helps with the prediction when there are missing values. For instance if the decision tree did choose height as a split point but that predictor was not captured in the record (a null value) but shoe size was the rule induction system would still have a matching rule to capture this record. Decision trees do have ways of overcoming this difficulty by keeping "surrogates" at each split point that work almost as well at splitting the data as does the chosen predictor. In this case shoe size might have been kept as a surrogate for height at this particular branch of the tree.

Another thing that decision trees and rule induction systems have in common is the fact that they both need to find ways to combine and simplify rules. In a decision tree this can be as simple as recognizing that if a lower split on a predictor is more constrained than a split on the same predictor further up in the tree that both don't need to be provided to the user but only the more restrictive one. For instance if the first split of the tree is age ≤50 years and the lowest split for the given leaf is age ≤30 years then only the latter constraint needs to be captured in the rule for that leaf.

Rules from rule induction systems are generally created by taking a simple high level rule and adding new constraints to it until the coverage gets so small as to not be meaningful. This means that the rules actually have families or what is called "cones of specialization" where one more general rule can be the parent of many more specialized rules. These cones then can be presented to the user as high level views of the families of rules and can be viewed in a hierarchical manner to aid in understanding.

Which Technique to Choose and When?

Clearly one of the hardest things to do when deciding to implement a data mining system is to determine which technique to use, and when. When are neural networks appropriate, and when are decision trees appropriate? When is data mining appropriate at all as opposed to just working with relational databases and reporting? When would just using OLAP and a multi-dimensional database be appropriate?

Some of the criteria that are important in determining the technique to be used are determined by trial and error. There are definite differences in the types of problems that are most conducive to each technique but the reality of real world data is constantly changing. These dynamics mean that, it no longer makes sense to build the "perfect" model on the historical data since whatever was known in the past cannot adequately predict the future because the future is so unlike what has gone before.

In some ways this situation is analogous to the business person who is waiting for all information to come in before they make their decision. They are trying out different scenarios, different formulae and researching new sources of information.

But this is a task that will never be accomplished at least in part, because the business, the economy and even the world is changing in unpredictable and even chaotic ways that could never be adequately predicted. Better to take a robust model that perhaps is an under-performer compared to what some of the best data mining tools could provide with a great deal of analysis and execute it today rather than to wait until tomorrow when it may be too late.

END POINTS

There is always the trade-off between exploration (learning more and gathering more facts) and exploitation (taking immediate advantage of everything that is currently known). This theme of exploration versus exploitation is echoed also at the level of collecting data in a targeted marketing system: from a limited population of prospects/customers to choose from how many do you sacrifice to exploration (trying out new promotions or messages at random) versus optimizing what you already know.

There was for instance no reasonable way that Barnes and Noble bookstores could in 1995 look at past sales figures and foresee the impact that Amazon books and others would have based on the internet sales model.

Compared to historic sales and marketing data the event of the internet could not be predicted based on the data alone. Instead perhaps data mining could have been used to detect trends of decreased sales to certain customer sub-populations - such as to those involved in the high tech industry that were the first to begin to buy books online at Amazon.

Enterprise data warehouses that integrate operational data with customer, supplier, and market information have resulted in an explosion of information. Competition requires timely and sophisticated analysis on an integrated view of the data. However, there is a growing gap between more powerful storage and retrieval systems and the users' ability to effectively analyze and act on the information they contain. Both relational and OLAP technologies have tremendous capabilities for navigating massive data warehouses, but brute force navigation of data is not enough. A new technological leap is needed to structure and prioritize information for specific end-user problems. The data mining tools and analytical processes can make this leap. Quantifiable business benefits have been proven through the integration of data mining and analytics with current information systems, and new products are on the horizon that will bring this integration to an even wider audience of users.

REFERENCES

Hubbard, Douglas W., *How to Measure Anything—Finding the Value of Intangibles in Business,* Wiley, April 2010.

May, Thorton, *The New Know: The Innovation Powered by Analytics,* Wiley and SAS Business Series, September 2009.

CHAPTER 3

EFFECTIVE DECISION MAKING AND ANALYTICS

> *Business decision-making has been predominantly a "craft." Each decision is its own ad hoc effort, including decisions supported by extensive data and analysis.*

The often-practiced sequence for analytics runs like this: The company stores data from transaction systems in data warehouses. A business user *hypothesizes and defines* what he/she is looking for and communicates this to an analyst. The analyst *reviews* the data available, *selects* the data required, *extracts* the data (sometimes with the help of IT teams), *analyzes* it with the help of statistical software, and *communicates* the results to the business user. The business user then *reviews* the various options, *makes* a choice and the "definition-extraction-analysis" sequence may *iterate*, until the business user is satisfied with the results.

The above approach is highly customized and often skilled labor-intensive and time-consuming. Given the nature of expanding businesses and much-desired business agility to adapt to changing business needs, it is essential that companies should follow an industrialized approach to analytics.

WHERE TO START—IDENTIFY THE OPPORTUNITIES

There are two fundamental approaches to finding business opportunities for applying analytics, and each one should be exercised regularly:

- *Outside-In Thinking* - Keeping tabs on what others in your industry are doing, using business decomposition and analysis frameworks to assess where performance can or must improve, and exploring your hunches about the business, what makes it tick, and where the next breakthrough may await.
- *Inside-Out Thinking* - Keeping a systematic inventory of your key business processes and how decisions are made within them, and of your key business decisions (e.g., to make an acquisition, developing a new product, going after a new market, etc.) and how they can be made more process oriented and benefit from more and better analytics.

Most businesses start the opportunity finding process by surveying what's happening elsewhere in their industry. Table 3.1 lists some of the most common applications of analytics that you're likely to find. Looking across your industry—

and scrutinizing the activities of your competitors—on a regular basis is essential. At a minimum, it keeps you alert and informed about what you must do to keep pace not only with the competition, but also with changing and rising customer expectations.

Let us first see what are the most common applications of analytics in the industry:

Table 3.1 Business analytics

Industry	*Analytical Applications*
Financial Services	Credit Scoring, Fraud Detection, Pricing Optimization, Trading Analytics, Claims Analysis, Underwriting Efficiency, Customer Profitability, Financial Fore-Casting and Budgetary Analysis, ROC and Working Capital Management, Shareholder Metrics
Retail	Product Promotions, Inventory Replenishment/Optimization, Shelf Management, Space Optimization, Demand Forecasting, Pricing Optimization, Merchandizing Optimization, Store Layout Analysis, Sales and Margin Rates, Shrink Analysis, Return Rates and Fraud Analysis, Credit Card Fault Detection, Assortment Optimization, Product Pricing, Seasonal Trends, Category Contribution, Hot Items Listing
Manufacturing	Supply Chain Optimization, Demand Forecasting, Inventory Replenishment, Warranty Analytics, Product Customization, New Product Development, Vendor Efficiency Model, Inventory Turns and Stock Levels, Fill Rates and Stock Outs, Storage Utilization, Network Utilization and Zone Routing, Inbound and Outbound Truck Load Analysis, SKU Velocity Analysis
Transportation	Scheduling Optimization, Routing Optimization, Yield Management
Healthcare	Drug Interaction, Preliminary Diagnosis Optimization, Disease Management
Hospitality	Pricing Optimization, Customer Loyalty, Yield Management
Energy	Trading, Supply Optimization, Demand Forecasting, Compliance
Communications	Price/Plan Optimization, Customer Retention, Demand Forecasting, Capacity Planning, Network Optimization, Customer Profitability
Services	Call Center Staffing, Service Optimization
Government	Fraud Detection, Case Management, Crime Prevention, Revenue Optimization
e-Commerce	Web Analytics, Site Design, Product Recommendations to Customers, Click Stream Analysis, Web Sales and Traffic Rates, Subscription Rates, Store Cannibalization Analysis, Web Traffic Segmentation and Target Marketing, ROI and Web Spend Effectiveness Analysis

Ironically, choosing your target process for analytics may be based on an intuitive hunch, for example:

➤ Something you've always suspected about your industry but have been unable to explore or verify. What are the implicit assumptions behind how industry players operate, and which of these may be obsolete or reversible?

- Something innovative that seems logical and doable, but for which you have no evidence to prove so. What business problems or challenges have proven resistant to solution by other means?
- Something that you (or someone influential in the business) passionately believe is important to customers. What needs or forms of value have customers themselves not yet discovered or articulated?

Note: There's nothing wrong with the informed hunch or educated guess at the start of opportunity finding, but you must verify your intuition by doing a small-scale test of the idea and expanding if it seems to be working and making a difference.

Critical Product Analysis

Data retrieved from various markets can indicate how well a product is received by the target audience and also what crucial changes must be made to it to maximize revenue. Furthermore, the organization can gain insight as to how a particular territory or market reacts to certain features of the product. This not only makes it possible to make minor alterations to the item for specific locations but also helps in studying trends associated with those regions.

Improved Customer Service

Organizations have learned through experience to keep track of their recurring customer queries and support issues. This tremendously helps them in enhancing performance by not repeating past mistakes while also enabling them to provide faster customer service and satisfaction.

Up-selling Opportunities

Tracking trends in customer behaviour can be very helpful in identifying the most prominent needs of a company's customer base. Hence it allows up-selling or cross-promotion of products that cater best to customers' needs.

Simplified Inventory Management

This is an often ignored yet very efficient application of business analytics. With the help of trend-tracking, business managers can minimize write-offs to a great extent, in turn, minimizing losses due to outdated inventory items. For example, analytic data gathered beforehand can help predict which products are on the verge of going obsolete in the near future. With this information, those specific products can be gotten rid of before they end up as write-offs.

Competitive Pricing Insights

This is yet another important highlight of business analytics that is ironically used by very few companies. Companies are known tracking trends in purchasing behaviour among customers to figure out price ranges that the target market is most comfortable in. Thus, businesses can effectively make their prices competitive without having to cut down too much on profits.

TAKING A PROCESS VIEW

In thinking about how analytics might support your business processes, it's important first to ensure that you are thinking about your business activities from a process standpoint. This means looking at the activities from an end-to-end perspective, with the primary customer of the activities as the recipient of the process outputs. Taking a process perspective allows organizations to identify all the possible ways in which analytics might be used to create a better outcome for a process customer.

For example, in a telecom industry an integrated process based approach including both customer and employee relationships could be thought of. A "customer experience lifecycle" consisting of six stages (aware/learn, need/buy, install/use, pay bill, seek help, renew/upgrade) provides an enterprise wide process view for the telecom industry. For each stage, identifying a series of attributes and metrics could be formulated. Then each stage and attribute in the entire customer experience could be further viewed as being potentially influential in determining customer loyalty. Thus, by having deeper insights into each one of these phases the company can make efficient decisions to result in reduction in customer turnover or "churn" and growing subscriber base. In addition, the company then can focus on up-sell and cross-sell substantially increasing lifetime customer value.

The same integrated, process-based approach to customer relationships could be also applied to employee relationships. Just as we investigate how customers learn about the company's offerings, how potential employees learn about the company could be explored.

Just as we attempt to reduce customer churn, reasons for employee departures could be addressed. For example, by analyzing employee attrition data for the last four years it was discovered quickly that employees were most vulnerable to leaving within 45 days of being hired. It was also learned that new employees during this period often felt ineffective because their computers weren't installed and configured quickly, and because supervisors didn't provide enough attention and direction. This discovery prompted addressing some of the on-boarding issues resulting in a rapid fall on employee turnovers. Analysis also suggested that signing up for the company's ESOPs was critical to new employees staying for more than a year. Which prompted an organizational directive to managers to intervene with employees slow to sign up, explaining details such as the company contribution match thus resulting in decreased turnover rates. Just as with customers, a process perspective was the key to better serving employees.

Most organizations already have some process orientation, be it Six Sigma, Lean, or reengineering. The key is to identify which attributes in the process are associated with satisfaction and value from the standpoint of the end-customer. The analytical work necessary to pinpoint the key attributes is not likely to be difficult once the process perspective has been adopted.

The Outside-in Approach

Broadly speaking, for any organization there are three areas that always remains in the focus: the business itself, its performance drivers, and the opportunities for differentiation. Interestingly these three areas can be also analyzed by applying three strategic tools:

- The first is the *Value Tree*, a formal decomposition of business or shareholder value most often used in decision alternative action analysis. The basic form of the tree has multiple layers of nodes (value-goals-objectives-criteria-attributes) and then how specific decisions or scenarios influence the attributes in these nodes. Figure 3.1 has a simple example adjusted to depict major business drivers and the processes whose performance most influences them. If the organization has a comprehensive measurement and metrics management system, it can perform statistical analysis on the value tree and determine the correlations among business drivers.
- The second is the *Service/Profit Chain*, a well-known business analysis framework that helps in documenting and quantifying specific linkages from what employees do, through customer satisfaction and value, to financial performance and share price. It is especially useful for exploring opportunities at the touch points with the customer and related to the customer's experience. Figure 3.2 below depicts the basic steps in the chain. In a service-oriented business, employee behavior can drive customer response, in turn driving increased loyalty and retention and business volume. Again, companies use analytics to understand the relationships among links in the chain, though a complete and quantitative set of relationships—all the way from employee satisfaction and engagement to share price—is difficult to pin down. Some skip the first two steps (at least initially) and start their investigation with customer loyalty.

Note: The original Harvard Business Review article introducing the framework, "Putting the Service Profit Chain to Work" (March 1994) has spawned a variety of books and articles exploring and extending the method, and some firms have made substantial progress at understanding relationships along the chain.

- The third tool explores the questions: "What kind of business are we really in?" and "How do we really create value?" Table 3.2 explains three basic business types:

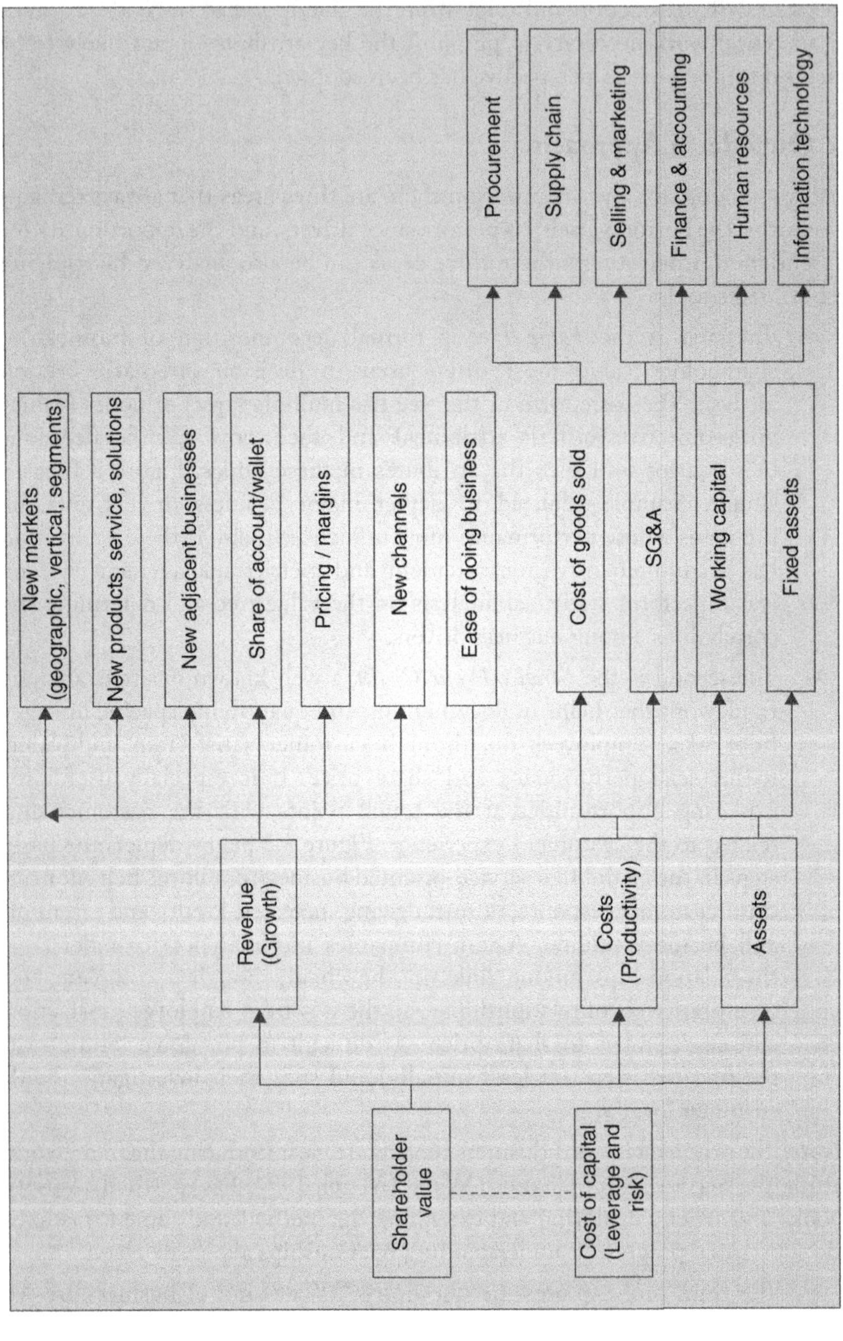

Figure 3.1 Value tree.

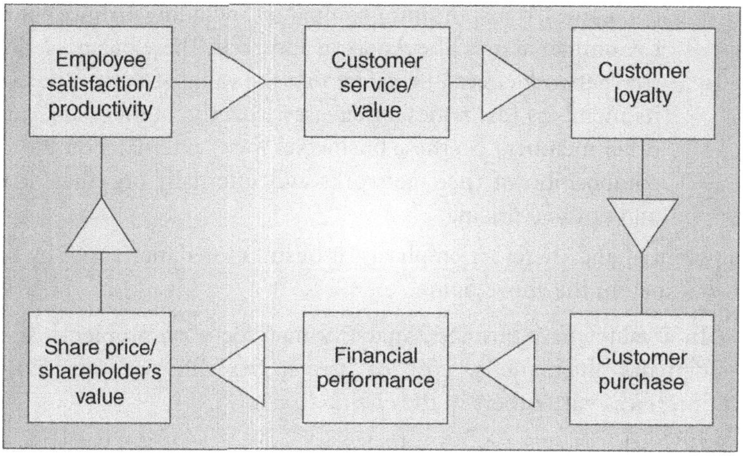

Figure 3.2 Service/Profit chain.

Table 3.2 Value chain

	Value Chain	*Value Shop*	*Value Network*
Business Types	Manufacturing	Consulting, Exploration, Construction, Hospitals	Banks, Insurance, Telecom, Airlines, Hotels
Managing Profits Managing Markets	Product Profitability Manage Brand: Expectations of Product Properties	People Profitability Manage Reputation: Trust in non-observable competencies	Network Profitability Manage Network Expectations: Expectations of network size and composition
Managing Efficiency	Capacity Utilization: Manage flow and Variation	Knowledge Leverage: Manage resource pyramid, Knowledge Management, IP leverage	Network Yield: Manage Prices and routing Optimally

- Value Chain businesses create value by producing physical products. Their external focus is on brand, their internal focus on efficient utilization of resources. Manufacturers are the classic examples. Chain businesses have been the traditional and dominant focus of most management theory, even though they are in the minority among corporations today.
- Value Shop businesses create value by solving problems (note that "shop" is in the sense of a "job shop" producing custom products, not a retail "shop"). Examples include hospitals, construction companies, and consulting firms. Externally, success depends on reputation, internally on the leverage of skilled people and their knowledge.
- Value Network businesses create value by bringing customers together to exchange or transport goods, capital, or information. Examples include financial institutions, telecommunications

companies, transportation companies including airlines, and online e-Commerce sites like Amazon and eBay. These businesses leverage the "network effect"—the fact that the value of a network to each of its members (or "nodes") increases with the number and quality of other members. So these businesses focus externally on the size and composition of their networks and internally on efficient routing and optimal pricing.

The potential and therefore emphasis of business analytics varies by business type, as outlined in the above figure.

- In a value chain business, analytics may focus on problems of supply/demand fluctuations, cost of assets, flexibility of operations, and interfaces with others in the chain.
- In a value shop business, which incorporates new information to solve new versions of problems, the most valuable analytics may be in support of exploration and solution and decision design.
- In a value network business, analytics may focus on understanding the network and its transaction patterns, the better to attract quality customers and minimize cost.

Note: For a complete description of these three business types, see "Casting off the chains: Value shops and value networks" by Fjeldstad and Andersen (European Business Forum, summer 2003).

Note that a business of one type may have major processes more akin to a different type. For example, back-office operations of a bank may have a lot in common with a value chain business, and its commercial loan department may function much like a value shop, while the bank as a whole is a value network, enabling the exchange of money. It's useful to apply this business type analysis to major processes within a corporation; however, one must keep in mind (and not work in opposition to) the overall purpose of the business. For example, telecommunications companies that run their customer service call centers, if focus too much on value chain businesses (pursuing efficient utilization over customer service), it may overlook other business aspects like customer experience thereby creating a disservice of driving customers out of the value network.

Value type analysis can serve two important purposes in finding opportunities to leverage business analytics. First, it can help you focus on the fundamental objectives of the business and how analytics can serve them. Second, it can suggest where to look outside your industry for fresh examples of analytical applications. When looking across industries for inspiration, your best hunting grounds are likely to be other industries within your value type (e.g., telecom companies learning from financial institutions). These are companies that face analogous business problems but in different contexts, and their analytical applications may be recognizable, relevant, and transferable.

Table 3.3 Value type analysis

	Value Chain	*Value Shop*	*Value Network*
Data	Data (part number, time, place, order, price) and data flow are fairly precise	Data is often voluminous, uncertain and context dependent	Underlying transactions (Calls, payments, shipments) are simple, but a high volume of transactions can happen anywhere
Objectives	Running at capacity, minimizing investment, forecasting demand, minimizing fluctuations	Assess problems and find resources to solve them	Minimize cost to select and serve best customers, both individually and collectively
Analytical Examples	Anticipating demand and supply, dealing with fluctuations	Creating frameworks and tests, enabling earlier and more decisions	Finding alternative views of transaction patterns, finding new customers outside the network

The Inside-Out Approach

Another way to find specific opportunities for applying analytics is by looking in detail at your processes and how decisions are made within them. What kinds of processes lend themselves to—or call for—business analytics?

At a broad level these processes are:

- Information-intensive—analytics reveal the meaning of information.
- Asset-intensive—analytics enable effective utilization and sharing of scarce or expensive resources.
- Labor-intensive—analytics enable decision-making and the leverage of expertise, especially where talent supply is short, talent demand is cyclical, and training times are lengthy.
- Dependent on speed and timing—analytics enable process acceleration and real-time decisions, especially where customer satisfaction or process competitiveness demand almost real time responses.
- Dependent on consistency and control—analytics enable consistent decisions even in unpredictable cases.
- Dependent on distributed decision-making—analytics enable decision makers to look upstream and downstream and anticipate the effects of their actions.
- Cross-functional or cross-business in scope—analytics reveal interdependencies and enable the parts to work together.

Specific opportunities could be also found for applying analytics by inventorying key business decisions (whether or not they are associated with well-defined business processes) and asking how better information and analysis would make for faster and better results.

In general, these could be:

- Complex decisions with lots of variables and steps within the decision process.
- Simple decisions where consistency is the key (or required for compliance).
- Places where you want to optimize the whole process or activity (i.e., if you simply decompose and optimize locally, you sub-optimize the whole).
- Decisions where you need to understand connections, correlations, and their significance.
- Places where you need better forecasts, anticipation, prediction, or downstream visibility.

Ask, for example, where are the places or business functions within the enterprise where we do forecasts—and are they of high and trustworthy statistical quality? Where do we need to optimize something? Where else would forecasts or optimization make a difference?

Be sure to cover different types of decisions and useful anticipations, for example:

- Strategic decisions—Should we acquire another company?
- Operational decisions—What are the likely sales for this quarter?
- Tactical decisions—Is this customer likely to buy this particular product?

Although few companies have as yet created an inventory of decisions, as you inventory and assess your important business processes and decisions, it may be useful to start with a realistic sense of their likely potential for embedded analytics.

Among the core operational processes, the potential of analytics is best established in supply chain and marketing. Sales and service are lagging behind but are areas of great opportunity. There may be lower analytical potential in the innovation process, given its unstructured and creative nature, except, of course, where analytical applications directly support simulation and/or engineering-type work.

Note: However, companies like Capital One apply experimental design to traditionally "creative" decisions—what color is the direct-mail envelope, where is the call-out box, is there a picture of someone in the mailing? Attributes like these—and their interactions—can be tested to understand their potential contribution to the outcome of interest.

Among the support activities, analytical potential is probably highest in performance management, where companies can make their scorecards more quantitative and analytical. The situation is similar in HR management, which is typically underserved by analytics but can accomplish a great deal by understanding and raising employee engagement. In IT management, operational activities may be highly automated and analytically measured, but the more creative work of finding new business uses of technology lends itself less to embedded analytics. In corporate development, key decisions (e.g., regarding M&A) may benefit greatly from analytics, but few companies take a process approach to such activities.

CATEGORIZATION OF ANALYTICAL APPLICATIONS

It's useful to categorize your current analytical applications and potential analytical opportunities—to understand your emphasis and "mix," to identify gaps and adjacent opportunities, and to set a realistic level of ambition. "Analytics alternative matrix" and "Ladder of analytical applications" are frameworks for doing so.

The "Analytics Alternatives" matrix categorizes applications according to timeframe—past or future—and content type—basic information versus new insight. The past-information quadrant is the realm of traditional business reporting, not really analytics. By applying statistical methods and modeling that information, however, you get insight into how and why things happened. Incorporating predictive analytics and simulations creates future information such as forecasts. And optimization models create future insight by addressing the question of what's the best that can happen.

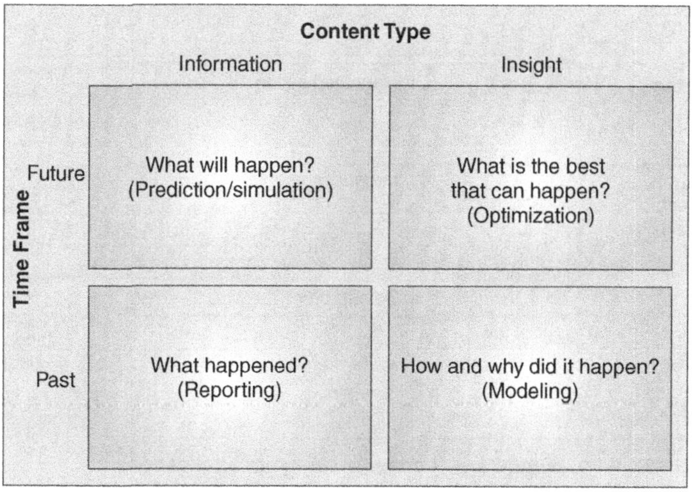

Figure 3.3 Analytics alternatives matrix.

This two-by-two matrix is a convenience. Any given analytical application may have elements of more than one category. However, you can learn a lot about what you are—and are not—doing analytically by using this matrix. And you can explore your options for turning past information into future insight.

The "Ladder of Analytical Applications," depicts how analytical capabilities and applications tend to build upon one another. Going up the ladder entails more sophisticated analytics. The foundation is good data—are they accurate, consistent, integrated, accessible, and relevant? Statistical analysis of that data yields useful segmentation (e.g., of customers, products, and transactions or other business events), which in turn enables differentiated action (e.g., treating customers differently, or calling upon the right "lane" in a flexible business process). Incorporating predictive analytics enables a business to optimally use its resources where opportunity is the greatest. At the institutional action area, differentiation and prediction are embedded in ongoing business processes and accomplished automatically. The top level is the domain of real-time optimization, where the process adjusts dynamically to maintain optimal business yield. As with any such classification, the higher levels tend to be less populated.

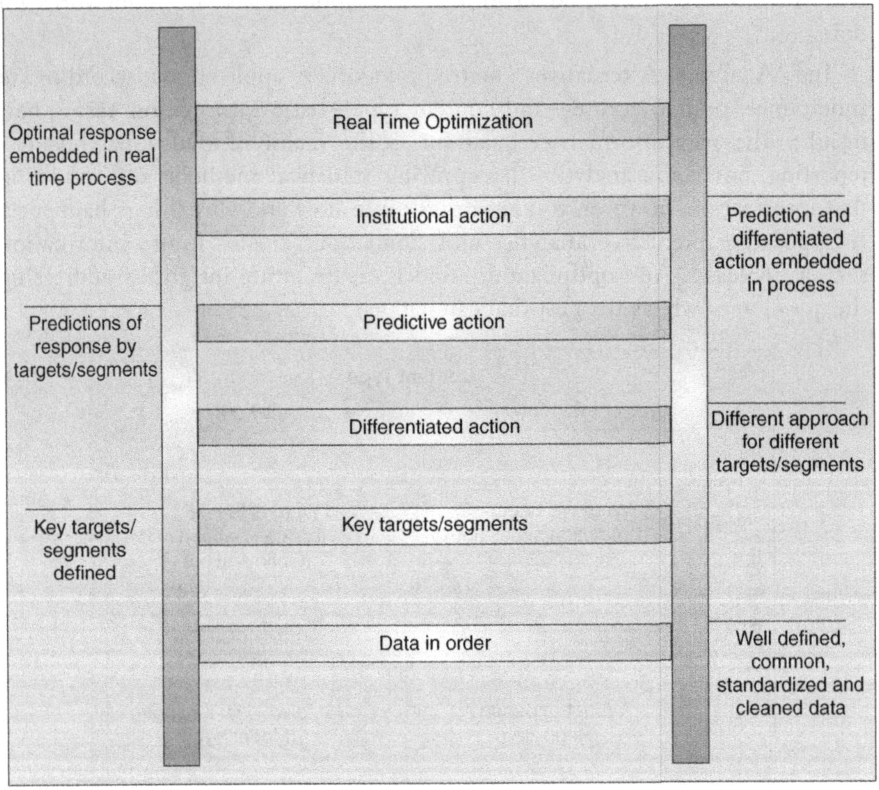

Figure 3.4 Ladder of analytics applications.

The ladder is a general pattern, not a set sequence. But within any major process area, it's enlightening to ask: How high have we climbed? How high can we climb? How high does the market want us to climb? Have we compromised our performance by skipping or only partially covering a level? Can we gain competitive advantage by moving up a level?

Qualify the Opportunities

For any analytical opportunity, the qualification step involves:

- Anticipating whether the application will make a significant difference in business performance.
- Anticipating whether the business will be able to implement the application and realize the opportunity.

We have discussed in general what attributes of processes lend themselves to business analytics. Formal qualification for embedded analytics requires examining the target process in greater depth, including:

- Does the process incorporate rational decision methods with well-defined parameters and well-understood business implications of decisions?
- Does the process call for or benefit from consistent decisions, including the need for exacting policy compliance or significant liability from inconsistently applied policies?
- Is the process high-volume and performed often, and are there significant cost savings from speeding decisions, eliminating steps, or selecting the best process variation?
- Will excelling at the process yield competitive advantage, or build a differentiated capability within the industry?

In the rest of this section, we will discuss three ways in which the qualification of a business analytics application differs from that of more conventional and predictable projects or initiatives.

DELTA Readiness Diagnosis

The DELTA framework captures five conditions that must be in place for an analytical initiative to succeed. Applied to process analytics, these are:

- *Data* - Do we have access to the necessary data of sufficient quality to apply analytics in the process? Do we have a rich data set for exploring, designing, and testing the embedded analytics? Do we have the technology to manage this data?
- *Enterprise* - Does the process have the cross-functional or cross-boundary scope to make a difference in overall business performance, including financially?
- *Leadership* - Does the process have a capable owner who can work across the affected functions and who has the backing of top management?
- *Targets* - Will analytics drive the performance of this process to a level that makes a difference in overall business performance, including financially? Do we have the metrics to track these results?
- *Analysts* - Do the analysts have sufficient analytical ability as well as process or domain knowledge? Who can bridge any gaps? Will process performers be prepared to work in an analytics-assisted manner?

Assess the readiness of the process and the organization in all five of these areas. You may need to fill gaps in order to have the foundation for succeeding with process analytics.

MOTIVATION AND MOMENTUM

Organizations face a variety of challenges in generating management motivation and organizational momentum for business analytics initiatives. Table 3.4 summarizes three common scenarios:

Table 3.4 Motivation scenarios

Scenario	*Business Problem*	*Impacted*
We have a problem of improvement opportunity	Need to raise performance, perhaps in response to a competitor. Need to lower cost, improve asset utilization or change cost structure. Need to increase innovation or accelerate time to market.	Mid to upper functional management, making targeting easier than investing
We have a data hoard	Sitting on an accumulation of potentially useful data that has yet to be explored and exploited. Ideally in combination with other assets—analysts and technology.	Who recognizes the potential? Helps if top management includes some business process owners and data stewards
We have a strategic opportunity	Determined to compete on a differentiation basis, to solve a problem nobody else has mastered, to be the best at something important. Determined to invest and seize the opportunity.	Top management, which puts the pressure on, especially if the assets are not ready

- Sometimes there's a well-defined business problem or improvement opportunity in a process that lends itself to analytics. Examples include logistics at Wal-Mart and revenue management at Marriott. Here the target may be clear, but management motivation may not be high enough if the problem is owned by functional managers. You may need to elevate sponsorship, especially if the analytical solution will be cross-functional.
- Sometimes a key executive or management team senses or recognizes that the business is sitting on a hoard of potentially valuable data associated with a business process (e.g., point-of-sale data, claims history, employee experience) that is not being put to good use, either operationally or predictively. This is often the case in financial institutions, and it was a big part of the momentum behind analytics at Harrah's. In this scenario, you need to do some exploration to uncover the specific potential of the data for process improvement, and you need

to get someone in top management to recognize the business value of exploiting it.

- Sometimes (often as the result of "Outside-In" thinking) top management senses or recognizes a strategic business opportunity that depends on analytics. As we mentioned earlier, this analytical opportunity may be sensed in only an intuitive way. This may seem the ideal scenario for generating momentum. However, any delay may frustrate management's expectations and drain momentum. And delay is common, especially when the opportunity needs further definition and qualification, the structure and management of the process are weak, or key assets (especially data) are not ready.

EXPERIMENTATION

One of the most challenging differences between a conventional information systems project or business change initiative and an analytics implementation is the inherently experimental nature of the latter. You can (and should) estimate the business value of any anticipated improvement in process performance. But if the analysis, decision steps, or process steps are new, you don't know the degree and value of success until you've given it a try. You don't know how a new mathematical model, the users of the model, and the established business processes will work together until they start to do so.

You may, for example, be confident that better decisions on the timing and priority of order-fulfillment will lower inventory and logistics costs and raise customer satisfaction. But you don't know how much effect a better decision system will have on each of those business goals. The first implementation of the decision system may just give a foretaste of the business value generated as the model is refined over time. And you may well discover new goals and new value over time.

An analytics initiative should be managed as a business experiment: a structured, controlled, cost-effective, and iterative approach to learning about the potential success or failure of a new product, service or process. A business experimentation initiative typically incorporates techniques such as iterative design, experimental design, rival designs, early pilots, stage-gate review, and periodic refunding. With a business experiment, sponsoring management must pay close attention, support adjustments on-the-fly, and be willing to pull the plug if the initiative stalls.

Thus, the final major question in qualifying a process analytics opportunity is "Can we handle a business experiment?" Do we have the right mindset and expectations, both among senior management and across the organizations affected by the analytical application? Are our project approval and management methods flexible enough to guide a business experiment through to conclusion, one way or the other? Are sponsors afraid to change course or pull the plug because they fear losing face?

If the company's project approval process (e.g., with strict financial hurdle rates), project management process (e.g., based on sequential milestones), and management mindset assume lockstep predictability in business projects, then an analytical initiative of any scope or scale is destined to run into a failure mode—no matter how good the concept, analysts, and technology behind it. In a situation like this, you should engage top management to break through the project approval and management obstacles, and then focus on the analytical model/application build up. Otherwise, you have to start small with process analytics—a local application entirely within the domain of an enthusiastic management sponsor.

END POINTS

Why Industrialize? Corporations have begun to "industrialize" knowledge-intensive processes in response to:

- *Customer expectations* - for real-time response and consistent decisions and actions.
- *Competitive pressures* - for increased agility and a faster "insight to action" loop.
- *Talent shortages* - the need to reduce dependence on costly, aging, or scarce human resources.

And keep in mind that there will still be important roles for *ad hoc* analytics in conjunction with processes that may not be ready for "industrial" analytics.

As businesses learn to adapt the disciplines of analytics and process management, however, many decisions can become more automated, embedded in the process flow, or, as we call it, "industrialized." Here the decision-maker decides to automate a decision with the right attributes (e.g., it is structured and repetitive) and works with the analyst to define the right information needs and decision rules. The analyst works with IT team to build an automated decision system, often incorporating a statistical model and tests and refines the system until it works well.

Once implemented, the decision system receives data from transaction systems in real or near-real time, makes decisions automatically and instantaneously, and thus determines subsequent process flow and triggers new transactions. Often the system is designed to discard the exceptional cases for the decision-maker to handle. Over time, the decision-maker and analyst would work to refine and optimize the decision system. The approach requires lots of skilled effort up front, but thereafter the decisions are automated with the flexibility to tune the system and adapt to changes as needed.

Table 3.5 Intuitive approach vs. industrial approach

	Intuitive/ad-Hoc	***Industrial***
Pattern	*ad-hoc*, siloed, project-by-project	Embedded in an ongoing process, streamlined and standardized
Purpose	One time decision or event support	Ongoing performance management
Benefit	One time	Recurring
Investment	Lower, one time	Higher up front, recurring to maintain the model
Time to implement	Brief	Longer
Speed of analysis	Same as time to implement	Once implemented fast or instantaneous
Skilled resources	Labor intensive, niche skill	Labor intensive upfront, analysis automated thereafter
Reusability	Can be saved for reuse but often found lost or not knowledge managed	Maintained and improvement upon, knowledge managed

Table 3.5 above contrasts the "Intuitive/*ad-hoc*" and "Industrial" approaches to employing business analytics. Intuitive/*ad-hoc* is a one-time effort, inherently slow. Industrial takes more time and effort up front, but then the decisions can be instantaneous. With intuitive/*ad-hoc*, the analysis is often discarded or forgotten after use. With industrial, it is maintained, improved, and available for reuse—thanks to investment in ongoing model management.

REFERENCES

Davenport, Thomas H., Harris, Jeanne G., and Morison, Robert, *Analytics at work—Smarter Decisions Better Results*. Harvard Business Press, February 2010.

Pyle, Dorian, "Business Modeling and Data Mining" (The Morgan Kaufmann Series in Data Management Systems), May 2003.

Fjeldstad, Andersen, "Casting Off The Chains: Value Shops and Value Networks" European Business Forum, summer 2003.

Heskett, James L., Jones, Thomas O., Loveman, Gary W., Sasser, W. Earl, Jr., and Schlesinger, Leonard A., "Putting the Service Profit Chain to Work", *Harvard Business Review*, March 2009.

CHAPTER 4

CHOOSING THE RIGHT ANALYTICS TECHNIQUE AND TOOLS

Successful analytics initiatives are not as simple as throwing a tool at a data set, clicking on a button, and watching it work. A successful analytics solution should utilize the best possible and most appropriate analytical technique and tool. But how does one select the best possible and most appropriate analytics technique and tool to develop the "right" analytics solution?

Like it or not, whenever we come across an analytics problem, the first thing that comes to our mind is—"To solve my customer churn problem what technique you are going to use? Are you going to run a neural net analytics or k-means algorithm?" Throughout this book, you will see, there is a conscious attempt to stay away from such conclusions and more or less guide you through the best practices. It is less of a "what technique you are going to choose" but more of a "how would you choose the right technique to solve a relevant analytics problem".

First let us discuss, what are the important characteristics of an analytics solution, and how these characteristics affect the choice of analytical techniques and tools? The approach to selecting an appropriate analytical technique and tool is based on two primary methods: Business Problem Analysis and Operational Readiness Analysis.

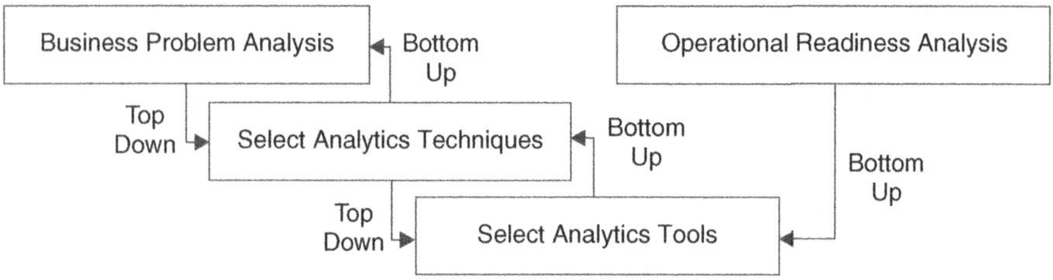

Figure 4.1 The approach to selecting an analytics technique and tool.

Business Problem Analysis is more of a top-down approach and helps the analyst select a technique and tool by looking at the features of the business problem (i.e., the analytics opportunity). Using this approach, the analyst can analyze the business problem in detail to determine the various constituents (what are the processes, what is influencing this problem, etc.) and also take advantage of prior experience, best practices employed to solve similar scenarios.

Operational Readiness Analysis is a bottom-up approach and starts the activities by considering the operational requirements and readiness (both skills as well as data availability) of the organization's IT environment before finalizing on the appropriate analytics techniques and tools to solve the business problem. In practice, there are many operational constraints that need to be considered, and any analytics solution will be forced to fit into these, regardless of which analytics techniques method one uses. Top down approach may narrow down the choices for analytics techniques and tools, but ultimately, operational and technical requirements will guide the final decision.

Note: The approach discussed here is not meant to be the definitive answer to the problem. Rather it should be used to guide the process of finding a good data analytics solution.

MAPPING ANALYTICS OPPORTUNITIES TO PROBLEM TYPES

Analytics solutions fall into a wide spectrum of categories: from problems that search for pre-defined patterns and data (e.g., loan approval, based on matching the applicant to known risk and profitability profiles), to problems that specify the data but not the patterns (e.g., fraudulent credit card usage, based on ever-changing usage patterns). Identifying the analytics opportunity provides a way to match the objectives of a specific solution to the objectives of a general class of applications (e.g., target marketing, fraud detection, and customer profitability, etc.).

Define Problem Types: There are five currently defined classes of problem types; the last of these is composed of combinations of the previous four problem types that require multiple modeling methods. Each problem type is distinguished by certain business and technical features discussed below.

Relationship Analysis

Relationship Analysis involves identifying associations or affinities between items within records of a database. Associations are occurrences that are linked in a single event. This is the most complex problem type because of the number of potential relationships that could occur. One drawback to Relationship Analysis is that the specific order or direction of the association is not usually known. For example, if the analysis discovers a link between hiking boots and tents, you would not be able to tell if hiking boots were bought first and tents second or vice versa.

Examples of Relationship Analysis include:

- *Market Basket Analysis* - Analytics can determine that in the summer, when someone purchases hamburgers or hot dogs and ice, they will also purchase barbecue charcoal 74% of the time. This association can be used to adjust promotions, store layout design or pricing.

- *Quality Control* - A manufacturing application may determine that 30% of all electrical switches with faulty wiring are manufactured on a Friday and are output during the afternoon shift.
- *Healthcare* - A healthcare application may analyze claim forms submitted by patients to determine relationships among medical procedures that are often performed together.

Classification

Classification entails grouping a collection of data records based upon the variables that comprise the records (e.g., credit rating data) and one key target variable (e.g., approval of a loan). In Classification problems, the desired grouping is known or pre-defined (in a target marketing example, customers are classified based on responses to previous marketing or purchase behavior). This is sometimes referred to as supervised learning. The resulting classification model is often used for prediction of outcomes for new data records. Classification is the most commonly used analytics today.

Other examples of Classification include:

- *Risk Assessment* - Analytics can be used in loan/insurance/credit card qualification or bankruptcy prediction applications. A bank may have history records indicating whether a customer is low, average or high risk for a loan. Analytics can analyze customer data to discover characteristics that make up a "high" risk person and characteristics that make up a "low" risk person.
- *Performance Management* - Classifying and predicting credit card customers (e.g., attriter, revolver, or transactor) based on customer attributes and spending patterns.

Clustering

Similar to Classification, Clustering groups a collection of data records, based upon the variables comprising the records such that each group is made up of similar records, but is distinctly different from the other groups. However, in Clustering, the key target variable is unknown (in an insurance fraud detection example, basing decisions only on previously identified fraudulent behaviour will miss any new abnormal behaviour), and groupings are defined by the analytics tool. This is sometimes referred to as unsupervised learning. One drawback of Clustering is that different tools and techniques may produce different segmentations of the input records.

Examples of Clustering include:

- *Fault Analysis* - Clustering can be used to analyze defects in product manufacturing where there may be no data on prior defects.
- *Customer Segmentation* - In problems such as customer attrition and target marketing, there may not be historical data to pattern knowledge

on and these problems can be solved only by identifying natural segments or clusters of customers.

- *Input to Classification Problems* - Clustering can also be used to determine the groupings for a Classification problem.

Sequential Pattern Analysis

Sequential Pattern Analysis is a modeling technique used to analyze collections of related records (i.e., all of one customer's purchases, cellular phone usage) to determine frequently occurring patterns over time (i.e., product purchase or usage patterns) and possibly predict future activity. Sequential Pattern Analysis can also determine "similar sequences," i.e., patterns similar to a given one. Typical examples include finding stocks with similar price movements, products with similar sales patterns, or stores/departments with similar revenue streams. Sequential Pattern Analysis differs from Relationship Analysis in that the order or sequence of the attributes matters when discovering patterns.

Other examples of Pattern Analysis include:

- *Performance Management* - Analytics can be used for cost reduction by analyzing insurance claims to determine frequently occurring sequences of medical procedures to target for better management or control.
- *Quality Control* - Analyzing sales patterns for better inventory forecasting and purchasing decisions.

Composite Modeling

Some problems require the use of multiple techniques listed above. Composite Modeling uses two or more of the problem types described above to solve the data mining problem.

Examples include:

- *Cross-Selling* - A two-step analytics solution consisting of classification of customers into segments, followed by relationship analysis to determine cross selling possibilities.
- *Fraud Detection* - Another two-step analytics—identification of frequently occurring sequential patterns of medical procedures, followed by classification of claims into normal and abnormal.

Table 4.1 provides a summary of analytics opportunities mapping to problem types. This is by no means is an exhaustive list of opportunities. The contents of the table give some indication of which problem type is appropriate for which analytics solution.

UNDERSTANDING INFORMATION TYPE AND USAGE

Since analytics techniques sometimes solve more than one business problem, the problem type alone does not necessarily uniquely determine a technique or

Table 4.1 Summary of analytics opportunities

Business Problem Type	*Relationship Analysis*	*Classification*	*Clustering*	*Sequential Pattern Analysis*
Target Marketing	Yes	Yes	Yes	
Marketing Channel		Yes	Yes	
Management				
Micro-Marketing		Yes	Yes	Yes
Customer Evaluation		Yes	Yes	Yes
Fraud Detection		Yes	Yes	Yes
Risk Assessment		Yes	Yes	
Profitability Analysis		Yes	Yes	Yes
Customer Attrition		Yes	Yes	Yes
Market Basket Analysis	Yes			Yes
Cross-Selling	Yes	Yes		
Product Displacement	Yes			
Delivery Channel Management		Yes	Yes	
Customer Gap Analysis		Yes	Yes	
Product Gap Analysis	Yes			Yes
Performance Management		Yes	Yes	Yes
Quality Control	Yes			Yes
Fault Analysis				Yes
Inventory Management	Yes			Yes

tool. The second step in business problem analysis is to understand and assess the information type and usage type of the analytics opportunity. Information type describes the type and format of the input and output required to solve the problem. Usage type describes who, how, and when the data analytics solution will be used. Unfortunately, most analytics techniques support multiple information and usage types and there is no easy way to directly map techniques to information and usage types.

Define Information Types

Information type describes how the data sources and problem relate and how the output and problem relate. This does not include traditional data features such as data volume, location, etc. which are covered under operational readiness analysis. There are three basic classes of information types: input dependencies, knowledge transformation type, and problem complexity.

Input Dependencies

This class of information type describes how the input records relate to one another within the data sources. The relationships between data sources can have an important effect on which technique(s) is(are) chosen. Examples include:

- *Independent* - All the data is contained within a single table or file, and each record contains all the necessary information to discover relationships (e.g., customer records for insurance policy approval/profitability analysis).

- *Hierarchical* - The data is contained in several tables or files, but the relationships between these tables or files are simple one-way, fixed dependencies (e.g., customer detail table with direct join to product detail table for direct marketing analysis).
- *Network/Complex* - Data is spread over many tables or files with multiple relationships and interdependencies.

Knowledge Transformation Type

This class of information type describes the type or format of output that the business process and/or problem type both desire and require. Certain techniques support specific knowledge transformation types, while others support multiple formats.

Problem Complexity

This class of information type refers to the complexity of the analytic problem. There are two features: 1) how complicated is the problem in terms of dependent variable(s), and 2) what is the number of attributes and types of inter-attribute relationships within the records. Examples include:

- *Simple dependent variable* - Dependent variable maps directly to records (e.g., new customer credit limit setting based on historical customer base).
- *Complex dependent variable* - May have more than one dependent variable or hierarchical dependent variables (e.g., mass personalization of advertisements in a magazine based on customer profiles).
- *Number of attributes* - Cellular phone fraud detection is based on few attributes (customer id, call source/destination, length); direct market analysis is based on many attributes (sex, age, income, location, education, martial status, etc.).

Define Usage Types

Usage type identifies how, when, and by whom the analytics application and its discovered knowledge will be used. There are four basic classes of usage types: type and number of users, level of user input, frequency of use, and domain variability.

Type and Number of Users

The type of user may influence the choice of analytical technique, since some techniques are easier to understand than others. The expected number of users (e.g., enterprise-wide or single-user) may also influence which analytical technique and tool is chosen. Some possible users include:

- *End user* - The end user only uses the transformed output from the analytics application and will have minimal input into the creation and business functions (e.g., a warehouse manager for inventory forecasting).

- *Business analyst* - The business analyst understands many business functions very well, but doesn't have the detailed analytic background necessary to develop analytics solution alone (e.g., a sales manager for sales force incentive programs).
- *Analytical specialist* - The analytical specialist is an expert in mining algorithms and techniques, but may not possess the business knowledge necessary to create appropriate models (e.g., a database marketing analyst for a telecommunications company).
- *Technical analyst* - The technical analyst is most likely to be developing the analytics applications and models (e.g., an IT employee dedicated to the marketing department). They are responsible for working closely with the business analysts and analytical specialists to create and evaluate models and, then, for the on-going maintenance of the analytics solution.

Level of User Input

This usage type defines the level of user involvement in defining the problem (i.e., reactive or proactive). Examples include:

- *Undirected pattern queries (bottom-up discovery)* - User input is minimal and the analytics target is broad (e.g., find product purchasing relationships for cross selling).
- *Detailed requirements (top-down directed)* - The user has a well defined problem and precisely directs the analytics application (e.g., in direct marketing, find the customers most likely to purchase this product in the next 6 months who may require financing assistance).
- *"Expert" user input/opinions* - The current ability of user-directed procedures to solve the problem may contain valuable explicit knowledge that should be incorporated into the construction of the analytics solution (e.g., classifying employment of applicant in loan approval analysis).
- *Model validation/refinement* - The analytics application requires frequent user input of "soft" information to increase accuracy (e.g., add knowledge about new marketing campaigns or products for inventory forecasting).
- *What-if analysis* - The analytics application allows the user to iterate through various solutions to weigh the benefits (e.g., in direct marketing campaign, if we contact more customers, what would the cost/benefit ratio be?).

Frequency of Use

How often the analytics model is used by the application can be a major influence on the analytics technique chosen. Possibilities include: one time use, infrequent use of same model, infrequent use of similar model, daily heavy usage, and operational usage.

Domain Variability

This feature refers to how the analytics problem domain is changing and considers both problem characteristics (variables) and problem relationships (solutions).

Examples include:

- *Static problem domain* - In this scenario neither the problem characteristics nor the solution relationships are changing, or they are changing very slowly.
- *Changing within problem domain* - The problem characteristics are not changing, but the relationships in the solution sets are changing (e.g., new fraudulent methods may continue to occur in a fraud detection system).
- *Growing within problem domain* - The problem characteristics are changing (e.g., insurance policy approval with future new policy attributes from external sources).
- *Expanding across problem domains* - The original analytics solution is expanding to include related problems (e.g., sales forecasting with future inventory forecasting application).

Once the business problem analysis is completed, the next step is to identify which analytical technique can solve the business problem. The first consideration is to map the applicable problem type to analytical techniques. As discussed earlier, the information and usage type should be considered here as well. But first, we must familiarize ourselves with several terminologies and approaches.

Similar to the previously defined classification scheme for analytics opportunities (based on problem type, information type and usage), analytical techniques can be classified and compared by certain features. Some of these features help narrow the search for the best techniques, while others are used to help pinpoint the best technique. The following terms are defined below: explicit versus implicit knowledge, supervised versus unsupervised learning, and opaque versus transparent modeling. Then, we discuss the major analytical techniques and how these features apply to each of them.

EXPLICIT KNOWLEDGE VS. IMPLICIT KNOWLEDGE

The analytical technique should allow users to include both explicit and implicit knowledge (if desired) when creating the data mining model.

- *Explicit knowledge* - Knowledge from domain experts or documents (e.g., rules the experts may know and use when analyzing data, but which may not be written down anywhere). Explicit knowledge is particularly useful when combined with implicit knowledge.
- *Implicit knowledge* - Knowledge that comes directly from data (i.e., derived specifically from data mining). May provide insight to new knowledge and is particularly powerful when combined with explicit knowledge.

SUPERVISED LEARNING VS. UNSUPERVISED LEARNING

Most analytical techniques can perform either supervised or unsupervised learning, but not both. Determining which type of learning is applicable to a problem can significantly narrow down the choice of techniques.

- *Supervised learning* - A set of actual target outputs is used to compare actual with produced output during learning (i.e., model construction). Supervised learning is used for constructing predictive models. Supervised learning methods often accept explicit knowledge when constructing models.
- *Unsupervised learning* - Models are constructed independent of any supplied performance criteria; there is no target field/value available. Unsupervised learning is used to search for new and inherent patterns in the data. Often, unsupervised learning methods provide results that are not particularly explainable by the user (i.e., doesn't produce transparent models).

OPAQUE MODELING VS. TRANSPARENT MODELING

Similar to supervised versus unsupervised learning, most analytical techniques can produce results either as opaque or transparent models, but not both. Determining which type of output model is required can also significantly narrow down the choice of techniques.

- *Opaque modeling* - The analytical technique provides limited, if any, explanation of how the results were derived. For example, when predicting responses to a direct mail campaign, the analytics results might state that one customer's score is 92/100 and another customer has a score of 54/100. The first customer would be more likely to respond to the mailing in this case.
- *Transparent modeling* - The results of the analytical technique clearly explain how decisions are reached. For example, when determining high or low-risk insurance candidates, the analytics results might state that a driver with more than two at-fault accidents is high-risk and a driver with less than two at-fault accidents is low-risk. Transparent modeling techniques are often preferred for those applications where legal or business needs require full explanation of decisions.

NEURAL NETWORKS

Neural networks attempt to simulate the way the human brain works—they "learn" how to solve a problem by examining and processing data values. They are made up of a collection of nodes with inputs and outputs—simple processing is performed at each node. Between the visible input and output layers, there may be several additional hidden intermediate layers.

Neural networks are not explicitly programmed with procedural knowledge. Instead they are trained through exposure to real-time or historical data. They are characterized by powerful pattern-matching and predictive capabilities in which input variables interact heavily (non-linear, complex problems).

There are over 50 different neural network architectures. Parallel processing characteristics and unique knowledge representation make neural networks capable of handling large amounts of nonlinear, multidimensional, and complex data. Many applications for neural networks go beyond the typical commercial arena. For example, neural networks may be applied to interpret electrocardiograms, voice recognition and synthesis, and handwriting recognition.

Summary

- Traits: Neural networks cannot handle explicit knowledge, performs both supervised and unsupervised learning outputs, opaque models only.
- Pros: Neural networks are well established and robust.
- Cons: Most neural networks are designed for specific problems; the domain of their application is narrow. Very little to no explanation of results is provided. Implementation and application require deep mathematical skills.

RULE DISCOVERY

Rule discovery implements any one of the several learning routines or algorithms that start with specifics (database records) and create generalities (decision trees, if/then rules) to divide the data on meaningful criteria. Learning routines include CART and ID3 algorithms, as well as many others. Most of these techniques evolved from statistical techniques to classify, generalize and summarize large data sets. Parameters such as rule length, factor importance, maximum/minimum number of rules to generate, rule confidence, minimum percent of database to use, and margin of error are used to control the induction routine.

The constructed models are in the form of deterministic or probabilistic logic trees. One of the key advantages of techniques based on decision trees is that, in addition to using a decision tree to make a prediction, the user may visually examine the tree itself. Rule discovery is not suitable for all kinds of problems, and may not work with some types of data. Some rule discovery tools have problems dealing with continuous sets of values, like revenue or age, and may require that these values be grouped into ranges. In addition, the way the ranges are specified may inadvertently hide patterns inherent in the data.

Rule discovery supports an iterative development process. For example, a model with too many rules (due to over-fitting or rules that are not general enough) can be corrected by rerunning with different control parameters or pruning if a decision tree algorithm is implemented.

Summary

- Traits: Rule discovery can handle explicit knowledge, incapable of unsupervised learning, outputs transparent models.
- Pros: Rule discovery algorithms can deal with high-dimensional data; ignores dimensionality of problem. Models are easy to understand (i.e.,

transparent). Prediction is fast and explanation facilities are readily available.

- Cons: Quick partitioning of data results in fast deterioration in quality of attribute selection. Model size can often become unmanageable if the model construction process is automated.

STATISTICS

Statistics have long been the traditional method for clustering, factor analysis, linear regression, and prediction. Some algorithms like CHAID, LOGIT, and Bayesian statistics are knowledge or hypothesis-generating; others such as ANOVA, polynomial regression, and Multiple Discriminant Analysis are primarily hypothesis-driven and are not considered to be true analytics techniques. Statistics are frequently used in combination with other analytical techniques.

Statistical models are based, in general, on continuous, linear data. Traditional statistical algorithms attempt to fit the data to an expected function or pattern and don't account for data points that lie outside of the function. These outliers are typically discarded from the analysis. Newer algorithms begin by clustering the data points and finding the best fitting functions for each cluster without requiring a pre-determined function. Outputted models are a mathematical formulation of problems or tabulated statistical information which may require further interpretation.

Summary

- Traits: Cannot handle explicit knowledge, incapable of unsupervised learning, outputs opaque models.
- Pros: Statistics are well established and robust. Resources (i.e., tools and personnel) are available in the market, and are well established.
- Cons: The scope of the application of statistics is narrow and is limited to problems of few dimensions. A process which employs statistical techniques can only be automated to a very low degree.

NEAREST NEIGHBOUR

Nearest neighbor is a technique for classifying records in a database by comparing them with similar records that are already classified. The technique predicts that a given record will have the same output value as most of its closest neighbors, with a confidence such that if the closest neighbors all have the same output value, then confidence is high in predicting that the given record will also have that output value. "Closeness" is measured by the weighted distance of the normalized values of the independent fields (one field per axis). Weights can be pre-specified or derived automatically.

Summary

- Traits: Can handle explicit knowledge, incapable of unsupervised learning, outputs transparent models.
- Pros: Nearest neighbor parallels human classification method—decisions are based on weighing the similarity to previous experience decisions and importance of each problem feature. Allows for range of classification instead of limiting to yes or no.
- Cons: Determination of optimal weights is difficult and can be very processing intensive if automated. A single record can influence the classification of the examined record. This can be an advantage or disadvantage depending on the problem.

FUZZY LOGIC

Fuzzy logic is a method of reasoning that attempts to deal with approximate or imprecise information by allowing variables to be described (often linguistically) and acted upon in terms of their degrees of membership in multiple sets. Instead of "one or zero," "on or off," and "true or false," fuzzy logic is based on the notion that many real-world decisions are not so clean cut. When we say someone is "tall," what does that mean? If someone stands about 2 meters in height, are they tall? What if they are in a room of professional basketball players? Are they still tall?

Fuzzy logic defines a formal method of answering such questions, and allows for the inherent "fuzziness" of human language. This technique is usually used as an extension of other analytics techniques to allow or interpret incomplete or imprecise data. It is also widely used as an embedded technology in consumer products, such as cameras and washing machines.

GENETIC ALGORITHMS

Genetic algorithms involve the mutation of parts of an initial solution. Elements and collections of elements adjust themselves and influence each other in ways that often give way to distinct patterns of activity. Genetic algorithms could be utilized to assist in generating an initial query using mutation/reproduction operations, examining the result, and determining new input parameters (possibly new mutation/reproduction scenarios). Genetic algorithms lend themselves to problem types that exhibit a known solution path but unknown location of the optimal solution along the path.

ANALYTICS AND VISUALIZATION

Visualization is an essential technique to bring the user into the discovery loop. Even the best set of rules or tables of data will be more understandable when visualized with color, relief, texture, 2D, 3D, or 4D representations. The primary goal of visualization is to inspire questions about a data set, questions users might not have thought of in the absence of the visualization. One obvious problem with visualization techniques is the difficulty of depicting relationships among more than three or four variables. Time is often the fourth dimension that is portrayed, resulting in animated date/time series of displays. In addition, data visualization relies heavily on the business analyst for the analysis and pattern recognition.

Visualization techniques can be applied throughout all the phases of the analytics process, and is particularly useful during the initial stages of knowledge exploration when a high-level view of data and relationships may be needed. The power of visualization can be also helpful in model evaluation phase—such as showing the relationship between neural network weight distributions and model error, or showing the number of rules generated versus certain inductive learning parameter settings.

ROUGH SETS

Rough sets is a technique that analyzes logical and probabilistic patterns in data, establishes strong relationships among variables, and allows fine tuned modeling of weaker relationships. Rough set theory is fairly intuitive and interactive. It is especially applicable to problems involving vague, imprecise, uncertain or incomplete information. In particular, rough sets are used to model and analyze data at various levels of abstraction to better expose data regularities; it provides techniques to analyze data dependencies, to identify fundamental factors and to discover rules from data.

Table 4.2 summarizes how the various analytics techniques discussed here can be classified in terms of each main problem type. The contents of the table give some indication of the level of support for analytics functionality that each technique provides. Again, information type and usage type should be considered to choose the actual analytical technique.

Table 4.2 Summary of analytics techniques

Analytical Technique	*Neural Networks*	*Rule Discovery*	*Statistics*	*Nearest Neighbor*	*Others*
Relationship Analysis	Yes	Yes	Yes	Yes	Yes
Classification	Yes	Yes	Yes	Yes	Yes
Clustering	Yes				Yes
Sequential Pattern Analysis	Yes	Yes	Yes		Yes

Table 4.3 Analytics algorithms and tools mapping

Algorithm	Decision Trees	Linear/Statistical	Multi Layer Perceptions	Nearest Neighbor	Radial Basis Functions	Bayes	Rule Induction	Polynomial Networks	Generalized Liner Models	Time Series	Sequential Discovery	K means	Association Rules	Kohonen
Angoss Mining Manager	Y	Y	Y	Y		Y	Y			Y	Y	Y	Y	
CA Clever Path Predictive Analysis	Y	Y	Y	Y		Y	Y			Y	Y	Y	Y	
Fair Issac Decision Management Suite	Y	Y	Y	Y		Y	Y			Y	Y	Y	Y	Y
Genalytics Predictive Suite	Y	Y					Y		Y	Y		Y	Y	
IBM Intelligent Miner	Y	Y	Y	Y	Y	Y	Y		Y	Y	Y	Y	Y	Y
Insightful Miner	Y	Y				Y	Y			Y	Y	Y	Y	
KXEN Analytic Framework	Y	Y	Y	Y		Y	Y	Y		Y	Y	Y	Y	Y
Oracle Data Miner	Y	Y	Y	Y	Y	Y	Y		Y	Y	Y	Y	Y	
Quadstone System	Y	Y		Y		Y	Y			Y	Y	Y	Y	
RapidMiner	Y	Y	Y		Y	Y				Y		Y	Y	
SAS Enterprise Miner	Y	Y	Y	Y	Y	Y	Y	Y	Y	Y	Y	Y	Y	Y
SPSS Clementine	Y	Y	Y	Y		Y	Y	Y	Y	Y	Y	Y	Y	Y

END POINTS

In this chapter, an attempt has been made to associate each analytical technique discussed in the above sections with a list of representative analytics tools. These associations were made based on vendor literature and product use. The list of representative tools in Table 4.3 is by no means complete, and will be updated as more vendors enter the market or gain greater acceptance. In addition, this section should not be viewed as a tool evaluation reference list; tools incorporating the analytical techniques presented here may be better or worse at supporting a particular feature.

REFERENCE

Nisbet, Robert, Elder, John, IV, and Miner, Gary, *Handbook of Statistical Analysis and Data Mining Applications*, Academic Press, June 2009.

CHAPTER 5

TECHNICAL ARCHITECTURE FOR ANALYTICS SOLUTIONS

An analytical solution should be constructed on the basis of the services needed to be delivered as outcomes. The environment should support the creation, maintenance, tracking, and deployment of one or more analytical models.

In this chapter we will discuss the technical architecture components that are necessary to implement a successful analytics solution. It is intended for the technical architect(s) responsible for constructing the analytics environment. This section outlines each technology component, how it fits into the architecture, the required inputs and generated outputs, and the characteristics of its use.

The technical architecture as described in Fig. 5.1 provides an exhaustive list of components required to deliver an analytics solution.

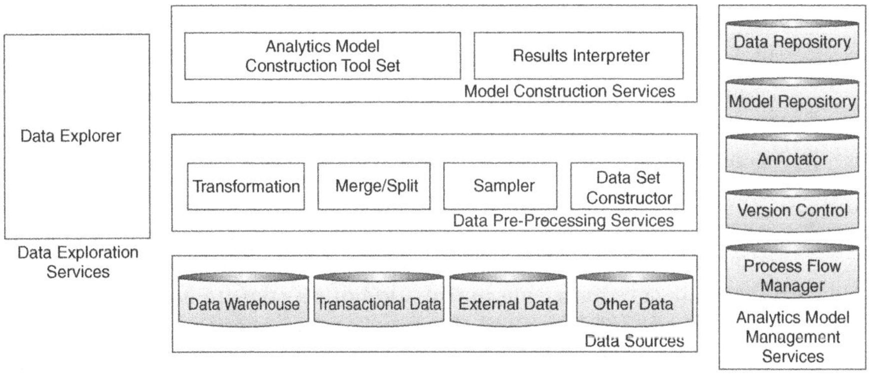

Figure 5.1 Analytics technical architecture components and services.

The architecture at a conceptual level consists of the following six key service areas.

- Data Sources
- Data Exploration Services
- Data Extraction Services
- Data Preprocessing Services
- Model Construction Services
- Analytics Management Services

Each of these services contains one or more technical components. The component metaphor was chosen to emphasize that an analytics solution should be constructed on the basis of the services needed to be delivered as outcomes. The architecture simply employs the components that provide the services desired. This implies that a given solution may use all of the components, while another may not. However, most solutions will require that all of the components be supported at some level.

Note: It is also obvious that, a data warehouse can be both a source for and a component of an analytics architecture.

DATA SOURCES

It is expected that companies exploring analytics opportunities must have already implemented a data warehousing solution. As a result of this fact, one of the primary goals while looking for a data source for analytics is to explore how an existing data warehouse infrastructure could be leveraged in building the analytics solution.

In gathering the requirements for the design of an analytical application, one of the main objectives is to determine where is the required data? This is often a tedious process and is performed at an attribute by attribute level. In general, there are four high level types of data that can be the focus of an analytical application. They are:

- *Data Warehouse* - The data warehouse data store is a cleansed and summarized repository of enterprise data. It is typically read-only, and is highly tuned to support complex queries that are generated to support multi-dimensional business questions (i.e., total sales by year, by product line, by region).
- *Transactional/Operational Data* - These types of data stores are typically the major source for data warehouse and analytics applications.
- *External Data* - External data can represent any type of information that comes from a source outside the enterprise boundaries of an organization. The challenges in getting information of this type in a format so that it can be used in data analysis architecture can be extreme.
- *Other Data* - For quite a number of business problems, there could be a need to collect data which are not usually mainstream business data and not paid importance in the first instance. Examples could be unstructured data like emails, documents, etc.

It is important to note that regardless of the data source, some form of manipulation/refining of extracted data will be necessary to support an analytics application, even if this information comes from a relatively "clean" data source like a data warehouse. Many projects overlook this fact when designing their data access architecture.

Given the scale and diverse nature of businesses today, it is an extremely complex and challenging task to extract raw data from diverse operational systems and to transform it to valuable information. In essence there is a need to establish a data acquisition and information delivery framework which includes components that take raw data from various sources, transform it, and make it usable for a business user. It is also obvious that several of these components would also be required by an analytics architecture. Therefore an architect needs to understand which components of the analytics architecture should be designed with information delivery requirements in mind and vice-versa. Data Exploration Services, Data Extraction Services, and Data Preprocessing Services all have information delivery components within them. One would expect, however, that an existing information management infrastructure could be heavily leveraged in the creation of these components.

DATA EXPLORATION SERVICES

Throughout the analytics process the data is constantly analyzed to find relationships, patterns, and information that is vital to the success of the effort. The Data Exploration components enable the analyst to perform hypothesis-driven analysis. For example, an analyst might hypothesize that third quarter sales contributed to forty percent of last year's revenues. This hypothesis would be tested using Data Exploration components. Thus, data exploration differs from discovery driven analysis because the analyst must formulate a hypothesis to guide the analysis.

In addition to hypothesis-driven analysis, the Data Exploration components allow the analyst to collect basic statistics and information about the data being studied. This might include histograms, data distributions, and results from simple queries.

The analyst will need the ability to study the data before, during, and after a model has been constructed. To do this, the *Data Exploration* components must be able to access data in the original data stores and preprocessed data sets in the *Data Repository*. One should note that the *Data Exploration* components are not typically used to update or insert data into the original data stores. Rather, they are used in a read-only fashion.

Explorer—The Explorer component provides one or more of the following functions:

- *Ad hoc* Query
- Reporting
- Basic Statistics
- Multi-dimensional Analysis
- Visualization

A number of *Model Construction Tools*, such as SAS, KXEN, Clementine, etc., provide data exploration capabilities as an integrated part of the analytics tool. However, these tools are typically limited to exploring data that has been brought into the tool's environment, either in memory or in a flat file format.

Table 5.1 Data exploration services

Inputs	Data from data sources or data repository, business rules and hypothesis.
Outputs	Verified or un-verified hypothesis.
Usage	Used manually by a user who has knowledge about the business problems and modeling techniques providing business understanding of the data.
Other considerations	Data exploration is a process that needs to access both data in the original data sources and pre-processed data sets and loaded into data warehouses and data Marts.

Relying solely on the tool's exploration capabilities will greatly limit the ability to explore the data in the original data sources. It is recommended that other tools be included to supplement the exploration capabilities provided by the *Model Construction Tools*.

DATA PRE-PROCESSING SERVICES

The data pre-processing components are responsible for extracting data sets from data sources, transform the data, and load them to the data repository. To collect raw data for analytics, the data transformation components may pull data from external sources, legacy databases and/or from analytical data stores within a data warehouse.

The data pre-processing components are utilized to transform the raw data from the data sources to data which is suitable for analytics purposes. This may involve manipulating the data to eliminate noise or to provide missing values, and/or consolidating data from one or more data sources. The changes made during data pre-processing are made specifically to the data in the data repository, not the original data source.

Data Extraction/Collection—Most often, the data set required for analytics will be a subset or block of data from the data source. For example, that we may need to collect data from the data source by a specific time period, marketing region or line of business. To effectively collect the right data, analysts most often use ETL capabilities and/or SQL or procedure languages.

When defining the data requirements for analytics, one should consider whether the data collection process will need to be scheduled or not. It may be desirable to initiate the extraction process overnight when processors are idle. If the extraction process is scheduled, then it is critical to monitor to track any exception conditions that occur and in case of exceptions should plan to initiate restart and recovery capabilities. Another consideration should be whether to select only new records (changed data from previous extraction) from a data source or only those records which have changed since the last extraction.

Data Transformation—Rich data transformation capabilities are required for performing analytics specific preprocessing of the source data sets. At a

Table 5.2 Data extraction/collection services

Inputs	Source system details, attributes and the records to be selected.
Outputs	Data subsets and their respective descriptions are produced. The description file lists the attributes included in the data set, their data type and length, and how each record is uniquely identified.
Usage	Additional data may be requested on demand by the analysts or by a scheduled process. The user must construct ETL modules or SQL procedures to extract records to meet user requirements like all customer orders in the north west region as recorded in the order entry system for the last five years.
Other considerations	If a data warehousing system exists, its extraction components may be leveraged to perform the extraction functionality needed for the analytics solution.

broad level the following four specific functions should be available during pre-processing. They are:

- *Cleanse* - The cleanse function is responsible for cleaning the source data by removing duplicate records, eliminating noisy data, and deriving missing values (when possible).
- *Transform* - The transform function is responsible for performing transformations of variables. A common transformation is to express a continuous variable as a discrete variable. This transformation is referred to as binning. One method for binning continuous variables is by "bucketing" them into ranges. For example, someone who is age 25 is placed in the 25-34 age bucket.
- *Derive* - The derive function is responsible for deriving new attributes from existing attributes. For example, the loss ratio, a common factor for measuring insurance profitability, is computed by dividing claims by premium.
- *Normalize* - The Normalize function is responsible for normalizing continuous variables, i.e., adjusting the values to fit on a normal curve (between 0 and 1). This is a common operation in statistics, and often required for construction of data mining models. However, it is highly

Table 5.3 Data transformation services

Inputs	Data structures, Data sets, Data demographics, Volumetrics.
Outputs	Transformed data sets.
Usage	The user or analytics requirements must define how the data is to be transformed. This includes defining derived attributes, the method for supplying missing values, means to eliminate noise, the variables to be normalized and specifying how to discretize continuous variables, if required.
Other considerations	Often existing components of a data warehouse architecture can be leveraged to satisfy the needs of these activities. If present, the data warehouse may have components that perform cleanse, transform and derive functionality.

unlikely that this function will be present in a data refinery, and therefore must be specifically accounted for in the analytics solution architecture.

Merge/Split—When data sets from more than one data source have been extracted, the merging/splitting activities are used to consolidate them into a single data set. As stated above, the data sets may be in a flat file format or in a relational format. If the data is in a relational format, then decomposing parent-child relationships and consolidating the data into a single data set is required to be done. For example, an order heading table could be merged with an order detail table to create a single order data set for analytics purposes.

If the data being merged is in a flat file format, some intervention will be necessary to specify how data sets are consolidated. When the merge is complex, a custom program will be needed to perform the merge. This may be the case when customer data from internal sources is merged with demographic data purchased from external data sources.

Table 5.4 Merge/Split services

Inputs	Data structures, Data sets, Data demographics, Volumetrics
Outputs	A single data set or table containing consolidated records from the data sources. A description of the merged data set will also be generated which states the attributes included in the data set, their data type and length, and how each record is uniquely identified.
Usage	Merging may be requested on demand by the user or by a system process. The user must state the means for merging the data sets by specifying how the records in each are uniquely identified and how the unique identifiers relate to one another. The user will also construct the definition of the data set to be created. The definition explains how records are to be identified, the order of the attributes and their data type and data length.
Other considerations	Often existing components of a data warehouse architecture can be leveraged to satisfy the needs of these activities. If present, the data warehouse may have components that perform cleanse, transform and derive functionality.

Sampler—This component is responsible for selecting a sample from the data set specified. The method of sampling is dependent on the modeling technique employed and business context of the analytics effort. The sampling method could be random or determined by explicit means to reduce bias in the data.

Table 5.5 Sampler services

Inputs	Data structures, Data sets, Data demographics, Volumetrics
Outputs	Data sample
Usage	This component could be requested on demand by the user or system process. The sampling method must be specified.
Other considerations	In some analytics efforts, the Sampler is used to determine which data to extract, typically by determining that a particular

	population is not well represented in the data. For example, in the case where most respondents answered no, a larger number of respondents who answered yes must be extracted to create a sample with equal distributions of yes and no respondents. This implies that the data collection and sampling activities may be used iteratively throughout the analytics process to construct an appropriate data set for model construction.

Data Loading/Storing—While the pre-processing services focus on collecting data and transforming data, they do not necessarily store any data. All the preprocessed data needs to be transferred to the data repository. The data transfer process should support heterogeneous platforms and network architectures, including transfer via the Internet. This may be a stand alone middleware component or a component of the client/server architecture. Scheduling may be necessary to transfer data at specified times. The data transfer process can be designed to perform record level data transfer or file transfer. Either way, it must have restart and recovery capabilities. Also, exception management processes need to be developed to report success of the data transfer or to report any exceptions.

Table 5.6 Data loading/storing services

Inputs	Source and target locations for data transfer, source data sets, target structure, control files
Outputs	Transformed data, data loaded to data repository, log files
Usage	Ideally, data transfer will be transparent to the user and require no intervention. However, in analytics environments lacking a robust architecture the user may have some degree of interaction with the custom data transfer component. For example, the user may be required to FTP a file from the extraction server to the desktop PC where analysis will occur.
Other considerations	Usually bulk data loading components such as Oracle's SQL*Loader are used. Data may be loaded immediately after it has been transferred or after some data preprocessing has been performed.

Data Set Constructor—The Data Set Constructor component is responsible for dividing sample data into multiple data sets for model construction. The number of data sets needed will vary depending on the analytics technique being employed and the needs of the Model Construction Tool. Typically, separate training and testing data sets will be required for model construction and evaluation. The data set constructor should also contain functionality to randomize the data before partitioning it to the construction data sets.

Table 5.7 Data set construction services

Inputs	Source and target locations for data transfer, source data sets, target structure, control files
Outputs	Data sets

Usage	The user or system process interacting with the Data Set Constructor must specify the number of data sets needed and the proportion of the source data to be partitioned to the sets. The user can also request that the data be randomized before it is partitioned.
Other considerations	Often existing components of a data warehouse architecture can be leveraged to satisfy the needs of these activities. If present, the data warehouse may have components that perform selective data extraction functionality.

MODEL CONSTRUCTION SERVICES

The *Model Construction* components provide the functionality to build analytics model and evaluate its results. These components provide a graphical working environment to interactively work with data, modeling algorithms and results.

Model Construction Tool—The Model Construction Tool is the primary component used to build and evaluate an analytics model. The component may provide multiple techniques for constructing the model. If so, it must allow the user to select the technique to be used for model construction. The Model Construction Tool contains the source code to configure and execute the statistics and data mining algorithm being employed by the model. Typically, the Model Construction Tool utilizes a graphical user interface to ease interaction with the model and its configurable parameters.

To shield the analyst from the complexity of the statistics and data mining algorithm, the Model Construction Tool should provide a construction mode that requires only a few parameter settings to configure the model. For more experienced users, the Model Construction Tool should have an "Expert" mode that permits the user to configure all the parameters that were defaulted in the construction mode.

Once the model is generated, the Model Construction Tool must provide a means for computing the accuracy and precision of the model. Typically this is computed by the Model Construction Tool when the model is exposed to a new data set, generally the test data set. Based on the accuracy and precision of the model, the user will need the ability to modify the model's architecture. Although the architecture will depend on the algorithm used, the user could modify the model's rules, change the number of hidden layers, prune the tree, etc. within the Model Construction Tool.

Table 5.8 Model construction services

Inputs	Business rules and information, construction data sets and previous mining results
Outputs	Analytics Results
Usage	The user must configure the model construction tool by specifying the input and output variables (if the problem is supervised),

	selecting the modeling technique and configuring its parameters, training the model and testing it using the test data set. Additional evaluation may be performed with the evaluation data set. Once a technique is proven, the process of model construction may be automated for a particular problem or task.
Other considerations	Often a requirement of the Model Construction Tool is the ability to clearly explain its results. There are two classes of Model Construction Tools: opaque and transparent. Opaque models give little, if any, explanation to the results. A neural network is an example of an opaque model. Transparent models explain how the results are derived, often by expressing if/then rules. A decision tree is an example of a transparent model. The requirement for result explanation may be driven by industry requirements or by the business users interpreting the results. This will affect the selection of modeling algorithms and influence the requirements for the Result Interpreter component.

Note: To preserve the models generated by the Model Construction Tool and to clearly document the process used to generate the model, the Model Construction Tool must be closely tied to the Model Annotator and the Version Control components. Version Control should be employed to preserve the models and the data sets used to build them. The Model Annotator will allow the analyst to document the process used in analytics.

Result Interpreter—To effectively interpret the results of an analytics model, they must be presented in a form which can easily be understood. This is the responsibility of the Result Interpreter component. The Result Interpreter takes data mining results (which could be in the form of the model itself and/or data files) and presents them in one or more of following forms:

- *Graphical representation* - A graphical representation is a means for visually displaying an analytical model or its results to the analyst. A common technique is to graphically display a decision tree and color code certain outcomes.
- *Natural language text* - Some analytics tools have the ability to generate natural language text that explains the analytical model or its results. An example is a textual report that explains the associations found from an associative model. The natural language text might read "When orange juice is purchased vodka is purchased 80% of the time."
- *Reports* - Often reports will be generated to express the results of an analytics model such as expressing the results in terms of business metrics or key performance indicators.
- *Procedural code* - Many times procedural code will be extracted from the analytics tool to represent the analytics model constructed. This is common when working with decision trees. Formats include SQL, C, and others. The procedural code can be used to build an application which performs the work of the generated model.
- *Data manipulation language* - Frequently, the results of executing an analytics model will need to be recorded in the transaction or operational

database from where the data originated. To effectively update the source database, many analytics tools have the ability to express the results in data manipulation language (SQL) which will insert, update or delete database records. As an example, the customer score generated by the model is recorded in the marketing database used to build catalog mailing lists. An update statement would be written for each customer scored.

Table 5.9 Result interpreter services

Inputs	Analytics Results
Outputs	Graphical representations, natural language text, reports, code and/or data manipulation language.
Usage	The user uses the output of the Result Interpreter to gain an understanding of the data mining results and how they were derived.
Other considerations	It requires a good amount of business understanding of the data to interpret the analytics results and validate the findings.

ANALYTICAL MODEL MANAGEMENT SERVICES

Since analytics is an iterative and data intensive process it is imperative that controls are in place to prevent lost work, to allow for the restoration of previous work, to provide adequate storage and to monitor transactions. The *Analytical Model Management* components of the analytics architecture provide these services for analytics models and data sets. Effective management is particularly important for the *Data Preprocessing* and the *Model Construction* services which will be tightly coupled to the *Analytical Model Mining Management* services.

Data Repository—The Data Repository is the storage component for processed data sets and results. The repository must be able to store data sets that have been extracted and those that have been through the data preprocessing routines. Significant storage space may be required as it is not uncommon to work with data sets that have millions of records.

Table 5.10 Data repository services

Inputs	Data sets, result sets
Outputs	Stored data sets
Usage	The user will access the Data Repository and its objects via the Version Control component and Annotator component. The Data Repository will also be explored using components in the Data Exploration services during the data mining process.
Other considerations	The Data Repository must be integrated with the Version Control and Annotator components to version data sets and to store descriptive information about them.

Model Repository—The Model Repository is the storage component for the analytical models. The model repository will depend heavily on the model construction tool(s) chosen because the models are often stored in a proprietary format. For this reason, the model construction tool and model repository are tightly coupled. Regardless of the model's format, significant storage may be needed to store models during construction and testing. Additional space may be required to store deployed or production models.

Table 5.11 Model repository services

Inputs	Models
Outputs	Stored Models
Usage	The user will access the Model Repository and its objects via the Version Control component and Annotator component.
Other considerations	The Model Repository must be integrated with the Version Control and Annotator components to version models and to store descriptive information about them.

Annotator—Since model construction and validation is an iterative task, the user should maintain detailed information regarding the analytical models constructed and the steps used to construct them. The Annotator serves as the facility for recording and editing this dialog. Specifically, information should be recorded to support the modeling technique selected, to explain the parameter settings chosen and to justify the model as a solution to the defined problem. In addition, detailed information should be captured about the data selected for mining and the steps required in preprocessing.

It should be noted that the functionality desired from the Annotator may be provided by the Model Construction Tool or the Version Control component.

Table 5.12 Annotator services

Inputs	Model, Construction data sets
Outputs	Model annotations
Usage	The user should interactively use the Annotator during the analytics process to record the steps taken and to justify them. Detailed information should be maintained on the modeling technique chosen and the parameters used to construct the model.
Other considerations	Implicit to the Annotator is the ability to view and edit the dialog throughout the Analytics process. The information captured should be accessible to others in a shared environment.

Version Control—Version Control should be employed to manage multiple models, their parameters and data sets used to build and test them. Version Control also allows multiple developers to work on model construction efforts without interfering with one another. The Version Control facility should be tightly coupled to the Model Repository and the Data Repository where models and data sets are stored, respectively.

Table 5.13 Version control services

Inputs	Data sets and models
Outputs	Version controlled and managed artifacts/objects
Usage	During construction and testing the user would use check-in/check-out facilities to build the model. Once a model is ready to version, its construction and test data sets should be versioned with it.
Other considerations	Most tools provide some way of version managing the models, in absence of such functionality every process and created artifacts should be documented rigorously.

Process Flow Manager—Ideally, robust analytics architecture would include a component as Process Flow Manager, which monitors and manages the various tasks of analytics processes. By coupling the information gathered by the Annotator and by Version Control with the metadata collected by the Process Flow Manager, the analyst is presented with a complete view of the analytics process.

Table 5.14 Process flow manager services

Inputs	Parameters that identify the level of detail to collect, the transaction types to monitor and the actions to take when defined conditions are met. Additionally, information for the Annotator and Version Control should be accepted.
Outputs	Transaction processing history as metadata.
Usage	The user monitors the data preprocessing effort using the information captured by the Process Flow Manager component. Access to this collected information could be via a simple reporting tool or through an OLAP tool.
Other considerations	The Process Flow Manager should be capable of collecting various levels of detailed information as specified by the user. In addition, the Process Flow Manager may be required to execute an action when a defined event has occurred, such as e-mail the analyst when data extraction has been completed.

ARCHITECTURE DEPLOYMENT CONSIDERATIONS

The components of the analytics architecture are intended to support both the development and deployment of the analytics solution. This section discusses some additional architectural considerations when deploying a solution.

When a solution is deployed, the functionality of several components may be tied together as an automated process. For example, a data collection routine could be written to extract, transfer, load and preprocess data for the next analytics run. Obviously, this requires the integration of several architectural components so that the components can communicate with one another and that the output of one component be accepted as the input of another.

An emerging trend among analytics and data mining vendors and solution providers is to create frameworks for analytics. These vertical applications are typically focused on a particular industry. For example, an analytics framework is built for the Telecommunications Industry that includes applications for customer segmentation, target marketing campaigns, etc. Such a framework masks the complexity of the model construction tool's algorithms by wrapping them in industry specific applications. The target user of such a framework or analytics workbench is a business analyst.

INTEGRATION WITH OTHER BUSINESS INTELLIGENCE TOOLS

Often an analytics solution will need the ability to integrate the results with other Business Intelligence tools, such as DSS, EIS, OLAP, etc. To facilitate this need, the results must be readily accessible and organized in a fashion that can be easily understood.

Note: The components of the analytics architecture collectively provide the services needed to deliver a robust architecture for delivery of an analytics solution. To assist the architect in constructing the analytics architecture, a component inventory matrix has been constructed below. It presents each of the technical components with a list of the basic functions provided by each. A priority for each function has been suggested as a guideline: 1 - Critical, 2 - Important, and 3 - Nice to Have.

Table 5.15 Summary of analytics architecture and services

Service	*Technical Component*	*Function*	*Priority 1-Critical, 2- Important, 3 - Nice to Have*
Data Exploration	Explorer	*Ad hoc* query	1
		Reporting	1
		Basic statistics	1
		Multi-dimensional Analysis	3
		Visualization	3
Data Extraction	Extractor	Data extraction	1
		Scheduled	2
		Ability to select only new row from data source since last extraction	3
		Ability to select modified rows from data source since last extraction	3
		Restart/Recovery	2
	Data Transfer	Data transfer from source to Data Repository	1
		Support heterogeneous platforms and network architectures	2
		Transfer via Internet	3
		Restart/Recovery	2

Data Preprocessing	Data Manipulator	Cleanse	1
		Transform	1
		Derive	1
		Normalize (Fit values to Normal curve)	1
	Merger	Merge native files, i.e., ASCII	1
		Decompose parent-child relationships and merge from relational data sources	1
		Write data in native format, i.e. ASCII	1
	Sampler	Random Sample	1
		Allow Explicit Sampling	2
	Data Set Constructor	Partition data into data sets	1
		Randomize data	2
Model Construction	Model Construction Tool	Configure mining algorithm	1
		Execute mining algorithm	1
		Graphical user interface	2
		Default parameters	2
		Expert mode	3
		Compute model accuracy, precision	2
		Modify model architecture	2
	Result Interpreter	Graphical representation	2*
		Natural language text	2*
		Reports	2*
		Procedural Code	2*
		Data Manipulation Language	2*
Model Management	Data Repository	Data set, result set storage	1
	Model Repository	Model storage	1
	Version Control	Check-in/Check-out facility	2
		Restoration of previous versions	2
		Comments	2
	Annotator	Annotation facility	1
	Process Flow Monitor	Transaction monitoring	3
		User specified level of data collection	3
		Ability to take action when event conditions are satisfied	3

Note: * Singularly, the various output formats of the Result Interpreter are each considered to be important. However, it is imperative that the Result

Interpreter presents the analytics results in one of the forms described. For that reason, at least one of the forms will be designated as critical when the analytics architecture is implemented. Likewise, some of the formats may not be necessary and deemed as "Nice to Have".

ADDRESSING TECHNICAL ISSUES

The purpose of this section is to discuss specific technical issues that can surface as robust analytical and data mining solutions are designed and implemented. It is intended to provide information to the technical architect who is responsible for making system design and construction decisions on an analytics and data mining engagement. It is also necessary for the reader to have a basic understanding of the environments that typically reside within any technical architecture. These environments are briefly described below:

- *Development Environment* - A development environment is a unified combination of standards, procedures and tools used to build business solutions in a consistent re-usable manner.
- *Execution Environment* - An execution environment is a unified collection of run-time services and control structures that provide an infrastructure for business systems to operate.
- *Operations Environment* - An operations environment is a unified combination of tools, support services, procedures and controls required to keep a production system operating. It differs from an execution environment in that its primary users are system administrators and production support personnel.

Development Architecture

The development architecture is a combination of development tools, methods, standards, and procedures essential to enable a comprehensive, integrated environment for developing and maintaining systems. It is primarily used by the system architects and developers. This section discusses the various considerations to support the high degree of integration which is required in a robust analytics solution.

Build versus Buy—Many of the leading tools on the market contain a wide range of functionality. However, they do not support all of the components which are necessary in robust analytics solutions. An infrastructure to support the analytics process will probably consist of multiple tools which integrate with each other to make up a complete solution. Even with the wide variety of tools in the market, it is likely that some smaller custom components will need to be built. Commonly, model annotation, model and data set version control, and process flow monitor components need to be built to complete an analytics application.

The requirements that are generated when integrating purchased components with custom developed components should be clearly communicated to the group or individual that maintains an enterprise's development environment. This will allow any analytics development to occur within a common development environment framework.

Developing Support for Data Access—While looking at the availability of required data, it is important to identify all of the data that will be required for analytics. Specifically, any data which is needed for analytics that can not be acquired should be identified and documented. Additionally, any external data which is being purchased from an outside source should be analyzed and the process for incorporating it into the analytics process should be documented. This is likely to be an iterative process.

The existence of a data warehouse or operational data store is important because much of the work done to prepare this data could be leveraged by an analytics process. For example, the extract and cleanse components of a data warehouse could be put to use so that these steps do not have to be duplicated, and the analytics process could pull its data directly from the data warehouse instead of transactional systems.

Using a New or Existing Platform—As the project team gathers requirements for a development environment to support the construction phase of analytics application, one of the most important questions will be around the technology platform. If resources are available to support analytics on existing platforms, this becomes a non-issue. If, on the other hand, the analytics solution will be constructed on a new platform, several development environment issues may surface. Obviously, if the platform is new to an organization, a completely new development environment may be required. It is also important to note that some analytics products are sold in conjunction with hardware. And in some cases, this hardware is of a proprietary nature and may be difficult to integrate into an existing development environment.

Execution Architecture

The execution architecture consists of run-time services and control structures coupled with an application infrastructure. It is primarily used by business analysts or others accessing the system to run data through an analytics model. This section discusses configuration management, tool integration, and hardware issues surrounding an analytics system's execution architecture.

Execution Architecture Components and Analytics Processes—Analytics processes have many commonalties with traditional client/server systems. However, there are some notable differences that are highlighted below:

Although it may seem obvious, it is important that analytics tools be integrated with the same interface or operating system that the rest of the application architecture uses. The more the model construction and deployment tools are integrated into the analytics application developers current tool set, the less time and effort will be needed to construct an analytics solution. For example, the code generated by the model construction tool should be the same type of code with which analytics application developers are familiar. In this way, any code maintenance would be easily accomplished by leveraging existing competencies.

An analytics project requires the ability to manage multiple versions of models and data sets. These objects need to be managed in the same way that source code does on a traditional engagement. Change control, migration control, and version control capabilities and procedures need to be applied across these development objects. This gives an analytics engagement team the same security and flexibility that traditional engagement teams enjoy. Although we see this capability as a critical component to an analytics architecture, most model construction tool vendors support only limited analytics model management services. An analyst must manage the different versions of these objects using unique file names and directories for storage since most tools do not provide more sophisticated versioning capabilities. In order to provide these services, a customized solution or procedure must be created; however, the cost of building this component may be prohibitive.

Although most quality management tools can still be used in an analytics environment, some additional metrics are needed. Metrics such as frequency of creating a new model or refreshing an obsolete one, accuracy and precision of given models, and number of iterations before a model can be validated should be kept to ensure quality in the model creation and deployment processes and that benefits are being realized.

Purchasing Hardware—The analytics system could be a large high-volume system, a small low-volume system, or a simple proof-of-concept. Each of these types of systems requires different hardware environments to support them. Some of these requirements are discussed below:

- In a large, high-volume system, analytics should be done from a data repository which is an off-line copy of a portion of the legacy data store. This repository can sometimes reside on existing hardware which is currently not being used to capacity. However, many times it may be necessary to purchase new, more powerful server hardware to support the analytics system. Some of the primary factors in this decision are: hardware support of the chosen analytics software, volume of data or records to be analyzed, frequency with which the analysis must be performed, and the hardware strategy of the organization. It is important that the analytics tool(s) selected take advantage of the hardware on which it runs. In general, mining algorithms may require significant resources to process a large number of records (large in this case would be anything over millions records). Often the processing power necessary to support this large requirement for resources can be provided by parallel processing server technology.
- Generally, a small, lower-volume analytics system does not require a powerful server. However, the system may require one or more high-powered workstations. This kind of analytics solution can suffice in

situations where there is a relatively low volume of data to be analyzed, a limited number of analytics techniques will be utilized, and/or frequency of analytics model runs is very low. This type of solution is also more relevant in situations where a small number of models, which do not change often, are being used. Obviously, the cost of designing and setting up this environment is much smaller than in a full-blown system.

- When developing a proof of concept for a feasibility study, powerful server hardware is rarely needed. Generally, these situations require a couple of standard workstations with a Pentium processor or equivalent and the proper tools.

DO I NEED PARALLELISM?

One of the more popular technologies available for high-end servers is parallel processing. Parallel processing can give an analytics solution the ability to perform frequent, high volume analysis of business data. It also keeps the door open for future analytics requirements, such as the need to build new models in a short amount of time. But, if not truly needed, parallelism can add significant cost for an incremental gain.

The data preprocessing and model construction components are most likely to benefit from the power of parallel processing. If the decision is made to use parallel processing, the project team should ensure that the parallelized mining algorithms provided by the model construction tool are scalable; that is, their performance should not degrade as the size of the input data set increases.

Some factors that should be considered when deciding on the use of parallel processing architectures are:

- Does the analytics tool support parallel processing servers and/or parallel databases?
- Does the analytics tool need to run in a shared workload environment?
- Is there a requirement to analyze high volumes of data at frequent intervals?
- How many analytics models are going to be created?
- Are models going to be frequently recreated with new data? i.e., is the business environment volatile?
- Will the analytics system need to expand beyond the limits of single processor servers?
- Does the client's hardware strategy include parallel processing servers?

Above all, parallel processing servers should not be used simply because they are the most powerful platforms available. They should only be used when a business requirement, like the ones listed above, dictates its use.

USING API'S IN DEVELOPING AN ANALYTICS SOLUTION

Since every tool in the marketplace does not support all of the capabilities found in the analytics architecture framework, programmer access to the services of an analytics tool is necessary to create a robust, fully integrated analytics solution. This access generally comes in the form of an open API set published by the tool vendor. These APIs can give a developer access to data preprocessing, model construction, model testing, and model usage functions of a tool. Also, if the analytics tool can export a model to a more embeddable format, generally source code or rules, then the appropriate languages or systems (e.g., knowledge base systems) must also be in place to take advantage of this functionality.

Some of the requirements which point to the need for an API set are:

- The need for a large, integrated analytics system.
- The ability to add additional functionality around the model construction tool.
- The ability to run the entire system in a production setting with little or no user intervention.
- The need to present results in an intuitive, user-friendly manner outside of the model construction tool, i.e., in another system.

Most often the capabilities that are missing are the interfaces to a process flow monitor and model management tools.

Many of the tools in the market package analytics techniques within a graphical interface. This gives the user greater ability to use the analytics techniques and results without having deep technical knowledge in the specific algorithm. Small analytics engagements which have short time frames and are performing one-time studies will probably not require an open API set. The analysis on these projects tends to be manual in nature with a high degree of interaction with the model. One reason why a tool with an API set might be chosen for these shorter engagements is if the tool was going to be used for future work which might need the flexibility of a programming interface.

Some situations may require the output of one model construction tool to be used as the input to another. This is called composite modeling. It is common for an analyst to use an opaque mining algorithm (e.g., a neural network) to do some initial analysis and then use a transparent algorithm (e.g., a decision tree) to explain the results. These algorithms may be part of different model construction tools or they may be part a tool which contains a suite of algorithms.

It is possible that different mining algorithms and tools may require their input data to be in different formats. In this case, the system may need to have multiple data pre-processing components, one set for each different format that must be generated. Therefore, an increased number of mining tools or algorithms in a system can increase the complexity of other system components. This higher complexity situation would be desirable if the benefits of having different sets of data analysis capabilities offset the cost and complexity of maintaining multiple components.

ANALYTICS AND IMPACT OF INTERNET TECHNOLOGIES

There are three areas where internet technologies can be used as a part of an analytics solution. First, external data vendors can supply data to their customers via the internet (e.g., data sets could be distributed using FTP at specified intervals). This can solve the problem of how to receive external data used for analytics.

The second impact the internet has on analytics is on the volume and structure of data that is accessible. The internet provides access to data that has never before been available to the business world. For example, the amount of demographic information about individual consumers that resides on the internet can be overwhelming. In addition to the new information itself, it is often organized using images, video, and other complex forms. Both of these factors add to the complexity of any analytics architecture that will attempt to tap into this wealth of data.

The third use for or of Internet technologies is as a method for deploying the "mined" knowledge. A company could create an application which incorporates an analytics model or the results of analysis and then deploy it on a corporate intranet or the public Internet. For example, a company could create a "smart" on-line catalog which tailors the products and services shown to the user according to his or her personal tastes.

These examples illustrate that the role of Internet technologies in analytics is really at both the front and the back end of the process. The core analytics process is not significantly altered by the inclusion of Internet concepts.

INTELLIGENT AGENTS IN ANALYTICS

Intelligent agents are active pieces of code which use data analysis algorithms to solve a problem or answer a question, and perform an action based on the answer. These agents can provide complimentary capabilities to an analytics system. Agents can be used for marketing, information retrieval, checking a model's validity, or notifying someone that a particular event has been detected.

Agents can also be used to target information, products, or services to a specific customer. Companies are now using agents which ask a few non-obtrusive questions about a person in an attempt to determine their preferences based on the preferences of other people with similar traits. Another slightly different application of this idea is to use agents to proactively market newspapers or information services to non-subscribers who have traits and interests similar to those of current subscribers.

Intelligent agents can also search and retrieve information from the internet. Companies can perform searches for potential customers, new data sources, or on-line documents. This information could be used to create mailing lists for a marketing or sales department, perform research in a specific area, or identify additional data sources for use in building mining models.

Agents can also actively validate the input data for a model to detect if a model may be "going stale." These agents analyze the latest set of input data and compare its traits to the traits of the original data set that was used to construct the model. If the traits of the current input data set are found to be outside of acceptable ranges, an agent indicates that the model may no longer be accurate for the new data set. The agent then alerts the model construction team that a new model may need to be built. This scenario would likely occur in a production setting.

A more simplistic use for intelligent agents in analytics is as a notification mechanism. An agent can trigger a notification via e-mail or other mechanism to a specified person or group. Some common events which may require immediate notification are: detection of an obsolete model, completion of scoring of a set of customers, or detection of fraudulent activity. This scenario would also be found in a production environment.

OPERATIONS ARCHITECTURE CONSIDERATIONS

The operations architecture is a combination of tools, support services, procedures, and controls required to keep a production system available and running efficiently. Its primary users are system administrators and production support personnel. This section discusses system management issues specific to analytics solutions.

The development and usage of an analytics system may require that support for both developers and end users be available through a helpdesk. The decision on whether or not to add helpdesk support for analytics would center on the number of end-users and/or developers that will actually be using the analytics system and the complexity of training the help desk personnel would require allowing them to support analytics tools. In most cases, help desk personnel would not be able to support the developers of analytics solutions due to its high level of complexity and specialization. In some cases, end-user support may be possible and necessary if the use analytics techniques have spread to a corporation's general end-user community, rather than a few power users.

Additionally, the database which holds the data sets (data repository) needs to be managed like other production databases. It needs recovery capabilities for both physical and logical failures; it should be included in the enterprise's backup/recovery strategy; and, it should be able to handle batch data processing runs. Furthermore, capacity planning should be performed if the system is intended to manipulate and store large data sets. Although, these tasks are not new or specific to analytics, they require special consideration during the construction of an analytics solution.

Finally, running large amounts of data through mining algorithms can often take large amounts of both memory and I/O resources. If an analytics application is accessing existing computer resources, a careful review of the current batch run schedule is necessary. It is also important to communicate to operations personnel that the batch runs can be extremely resource intensive.

END POINTS

Current business processes often use data from several sources. Data is characterized to be heterogeneous, incomplete, and usually involves a huge amount of records. This implies that data must be transformed in a set of patterns, rules or some kind of formalism, which helps to understand the underlying information. The participation of several organizations in this process makes the assimilation of data more difficult.

In addition, new communication scenarios, mainly internet, have appeared and delivered great units of information everyday, which must be properly managed and tackled. Many scientific and industrial fields generate enormous amounts of data. This trend seems to be increasing and there is no end in sight. However, the number and diversity of these data items may cause the opposite effect, that is, they can hide the underlying information, avoiding the understanding of such information. For this reason, it is necessary to use data abstractions in order to discover the essence of the information. Analytics as a process of discovering useful patterns in data helps in delivering comprehensive knowledge of the concrete domain information. This process must be automatic, or at least, semi-automatic, since a manual process would be excessively costly and prone to error. At the same time, centralized solutions to the analytics problem are not suitable for most of the current scenarios, because of the complexity of the analytics tasks and security issues related to data, which is distributed among several organizations. Distributed analytics systems provide an efficient use of multiple processors and databases to speed up the execution of data analysis and enable data distribution. However, there is no universal strategy to configure a distributed analytics environment to be optimal in the resolution of every process.

Grid computing has emerged as a new technology, whose main challenge is the complete integration of heterogeneous computing systems and data resources with the aim of providing a global computing space. Extending the concept to analytics, analytics grid could be a solution allowing analytics processes to be deployed in a grid environment, in which data and services resources are geographically distributed, belong to several virtual organizations and the security can be flexibly solved.

A wishful thinking, may be!

REFERENCES

Tan, Pang-Ning, Steinbach, Michael, and Kumar, Vipin, "Introduction to Data Mining." May 2005.

Bramer, M. A., "Principles of Data Mining" (Undergraduate Topics in Computer Science), March 2007.

CHAPTER 6

IMPLEMENTING ANALYTIC SOLUTIONS

Implementing an analytics solution is an iterative process with several interconnected steps that need to be executed in a perfect harmony.

The purpose of this chapter is to provide a generalized implementation approach for the development and implementation of an analytic solution. By no means is the approach and methodology discussed here a definitive guide, as analytics and data mining solutions gain wider industry acceptance, further evolution of the approaches discussed here will indeed refine and enhance the implementation best practices.

This section begins by discussing the overall implementation approach and then focuses on each of the specific phases within an analytics project. For each phase, an overview is given, followed by a discussion of the appropriate task packages, deliverables, exit criteria, and next steps.

You may find certain similarity and overlapping concepts with Chapters 3 and 4, where we discussed the analytics methodology at a high level.

Before addressing the overall implementation approach, one must realize that its success relies on strong capabilities, such as:

- Clearly defined business objectives for analytics, derived from the organization's vision and strategy
- Appropriate combination of skills (business, analytical and technical) within the organization
- Suitable means for deploying and integrating analytics within the organization's business processes
- Relevant internal and external information and data analysis (i.e., analytics) techniques available to the organization

When developing an analytics solution a union of these domains should be always kept at the forefront. This couples the attainable business objectives with the right analytical techniques accessing the appropriate information to deploy meaningful knowledge to skilled analysts within the organization.

If the developed solution falls outside of the union of these domains, it is unlikely to meet all of its objectives. A solution falls outside of the union when inappropriate analytical techniques are chosen (i.e., technology for technology's sake), when the solution is based on irrelevant information, or when the business objectives are not kept in sight. While no approach is fail safe, risk can be mitigated by the implementation approach outlined below.

ANALYTICS SOLUTION IMPLEMENTATION PROCESS FLOW

To begin with, business knowledge is a very important step which helps in understanding the business problem and sets the objectives and goals the business would wish to achieve. These inputs are then taken to create a preliminary plan clearly defining the analytics project scope. The next important aspect is to understand and analyze what data are available, in what state they are, how much effort is required to bring the data into a cleansed and standardized environment, etc. If you do not have a good understanding of data, you will run into many challenges when you start developing the analytics models. Thus, data preparation becomes a critical activity of any analytic project. Once you have got the right data, next step is to develop analytic models and validate the outcomes with business users. There are various modeling techniques like decision trees, rule induction, case base reasoning, visualization techniques, nearest neighbor technique, clustering algorithms etc. Usually, this becomes an iterative activity till a model is finalized based on accuracy, coverage and validity.

The diagram above depicts the various phases, tasks and sub-tasks. In the following sections we will cover these with details.

OPPORTUNITY ASSESSMENT AND FEASIBILITY ANALYSIS

This initial phase focuses on understanding the objectives and requirements from a business perspective, and then converting this information into a problem definition, and a preliminary plan designed to achieve the objectives.

An opportunity assessment is conducted as the first phase of analytics projects to define the vision and strategy of the organization, as well as the subsequent direction of the analytics solution. Beginning a project with an opportunity assessment, as opposed to going directly to the development of a production-ready system, can mitigate risk to the overall organization. The benefits may include a clear understanding of the business direction, a sense of what is most important, an understanding of the benefits of change, or all of the above. An opportunity assessment is particularly appropriate when an organization needs a response to a business problem, an appraisal of a particular technology, an examination of present and future industry position, or an evaluation of strategic direction.

The objectives of an opportunity assessment are as follows:

- Create a list of key questions that the organization would like addressed and answered.

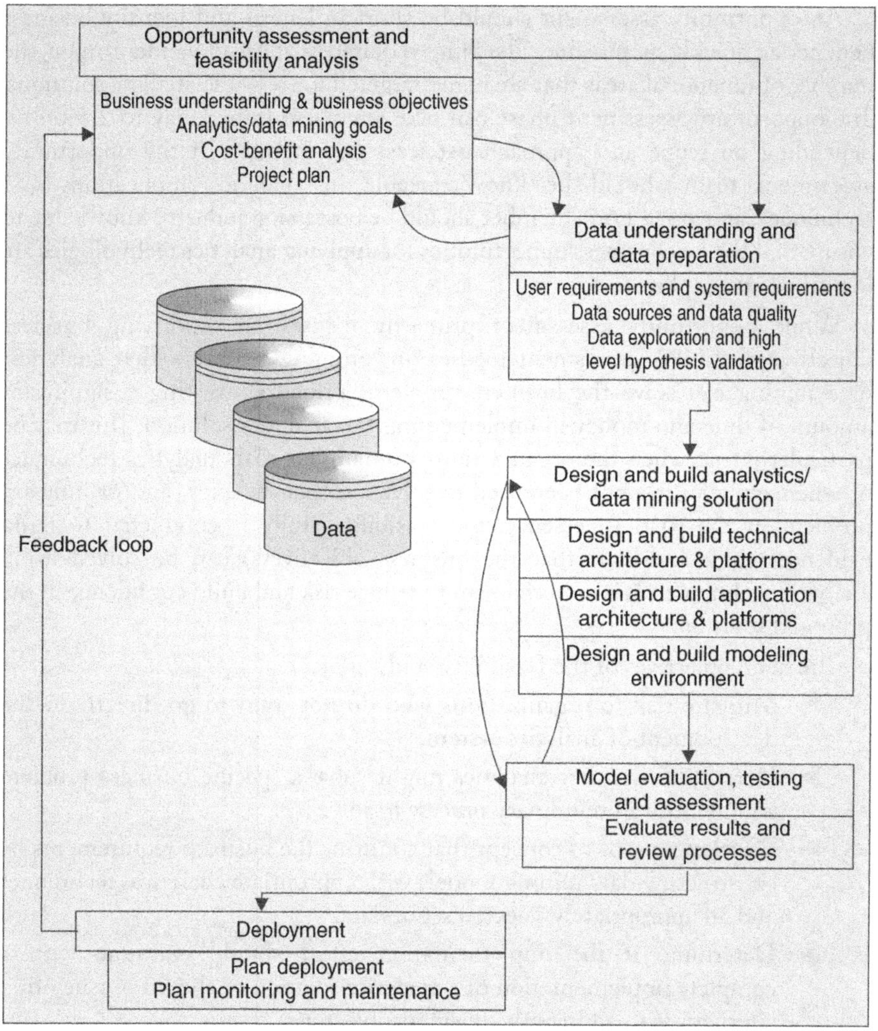

Figure 6.1 Analytics methodology and framework.

- Establish a clear context, which includes an understanding of what is most important for the business and its use of analytics.
- Determine how an analytic solution fits into the organization's vision and strategic plan.
- Define the preliminary business case, including a cost/benefit analysis, for analytics.
- Determine if the business processes are in place to achieve and sustain the benefits of an analytic solution.
- Determine if the technical architecture and resources, including data, needed to support the implementation effort exist in the organization.
- Recommend how to continue the development of the analytics solution.

An opportunity assessment should be short in length and identify business benefits as quickly as possible. The time required is most dependent upon the number of functional areas that are being targeted for possible analytic solutions. The opportunity assessment phase can take anywhere from 1 day to 2 months, depending on scope and approach. At least one member of the opportunity assessment team should be knowledgeable in analytics applications and techniques, and at least one member should be possessing industry knowledge to ensure that the key business opportunities for applying analytics technologies are identified and explored.

While opportunity assessment primarily focuses on solidifying business objectives, feasibility assessment focuses on "proofing" aspects—that analytics/data mining can solve the business problems prior to investing a significant amount of time and money in implementing the analytics solution. This may be particularly true when the organization is unfamiliar with analytics techniques or when analytics has not been used to solve a similar business and/or industry problem in the past. In essence, the feasibility study is conducted to build evidence which indicates that the business objective(s) can be solved using analytics techniques. It is a mechanism to reduce risk and build confidence in the proposed solution.

The main objectives of the feasibility study are to:

- Mitigate risk to organizations who do not want to go directly to the development of analytics system.
- Determine whether analytics might solve a specific business problem and identify a preliminary process to solve it.
- Develop a proof of concept that confirms the business requirements by constructing data mining models with appropriate analytical techniques and an appropriately selected set of data.
- Determine if the implementation effort should continue with a complete implementation of a analytics solution or should pursue other alternatives to address the business objectives.

During a feasibility study, a proof of concept is created to serve as a model of the behavior and functionality of an application prior to its creation. At the core of the proof of concept is a light weight analytics model that effectively addresses the business problem and demonstrates the capabilities of the selected analytics techniques and tools. However, the proof of concept is not intended to be a fully functional application and may even be discarded before the design and build phase.

After the feasibility study is complete, the scope of the application and the potential costs and benefits can be better determined. To be successful, the feasibility study should have clear measures of success defined, i.e., statistics and metrics. In addition the feasibility study should focus on target outcomes rather than process internals.

As technologies mature, organizations will become more familiar with analytics solutions, and the need to perform feasibility studies will likely diminish. In the meantime, a feasibility study remains an effective way to build client confidence and mitigate risk when implementing an analytics solution.

Some of the deliverables created during this phase are:

- A Business Case, which includes the business goals of an organization, narration of how an analytics solution can improve the overall business situation and solve a specific business problem, and a costs/benefits proposal and the compelling reason for proceeding.
- A High-Level Roadmap, including technical, process and organization design, which indicates how the business problem will be solved.
- A Project Definition and Plan, which defines the scope of the project and develops a high-level work plan for the analytics solution.
- An assessment of organization readiness consisting of preliminary personnel and skill requirements.

DATA UNDERSTANDING AND DATA PREPARATION

It is interesting to note that, during the feasibility analysis, the team usually does some amount of high level data understanding and data preparation activities in order to probe the analytics solution.

In reality, the data understanding and data preparation phase is all about identification of right data sources, collection of the required data elements, identifying data quality problems, discovering first insights into the data, detecting interesting subsets to form hypotheses for hidden information, and constructing ion of the final data set (data that will be fed into the modeling tool(s)) from the initial raw data.

The data understanding and data preparation tasks are likely to be performed multiple times, and not in any prescribed order. Tasks include table, record, and attribute selection as well as transformation and cleaning of data for modeling tools.

DESIGN AND BUILD ANALYTICS/DATA MINING SOLUTION

This phase takes the inputs from the previous phase and starts looking deeper into the user requirements, prioritized business needs, system requirements, application architecture, technical architecture, test strategy, etc.

In this phase, the other most important activity is fit-gap analysis of various modeling techniques. Typically, there are several techniques for the same analytics problem type. Some techniques have specific requirements on the form of data. Therefore, stepping back to the data preparation phase is often needed.

The development approach focuses on the delivery of an analytics solution to solve the business problem(s) identified in the opportunity assessment and feasibility study phases. The objective is to design, build and deploy an analytics solution. The solutions developed can take a number of forms. These range from constructing a pilot to be used when addressing a narrow business problem to delivering a comprehensive solution that has a robust technical architecture for an end-user applications.

Success factors for the development phase include the following:

- Direct attention should be paid to the experience and number of users of the application.
- Determine how frequently the application will use the analytics results and how frequently the model will be reapplied to discover new information or a new problem.
- The infrastructure and architecture should be designed in such a way that future expansion needs, in terms of processing power and capacity, can be addressed.
- The needs of the current technical environment and applications which will interact with the data mining architecture should be supported.

This phase may vary greatly in length but, in general, the data extraction, preprocessing, and analysis tasks are typically 70%–80% of the overall data analysis effort.

Since the model construction activity is at the core of the analytics solution and is often an iterative model till the final state is reached, the technical architecture needs to enable the following functionalities as services so that the iterative nature of the model development is adequately accommodated without impacting the other phases and activities.

- Model Construction Services
- Data Exploration Services
- Data Extraction Services
- Data Preprocessing Services
- Data Repository Services
- Management Services
- Deployment Services

MODEL EVALUATION, TESTING, AND ASSESSMENT

At this stage in the project you have built a model (or models). Before proceeding to final deployment of the model, it is important to more thoroughly evaluate the model, and review the steps executed to construct the model, to be certain it properly achieves the business objectives. A key objective is to determine if there is some important business issue that has not been sufficiently considered. At the end of this phase, a decision on the use of the data mining results should be reached.

This phase also consists of an important activity—preparation and execution of benefits realization test to prove that the delivered solution solves the business objectives that were defined in the opportunity assessment and feasibility assessment phase.

As a component of the benefits realization test, the results created by the data mining model should be compared to the actual business outcomes. This is a function of knowledge evaluation discussed at length in the earlier chapters of this book.

DEPLOYMENT

Creation of the model is generally not the end of the project. Even if the purpose of the model is to increase knowledge of the data, the knowledge gained will need to be organized and presented in a way that the user can use it. Depending on the requirements, the deployment phase can be as simple as generating a report or as complex as implementing a repeatable analytics process. In many cases it will be the business users/knowledge workers, not the data analyst, who will carry out the deployment steps, hence a step by step documentation elaborating on various aspects of the model created, how to use it, how to test it, how to deploy it, how to troubleshoot etc. is required. This will help them understand up front what actions will need to be carried out in order to actually make use of the created models.

In the following sections we will discuss the various activities, tasks and sub tasks that constitute each of the phases discussed above.

OPPORTUNITY ASSESSMENT AND FEASIBILITY ANALYSIS

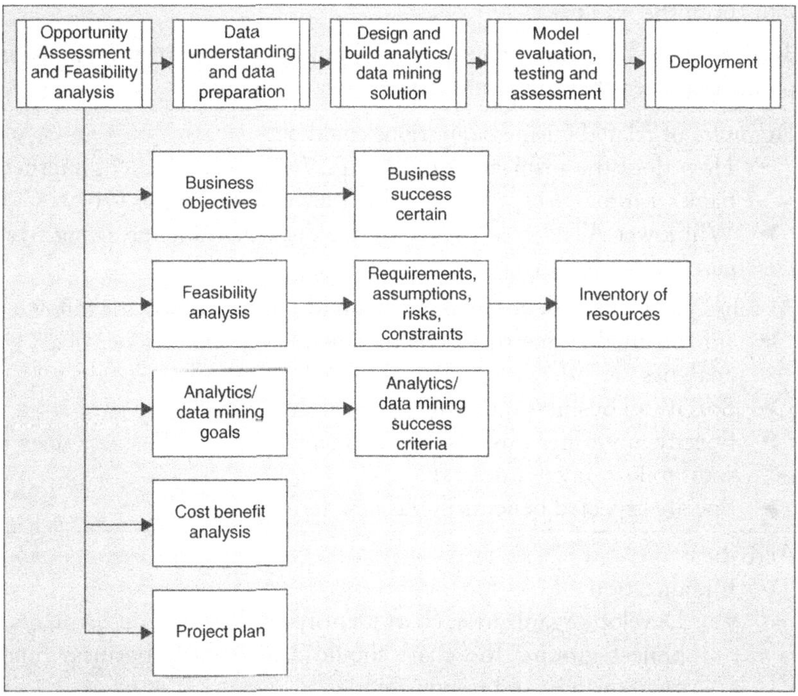

Figure 6.2 Opportunity assessment and feasibility analysis phase.

Determine Business Objectives

Task: Determine Business Objectives—The first objective of the data analyst is to thoroughly understand, from a business perspective, what the organization really wants to accomplish. Often there are many competing objectives and constraints that must be properly balanced. The analyst's goal is to uncover important factors, at the beginning, that can influence the outcome of the project. A possible consequence of neglecting this step is to expend a great deal of effort producing the right answers to the wrong questions. An analytics opportunity assessment should concentrate on fully analyzing an organization's current data and data analysis. This in-depth evaluation provides valuable information that helps derive the appropriate vision and strategy for the organization. Available hardware and software for analyzing and manipulating data should also be examined, as well as the functional data analysis capabilities that exist within the organization. The data itself may also be a useful source of information during this task.

It is during this phase that evaluation criteria (e.g., cost/benefit analysis) are developed to identify strategic options and select the best option for going forward. However, it is usually very difficult to quantify the benefits of analytics, and commonly used evaluation criteria do not always provide this information. This is particularly true in industries and areas where analytics engagements have not been performed before. In these cases, the best way to quantify analytics benefits is to perform a proof of concept with a sample set of data and extrapolate benefits from the results.

To illustrate—The primary business goal might be to keep current customers by predicting when they are prone to move to a competitor.

Examples of related business questions could be:

- How does the primary channel (e.g., ATM, visit branch, internet) a bank customer uses, affect whether they will stay or go? Or
- Will lower ATM fees significantly reduce the number of high-value customers who leave?

As subsequent activities, the analytics team would start doing the following –

- Informally describe the problem which is supposed to be solved with analytics
- Specify all business questions as precisely as possible
- Specify any other business requirements (e.g., the business does not want to lose any customers)
- Specify expected benefits in business terms

Activities:

- Organization
    - Develop organization chart identifying divisions, departments, and project groups. The chart should also identify business function owner names and responsibilities.
    - Identify key persons in the business and their roles.

- Identify an internal sponsor (financial sponsor and primary user/domain expert).
- Is there a steering committee and who are the members?
- Identify the business units which will be impacted by the data mining project (e.g., Marketing, Sales, Finance).

➤ Problem Area
- Identify the problem area (e.g., Marketing, Customer Care, Business Development, etc.).
- Describe the problem in general terms.
- Check the current status of the project (e.g., Check if it is already discussed within the business unit that we are performing an analytics project, or do we need to advertise analytics as a key technology to the business?).
- Clarify prerequisites of the project (e.g., what is the motivation of the project? Does the business already use analytics?).
- If necessary, prepare presentations and present analytics to the business.
- Identify target groups for the project result (e.g., Do we expect a written report for top management, or do we expect a running system that is used by naïve end users?).
- Identify the users' needs and expectations Current Solution.
- Describe the solution currently in use for the problem.
- Describe the advantages and disadvantages of the current solution, and the level to which it is accepted by the users.

Task: *Business Success Criteria*—Describe the criteria for a successful or useful outcome to the project from the business point of view. This might be quite specific, such as reduction of customer churn to a certain level, or could be generic and subjective such as "give useful insights into the relationships". In the latter case it should be indicated who will make the subjective judgment.

Activities:

➤ Specify business success criteria (e.g., improve response rate in a mailing campaign by 10%, and sign-up rate increased by 20%).

➤ Identify who will assess the success criteria.

Note: Each of the success criteria should relate to at least one of the specified Business Objectives.

Feasibility Analysis

Task: *Feasibility Analysis*—This task involves more detailed fact-finding about all of the resources, constraints, assumptions, and other factors that should be considered in determining the analytics goal and project plan. In the previous task, your objective is to quickly get to the crux of the situation. Here, you want to flesh out the details.

Activities:

- Sources of Data and Knowledge
- Identify data sources
- Identify type of data sources (on-line sources, experts, written documentation, ...)
- Identify knowledge sources
- Identify type of knowledge sources (on-line sources, experts, written documentation, etc)
- Check available tools and techniques
- Describe the relevant background knowledge (informally or formally)
- Hardware Resources
- Identify the base hardware
- Establish the availability of the base hardware for the analytics project
- Check if the hardware maintenance schedule conflicts with the availability of the hardware for the analytics project
- Identify the hardware available for the analytics tool to be used (if the tool is known at this stage)
- Personnel Sources
- Identify project sponsor (if different from internal sponsor as in Section 1.1.1)
- Identify system administrator, database administrator and technical support staff for further questions
- Identify market analysts, data mining experts and statisticians and check their availability
- Check availability of domain experts for later phases

Note: Remember that the project may need technical staff at odd times throughout the project, e.g., during Data Transformation.

Task: ***Requirements, Assumptions, and Constraints:*** Gathering User and Usability Requirements is a critical activity. Following are the key aspects that needs to be kept in mind while eliciting requirements.

- *User requirements and usability requirements* - Used to identify the system's users, their business needs and usability requirements. The user requirements for data exploration must also be collected. The data analyst and even the end-user will have requirements for examining the data and performing user directed discovery. The capabilities needed will be used to select exploration tools for inclusion in the architecture.
- *Gather user skill inventory* - When delivering an analytics solution, it is imperative to inventory the data analysis skills that the analysts and end-users have and to identify any gap between those and the skills needed to work in an analytics environment. The gap indicates skills that must be addressed in the solution's design and subsequent training programs.
- *How should the results be presented to the users?* - When defining the usability requirements for an analytics solution, consider how an analytics model and its results will be presented to the users. An analytics model and its

results can be presented in a number of ways including reports, code, graphical representations, etc. It is important that the analytics model be presented to the user in a meaningful and easily interpreted fashion. The usability requirements defined will affect selection of modeling techniques, selection of model construction tools and the design of the user interaction with the model and its results.

- *Should an opaque or transparent modeling technique be used?* - Another consideration to be addressed is the level of explanation that must be given by the model. The goal here is to understand how a decision is made by the model. This requirement will greatly influence the selection of analytical techniques for mining and the model construction tool used to build the model.
- *Gather System Quality Requirements* - This is used to formalize the quality requirement for the solution in terms of the system's metrics and goals. Several questions should be resolved during this task:
- *State the accuracy/precision requirements of the model* - When a model is constructed, its accuracy and precision must be determined during the model validation phase. The desired level of accuracy and precision should be stated as part of the system quality requirements. Although there is no single answer to what level of accuracy and precision is valid for all business cases, it will be influenced by how clearly the business context is defined, the quality of data and the analytical technique employed.

Best Practice: Data mining models can be considered either opaque or transparent. Opaque models can only give limited explanation, if any at all, to the decision made. An opaque model usually, only gives the answer. An example of an opaque model is a customer scoring system built with a neural network. The model would state that the customer's score is, say, 98.

On the other hand, transparent models clearly explain how decisions are reached. For example, a decision tree gives a set of rules to explain how customer segmentation is made? This model would state that the customer is a "Churner" based on rules like the customer has changed long distance carriers more than twice in the last year and has carried a balance on her credit card for more than six months.

The usability requirements and the business context will help define the level of explanation needed. Some business problems, such as underwriting insurance policies, will require full (transparent) explanation of the decision reached due to government regulation, state law, etc. Others, such as predicting responses to a direct mailing campaign, will be interested only in the answer (opaque) and not care about the means of reaching it.

- List all requirements of the project including schedule of completion, comprehensibility and quality of results, and security as well as legal issues. As part of this output, make sure that you are allowed to use the data.

- List the assumptions made by the project. These may be assumptions about the data which can be used during data mining, but may also include other assumptions about the business upon which the project rests. It is particularly important to list the latter if they form conditions on the validity of the results.
- List the constraints on the project. These may be constraints on the availability of resources, but may also include technological constraints such as the size of data, which it is practical to use for modeling.

Activities:

- Requirements
    - Capture requirements on comprehensibility, accuracy, deployability, maintainability, and repeatability of the analytics project and the resulting model(s).
    - Capture requirements on security, legal restrictions, privacy, reporting, and project schedule.
    - Specify target group profile.
    - Capture all requirements on scheduling.
- Assumptions
    - Clarify all assumptions (including implicit ones) and make them explicit (e.g., To address the business question, a minimum number of customers with age above 50 is necessary).
    - List assumptions on data quality (e.g., accuracy, availability).
    - List assumptions on external factors (e.g., economic issues, competitive products, technical advances).
    - Clarify assumptions that lead to any of the estimates (e.g., the price of a specific tool is assumed to be lower than $1000).
    - List all assumptions on whether it is necessary to understand and describe or explain the model. (e.g., How should the model and results be presented to senior management/sponsor.)
- Constraints
    - Check general constraints (e.g., legal issues, budget, timescales and resources).
    - Check access rights to data sources (e.g., access restrictions, password required).
    - Check technical accessibility of data (operating systems, data management system, file or database format).
    - Check whether relevant knowledge is accessible.
    - Check budget constraints (Fixed costs, implementation costs, etc.).

Note: The list of assumptions also includes assumptions at the beginning of the project, i.e., what has been the starting point of the project.

Task: ***Risks and Contingencies:*** List the risks, events which might occur to delay the project or cause it to fail. List the corresponding contingency plans; what action will be taken if the risks happen.

Activities:

- Identify business risks (e.g., competitor comes up with better results first).
- Identify organizational risks (e.g., department requesting project not having funding for project).
- Identify financial risks (e.g., further funding depends on initial analytics results).
- Identify technical risks.
- Identify risks that depend on data and data sources (e.g., poor quality and coverage).
- Determine conditions when each risk may occur.

Task: *Outputs Inventory of Resources*—List the resources available to the project, including: personnel (business experts, data experts, technical support, analytics personnel), data (fixed extracts, access to live warehoused or operational data), computing resources (hardware platforms), software (analytics tools, other relevant software).

Determine Analytics and Data Mining Goals

Task: *Determine Analytics Goals*—A business goal states objectives in business terminology. An analytics goal states project objectives in technical terms. For example, the business goal might be "Increase catalog sales to existing customers" while the analytics goal would be "Predict how many widgets a customer will buy, given their purchases over the past three years, demographic information (age, salary, city, etc.), and the price of the item".

Activities:

- Translate the business questions to analytics goals (e.g., a marketing campaign requires segmentation of customers in order to decide whom to approach in this campaign; it should be specified by the level/size of the segments).
- Specify problem type (e.g., classification, description, prediction and clustering).

Task: *Success Criteria:* Define the criteria for a successful outcome of the project in technical terms, for example a certain level of predictive accuracy, or a propensity to purchase profile with a given degree of "lift". As with business success criteria, it may be necessary to describe these in subjective terms, in which case the person or persons making the subjective judgment should be identified.

Activities:

- Specify criteria for model assessment (e.g., model accuracy, performance and complexity).
- Define benchmarks for evaluation criteria.
- Specify criteria which address subjective assessment criteria (e.g., model explainability and data and marketing insight provided by the model).

Cost Benefit Analysis

Task: *Costs and Benefits:* A cost-benefit analysis for the project compares the costs of the project with the potential benefit to the business if it is successful. The comparison should be as specific as possible, for example using monetary measures in a commercial situation.

Activities:

- Estimate costs for data collection.
- Estimate costs of developing and implementing a solution.
- Identify benefits when a solution is deployed (e.g., improved customer satisfaction, ROI, and increase in revenue).
- Estimate operating costs.

Note: Remember to identify hidden costs such as repeated data extraction and preparation, changes in work flows, and training time during learning.

Produce Project Plan

Task: *Produce Project Plan*—The project plan should ideally cover a high level roadmap for achieving the analytics goals, key milestones, dependencies, management review checkpoints and anticipated set of steps to be performed during the rest of the project including an initial selection of tools and techniques.

List the stages to be executed in the project, together with duration, resources required, inputs, outputs and dependencies. Where possible make explicit the large-scale iterations in the analytics process, for example repetitions of the modeling and evaluation phases.

As part of the project plan, it is also important to analyze dependencies between time schedule and risks. Mark results of these analyses explicitly in the project plan, ideally with actions and recommendations if the risks appear.

Activities:

- Define the initial process plan and discuss the feasibility with all involved personnel.
- Put all identified goals and selected techniques together into a reference framework that solves the business questions and meets the business success criteria.
- Estimate effort and resources needed to achieve and deploy the solution. It is also useful to consider past experiences when estimating timescales for data mining projects. It is also advisable to refer to any organizational directives/standards such as for any analytics/data mining project, 50%–70% of the time and effort in a data mining project is used in the data preparation and data understanding phase, and 30%–50% in the Modeling, and 10%–20% in opportunity assessment and feasibility analysis phase.
- Identify critical steps.

- Mark decision points.
- Mark review points.
- Identify major iterations.

Note: The project plan is a dynamic document in the sense that at the end of each phase a review of progress and achievements is necessary and an update of the project plan accordingly is recommended.

Best Practice: It is always useful to create an exhaustive list of business terminologies and analytics terminology and make this available for the subsequent phases of the project. This helps in establishing a standardized taxonomy for the project.

1. Terminology—A glossary of terminology relevant to the project. This may include two components:
   (a) A glossary of relevant business terminology, which forms part of the business understanding available to the project. Constructing this glossary is a useful "knowledge elicitation" and education exercise.
   (b) A glossary of analytics terminology, illustrated with examples relevant to the business problem in question.

Activities:

1. Check prior availability of glossaries, otherwise begin to draft glossaries.
2. Talk to domain experts to understand their terminology.
3. Become familiar with the business terminology.

While the opportunity assessment and feasibility analysis activities are underway, in parallel, a team of technology experts can start doing a high level assessment of various products and tools as relevant to the analytics goals and business objectives.

Initial Assessment of Tools and Techniques – This activity is primarily driven by technology experts and with assistance from few business users to identify analytics tools which can support the business objectives and data mining goals.

Activities:

1. Create a list of selection criteria for tools and techniques (or use an existing one if available).
2. Choose potential tools and techniques.
3. Evaluate appropriateness of techniques.
4. Review and prioritize applicable techniques according to the evaluation of alternative solutions.

Data Understanding and Data Preparation

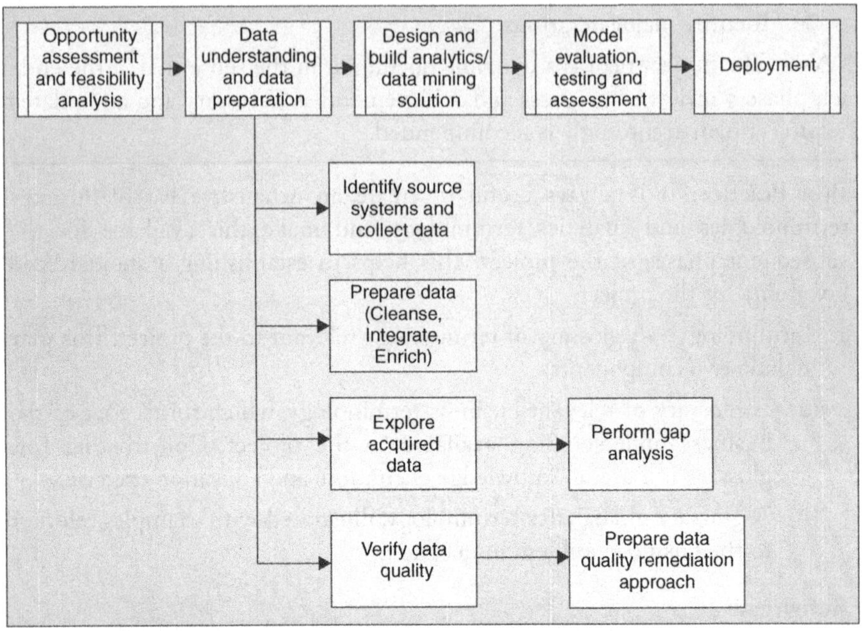

Figure 6.3 Data understanding and data preparation phase.

Identify Source Systems and Collect Data

Task: *Identify Source Systems and Collect Data*—Identify data sources that would provide the desired data elements to perform analytics. The data collection process is also equally important so that any dependencies on source systems are eliminated. Identifying data sources is a nontrivial task which involves determining the data requirements and identifying where that data resides. Ideally, all of the data requirements will be satisfied by data in transactional, operational, data warehouses, data marts or analytical stores within the organization. Additional information, such as market intelligence and demographic data, may be purchased from external sources.

If the data requirements are not fully satisfied, then one must determine if the missing data will jeopardize the results of the analytics effort. In certain cases, the analytics effort can continue without all of the desired data; doing so may result in a solution that does not deliver its full benefit to the organization. However, if the missing data is vital to the success of the data mining effort then additional work may be required to acquire it. The data might be acquired by modifying existing systems to capture additional fields, by designing new systems to gather information or by pursuing new external sources.

Regardless, the time and cost needed to acquire the data must be weighed against the benefit that will be gained by using it in the analytics effort.

Note: If you acquire data from multiple data sources, be prepared for additional activities during the system development phase—for example, data integration and consolidation of same type of data elements coming from multiple sources.

Having a well thought out data selection criteria helps in narrowing the search for data; some of the criteria may be: relevance to the analytics goals, quality, and technical constraints such as limits on data volume or data types. The criteria should include selection of attributes (columns) as well as selection of records (rows) in a table.

List the data set(s) acquired, together with their originating source systems, the methods used to acquire them, any special considerations should be applied and any problems encountered. Problems encountered, and any solutions achieved, are listed to aid with future replication of this project or with the execution of similar future projects. Document the data to be included/excluded and the reasons for these decisions.

It is also important to have a rigorous documentation process describing the data, which has been acquired, including: the format of the data, the volumetric of data, for example number of records and fields in each table, the identities of the fields, and any other features of the data, which have been discovered.

Activities:

- Identification of data sources and data selection criteria
  - Plan which information is needed (e.g., only given attributes, additional information).
  - Check if all the information needed (to solve the data mining goals) is actually available.
- Which attributes are necessary for the specified analytics goals? Which attributes have been identified as being irrelevant? How many attributes can we handle with the chosen techniques?
  - Select tables/files of interest.
  - Select data within a table/file.
  - Think about how long history one should use even if available (e.g., even if 18 months data is available, maybe only 12 months is needed for the exercise).
- Data preparation
  - If the data contains free text entries, do we need to encode them for modelling, or do we want to group specific entries?
  - Are there missing attributes? How would we get them, if they are critical?
  - Describe how to extract the data, collect appropriate additional data (from different sources—in-house as well as externally).
  - Perform significance and correlation test to decide if fields should be included.
  - Select different data subsets (e.g., Different attributes, only data which meet certain conditions).

- Consider use of sampling techniques (e.g., a quick solution may involve the reduction of the size of the test data set or the tool may not be able to handle the full data set, splitting test and training data sets). It may also be useful to have weighted samples to give different importance to different attributes or different values of the same attribute.
- Document the rationale for inclusion/exclusion.
- Check available techniques for sampling data.

➢ Volumetric Analysis of Data
- Identify data and method of capture.
- Utilize statistical analyses if appropriate.
- Document tables and their relations.
- Document data volume, number of records/attributes, complexity.
- Do the data contain unstructured data/free form text entries?

➢ Attribute Types and Values
- Check accessibility and availability of attributes.
- Check attribute types (numeric, symbolic, taxonomy etc.).
- Check attribute value ranges.
- Analyze attribute correlations.
- Understand the meaning of each attribute and attribute value in business terms.
- For each attribute, compute basic statistics (e.g., compute distributions, averages, max, min, standard deviations, variances, skewness etc.).
- Analyze basic statistics and relate the results to their meaning in business terms.
- Is the attribute relevant for the specific analytics goal?
- Is the attribute meaning used consistently?
- Interview domain experts on their opinion of attribute relevance.
- Is it necessary to enrich the data, which has missing or incomplete values? (Depending on the modeling technique used)

➢ Keys
- Analyze key relations.
- Check amount of overlaps of key attribute values across tables.
- Review Assumptions/Goals.
- Update list of assumptions if necessary.

Note: Data collected from different sources may give rise to quality problems when merged (e.g., address files merged with customer base may show up inconsistencies of format, invalidity of data, etc.). Also important to be aware of the impact of acquiring free flow text data. It may be also necessary to pre-process the data (time series data, weighted averages, etc.)

Prepare Data

Task: *Prepare Data*—This task includes constructive data preparation operations such as the production of derived attributes, flattening of records, or transformed values for existing attributes. Another important consideration is to raise the data quality to the level required by the selected analysis techniques. These are methods whereby information is combined from multiple tables or records to create new records or values. This may involve selection of clean subsets of the data, the insertion of suitable defaults or more ambitious techniques such as the estimation of missing data by modeling.

In many cases there will be situations where creation of derived attributes will be required; these are new attributes that are constructed from one or more existing attributes in the same record.

> **Example:** Create records for customers who made no purchase during the past year. There was no reason to have such records in the raw data, but for modeling purposes it might make sense to explicitly represent the fact that certain customers made zero purchases.
>
> **Best Practice:** Why do we need to construct derived attributes during the course of an analytics process?
>
> It should not be thought that only data from databases or other sources is the only type of data that should be used in constructing a model. Derived attributes might be constructed because: Background knowledge convinces us that some fact is important and ought to be represented although we have no attribute currently to represent it.

Before adding derived attributes, it is always advisable to determine if and how they will ease the model process or facilitate the modelling algorithm, Perhaps "income per head" is a better/easier attribute to use than "income per household". Do not derive attributes simply to reduce the number of input attributes.

Another type of derived attribute is single-attribute transformations, usually performed to fit the needs of the modelling tools. Specify necessary transformation steps in terms of available transformation facilities; for example, transformations may be necessary to change ranges to symbolic fields (e.g., ages to age ranges) or symbolic fields ("definitely yes", "yes", "don't know", "no") to numeric values. They are often required by the modelling tools or algorithm.

Other integration activities like merging different source data is also not ruled out. Merging refers to joining together two or more data sets that have different information about the same objects.

> **Example:** A retail chain has one table with information about each store's general characteristics (e.g., floor space, type of mall), another table with summarized sales data (e.g., profit, percent change in sales from previous year), and another with information about the demographics of the surrounding area. Each of these data sets contains one record for each store. These data sets

can be merged together resulting in one record for each store, combining fields from the source tables. Merged data also covers aggregations.

Similarly, aggregation operations also need to be performed on data sets; aggregation refers to operations where new values are computed by summarizing together information from multiple records and/or tables.

Example: Converting a table of customer purchases where there is one record for each purchase into a new table where there is one record for each customer, with fields such as number of purchases, average purchase amount, percent of order charged to credit card, percent of items under promotion, etc

There could be some tool related constraints or specific requirements like order of the attributes, such as the first field being a unique identifier for each record or the last field being the outcome field the model is to predict. It might be important to change the order of the records in the data set. Perhaps the modeling tool requires that the records be sorted according to the value of the outcome attribute. Most common situation is that the records of the data set are initially ordered in some way but the modeling algorithm needs them to be in a fairly random order.

Example: When using neural networks it is generally best for the records to be presented in a random order although some tools will hand this automatically without explicit user intervention.

Additionally, there are purely syntactic changes made to satisfy the requirements of the specific modeling tool. Examples: removing commas from within text fields in comma-delimited data files, trimming all values to a maximum of 32 characters.

Activities:

- Check available data preparation functionality with the list of tools suggested for the project.
- Decide whether it is best to perform the data preparation activities inside the tool or outside (i.e., which is more efficient and repeatable).
- Decide if any attribute should be normalized (e.g., when using a clustering algorithm with age and income, the income will dominate).
- Consider adding new information on the relevant importance of attributes by adding new attributes (e.g., attribute weights, weighted normalization).
- If there are missing attributes, how would they be constructed? (decide type of construction (e.g., aggregate, average, induction)), add new attributes to the accessed data.
- Check for available techniques if needed (e.g., mechanisms to construct prototypes for each segment of segmented data).
- Check integration facilities if they are able to integrate the input sources as required.
- Integrate sources and store result, some tools have requirements on the

order of the attributes, such as the first field being a unique identifier for each record or the last field being the outcome field the model is to predict.

- Reordering records, it might be important to change the order of the records in the data set. Perhaps the modeling tool requires that the records be sorted according to the value of the outcome attribute. These are purely syntactic changes made to satisfy the requirements of the specific modeling tool.
- Reconsider data selection Criteria in light of experiences of data preparation (i.e., may wish include/exclude other sets of data).

Note: Data Preparation activities refer to primarily syntactic modifications made to the data that do not change its meaning, but might be required by the modeling tool.

Explore Acquired Data

Task: ***Explore Acquired Data***—This task primarily focuses on querying, visualization and reporting of the acquired data covering key findings around distribution of key attributes, for example the target attribute of a prediction task; relations between pairs or small numbers of attributes; results of simple aggregations; properties of significant sub-populations; and other simple statistical analyses. These analyses helps address the analytics goals; they may also contribute to or refine the data description and quality reports, and feed into the transformation and other data preparation needed for further analysis.

Based on the analytics requirements data exploration tools should be selected to provide the necessary functionality. Prior to selection of specific tools, determine if the exploration needs are met by the model construction tool or components of an existing data warehousing architecture. For those needs which were not satisfied by existing tools, one or more tools may be required to meet the remaining requirements.

In essence, through data exploration activities the initial hypothesis is validated at a high level and if there are any gaps, those are documented and remedial strategies formulated.

Activities:

- Data Exploration
  - Analyze properties of interesting attributes in detail (e.g., basic statistics interesting sub-populations).
  - Identify characteristics of sub-populations.
  - Consider and evaluate information and findings in the Data.
- Descriptions Report
  - Form hypothesis and identify actions.
  - Transform hypothesis into an analytics goal if possible.
  - Clarify analytics goals or make them more precise. Blind search is not necessarily useless but a more directed search towards business objectives is preferable.

- ♦ Perform basic analysis to verify the hypothesis.
- ♦ Perform gap analysis on acquired data and analytics goals.

Verify Data Quality

Task: *Verify Data Quality*—Examine the quality of the data, addressing questions such as: Is the data complete (does it cover all the cases required)? Is it correct or does it contain errors, and if there are errors how common are they? Are there missing values in the data? If so how are they represented, where do they occur and how common are they?

List the results of the data quality verification; if quality problems exist, list possible solutions. Solutions to data quality problems will generally depend heavily of both data and business knowledge.

Activities:

- ➤ Identify special values and catalogue their meaning
  - ♦ Review Keys, Attributes.
  - ♦ Check coverage (e.g., are all possibly values represented).
  - ♦ Do the meanings of attributes and contained values fit together?
- ➤ Identify missing attributes and blank fields
  - ♦ Check for attributes with different values that have similar meanings (e.g., low fat, diet).
  - ♦ Check spelling of values (e.g., same value but sometime beginning with a lower case letter, sometimes with an upper case letter).
  - ♦ Check for deviations, decide whether a deviation is noise or may indicate an interesting phenomenon.
  - ♦ Check for plausibility of values, e.g., all fields have the same or nearly the same values.
  - ♦ If the data is stored in flat files, check which delimiter is used and if it is used consistently within all attributes.
  - ♦ If the data is stored in flat files, check number of fields in each record.
- ➤ Noise and inconsistencies between sources
  - ♦ Check consistencies and redundancies between different sources.
- ➤ Plan how to deal with noise
  - ♦ Detect type of noise and which attributes are affected.
  - ♦ Reconsider how to deal with observed type of noise.
  - ♦ Correct, remove or ignore noise.
- ➤ Decide how to deal with special values and their meaning. The area of special values can give rise to many strange results and should be carefully examined. Examples of special values could arise through taking results of a survey where some questions were not asked or nor answered. This might result in a value of '99' for unknown data e.g., 99 for marital status or political affiliation. Special values could also arise

when data is truncated—e.g., '00' for 100 year old people, or all cars with 100,000 km on the clock.

Note: Reconsider Data Selection Criteria in light of experiences of data quality issues (i.e., one may wish include/exclude other sets of data).

Prepare Data Quality Remediation Approach

Task: ***Verify Data Quality***—Prepare a set of reports describing what decisions and actions were taken to address the data quality problems. Transformations of the data for cleaning purposes and the possible impact on the analysis results should also be considered. Document review comments of any attributes that may give answers which conflict with common sense (e.g., teenagers with high income). Use visualization plots, histograms, etc. to show up inconsistencies in the data in a graphical way.

Note that some fields may be irrelevant to the analytics goals and therefore noise in those fields has no significance. However, if noise is ignored for these reasons, it should be fully documented as the circumstances may change later!

It is also important to acknowledge that it may be necessary to exclude some data since they do not exhibit either positive or negative behavior (e.g., to check on customers loan behavior, exclude all those who have never loaned, do not finance a home mortgage, those whose mortgage is nearing maturity, etc. Any such inclusions/exclusions should also be documented.

Note: Any assessment of data quality should be made not just of the individual data sources but also of any data that comes from merging data sources. Merged data may present problems that do not exist in the individual data sources because of inconsistencies between the sources.

Design and Build Analytics Solution

The objective of this phase is to design and build an analytics solution. The solutions developed can take a number of forms. These range from constructing a pilot to be used when addressing a narrow business problem to delivering a comprehensive solution that has a robust technical architecture for end user applications.

Success factors for this phase include the following:

- Direct attention should be paid to the experience and number of users of the application.
- Determine how frequently the application will use the analytics results and how frequently the model will be reapplied to discover new information or a new problem.
- The infrastructure and architecture should be designed in such a way that future expansion needs, in terms of processing power and capacity, can be addressed.

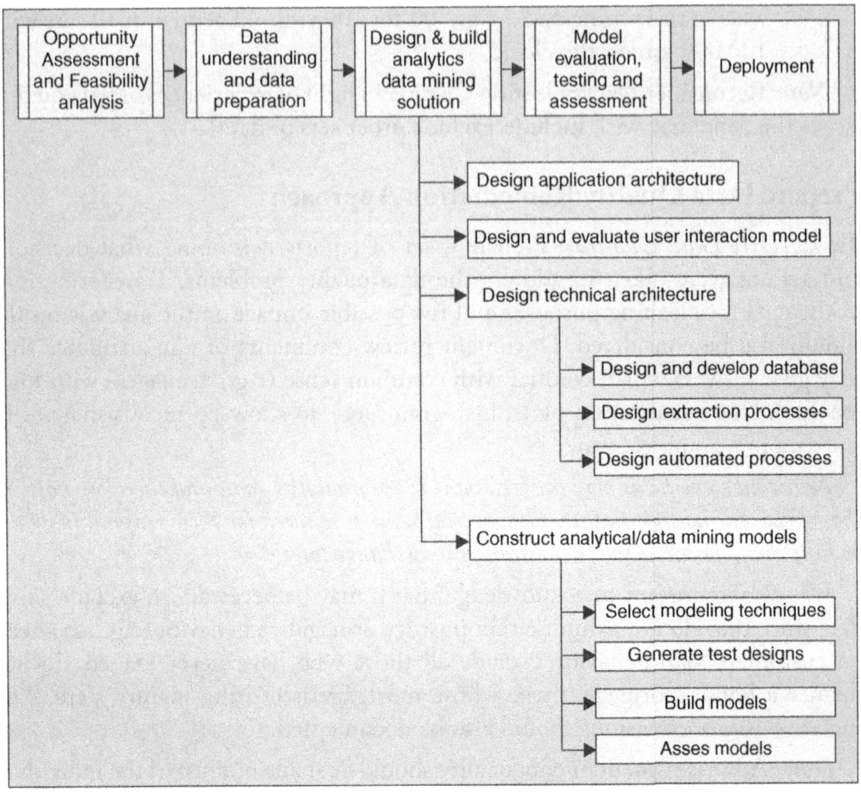

Figure 6.4 Design and build analytics solution phase.

➤ The needs of the current technical environment and applications which will interact with the architecture should be supported.

Duration of this phase may vary greatly in length but, in general, the data extraction, preprocessing, and analysis tasks are typically 70%–80% of the overall data analysis effort.

DESIGN APPLICATION ARCHITECTURE

The design application architecture task is performed to identify and resolve overall design issues and to document the overall application structure.

One of the more important decisions to be made when delivering an analytics solution is the choice of analytic technique(s) to be used. The chosen technique must fit the business context and the available data. In addition, it must provide the desired level of model explanation. It is imperative that the analytic technique(s) be chosen during this task package as it will influence the selection of a model construction tool.

To aid in the selection of an analytical technique, it is often necessary to extract and analyze a subset of the data to determine if it is appropriate for the desired technique. Based on a general sample of historical and/or external data, one should inventory the available entities and determine their data structure. Then, identify the independent variables and determine if a representative sample can be constructed for the mining algorithm to be used. In most cases, one technique will fit the data better than other techniques.

Task: *Design Application Architecture*—Contains tasks which determine how the application will be architected (inclusive of models), tested and rolled-out. Following are few key questions that must be addressed:

- Should a pilot application be released first?—One way of reducing risk to the overall project outcome is to release a pilot solution. A pilot solution focuses on a very narrow business problem. Upon completion, the pilot solution should provide a framework for developing a more robust solution that addresses the remaining business problems. This approach is frequently used when building client/server systems. For example, a pilot application is built to underwrite insurance policy renewals. After the renewal pilot is proven successful, the remaining business problems are addressed, say new business applications and policy endorsements. A similar approach could be adopted when delivering the data mining solution.
- How often the models should be generated and released?—An analytic implementation may differ dramatically from a traditional implementation because analytic models are often extremely sensitive to subtle changes in the input data. As the business conditions and data change, so must the model. If the model is not sensitive to these changes, its validity may be reduced or negated. For this reason, controls must be designed to determine when new models should be generated and released to reflect the current business conditions.
- What is the expected time frame for generating a new model?—Some problems will dictate that a model must be constructed or regenerated within a certain time frame. Therefore, the expected cycle time for generating a model should be expressly stated. This will be influenced by the frequency of business changes, the data volume, the number of variables and the analytical technique chosen. The expected cycle time should then be used as a requirement for the technical architecture as it will influence the choice of hardware and software components.

The following steps considerations are usually required during the application design phase. The decisions made for each of these, can have a direct impact on how the other steps of the methodology are implemented. Below we provide a short description of the above steps and some of the issues that need to be addressed.

Computation of statistics—This step gathers information about the number of attributes, number of records, and detailed information at the attribute level, such as: number of distinct values and range of values. This information is used to make decisions on the data types of the target and the other attributes, as well as to guide the required data transformations.

Sampling—Sampling can be used to improve model build time when dealing with large data sets. Short run time for completing the whole methodology is as important as ease of use. When sampling for a task that has a categorical target column it is necessary to ensure that all the target values are represented in the sample. This can be accomplished with stratified sampling. If the algorithm used in the methodology relies on prior probabilities (e.g., Naïve Bayes) the information about the original target distribution needs to be incorporated in the model.

Attribute data type identification—The identification of an attribute's data type (e.g., categorical vs. numeric) is an important and challenging step. Some algorithms (e.g., Support Vector Machines) cannot work with categorical data. Other algorithms (e.g., Association Rules) treat all attributes as categorical. Finally, some algorithms (e.g., CART) process numeric and categorical attributes differently. Incorrect identification of data type may lead to poor performance and incorrect data preparation. An example of simple heuristic is to consider columns containing floating-point data as numeric.

Attribute selection—The elimination of irrelevant attributes can help improve performance and, for methodologies that return explanations, improve explanatory power. Methods are usually divided into filter and wrapper methods. Filter methods remove attributes before a model is built and involves a single model build. Wrapper methods build multiple models each with a different combination of attributes. The model/attribute set with best performance is then selected. Given the design goals outlined above (reasonable accuracy within acceptable execution time) a filter method is the preferable approach for the type of process automation proposed here.

Algorithm selection—Many times the same high-level concept, depending on the characteristics of the data, requires the use of different techniques for best results. For example, predicting an unknown value requires either a classification or a regression algorithm depending on the target data type (categorical or numeric). An automated approach should be able to switch algorithms according to the nature of the data.

Data transformation—Most algorithms require the data to be suitably transformed in order to produce good results. Some common data transformations are: binning, normalization, missing value imputation, and outlier removal. The techniques used for transforming the data are selected based on attribute data type, attribute value range, attribute cardinality, and percentage of missing values for an attribute or a record.

Since data transformation steps can interact, it is necessary to carefully plan the sequence and the types of transformations that are followed in methodology. For example, outlier removal can be accomplished by transforming the data and missing value replacement can be done after outlier removal in order to eliminate the impact of outliers on the replacement values. Binning (e.g., quantile binning) may also be used to minimize the impact of outliers.

Model selection and quality assessment—Model selection involves evaluating a set of models using different techniques or using a single technique and different parameter values. Evaluation requires either splitting the data in two (training and evaluation data sets) or using cross-validation. The model with the best figure of merit in the evaluation data set is used to generate the final results. The data mining process needs to implement model selection in order to tune algorithm settings and ensure reasonable performance. It is also desirable to return a figure of merit that indicates the reliability of the results.

Output generation—Many of the goal-oriented tasks defined in the previous section require output explanations or descriptive information. For example, GROUP should return some description of the groups alongside the assignment of records to groups. It is important to take into account the effect of the transformation used in the data preparation steps in order to reverse those transformations before returning details. Descriptive information should be provided on the same scale and within the ranges of the original data.

Task: *Design and Evaluate User Interaction Model*—This is performed to design how users will interact with the solution and how it will be integrated into their work. The primary task is to determine the user metaphor for interacting with data, model and results. When designing an analytics solution, one must determine how a user will interact with the data, the analytics model and the modeling results. The design must be appropriate to the classes of users and meet the overall business needs. Most, but not all, model construction tools will provide an interface for interacting with the model. This will generally satisfy the needs of the model constructor but may not satisfy the needs of all users.

In the next few paragraphs, the common steps used in data preparation process are outlined.

The analyst needs to identify a table in the database and a column of interest (to be analyzed). The rest of the process as explained in the diagram below, performs the necessary data preparation activities to the provide data for model building and generating results. For example:

- Attributes of date data type are further categorized into day of the week, hour of the day, etc by extracting specific pieces of information from the original date attribute.
- Numeric attributes may be discretized depending on statistics of the input data set. Quantile binning is widely used for such purpose, which has the added functionality of handling outliers.

The resulting output contains one row for each of the independent attributes. For each attribute, the results also provide a measure of value indicating how useful the column is for determining the value of the analyzed column. Higher values indicate greater potential. Values range from 0 to 1. In addition the results should also provide a rank indicating the attribute's importance relative to the other attributes.

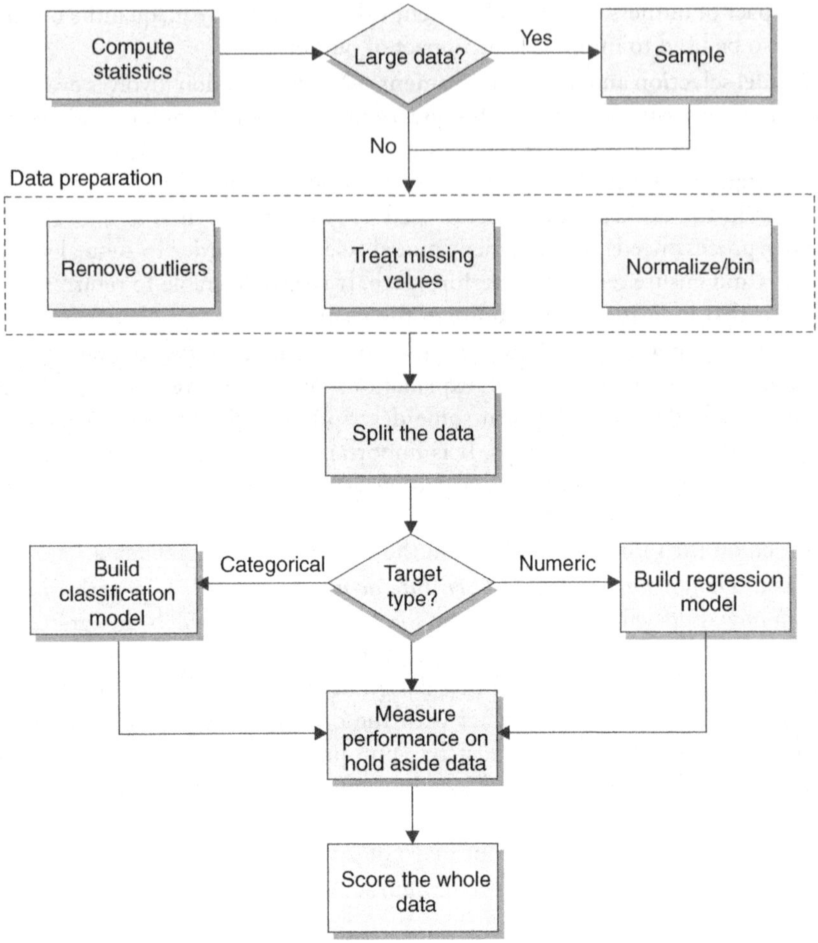

Figure 6.5 Data preparation process flow.

If the target attribute is identified as categorical, a classification model is built otherwise a regression model is built instead. The model-building step includes algorithm selection and model selection (parameter tuning). For classification models, it is necessary to adjust the parameters to avoid returning trivial results for heavily skewed target distributions. For example, this can be achieved by using a cost matrix or using a decision probability threshold other than 0.5 in the case of binary target values. Once a model is built it is necessary to measure its generalization performance on the test data set. The performance measure used is calculated based on the model's performance improvement over a "naive" baseline model. The value is returned using the accuracy percentages. Finally, the model is applied to the complete input data set in order to provide predictions for all the records in the input data.

Design Technical Architecture

Task: *Design Technical Architecture*—The Design Technical Architecture task is performed to design a technically feasible, affordable architecture that satisfies the solution's requirements. This task should address the following issues:

- Determine if data warehousing components can be leveraged or reused—When designing the technical architecture, seek opportunities to leverage or reuse components of a data warehouse. Commonly, the components of a data warehouse will perform functions similar to the components described in the data preprocessing services. Other opportunities may be present as well.
- Is parallelism a requirement?—When designing the components of the technical architecture, one should consider the needs for parallel processing. A few of the robust model construction tools have parallelized their algorithms and preprocessing functions. A parallel environment will greatly reduce the time to construct models when working with large data sets. Similarly, one should consider the scalability of the model construction tool. If a tool is scaleable, an increase in the size of the data set will result in a linear increase in the time required to construct the model.

Note: The requirements for parallelism and scalability will vary depending on the frequency of model construction. If the organization will be building multiple models on a frequent basis, the time savings in model construction may clearly justify the additional expense of purchasing a parallel environment. However, if the organization performs "one-time" studies on an infrequent basis, the length of time needed to create the model may not matter and therefore not justify the need for a parallel environment. Either way, the organization should consider its current and future needs when determining this requirement.

- Determine gaps in architecture (if any)—A gap analysis is required to identify where additional architecture design will be necessary. The gap analysis should compare what services are provided by the designed architecture to the user requirements and usability requirements discussed earlier. The gap analysis will identify areas where the packages chosen, such as the model construction tool, do not meet all of the needs as stated in the requirements. If this gap must be overcome, then additional design considerations will be necessary to provide interfaces or integrate additional functionality into the architecture.
- When planning the construction of the technical architecture, one should consider the interdependencies of the services and schedule them accordingly. Often, the project requirements will dictate when each service components must be built and tested. In the absence of stringent requirements, the following order of precedence is suggested:
    - Model Construction Services
    - Data Exploration Services

- Data Extraction Services
- Data Preprocessing Services
- Model Management Services

Since the model construction tool is often the centerpiece of the analytics architecture, it is recommended that it be installed and tested before proceeding with the build/install of other components. In addition, the model construction tool will often have functionality which satisfies the needs of other services. For example, the model construction tool may have data preprocessing functions or rudimentary data exploration functions. This will be particularly true of the high-end tools.

The collection of tools used for data exploration services should be installed next. These tools will be used to explore the source data, data extracted by the extraction services and the data in the data repository.

The Data Extraction Services should be built/installed next because they are a prerequisite to the data preprocessing services. However, there may be opportunities to build the two in parallel. The data extraction services contain components which are necessary to extract and transfer data from its source to the data repository.

The data preprocessing components are required to make source data mineable. The preprocessing components may be tightly coupled to the RDBMS which supports the data repository and the model construction tool.

Finally, the remaining components of the Model Management Services should be built before model construction can begin. This includes construction of the Model Repository.

Task: *Design and Develop Database*—The activity contains tasks to design the logical and physical database and its conversion processes. In many mining environments, the data repository will be a relational database. However, in some cases the mining environment may work with flat files. If so, one sacrifices the management services provided by the RDBMS engine. The following tasks are performed during this task package:

- Design data repository—The database in the data mining architecture is referred to as the data repository. The logical and physical database design should be performed with attention to management of data from multiple data sources. In addition, one should consider how model construction data sets will be stored in the database.
- Build the logical data model of the data repository—The data repository is where mining data will be stored.
- Build Data Repository—After the logical and physical design of the data repository has been completed, the data repository should be built.

Task: *Design extraction processes*—Prior to populating the repository, the Data Extraction services must be designed. The data extraction services are responsible for extracting data from the disparate data sources and transferring them to the mining environment where they can be loaded into the Data Repository. These services may be provided by purchased components, leveraged from data warehousing components or custom built.

Task: *Design Model Repository*—Careful consideration should be given to how models will be stored in the mining environment. A Model Repository should be designed for this purpose.

Task: *Design Analytical and Data Mining Models*—This task is performed to design the architecture components required to begin system implementation.

Task: *Design Automated Processes*—The Design Automated Processes task is all about designing the automated components of the solution and the development of an approach for performing the component test. The following tasks are performed during this task package:

Task: *Select processes to be automated*—When designing the automated processes of a data mining solution, one should focus on the data extraction and data preprocessing services. Although they are not required to be automated, they are utilized frequently and ideally should require little manual intervention. In many cases, they will be built with a batch architecture for execution during non-peak hours. Therefore, these services should be designed for reuse and automation.

Another area to consider for automation is the process of deploying models. Although this is dependent on the specific solution, it is possible that a model might be constructed and automatically nested within another system. For example, a model is constructed to assist call center representatives in cross-selling products.

Task: *Extract data and load the Data Repository*—Once the data repository has been designed and constructed, the data should be extracted and loaded. It is imperative that the data repository is populated before model construction begins. This differs from traditional development of custom systems which require that only common test data be loaded into the database. For model construction, all of the mining data must be present.

Task: *Perform data preprocessing*—Once the data preprocessing components have been designed, the data loaded in the data repository should be processed prior to beginning the construction of the models. All the preprocessing should be performed to ensure that the data is suitable for mining. This includes sampling the data and dividing it into model construction data sets. The analytical technique chosen and the component testing approach will influence how data is sampled and the requirements of construction data sets.

Task: *Determine approach for evaluating ("component testing") models*—When developing the component testing approach, particular attention must be given to the approach for evaluating models. The approach should include validating the models accuracy/precision and verifying its results against explicit business knowledge.

Construct Analytical and Data Mining Models

There are three key activities to be completed during this task:

- *Perform data analysis* - Prior to constructing a data mining module, detailed data analysis should be performed on the mining data. This analysis includes insuring that the data preprocessing has been executed properly, collecting fundamental statistics on the data, viewing data distributions, etc.
- *Model validation* - Once a model has been built, validated and verified to meet the business objectives, it must be transformed into a deployable format. Common formats include reports, procedural code, graphical representations, data manipulation language and natural language text.
- *Training task packages* - It is particularly important to create meaningful and complete training procedures and materials during a data mining project given the complex nature of the analytical techniques used. Special attention should be given to users who have not previously had experience with advanced decision-making systems. In addition, the training information should address ongoing maintenance of both the data mining system and models.

Select Modeling Techniques

Task: *Select Modeling Technique*—As the first step in modeling, select the actual modeling technique that is to be used initially. If multiple techniques are applied, perform this task for each technique separately. It should not be forgotten that not all tools and techniques are available for each and every task. From amongst these tools and techniques, there could be other constraints which further limit the choice available to the analyst. It may be that only one tool or technique is available to solve the problem in hand—and even then the tool may not be the absolutely technical best for the problem in hand.

Select model construction tool(s)—Once the requirements have been collected and the analytical technique chosen, a model construction tool(s) must be selected.

Activities:

- Decide on appropriate technique for exercise bearing in mind the tool selected.
- Define any built-in assumptions made by the technique about the data (e.g., quality, format, distribution).
- Make sure that these assumptions hold and step back to Data Preparation Phase if necessary.

Generate Test Designs

Task: *Generate Test Design*—Before we actually build a model, we need to generate a procedure or mechanism how to test the model's quality and validity.

For example, in supervised data mining tasks such as classification, it is common to use error rates as quality measures for data mining models. Therefore, we typically separate the data set into train and test set, build the model on the train set, and estimate its quality on the separate test set.

A primary component of the plan is to decide how to divide the available data set into training data, test data, and validation data sets.

Activities:

- Check existing test designs for each analytic goal separately.
- Decide on necessary steps (number of iterations, number of folds etc.).
- Prepare data required for test.

Build Model

Task: *Build Model*—Run the modeling tool on the prepared data set to create one or more models. With any modeling tool, there are often a large number of parameters that can be adjusted. These parameters and their chosen value, along with rationale for the choice of parameter settings should be documented and version managed.

Activities:

- Set initial parameters.
- Document reasons for choosing those values.
- Run the selected technique on the input data set to produce the model
- Post-process data mining results (e.g., Editing rules, Display trees).
- Describe any characteristics of the current model that may be useful for the future.

Assess Model

Task: *Assess Model*—The data mining analyst interprets the models according to his/her domain knowledge, success criteria, and the desired test design. This task interferes with the subsequent evaluation phase. Whereas the analyst judges the success of the application of modeling and discovery techniques more technically, he/she validates the results with business analysts and domain experts. Moreover, this task only considers models whereas the evaluation phase also takes into account all other results which were produced in the course of the project.

The analyst also tries to rank the results. He/she assesses the models according to the evaluation criteria. As far as possible he/she also takes into account business objectives and business success criteria. In most analytics projects, the analyst applies a single technique more than once or generates results with different alternative techniques. In this task, he also compares all results according to the evaluation criteria.

Summarized results of this task including qualities of generated models (e.g., in terms of accuracy), and ranks etc are documented for review purpose.

Activities:

Evaluate result with respect to evaluation criteria—"Lift Tables" and "Gain Tables" can be constructed to determine how well the model is predicting.

- Test result according to a test strategy (e.g.: Train and Test, Cross validation, bootstrapping etc.).
- Compare evaluation results and interpretation.
- Create ranking of results with respect to success and evaluation criteria
- Select best models.
- Interpret results in business terms (as far as possible at this stage).
- Check plausibility of model.
- Check impacts for analytics goal.
- Check model against given knowledge base to see if the discovered information is novel and useful.
- Check reliability of result.
- Analyze potentials for deployment of each result.
- If there is a verbal description of the generated model (e.g., via rules), assess the rules; are they logical, are they feasible, are there too many or too few, do they offend common sense?
- Assess results.

Note: According to the model assessment, revise parameter settings and tune them for the next run in task build model. Iterate model building and assessment until you strongly believe that you found the best model(s). Iterate model building and assessment until you find the best model.

Evaluation

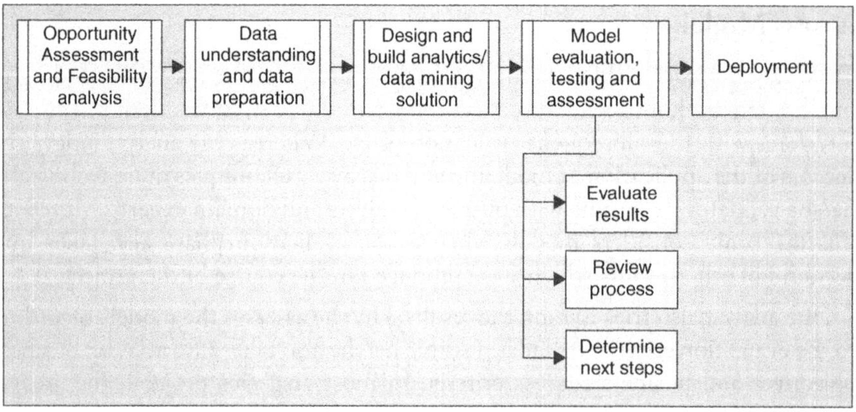

Figure 6.6 Evaluation phase.

In the previous phases the model assessment and evaluation activities were primarily focused on factors such as the accuracy and generality of the model. In this phase the focus is primarily on assessing the degree to which the model meets the business objectives and seeks to determine if there is some business reason why this model is deficient. The results need to be compared with the evaluation criteria defined at the start of the project.

A good way of defining the total outputs of the model is to use the equation:

RESULTS = MODELS + FINDINGS

In this equation we are defining that the total output of the data mining project is not just the models (although they are, of course, important) but also findings which we define as anything (apart from the model) that is important in meeting objectives of the business (or important in leading to new questions, line of approach or side effects (e.g., data quality problems uncovered by the data mining exercise).

Note: that although the model is directly connected to the business questions, but the findings need not be related to any questions or objective, only that they are important to the initiator of the project.

Moreover, evaluation also assesses other results generated. Analytics results cover models which are necessarily related to the original business objectives, and all other findings which are not necessarily related to the original business objectives but might also unveil additional challenges, information, or hints for future directions.

Activities:

- Understand the analytics result.
- Interpret the results in terms of the application.
- Check impacts for analytics goal.
- Check the result against the given knowledge base to see if the discovered information is novel and useful.
- Evaluate and assess result with respect to business success criteria.
- Compare evaluation results and interpretation.
- Create ranking of results with respect to business success criteria.
- Check impacts of result for initial application goal.

Review Process

Task: *Review Process*—At this point the resultant model hopefully appears to be satisfactory and to satisfy business needs. It is now appropriate to do a more thorough review of the analytics models in order to determine if there is any important factor or task that has somehow been overlooked. This review also covers quality assurance issues, e.g., did we correctly build the model? Did we only use attributes that we are allowed to use and that are available for future analyses?

Activities:

- Analyze the analytics processes.
- Identify failures.
- Identify misleading steps.
- Identify possible alternative actions, unexpected paths in the process.

According to the assessment results and the process review, the project decides how to proceed at this stage. The project needs to decide whether to finish this project and move on to deployment if appropriate, or whether to initiate further iterations or set up new data mining projects.

- Analyze potential for deployment of each result.
- Estimate potential for improvement of current process.
- Check remaining resources to determine if they allow additional process iterations (or whether additional resources can be made available).
- Recommend alternative continuations.
- Refine process plan.
- Rank the possible actions.
- Select one of the possible actions.
- Document reasons for the choice.

Deployment

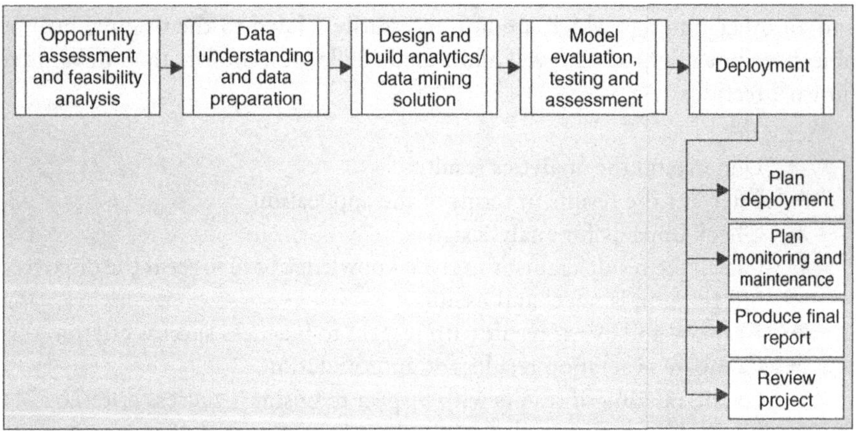

Figure 6.7 Deployment phase.

Plan Deployment

Task: *Plan Deployment*—In order to deploy the analytics result(s) into the business, this task takes the evaluation results and concludes a strategy for deployment. If there has been identified a general procedure to create the relevant model(s), this procedure is documented here for deployment later.

Activities:

- Develop and evaluate alternative plans for deployment.
- Identify possible problems when deploying the data mining results (pitfalls of the deployment).

Plan Monitoring and Maintenance

Task: *Plan Monitoring and Maintenance*—Monitoring and maintenance are important issues if the analytics result becomes part of the day-to-day business and its environment. A careful preparation of a maintenance strategy helps to avoid unnecessarily long periods of incorrect usage of analytics models. In order to monitor the deployment of the result(s), the project needs a detailed plan on the monitoring process. This plan takes into account the specific type of deployment.

Activities:

- Check for dynamic aspects (i.e., what things could change in the environment?)
- When should the result or model not be used any more? Identify criteria (validity, threshold of accuracy, new data, change in the application domain, etc.)? What should happen if the model or result can no longer be used? (Update model, set up new data mining project, etc.)
- Will the business objectives of the use of the model change over time? – fully document the initial problem the model was attempting to solve
- Develop Monitoring and Maintenance Plan.

Produce Final Report

Task: *Produce Final Report*—At the end of the project, the project leader and his team write up a final report. It depends on the deployment plan, if this report is only a summary of the project and its experiences (if they have not already been documented as an ongoing activity), or if this report is a final presentation of the analytics result(s).

Identifying the results obtained, the report should also describe the process, showing costs incurred, define any deviations from the original plan, describe implementation plans and make any recommendations for future work.

Activities:

- Identify what reports are needed (slide presentation, management summary, detailed findings, explanation of models ....).
- Analyze how well initial analytics goals have been met.
- Identify target groups for report.
- Outline structure and contents of report(s).
- Select findings to be included in the reports.
- Write a report.
- Decide on target group for final presentation (will they already have received final report?).
- Select which items from final report should be included in final presentation.

Review Project

Task: *Review Project*—Assess what went right and what went wrong, what was done well and what needs to be improved.

This phase summarizes important experiences made during the project. For example, pitfalls, misleading approaches or hints for selecting the best suited analytics techniques in similar situations could be part of this documentation. In ideal projects, experience documentation covers also any reports that have been written by individual project members during the project phases and their tasks.

Activities:

- Interview all significant people involved in the project and ask them about their experiences during the project.
- If end users in the business work with the analytics result(s), interview them—are they satisfied? What could have been done better? Do they need additional support?
- Summarize feedback and write the experience documentation.
- Analyze the process (things that worked well, mistakes made, lessons learned, etc.).
- Document the specific analytics processes (How can the results and the experience of applying the model be fed back into the process?)
- Abstract from details to make the experience useful for future projects.

END POINTS

Why such an elaborate implementation guideline? More often we rush into developing an analytic solution and do not realize the implications of such an ad-hoc approach. As we discussed throughout this chapter, the actual development of analytic solution is probably a smaller part of the larger effort. Key considerations such as, do we really understand what the business wants to achieve, do we have the right data, is the data quality good enough for our analytics purpose, how do we validate the results, how do we deploy the solution, etc, are extremely important to deliver a meaningful and sustainable analytics solution.

REFERENCES

Tan, Pang-Ning, Steinbach, Michael, and Kumar, Vipin, "Introduction to Data Mining", May 2005.

Bramer, M.A., "Principles of Data Mining" (Undergraduate Topics in Computer Science), Aug 2001.

CHAPTER 7

BUSINESS ANALYTICS AND APPLICATIONS

Actionable insights, if not applied to solve real-world business problems, are, of no use. Analytics is not a novelty anymore; it is an important asset and a differentiator to compete in a globalized economy.

Analytics comprises a great many techniques that deal with statistics, most of which we have already discussed in the earlier chapters of this book. So, why are we devoting a whole chapter on business analytics? The answer lies in industry vertical alignment of analytics as a solution to optimize and augment their business model. A few such possibilities are explored below:

Critical product analysis—Data retrieved from various markets can indicate how well a product is received by the target audience, and also what crucial changes must be made to it to maximize revenue. Furthermore, the organization can gain insight as to how a particular territory or market reacts to certain features of the product. This not only makes it possible to make minor alterations to the item for specific locations but also helps in studying trends associated with those regions.

Improved customer service—Organizations have learned through experience to keep track of their recurring customer queries and support issues. This tremendously helps them in enhancing performance by not repeating past mistakes while enabling them to provide faster customer service and satisfaction.

Up-selling opportunities—Tracking trends in customer behavior can be very helpful in identifying the most prominent needs of a company's customer base, hence allowing it to up-sell or cross-promote products that cater best to customers' needs.

Simplified inventory management—This is an often ignored yet very efficient application of business analytics. With the help of trend-tracking, business managers can minimize write-offs to a great extent, in turn, minimizing losses due to outdated inventory items. For example, analytic data gathered beforehand can help predict which products are on the verge of going obsolete in the near future. With this information, those specific products can be gotten rid of before they end up as write-offs.

Competitive pricing insights—This is yet another important highlight of business analytics that is, ironically, used by very few companies. Companies are known tracking trends in purchasing behavior among customers to figure out price ranges that the target market is most comfortable in. Thus, businesses can effectively make their prices competitive without having to cut down too much on profits.

In the sections below, we will discuss business analytics as applied to various industry verticals ranging from Smart Metering to Stock Market to Travel and Tourism.

GETTING SMART—METER DATA MANAGEMENT AND ANALYTICS

There is an unprecedented focus on how to better manage the natural resources and how to smartly manage the limited energy resources we have on our hand. As a utility company, if you distribute multiple products—electricity, water, natural gas, etc. or serve a diverse service area, you may have installed multiple types of meter reading solutions. Today your utility may have tens or even hundreds of thousands or millions of meters from multiple manufacturers generating data that are gathered in multiple ways. Your large investment in gathering meter data has helped your billing department keep pace with change and growth, but now other groups within your utility are asking for more data. Or, perhaps you are looking for ways to share the operational costs of deploying Automated Meter Reading (AMR) solutions across the multiple groups that can all gain some advantage with these data. Ideally, you need one simple way to collate and analyze all your meter data for forecasting, planning, energy delivery, maintenance, and more, to help keep your system reliable, profitable, and competitive.

Smart Metering may also include:

- At the customer site, an easy to read display helping customers check for leaks, reduce consumption, and monitor compliance with local restrictions. Interval meters on customer premises that measure consumption during specific time periods and communicate it to the utility, often on a daily basis. While in the electric industry, measurement intervals can be as short as every 10 or 15 minutes, water intervals of 30 to 60 minutes, or longer, generally provide adequate information.
- At the utility company, additional data collection and processing software, such as a meter data management application. This isolates the existing billing system from the increasing meter data volumes that smart metering introduces.

Properly managed meter data enable utilities to predict system load and usage to avoid imbalances and reduce off-network purchases. Data analysis can help pinpoint over- or under-utilized infrastructure, improve system throughput, speed service restoration after outages, and more. Properly managed data mean your utility can deliver more value to customers and shareholders for less overall cost. Data themselves becomes an asset. Meter data analytics can improve operational efficiency, cost reduction, and meeting current and future goals with fewer resources.

In this section we will discuss various challenges of implementing a robust meter data management strategy and how analytics can unlock the hidden potential. While each case will be slightly different, because each organization's collection of disparate meters, meter reading, and data processing systems is different, implementation of meter data management solutions usually includes these steps:

- Establish an enterprise meter data management strategy. Implementing a new system will have enterprise-wide ramifications, so the entire enterprise needs to support the implementation. For nearly every department in the utility, a business case should be made that accessible, accurate meter data can improve operations, reduce costs, and create new services.
- Identify all sources, destinations and formats for meter data. Conduct an enterprise-wide assessment of data needs. Understand the data complexity, quality of data, and define data ownership for source systems.
- Define a target centralized data model that would collate all these disparate data coming from various source systems. Careful considerations should be taken while designing the data model in conjunction with business so that the model remains scalable and also meets the data needs of the business users.
- Architect and design the data integration processes for population of the centralized data repository.
- In a phased manner start servicing various consumers of this centralized data like billing, forecasting, outage management, distribution planning, and revenue assurance.
- Develop analytic applications to provide predictive modeling around outages, revenue leakages, optimal distributions and customer relationship management.

A few illustrations of how an efficient meter data management would enable a whole host of other services that are beneficial to energy providers and their customers have been discussed below.

Outage Management

A single repository of meter data greatly eases the management of power outage data. With AMR systems that provide outage or restore information, a meter data management system can record outage start and restore times; organize events by meter, customer, fixed network collector, and transformer; push alerts to external outage management systems; and filter and present meter events to identify problem areas Having a central system provides standard interfaces to receive events from AMR systems and standard events codes, regardless of meter or collection system type. It insulates outage management systems from having to understand the details of how meter reading systems report events.

All of these abilities benefit both the energy provider and its customers by verifying power outages before sending field personnel to investigate (potentially saving money), diminishing revenue loss with early warning of problems from meters, and accurately counting outage durations for important public service scores.

Distribution Planning and Reliability

By combining historical customer data from the centralized repository with historical weather data and transformer capacity ratings, electricity providers can start to predict how transformers might perform under extreme weather conditions. Pinpointing a potentially overloaded transformer before it fails has several benefits. Crews can fix problems during scheduled work hours, saving the utility overtime. Utilities do not lose revenue because of a disruption to service. Customers enjoy continuous service; for the sick and the elderly, this can be critical during extreme weather conditions. Likewise, pinpointing potentially underutilized transformers means that utilities have the opportunity to right-size their equipment in an orderly fashion. This saves on labor and equipment costs, while possibly expanding the capacity of the distribution system.

Revenue Assurance

By relying on a central repository of historic meter data, analytics can pinpoint usage patterns that might indicate meter defect, meter tampering, or theft of service. If a customer's energy usage remains abnormally low during heat waves, cold snaps, or before and after outages, then the meter might be malfunctioning. If more energy is flowing past distribution points than is being billed for, then it's possible that someone is stealing service. Without meter data management, this type of revenue-assuring analysis is nearly impossible.

This not only generates more revenue to the utility, but also means better service and better costs to the customers. Utilities recapturing revenue from those people stealing services don't need to raise their rates to cover stolen services. In some parts of the world, theft of service accounts for 20% or more of power consumption. Tamper detection can make a huge difference to energy providers and to the vast majority of honest, paying customers.

Forecasting and Curtailment

By applying advanced statistical modeling to the historic data stored in meter data management repositories, utilities can generate highly accurate forecasts of future energy demand. Balancing supply and demand is the heart of a reliable and stable energy delivery system. Solid, accurate forecasts remove the guesswork from daily operations and long-term planning, lowering both risk and cost. Purchasing last-minute power on the spot market can be very expensive. Accurate and timely forecasts also provide energy intelligence that is directly applicable to infrastructure construction and maintenance, pricing contracts, supply schedules, load profiles, rate design, and energy efficiency.

With the ability to predict times of peak demand, utilities and their customers can form partnerships to reduce extreme loads, thus maintaining a reliable and affordable supply of power. Power-intensive C&I customers can voluntarily reduce their consumption during peak times in exchange for payments or credit from the utility. On the residential side, utilities that have addressable thermostats installed in homes can change heating or cooling thresholds by a degree or two over a large number of homes, thereby lowering the system stress while continuing service.

Smart metering is a term that has taken on a range of meanings in different contexts, from the interval metering of electricity, to the Automated Meter Reading technology used collect usage data, to real time monitoring of resources usage. This rapidly developing concept offers an ability to more frequently monitor residential and non-residential demand patterns for resources (water, energy, electricity, etc).

Taking water usage as an example, let us illustrate what are the challenges and how analytics can help in understanding the usage patterns so that companies and governments can proactively make informed decisions. In case of water usage, there remain several important parameters in end-use modeling that are difficult to determine or for which increased accuracy of measurement would be beneficial. For example:

- Indoor/outdoor split of water use
- Breakdown of outdoor end-uses
- End-uses in multi-residential dwellings
- Evaporative air conditioner usage
- Leak sources

Event recognition approaches require significant time by the analyst to manually identify events such as showers, toilets, washing machines and irrigation, which increases costs for processing several weeks of data in a home. It is also difficult to distinguish some overlapping events in this environment. The alternative to a single meter on the mains supply is to put individual meters on each appliances. However, this is costly and cumbersome at a large scale.

Consequently, in considering how the next generation of smart meters could be developed to best provide valuable information for usage measurement, the following elements are important:

- An ability to accurately identify indoor and outdoor end-use events
- Capacity to distinguish simultaneous (overlapping) events with reasonable accuracy
- An ability to automate capture and processing of end-use data

Technology components for end-use measurement can be broadly grouped by their functionality into:

- ➤ Data capture technologies
- ➤ Data transfer equipment
- ➤ Tools for data analysis

Data capture technologies enable collection of raw data from a household. They include water meters and data loggers. Technologies for data transfer facilitate the collection and delivery of data from the meter/logger to a site where processing and analysis can occur. Data transfer can be manual (e.g., a person physically visits house to read meter or download data) or automated. Data analysis technologies assist in the processing and interpretation of raw data into meaningful information about end-uses.

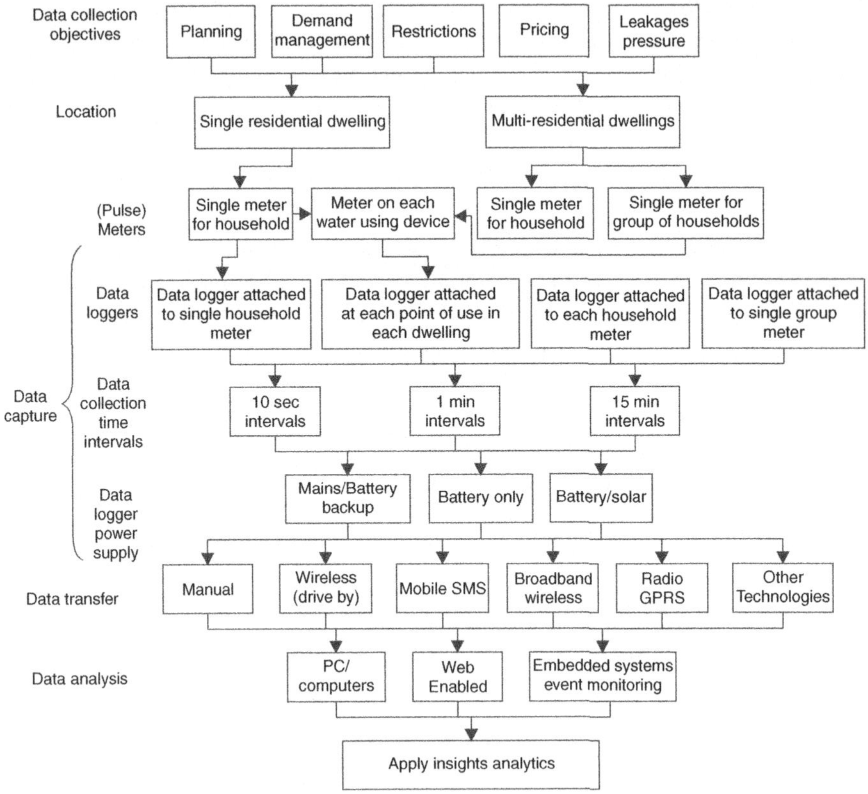

Figure 7.1 Data collection and analysis in utility industry.

The above diagram depicts smart metering topology linked to data collection and analysis activities. Various data collection objectives suggest different technological requirements for obtaining necessary data for analysis.

Location represents two options: end-use measurements on single residential dwellings (stand alone houses having one main meter per household); or end-use measurements covering multi-residential dwellings such as a block of units where there may be a single common meter for several households or a meter per household.

Data capture equipment includes water meters measuring flow rates, data loggers that can record and time stamp pulses from water meters and other sensors and recorders such as electricity meters that can provide relevant information. Meters could be installed to record total usage for the whole household at a single point or individual usage of defined appliances.

Data collection time intervals and power supply requirements need to be defined in an end-use study. Data on electricity consumption could be simultaneously collected to identify typical end-uses by matching a pattern of electricity usage with appliance usage.

In summary, a variety of devices and methods can be used to collect, transfer and analyze end-use data. At one end of the spectrum are methods that rely on manual measurement and reporting including house inspections, log books and questionnaires. At the more sophisticated end, automated data collection and real time data analysis elements helps companies optimize how they manage their resources and services. Once collected, data must be transferred to a central location for analysis. This transfer can be manual or automated using one-way or two way communication between the data collector, logger and the final data storage point.

Let us look at several examples of how it would help:

To analyze leak detection or to understand water savings associated with pressure regulation, total usage monitoring would be sufficient (measured at regular intervals). Total use monitoring is a common basis for long-term planning. Frequent information available through smart metering would add to the understanding of seasonal variability at the household level.

The ability to discern end uses enables more detailed end-use based planning to be undertaken. Differentiation between indoor and outdoor uses, for example, would assist in the monitoring of compliance with water restrictions targeting outdoor uses. The future development in this area could be real time differential pricing for indoor and outdoor uses or time-of-use pricing.

Let us look at few innovative usages of analytics in meter data management below.

In-Home Displays and Real-Time Analytics

Display devices that show water use in real time help customers detect leaks. While diligent customers may, a few times a year, turn off all water and check an outside meter to ensure there is no flow, most meters are deliberately located in out-of-the-way areas that make it hard to detect new, small leaks. A conveniently located on-premises monitor can help a customer notice a leak because, for instance, the reading is higher in the morning than it was at night even though no water was used in the day.

Prominently located displays serve as a constant reminder about the need for water conservation. They also enable jurisdictions to win customer compliance with water-use advisories or restrictions, such as a weekly maximum use per occupant. Displays tailored to the specific needs of the user, such as those comparing current water uses with neighborhood averages or with consumption in previous months, may help consumers further focus on conservation.

Analytics and data management enablers:

- A meter data management and/or customer information system that can process data rapidly so as to provide timely data to customers.
- A customer information or portal system that can format data into charts and tables that customers can readily understand.

Information Delivery Channels and Computer Portals

Installing monitors at each customer site may come with a price tag that water utilities find difficult to afford. As a result, many elect less expensive ways to provide consumption details, such as computer websites with individualized portals or even printouts enclosed with bills. Surveys appear to indicate that customers prefer the on-site display, which provides rapid and easily accessible data. Web portals, however, have an added advantage: they readily link concerned customers to information on how to lower consumption and/or bills.

In addition utility companies can use time-of-use or interval data to:

Detect customer-premises leaks - Leak detection for households is relatively simple. Leaks or faulty plumbing are the most likely culprits if hourly usage never drops to zero. Utilities can use more sophisticated algorithms, generally available from software vendors, to identify possible leaks at commercial and industrial properties with round-the-clock water use.

Preliminary experience indicates that substantial numbers of customers will sign up for voluntary leak notification if utilities offer it and will provide telephone numbers or email addresses where utilities can send automatic alerts. In communities with serious or growing water issues, mandatory notification may become the norm. In many cases, it appears, customers may already know about, for instance, a dripping faucet, but notification from the utility pointing out the cost and long-term community implications can encourage repair.

Utility notifications are even more welcome and effective when customers are unaware of leaks in walls and foundations that, left un-repaired, have the potential to damage structures significantly. As water issues escalate, utility companies can consider fines or penalties for customers who fail to fix leaks. In regions with competitive or partially competitive utility markets, utilities can use this leak detection ability to offer leak insurance to property owners. Examples could be:

- *Detect small leaks in mains* - A utility that compares a day's consumption for a group of customers (such as residences on a block) with readings from a water main serving that block may be able to identify small leaks (or possibly theft) before they become too large to be overlooked.

- *Identify the location and extent of a water main break* - Smart meters can activate the communication link to the utility and send "last gasp" messages when they detect a significant drop in pressure.
- *Monitor compliance with local water restrictions* - Water utilities and sister municipal agencies in drought-plagued areas may be under heavy pressure to identify possible violations of local restrictions on, for instance, outdoor watering or non-essential water use during daylight hours. Analyses of smart metering data can help them fulfill such public mandates.

The utility's ability to detect leaks is, in some regions, becoming a major financial factor for utilities. Regulators concerned about reducing water waste may establish performance-based incentives for utilities to reduce water loss. The faster utilities can detect, size, and prioritize repairs for leaks, the greater their ability will be to earn these incentives.

Analytics and data management enablers

- Integration that links leak detection with a mobile workforce management system so as to automatically dispatch field crews to the sites of suspected major leaks.
- An analytics application that can compare current meter readings with past and anticipated readings so as to readily predict consumption patterns that may result from leaks.
- A customer information system that, once provided with local use regulations, can be programmed to detect and report likely violations.
- Automatic customer contact systems (email, SMS, telephone) that alert customers to problems.

We discussed at length how smart meter data management supported by analytics can help us better manage water, a precious resource for all of us. The same concept can be extended to electricity as well.

The patterns (or profiles) of energy usage contained within the energy usage data are great for discovering where a building is wasting energy. Energy profiles show how much energy is being used at particular times-of-the-day and days-of-the-week - and what equipment is using that energy, and why one needs to be using it at the times in question.

If the profiles show energy being used on times or days when you are not aware of a good reason for energy to be used, that is an indication that energy is possibly being wasted and is something for you to investigate.

To make sense of the energy profiles, you need to have good idea about what goes on in the building that relate to energy consumption.

Every building is different, but the following factors are commonly relevant:

- Occupancy - when do people come and go?
- What are the core occupancy hours (e.g., 9 to 5)? Are there multiple shifts (e.g., a day shift and a night shift)?

- Do people ever work on-site outside of the core occupancy hours? or Do certain staff stay on after the official closing time?
- Does anyone come in on weekends or holidays?

HVAC—**heating, ventilation, and air conditioning**

- What fuels are used for heating (e.g., gas, electricity)?
- Is there air conditioning? Is it used just for cooling in summer, or is it used all year round (e.g., to keep equipment cool)?
- How is the heating controlled? Is it on a timer? When is it set to switch on and off? Are there different timer settings for weekends and holidays?

It is important to be aware that most forms of gas heating also use electricity for fans, pumps, and controls. For example, for a heating system consisting of a gas boiler connected to radiators, 5% or more of the total energy used will typically be electricity. This is particularly significant in cost terms because electricity usually costs several times more per kWh than gas.

Heating systems that involve ducted air will typically use a considerable amount of electricity (40% or so is not uncommon). Air conditioning also usually consumes a lot of electricity.

The upshot of this is that HVAC energy wastage can usually be identified from patterns of electricity consumption alone. But if you do have interval metering on your gas supply it is well worth taking a closer look at your patterns of gas consumption too.

Lighting

- What controls when the lights come on and off? Are they automatically controlled (e.g., by a sensor that detects movement or light-levels), or are they turned on and off by staff?
- Do lights remain on when they are not needed (e.g., when staff have gone home, or when they're on lunch-break)?
- Are there enough light-switches? For example, if one person is working late in a large open office, will they have to light the entire office just to light their desk?

Note: Most buildings have different sets of lights for different purposes (e.g., a set of lights in the main office, a set of lights in the meeting rooms, a set of lights in the warehouse, a set of security lights outside). Your answers to the questions above may depend on which set of lights you're talking about.

Office equipment

- Do staff turn their computers off when they leave work?
- Is there office equipment such as photocopiers / printers? Is it turned off when not in use?

Other energy-consuming equipment/processes

This could include anything from a printing room, to a fork-lift-truck charger, to specialist production-line equipment.

- What processes or items of equipment exist that use energy?
- What sort of energy do they use (e.g., electricity, or gas, or both)?
- When do they use energy? When do the processes run? When is the equipment switched on and off?

It's important to note that industrial processes can often dwarf all other types of energy consumption in a building. If a building has processes or items of equipment that consume a lot of energy, even small changes to the way that they're operated can often make a big difference to the energy bill. Following is a representation of energy consumption during regular office hours 7 AM to 7 PM.

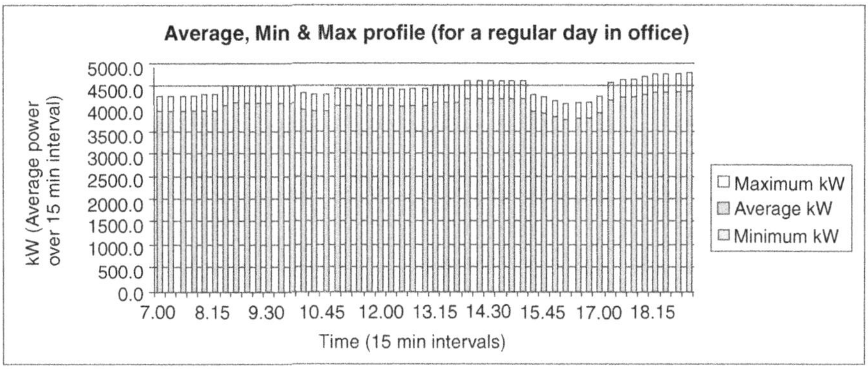

Figure 7.2 Time interval utility data and analysis.

High out-of-hours energy consumption

Energy wastage is very common during "out-of-hours" periods (e.g., at night and on weekends). In the out-of-hours periods (Saturday and Sunday), the building is using around 35% of the energy that it uses in peak consumption periods. It is often necessary for a certain amount of equipment to operate during out-of-hours periods (e.g., security lighting or a central computer room). However, it's rare for the out-of-hours consumption to need to be as high as is demonstrated by the above figure. Such patterns indicate that there is huge potential to save energy by reducing the out-of-hours energy consumption.

Poor automatic control (especially HVAC)

Energy uses such as HVAC (heating, ventilation and air conditioning) should usually be closely tied to the occupancy hours. Considerable energy is wasted if a building is heated or cooled when nobody is using it, or if an entire building is heated or cooled when only a couple of rooms are in use. A more severe example would be that of a building with a heating timer that only allows a single on-time and a single off-time (as opposed to allowing different times to be set on different days). It's not uncommon for buildings to have such a timer, even when they operate on Monday to Friday only - this results in considerable wastage as the heating comes on unnecessarily every Saturday and Sunday.

Analytics in Stock Exchange Market Manipulation Scenarios

Various frauds are committed in the transactions relating to shares and can be better explained by bifurcating them in relation to their relevance to the investigator.

Wikipedia defines Market manipulation as a deliberate attempt to interfere with the free and fair operation of the market and create artificial, false or misleading appearances with respect to the price of, or market for, a security, commodity or currency.

Market manipulation can occur in multiple ways:

- *Pools* - Agreements, often written, among a group of traders to delegate authority to a single trader in a specific stock for a specific period of time and then to share in the resulting profits or losses.
- *Churning* - When a trader places both buy and sell orders at about the same price. The increase in activity is intended to attract additional investors, and increase the price.
- *Runs* - When a group of traders create activity or rumors in order to drive the price of a security up.
- *Ramping (the market)* - Actions designed to artificially raise the market price of listed securities and to give the impression of voluminous trading, in order to make a quick profit.
- *Wash trade* - Selling and repurchasing the same or substantially the same security for the purpose of generating activity and increasing the price
- *Bear raid* - Attempting to push the price of a stock down by heavy selling or short selling.
- *Fainting the tape* - An illegal action by a group of market manipulators buying and/ or selling a security among themselves to create artificial trading activity, which, when reported on the ticker tape, lures in unsuspecting investors as they perceive an unusual volume.
- *Front running* - An illegal practice of a stock broker executing orders on a security for its own account while taking advantage of advance knowledge of pending orders from its customers. When orders previously submitted by its customers will predictably affect the price of the security, purchasing first for its own account gives the broker an unfair advantage, since it can expect to close out its position at a profit based on the new price level. Front running may involve either buying (where the broker buys for their account, before filling customer buy orders that drive up the price) or selling (where the broker sells for its own account, before filling customer sell orders that drive down the price).

  For example, suppose a broker receives an order from a customer to buy a large block of 400,000 shares of some stock, but before placing the order for the customer the broker buys 20,000 shares of the same stock for his own account at $100 per share, then afterward places the customer's order for 400,000 shares, driving the price up to $102 per share and allowing the broker to immediately sell his shares for, say, $101.75, generating a significant profit of $35,000 in just a short time. This $35,000 is likely to be just a part of the additional cost to the customer's purchase caused by the broker's self-dealing.

This example uses unusually large numbers to get the point across. It is, however, highly uncommon for brokers to process buy orders totaling $40,800,000 in a single transaction. In practice, computer trading splits up large orders into many smaller ones, making front-running more difficult to detect.

A practice similar to front running is called "tailgating". Tail gating means the action of a broker or adviser purchasing or selling a security for his or her client(s) and then immediately making the same transaction in his or her own account. This is not illegal like front running, but it is not looked upon favorably because the broker is most likely placing a trade for his or her own account based on what the client knows (like inside information).

➤ *Pump and dump* - "Pump and dump" is a form of stock fraud that involves artificially inflating the price of an owned stock through false and misleading positive statements, in order to sell the cheaply purchased stock at a higher price. Once the operators of the scheme "dump" their overvalued shares, the price falls and investors lose their money.

During the dot-corn era, when stock market fever was at its height and many people spent significant amounts of time on stock Internet message boards, a 15-year-old named Jonathan Lebed showed how easy it was to use the Internet to run a successful pump-and-dump. Lebed bought penny stocks and then promoted them on message boards, pointing at the price increase. When other investors bought the stock, Lebed sold his for a profit, leaving the other investors holding the bag.

➤ *Circular Trading* - Circular Trading is a method whereby buyer and seller of the shares / stocks come to an understanding whereby both sell order and buy order will be matched with both price and quantity and thereby creating large volumes in the trading of specific scrip of those companies with whom they both enter in to an agreement thereby pushing the share price of the company and thereby take undue advantage from the increase in prices.

Case Study—Concentration of Market in a Few Hands/ Inter Stock Exchange Dealings

The Stock market is concentrated in the hands of a few institutions and big stocks brokers whose transactions affect the whole market and also affect the buying and selling sentiments of the small investors and thus resulting in the raise or fall of the stock market. The market manipulators in the Stock Market do not restrict their operations to a single Stock Exchange, but they extend their hands to other Stock Exchanges and make circles with the help of other brokers listed on other Stock Exchanges. With this, the circular effect is not limited to a group of stock brokers of a particular stock exchange, but it extends to other stock exchanges and involves stock brokers from different stock exchanges.

This makes a bigger circle and develops frenzy amongst the individual investors across the country. By the time frenzy and the circle become bigger, the market manipulators leave the circle leaving behind gullible individual investors, who lose their money, because of the undue appreciation / fall in the prices of the shares. They make use of the non-uniformity in the settlement dates of various stock exchanges and shift their positions from one exchange to the other, with out transfer of funds.

As discussed above, the market becomes a situation of "weak hands" vs "strong hands." Prices are engineered by the strong hands to take advantage of the weak hands. Let's look at few scenarios depicting strong hands.

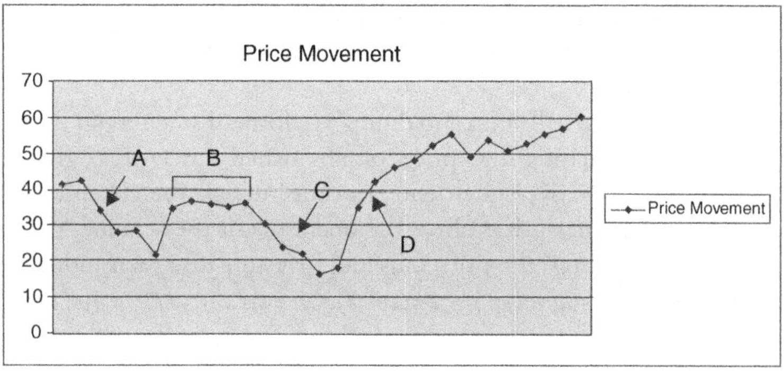

Figure 7.3 Monthly price movement and pattern detection.

Here is what to look for:

- "A" - Prices start dropping down into a major low area.
- "B" - Prices consolidate for an extended period of time. (Remember, this is a monthly chart.)
- "C" - Prices are squeezed even lower by the strong hands, sufficiently lower to drive out all of the weak hands. Anyone bullish on this market is now ready to or has already capitulated. During and following the squeeze, the strong hands accumulate everything available at low, low prices. The strong hands now own this market.
- "D" - Since there is no one left to sell, the only thing that can happen is for demand to take hold and prices to rise. The strong hands sell into rising demand. The transfer of wealth eventually changes from the strong hands to the weak.

How do we analyze and predict a market manipulation situation such as the one we just discussed? One can analyze the pattern and build induction rules:

- Descending prices, followed by a leveling off into congestion that appears to be as low as prices are going to go.

- A surprise further descent by prices (the squeeze), followed by another period of congestion prior to the start of a rise in prices.
- A steady rise in prices that eventually penetrates the former congestion. It is in this period of steadily rising prices that the manipulators make excellent trades in a market.

Let us look at another scenario. This time we will see it on daily prices.

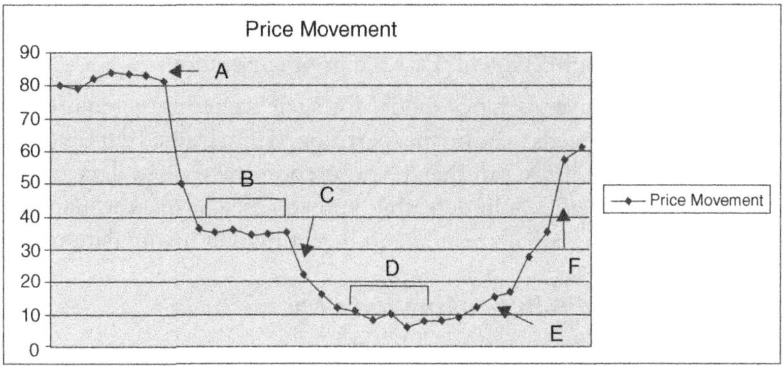

Figure 7.4 Monthly price movement and pattern detection.

- "A" - Prices begin a drop to what, at the time, were major lows.
- "B" - Prices consolidate at the major lows in what appears to be a bottom. It looks as if prices will not go any lower.
- "C" - To the dismay of anyone bullish, prices do drop lower. The squeeze is on. All weak hands are driven out of the market. It is a complete bullish capitulation.
- "D" - A period of consolidation forms once again. At this point and during the squeeze, we have had accumulation by the strong hands.
- "E" - Prices begin to rise on demand
- "F" - Prices rise higher than the former consolidation.

The above scenarios depicted bull squeezes. Sometimes the squeeze can be a bear squeeze. Below is a bearish squeeze scenario. This time we'll use a weekly scenario.

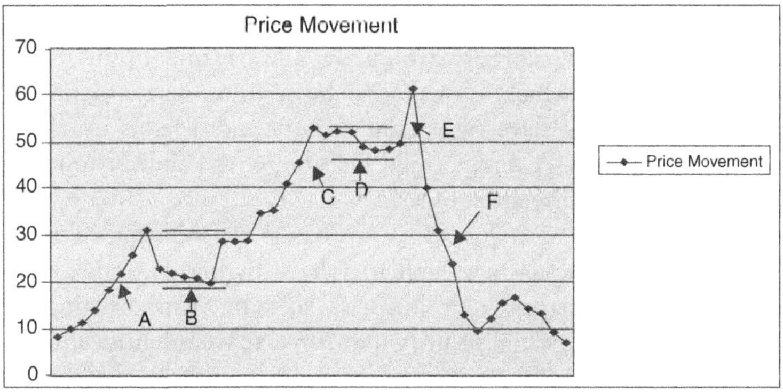

Figure 7.5 Weekly price movement and pattern detection.

- "A" - Prices climb to new all-time highs
- "B" - Prices consolidate, looks like perhaps the end of the bull rise.
- "C" - Prices rise again in an attempt to squeeze out the weak bears.
- "D" - Prices consolidate once again. Perhaps this is now distribution and prices will start down.
- "E" - Wrong! Prices make on final squeeze to even higher highs. You now have a complete bear capitulation. The strong hands have driven out the bears. There is only one way prices can now go.
- "F" - That's right! Down!! Past the prior congestion.

To develop predictive analytics model for such scenarios, it requires a lot of historical data, which needs to be further partitioned into trained data and test data. The rules as discussed above can then be exposed to the trained data and scoring done to reflect confidence % in detecting known cases of market manipulation. After that the model is run on test data to detect market manipulation cases.

Analytics Applications in Banking Industry

Traditionally the banking industry has been an early adopter of analytics, primarily to understand their customer's transactional patterns, and thus exploit the knowledge to cross-sell and/or up-sell various products to them. In the wake of increasing terrorism and fraudulent activities, banks also have started increasingly using analytics to detect and prevent fraud and money laundering cases. Below are few examples of how banks vise analytics:

- Interest rates greater than 14% or less than 4% would potentially identify a fraud in which a bank employee has given a friend, or themselves, a more than favorable market rate.
- Dormant and hold-mail accounts made current by an employee generally do not have significant, or any, activity flowing through them. This may be an indication that an employee is trying to misappropriate funds.
- Internal demand deposit accounts are instances where the opening of an account may be used for moving funds or for providing access to fund that could be stolen by an employee.
- Nondiscretionary accounts with more than 20 transactions per month can be a red flag. Nondiscretionary accounts are accounts whereby the customer has sole authority to initiate an investment transaction within their account, which is managed by a third party. Generally, these accounts do not have significant activity and a fee is usually assessed based on trades. A report could help target the auditor toward activity with a higher correlation of risk.
- Certain commission programs are based on the type of relationship (e.g., referral versus new) and may have higher commissions for new business. Comparing new business accounts with existing customer data (e.g., name, social security number, taxpayer identification number) may identify unethical activity resulting in inappropriate commission payouts.

Cross-Selling and Customer Loyalty in the Banking Industry

Financial institutions have been grappling with a question: how well do they know their customers? For example, while a bank may know that customers meeting certain criteria are likely to close their accounts, it is another matter to figure out a strategy to do something about it. In other words, it is essential to ensure that each customer interaction seizes the opportunity to increase customer satisfaction, loyalty, and revenue-generation potential. Traditionally, banks have focused on segmenting and courting high-value consumers.

Where they have fallen short is in taking that understanding of high value customers and using this information to predict the qualities that would raise the value of mid-level consumers, opening a large (and largely untapped) market opportunity. Predictive models can be effectively used to evaluate the right customer interaction message to be delivered to customers. Developing predictive models in conjunction with business rules enables calculation of probabilities of acceptance, indicating which offers are being accepted by which types of customers thus providing a competitive edge for the right offer at the right time.

By tailoring marketing options to consumers, banks can execute one-to-one campaigns that utilize predictive technologies to capture a sense of personalization and get a better response rate for their campaigns. Equally important, businesses can have an effective strategy for building loyalty and brand value, by tapping into customers' demands for personalized service, and their desire to escape the hassle of researching different service offerings. For example, a mortgage customer may tell the lending bank about an existing auto loan. An agent of the bank can add this information to the customer's profile, and present back a pre-approved refinance of the auto loan. This will save the customer money by consolidating the existing mortgage and auto loan with one bank. If the bank can calculate the savings on the fly, the customer can see a clear benefit.

Case Study—Developing Credit Scoring Models

Over the past 30 years, growing demand, stronger competition and advances in computer technology have meant that the traditional methods of making credit decisions that relied mostly on human judgment have been replaced by methods that employ statistical models. Statistical models today are used not only for deciding whether or not to accept an applicant (application scoring), but also for predicting the likelihood of defaults among customers who have already been accepted (behavioral scoring) and also predicting the likely amount of debt that the lender can expect to recover (collection scoring).

Credit scoring is performed because it provides a number of important business benefits, all of them based on the ability to quickly and efficiently obtain fact-based and accurate predictions of the credit risk of individual applicants or customers. For example, in application scoring, credit scores are used for optimizing the approval rate of credit applications.

Application scores enable an organization to choose an optimal cut-off score for acceptance, such that market share can be gained while retaining maximum profitability. The approval process and the marketing of credit products can be streamlined based on credit scores. For example, high-risk applications can be given to more experienced staff, or pre-approved credit products can be offered to select low-risk customers via various channels, including direct marketing and the Web.

Credit scores, both of prospects and existing customers, are essential in the customization of credit products. They are used to determine customer credit limits, down payments, deposits and interest rates.

Behavioral credit scores of existing customers are used in the early detection of high-risk accounts, and they enable organizations to perform targeted interventions, such as proactively offering debt restructuring. Behavioral credit scores also form the basis for more accurate calculations of the total consumer credit risk exposure, which can result in a reduction of bad debt provision.

Other benefits of credit scoring include an improved targeting of audits at high-risk accounts, thereby optimizing the workload of the auditing staff. Resources spent on debt collection can be optimized by targeting collection activities at accounts with a high collection score. Collection scores are also used for determining the accurate value of a debt book before it is sold to a collection agency. Finally, credit scores serve to assess the quality of portfolios intended for acquisition and to compare the quality of business from different channels, regions and suppliers.

The methodology of constructing credit scoring models generally involves the following process.

- First, a sample of previous customers is selected and classified as "good" and "bad" depending on their repayment performance over a given period.
- Next, data are compiled from loan applications, personal and/or business credit records and various sources if available (for example, credit bureau reports).
- Finally, statistical or other quantitative analysis is performed on the data to derive a credit scoring model. The model comprises of weights to apply to the different variables or attributes in the data and a cut-off point. The sum of the weights applied to the variables for an individual customer constitutes the credit score. The cut-off point determines if this customer should be classified as "good" or "bad".

Risk scoring, as with other predictive models, is a tool used to evaluate the level of risk associated with applicants or customers. While it does not identify "good" (no negative behavior expected) or "bad" (negative behavior expected) applications on an individual basis, it provides statistical odds, or probability, that an applicant with any given score will be "good" or "bad." These probabilities or scores, along with other business considerations such as expected approval rates, profit, churn, and losses, are then used as a basis for decision making.

In its simplest form, a scorecard consists of a group of characteristics, statistically determined to be predictive in separating good and bad accounts. Scorecard characteristics may be selected from any of the sources of data available to the lender at the time of the application. Examples of such characteristics are demographics (e.g., age, time at residence, time at job, postal code), existing relationship (e.g., time at bank, number of products, payment performance, previous claims), credit bureau (e.g., inquiries, trades, delinquency, public records), real estate data, and so forth.

The traditional form of a credit scoring model is a table containing a number of questions that an applicant is asked (called characteristics) and, for each question, a list of possible answers (called attributes). For example, one characteristic may be the age of the applicant, and the attributes for this characteristic are then a number of age ranges into which an applicant can fall. For each answer, the applicant receives a certain number of points—more if the attribute is one of low risk, fewer if the risk is higher. If the application's total score exceeds a specified cut-off number of points, it is recommended for acceptance.

Such a scorecard model usually is in the form of models, such as decision trees or neural networks. To begin with, a scorecard is easy to apply. If needed, the scorecard can be evaluated on a sheet of paper in the presence of the applicant. The scorecard is also easy to understand. The number of points for one answer doesn't depend on any of the other answers, and across the range of possible answers for one question, the number of points usually increases in a simple way (often monotonically, or even linearly). Therefore, it is often easy to justify to the applicant a decision that is made on the basis of a scorecard. It is possible to disclose groups of characteristics where the applicant has a potential for improving the score and to do so in broad enough terms not to risk manipulated future applications.

On the other hand, a decision tree may outperform a scorecard in terms of predictive accuracy, because unlike the scorecard, it detects and exploits interactions between characteristics. In a decision tree model, each answer that an applicant gives determines what question is asked next. If the age of an applicant is, for example, greater than 36 and less than 50, the model may suggest granting a credit without any further questions, because the average bad rate of that segment of applications is sufficiently low. If, on the other extreme, the age of the applicant is below 25, the model may suggest asking about time on the job next. Then, credit might be granted only to those that have exceeded 24 months of employment, because only in that sub-segment of younger adults is the average bad rate sufficiently low.

Thus, a decision tree model consists of a set of "if ... then ... else" rules that are still quite straightforward to apply. The decision rules are also easy to understand, perhaps even more so than a decision rule that is based on a total score that is made up of many components. However, a decision rule from a tree model, while easy to apply and understand, may be hard to justify for applications that lie on the border between two segments. There will be cases where an applicant will, for example, say: "If I had only been two months older, I would have received credit without further questions, but now I am asked for additional securities. That is unfair." That applicant may also be tempted to make a false statement about his or her age in the next application, or simply go elsewhere for financial services.

Even if a decision tree is not used directly for scoring, this model type still adds value in a number of ways. The identification of clearly defined segments of applicants with a particularly high or low risk can give dramatic new insight into the risk structure of the entire customer population. Decision trees are also used in scorecard monitoring, where they identify segments of applications where the scorecard underperforms.

With the decision tree, we could see that there is such a thing as a decision rule that is too easy to understand and thereby invites fraud. Ironically speaking, there is no danger of this happening with a neural network. Neural networks are extremely flexible models that combine characteristics in a variety of ways. Their predictive accuracy can be far superior to scorecards and they don't suffer from sharp "splits" as decision trees sometimes do.

However, it is virtually impossible to explain or understand the score that is produced for a particular application in any simple way. It can be difficult to justify a decision that is made on the basis of a neural network model. In some countries, it may even be a legal requirement to be able to explain a decision and such a justification must then be produced with additional methods. A neural network of superior predictive power is therefore best suited for certain behavioral or collection scoring purposes, where the average accuracy of the prediction is more important than the insight into the score for each particular case. Neural network models cannot be applied manually like scorecards or simple decision trees, but require software to score the application. However, their use is just as simple as that of the other model types.

To illustrate the use of analytics for credit scoring, consider a credit card issuer who is interested to develop a credit scoring model to predict the credit risk of credit card applicants as bad loss, bad profit and good risk. The credit card issuer intends to deploy the model at the time the credit card applications are processed. Assume that all applicants provide the following information in the application form:

- age
- annual income
- gender
- marital status
- number of children
- number of other credit cards held
- whether the applicant has an outstanding mortgage loan

For the purpose of our example, the target variable is credit risk and the input variables are the seven variables listed above, from age to whether the applicant has an outstanding mortgage loan. Prior to developing this application, the credit card issuer has categorized a representative sample comprising several one-year old credit card holders into three groups (bad loss, bad profit and good risk).

Table 7.1 Variables for credit scoring model

Characteristic Name	*Attribute*	*Scorecard Points*
Age	23	63
Age	23–25	75
Age	25–28	79
Age	28–34	85
Age	34–46	94
Age	46–51	80
Age	> 51	65
Income	2000	50
Income	10,000–30,000	62
Income	30,000–50,000	75
Income	50,000–1,00,000	92
Income	> 1,00,000	103
Existing Cards	American Express, Master, Visa	100
Existing Cards	Other	80
Existing Cards	None	50
Status	Married,Children	80
Status	Unmarried	75
Status	Married, No children	79
Loans	Yes	70
Loans	None	99

Each attribute ("Age" is a characteristic and "23-25" is an attribute) is assigned points based on statistical analyses, taking into consideration various factors such as the predictive strength of the characteristics, correlation between characteristics, and operational factors. The total score of an applicant is the sum of the scores for each attribute present in the scorecard for that applicant.

- For the score range 245–250, the expected marginal bad rate is 1.2%. That is, 1.2% of applicants with a score between 245 and 250 will likely be "bad."
- The cumulative bad rate—that is, the bad rate of all applicants above 245—is 0.84%.
- The acceptance rate at 245 is 17.44%, that is, 17.44% of all applicants score above 245.

Based on factors outlined above, a company can then decide, for example, to decline all applicants who score below 200, or to charge them higher pricing in view of the greater risk they present. "Bad" is generally defined using negative performance indicators such as bankruptcy, fraud, delinquency, writeoff/chargeoff, and negative net present value (NPV).

Risk score information, combined with other factors such as expected approval rate and revenue/profit potential at each risk level, can be used to develop new

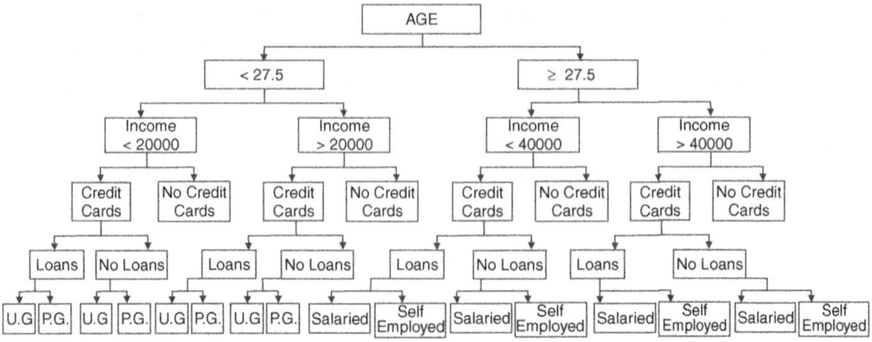

Figure 7.6 Decision tree for customer segmentation.

Table 7.2 Credit scoring process

Score Range	*Count*	*Cumulative Count*	*# of Goods*	*Cumulative # of Goods*	*# of Bads*	*Cumulative # of Bads*	*Marginal Bad Rate*	*Cumulative Bad Rate*	*Approval Rate*
273 ≤ Score <279	842	842	840	840	2	2	0.24	0.24	1.81
267 ≤ Score <273	511	1353	510	1350	1	3	0.20	0.22	2.91
262 ≤ Score <267	574	1927	570	1920	4	7	0.70	0.36	4.14
256 ≤ Score <262	2087	4014	2070	3990	17	24	0.81	0.60	8.63
245 ≤ Score <250	2338	8108	2310	8040	28	68	1.20	0.84	17.44
239 ≤ Score <245	2917	11025	2880	10920	37	105	1.27	0.95	23.71

application strategies that will maximize revenue and minimize bad debt. Some of the strategies for highrisk applicants are:

- Declining credit/services if the risk level is too high
- Assigning a lower starting credit limit on a credit card or line of credit
- Asking the applicant to provide a higher down payment or deposit for mortgages or car loans
- Charging a higher interest rate on a loan
- Charging a higher premium on insurance policies
- Asking the applicant to provide a deposit for utilities services
- Offering prepaid cellular services instead of postpaid

- Denying international calling access from telecommunications companies
- Putting the applicant into a "watch list" for potential fraudulent activity

Conversely, high-scoring applicants may be given preferential rates and higher credit limits, and be offered upgrades to premium products, such as gold or platinum cards, or additional products offered by the company.

Application scores can also help in setting "due diligence" policies. For example, an applicant scoring very high or very low can be declined or approved outright without obtaining further information on real estate, income verification, or valuation of underlying security.

The previous examples specifically dealt with risk scoring at the application stage. Risk scoring is similarly used with existing clients on an ongoing basis. In this context, the client's behavioral data with the company is used to predict the probability of negative behavior. Based on similar business considerations as previously mentioned (e.g., expected risk and profitability levels), different treatments can be tailored to accounts, such as:

- Offering product upgrades and additional products
- Increasing credit limits on credit cards and lines of credit
- Allowing some revolving credit customers to go beyond their credit limits
- Flagging potentially fraudulent transactions
- Offering better pricing on loan/insurance policy renewals
- Deciding whether or not to reissue an expired credit card
- Pre-qualifying direct marketing lists for cross-selling
- Directing delinquent accounts to more stringent collection methods or outsourcing to a collection agency
- Suspending or revoking phone services or credit facilities
- Put an account into a "watch list" for potential fraudulent activity

Generic or pooled data scorecards are those built using data from multiple lenders. For example, four small banks, none of which has enough data to build its own custom scorecards, decide to pool their data for auto loans. They then build a scorecard with this data and share it, or customize the scorecards based on unique characteristics of their portfolios. Scorecards built using industry bureau data, and marketed by credit bureaus, are a type of generic scorecards.

Risk scoring, in addition to being a tool to evaluate levels of risk, has also been effectively applied in other operational areas, such as:

- Streamlining the decision-making process, that is, higher-risk and borderline applications being given to more experienced staff for more scrutiny, while low-risk applications are assigned to junior staff. This can be done in branches, credit adjudication centers, and collections departments.
- Reducing turnaround time for processing applications through automated decision making
- Evaluating quality of portfolios intended for acquisition

- Setting economic and regulatory capital allocation
- Setting pricing for securitization of receivables portfolios
- Comparing the quality of business from different channels/regions/suppliers

Risk scoring, therefore, provides creditors with an opportunity for consistent and objective decision making, based on empirically derived information. Combined with business knowledge, predictive modeling technologies provide risk managers with added efficiency and control over the risk management process.

Analytics and Insurance Risk Management

The insurance industry has a unique business model unlike that of any other industry. Insurance is the one product that the manufacturer sells without knowing exactly how much it will cost to produce before the product is sold. For other industries, the costs of materials, labor, distribution and profit margin are known before a price is established. Therefore, Insurers must make educated guesses about their future costs, and the penalties for inaccurate guesses range from a loss of customers to insolvency. Insurers use predictive models in four primary areas — actuarial, marketing, underwriting and claims.

Actuarial - The actuarial function is tasked with setting rates and reserves. It tends to be staffed with professionals having strong statistical skills and insurance industry knowledge.

- *Marketing* - Marketing approaches modeling in much the same manner as other industries, with one exception. For insurance companies whose products are sold by independent agents and brokers, the company does not own the customer relationship and must obtain the intermediary's consent to contact the insured.
- *Underwriting* - Underwriting is tasked with the decision of whether to accept or decline a risk and, if accepted, what unique loss prevention actions must the insured make. For ages, underwriting function based its decisions on risk selection rules designed to ensure a consistent book of business. More recently, underwriting automation systems have been developed that incorporate rules engines to reduce the level of human involvement in the underwriting process. Underwriting can be optimized by having created highly accurate rate structures with pricing for every type of risk, thereby automating the manual tasks and optimally utilize the experienced underwriters to review specific risk mitigation areas.
- *Claims* - The Claims function is tasked to analyze the claims filed, subrogation management, resource allocation and fraud prevention type of activities.

We will discuss in greater detail the uses of predictive modeling in each of the four primary business areas of the insurance industry. This is not an exhaustive discussion of the uses of predictive models. It is intended to give the reader a basic understanding of the industry and modeling strategies adopted.

Virtually every aspect of the insurance business can benefit from an improved ability to predict the future. Actuaries attempt to predict loss probability, loss severity, required reserves, etc. using mathematical techniques. Similarly, underwriters attempt to predict which risks are most likely to be profitable and base their decisions on these predictions. Whether actuaries desire to create more accurate pricing models, underwriters hope to make better underwriting decisions, marketing wants to improve campaign results or claims needs to predict and avoid litigation, all of insurance business functions will benefit from predictive analytics.

Actuarial Analytics

Actuaries can be broadly divided into two categories. Casualty actuaries focus on the property and casualty (P&C) industry, which includes automobile, homeowners, health, liability, business and similar product lines. Life actuaries focus on life insurance and annuities.

Within these two categories, there are two classes of actuary that are determined by primary job function—pricing and reserving.

- Pricing actuaries are concerned with the calculation of rates for various insurance products. Due to regulatory differences between countries and even between states or provinces within countries, pricing actuaries must calculate rates for every product in every jurisdiction. Because pricing models tend to lose their effectiveness over time, new rates are often calculated several times per year.
- The responsibility of the reserving actuary is to calculate the amount of premium that should be held in reserve to meet the company's obligations for claims and unearned premium as well as to meet regulatory reserve requirements. For certain product lines that have claims that are paid out over long time periods, such as bodily injury claims or worker's compensation, the reserve prediction can be quite challenging.

Pricing

The insurance industry evolved long before the computer, and the techniques used for ratemaking were simple enough to be done by hand. For centuries, actuaries have relied on simplistic methods for calculating rates. Prior to 1960, almost all actuaries calculated rates based on one risk characteristic at a time and determined rate relativities for each characteristic independently of each other. The 1960s brought two major changes to actuarial science — the increased availability of computers and the use of the minimum bias procedure. Most practitioners use these methods to create multiplicative rating models, which are fairly easy to implement and are easy for agents to understand.

Note: The minimum bias procedure becomes useful when the classification system has multiple dimensions. For a two-dimensional classification system, this means each cell in a matrix. The observations can be average loss costs, loss frequencies, or loss ratios. In practice, the data would consist of losses and exposures (for loss costs), claim counts and exposures (for loss frequencies), or losses and premiums (for loss ratios).

The underlying principle of actuarial ratemaking is that the only bad risk is an under-priced risk. However, insurers must balance pricing adequacy with market and regulatory considerations. Except in rare situations, they are not permitted to charge any rate that the market will bear.

Traditionally, the process of rate-making involves the identification of risk factors and the computation of premiums based on expected claims and payments for the various combinations of predefined risks. Typical of this are one-page rate sheets showing automobile insurance rates based on automobile power and region, potentially modified by discounts for certain occupations or by age surcharges. This basic rate structure would be subject to penalties or reductions depending on accident frequency. Lately have insurers begun to construct more complex risk classes by considering additional factors, such as yearly mileage driven, number of other drivers in the household, use of a garage. Even with this extended structure, the basic model is to group customers sharing the same risk features together into one tariff, and separating them out on the basis of their accident behavior.

One major implication of this approach is the fact that among new customers lacking driving history the good drivers will subsidize the bad drivers for a substantial time, until the premium reduction of the good drivers takes effect, which may be a slow process extending over years. Similarly, the rate increase for new bad drivers will lag their actual loss costs. Compounding factors are common regulatory requirements on the industry, attempting to make sure that insurance is affordable. This will limit the maximum amount of premiums that can be asked of customers, irrespective of their accident behavior. Therefore, even when considering long standing customers it is unavoidable that good drivers subsidize bad drivers to some degree. In fact entire risk groups, such as young male drivers, or drivers from inner city locations may be charged a premium more reflecting the higher insurance costs for the entire risk group rather than the individual accident behavior, since regulatory requirement will not allow to set premiums high enough to offset costs for bad drivers. Again good drivers will subsidize bad drivers.

Like for any other data mining task, the most fundamental requirement is the availability of appropriate data. In the context of insurance policies, this requires information on the policyholder, on the risks covered, on cumulative risk behavior, and optionally on a variety of additional factors that may be relevant. A sample set of variables used in this context has been provided in Table 7.3.

This variable set originates from an actual insurance provider and illustrates the kind of data used for rate setting. Most of the variables are self-explaining and non-surprising; note, however, the inclusion of data on marriage status and number of children. The use of other personal data may soon become common place. The insurance data also contain information for various types of non-accident claims, such as glass, storm, theft, and vandalism.

Table 7.3 Typical variables used for Automobile Insurance

Variable Name	*Description*
Contract_id	Unique contract identifier
Period_begin	Beginning date for the period covered
Period_end	Ending date of the period covered
Premium Basic	Premium paid in the period
Damage_collision	Premium for additional damage collision paid in the period
Total_damage	Damage of all accidents, broken down into:
Vandalism	Vandalism damage
Storm	Storm damage
Glass	Glass damage
Fire	Damage caused by fire
Theft	Damage caused by automobile theft
Theft_parts	Damage caused by theft of accessories
Usage	Type of use for vehicle
Group	Vehicle group for insurance purposes
Z_tariff	Tariff zone
Z_damage	Damage zone
Z_theft	Theft zone
Z_glass	Glass damage zone
Previous	Duration of contract for previous vehicle
License_age	Time since license was obtained
Insurance_age	Length of time with this insurance
Driver_age	Age of the driver
Vehicle_age	Age of the vehicle
Possession_age	Time since the vehicle was obtained
New	Newly insured person?
Garage	Uses garage?
Num_vehicles	Number of vehicles
Licenses	Number of license class
Married	Marriage status
Children	Number of children
Gender	Male or female driver
Bonus	Fraction of rate reduction or increase
Region	Region of vehicle location

The primary business question to be addressed with these data is the setting of rates for new and existing customers. Several of the variables may not be available for new customers, in particular data on premiums, costs, and profitability. Data on previous accident behavior may be incomplete or entirely missing, e.g., when dealing with a newly licensed driver. In order to predict a rate in these cases, care must be taken to exclude these variables from any rate-predicting model. In addition to rate setting, there is also the issue of "rate monitoring", i.e., dynamically managing the rate structure for existing customers. This involves analyzing the profitability of the various risk classes, and may result in taking corrective action in case of under-performance or in the face of competitive pressures. It may also involve a change in the "bonus" system, i.e., the penalizing or rewarding of customers based on their yearly accident claims.

The basic concepts, which are used in rate setting and rate monitoring, are the "pure premium" and the "loss ratio". Pure premium is the premium that would be sufficient to offset all accident claim costs. For any given customer, it can be estimated as the product of (1) the likelihood of submitting a claim, and (2) the expected size of the claim.

The pure premium is the "rock bottom" of any premium structure: at that level an insurance company could not generate a profit, but ideally, would not lose any money either. In practice, of course, there are many operating expenses in a business, including buildings, equipment, and personnel that need to be covered, irrespective of how many claims occur,

None of these costs are included in the pure premium. Neither is underwriting costs, such as commissions to agents and brokers. The actual premium therefore is always substantially higher than the pure premium.

Variable Description

Loss ratio is another basic concept used in rate making and rate monitoring. It is defined as the fraction of claim costs to premiums. A realistic figure in automobile policies is in the order of 70%–80%, i.e., more than 70% of the premiums collected will be needed to pay for accident claims. Again, the loss ratio does not include the additional costs due to operating the insurance business. The loss ratio is only meaningful when calculated over several years, in order to take into account the varied propensity of the customers for accidents, thus generating claim costs. When calculated in this way, it is however, a very telling figure of the profitability of a company.

Lowering the loss ratio is the major goal of insurance companies. This lowering can be accomplished in two ways: adjusting the rate structure in order to increase premiums or adjusting the customer population to producing fewer claims. In practice both ways are realized through rate adjustments: penalize bad drivers and thereby discourage them from continued coverage, reward good drivers into loyal customers. This behavior will extend toward new customers as well, by predicting their similarity to good or bad drivers, ideally setting up conditions to attract good drivers and discourage poor ones.

As an example of a model generated by a decision tree we can inspect Figure 7.7 which shows the result of a decision tree analysis attempting to predict a target (pure premium) from input variables. The most important 3 variables to account for the target values are driving license date, period of driving, and zip code.

Initially (at the top of the tree) the analysis covered 4019 customers resulting in an average pure premium of 3109. This premium was much higher (96754) for a small group (43 customers) with driving license dates since 1991. Following the other branches we arrive at four terminal segments with different premiums, containing different numbers of customers. Taken together, the customers add

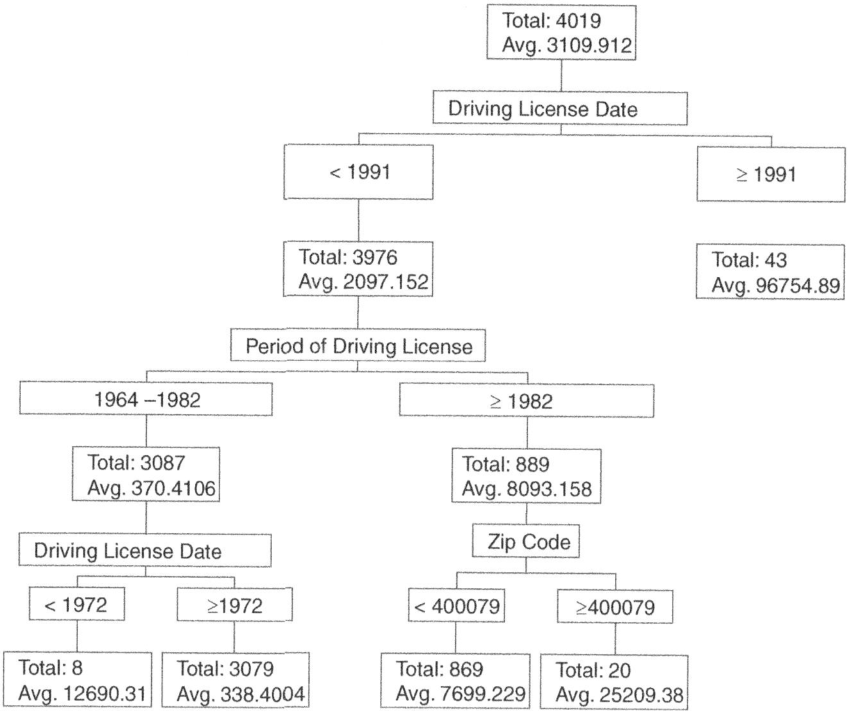

Figure 7.7 Decision tree for premium analysis.

up to the original 4019. One of the terminal segments still contains a large set of customers (3079) and could be subject to a more detailed subsequent analysis.

It is also important to realize, that variables higher up in the tree (such as driving license date in the current example) have been determined to be "more important" than variables further down in the tree (such as zip code). This importance of variables can be quantified by different measures. Sometimes it may improve results, if models are developed separately for different parts of the data. For example, if the driving behavior is different between genders or countries it may be useful to build a model for each of these cases. In order to predict the driving risk for a new customer, we would first have to determine the nationality and if he/she is male or female, and then use the appropriate model.

One of the recent prominent ways to devise a new rating structure is to focus on the "loss ratio", i.e., the ratio between claim losses and premiums. This requires the use of historical data covering multiple years, as losses are random events and cannot be modeled realistically by only focusing on a single rating period. Also provisions need to be taken that a rare single large loss does not bias the analysis unduly, usually therefore losses are "capped" at a certain amount. The rate making process consists of predicting the loss ratio from the risk variables and then focus on those rate groups that show a relatively high variance. This variance would indicate that there are subgroups with different business implications in a given rate class, which then will need to be subdivided in order to achieve a more homogeneous behavior.

We can inspect the decision rules produced by the decision tree analysis, with the purpose of focusing on those nodes with a high standard deviation in loss ratio, e.g., the following rule is found

IF Car brand IS ONE OF: CITROEN NISSAN AND Age of the car < 13.5 AND Driving license date $\leq$ 1982.5 THEN NODE: 13, N: 107, AVE : 4.12953, SD : 6.28759;

which can be summarized as follows: "there is a high loss ratio of about 413% coupled with a high standard deviation, if the conditions listed after the "IF" are met. When computing the loss ratios, we need to recall that it is defined as the ratio of costs to premium. A loss ratio of 1 then means that 100% of the premiums are needed to offset cost. In the rule above, the ratio is approximately 4.13, hence more than four times the collected premiums (i.e., 413%) are needed to offset costs.

Let us further analyze this; the purpose of such analysis would be to further reduce the variance of the loss ratio, by subdividing customers into separate risk groups.

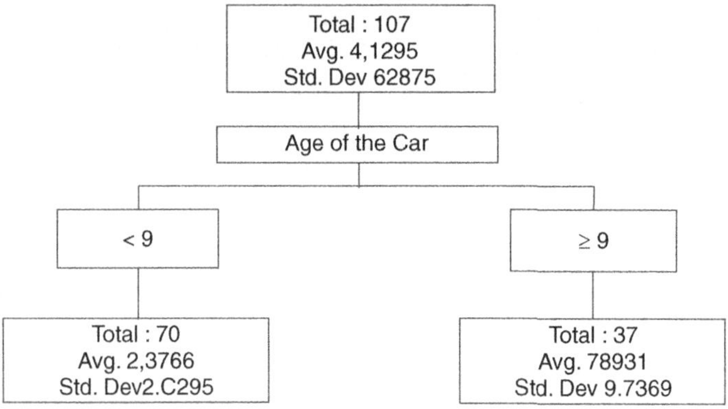

Figure 7.8 Decision tree for loss ratio analysis.

Pursuing the example above in more detail, we generate the potential variables for the first split of the decision tree, and may select "age of the car" as a splitting variable, as shown in figure above. As a result, we find a subset with a very high loss ratio (789%) and a high standard deviation for the customer group with "age of the car $ 9". Attempting an alternative split using the car location "zip code" we get a similar result as shown in figure below. Again there is a subgroup ("ZIP code $ 400079") with high loss ratios and high standard deviations.

By identifying additional characteristics that can segment existing rating cells into smaller cells with different rates, an insurer with a more granular structure can compete with other insurers using lower prices, while continuing to charge an appropriate premium. At the same time, they may charge more for other

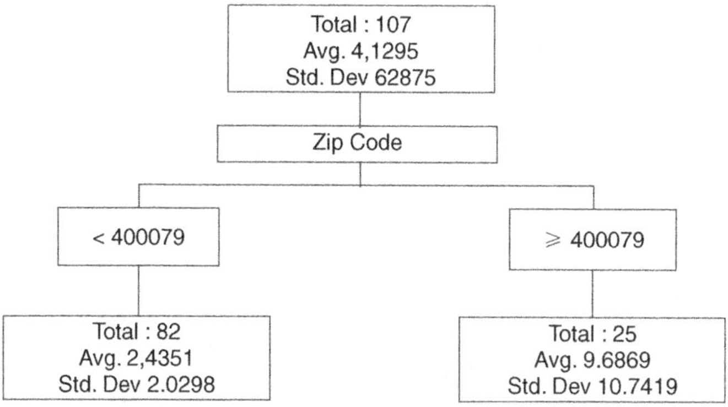

Figure 7.9 Additional criteria for segmentation.

sub-segments that have been identified as having a higher loss cost. The end result is that their competitor retains business that is under-priced — a situation described in the industry as "adverse selection." Ultimately the competitor with the larger rate cells will have poorer loss results, will lose profitable business and will gain unprofitable business.

Note: Tendency of people with significant potential to file claims wanting to obtain insurance coverage. Insurers protect themselves from adverse selection by attempting to measure risk and either charging more from the higher risks, or by refusing to cover them at all. For example, motor insurers charge higher premiums for cars and drivers that are statistically more likely to be involved in accidents. Medical insurers usually exclude pre-existing conditions (i.e., any illness that pre-dates the start of cover) from their cover in order to deter people from buying cover after a problem has been diagnosed. In part, the problem of adverse selection is dealt with by the insurers' attempts to measure risk, which is anyway necessary to setting premiums.

Severity forecasting

Another use for modeling is the forecasting of loss severity. For P&C lines of business, the amount that must be paid for each claim varies. Rarely do claim amounts reach the limits of coverage. Many factors impact loss severity. As the cost of vehicles rises, the loss cost for auto theft rises. The addition of airbags to vehicles may have mitigated bodily injury losses, but they increased the costs associated with relatively minor accidents. More advanced insurers use econometric time series forecasting techniques to predict trends in loss severity and incorporate these models into their ratemaking process.

Frequency forecasting

Yet another use of models is the prediction of loss frequency or the count of claims for a given exposure. For some lines of business, a single risk may be expected to have multiple claims; for others, such as life, there is but one. The ability to accurately forecast frequency has a direct bearing on the ability to calculate accurate rates, allocate staff and mitigate loss. Like severity, loss frequency is impacted by external factors. For example, as gasoline prices rise, mileage driven tends to decrease and the frequency for some types of accidents decreases as well. At the same time, the demand for expensive, gas-guzzling SUVs decreases and the frequency of theft and fire losses to such vehicles tends to rise.

Premium forecasting

For some P&C lines of business, premiums may rise independently of rate increases. Most home owner policies, for example, contain a provision that automatically increases the amount of coverage based on changes to the consumer price index. Because premium is based in part on the amount of coverage, premiums tend to rise automatically. For other property lines, such as auto comprehensive coverage, the cost of coverage is based on the value of the vehicle. As vehicles age, their value decreases, and the corresponding premium for physical damage coverage also decreases. An interesting development in the US recently involved the novel idea of charging different liability premiums depending on the type of vehicle driven. In the past, liability premiums were based on location, miles driven and the type of use. As SUVs grew in size and popularity, the injuries caused by these vehicles mandated higher rates. It will be interesting to see if higher gas prices cause reduced demand for these vehicles and a corresponding reduction in premium volume.

Reserving

The final area for modeling by actuaries is the forecasting of reserves. There are two reserves—unearned premium reserves and loss reserves. For most insurance policies, premiums are paid in advance and are not earned by the insurer until the policy has run its course. In the event that the insured cancels coverage, the insurer must refund the unearned portion of the premium. Loss reserves are established to pay for claims. In many cases, the amount that will be ultimately paid out for a claim is not known until months or years after the claim has occurred. When calculating rates, actuaries include losses paid as well as losses reserved in their loss cost calculations. An insurer who has excess reserves will tend to have rates that are higher than necessary and will increase their attrition risk. An insurer who is under reserved runs a greater risk of insolvency, downgrade by ratings bureaus and rate calculations that will result in excessively high loss ratios.

Most actuaries use a technique known as the loss development triangle to estimate how much money should be held in reserve. This technique involves the summarization of loss payments over the time that passed since the loss occurred, known as the development period. Once the development is known, actuaries then compare development periods. It is at this point that there is little agreement over which is the best method for analyzing development. It is also where the greatest flexibility is required and the actuary's knowledge of the history of the book of business under analysis comes into play.

Marketing Analytics

The primary role of marketing for insurance companies is not much different from other industries: to attract and retain profitable customers. It is the definition of what constitutes a customer that sets insurance apart from other industries. There are three basic types of insurance marketing systems: direct writers, captive agencies and independent intermediaries.

For direct writers, there is no middleman. The insurer maintains a staff of customer service representatives who have been trained and, in some cases, licensed to handle insurance products. Customers can purchase and modify their policies through the Web, phone or mail. In this type of arrangement, the company owns the customer relationship and can manage it as they see fit. They have the luxury of not having an agent or broker between the company and the customer—and no commission requirement.

Like direct writers, insurers who maintain a captive agency force also own the customer relationship. Generally, their agents are permitted to only write business for the company. The agent is an employee of the company and is viewed as a representative of the company.

The independent agency or broker is a very different situation. Independents have the ability to place business with any company with whom they have a contract. Not only is the company competing for the insured's business, but they are competing for the agent's business as well. The agent owns the customer relationship, and the company cannot contact the insured directly without the agent's consent. It is not uncommon for an insured to have a single independent agent, but have insurance products with multiple carriers. This situation complicates the marketer's job considerably.

It is a commonly held belief that it takes many months if not years to recover the cost to acquire a new insurance customer, with estimates ranging from a low of 18 months to a high of five years. Insurers also know that business that has been on the books for more than a year tends to be significantly more profitable than business that is in its first year of coverage. Because of this, insurers place great emphasis on retaining customers. Customer retention models are used by some companies to predict which customers are most likely to attrite and to take steps to retain them.

One well-known factor that has a positive influence on customer retention is the number of insurance products a particular customer holds. Armed with this knowledge, insurers go to great lengths to encourage cross-selling of their products within households. For most insurers, "companion policy" discounts are offered to lower premiums for multi-policy households. Cross-sell models are quite common in insurance.

Response modeling is also prevalent, but the methods used are different depending on the distribution channel used. For direct writers and captive agencies, the methodology is very similar to that used by retail, although campaigns tend to be smaller and more tightly focused. For insurers who use independent agents, response models must consider both the potential customer's response probability as well as the likelihood that the agent will place the business.

Underwriting Analytics

A basic requirement of insurance is to begin with a set of homogeneous exposures. The underwriter's job is to ensure the homogeneity of the book through risk selection and rate assignment. For many generations, underwriters have based their decisions on risk selection rules. Risks that violate one or more selection rules are declined unless the underwriter is willing to make an exception. Regulations govern which risk characteristics may be considered and prohibit unfair discrimination. In addition, regulations address the type of adverse action an insurer may take based on certain risk characteristics and these regulations differ for new applications versus existing business.

Insurers tend to alter their selection rules relatively frequently. If loss results deteriorate, they tighten rules and if results are good, rules are slackened. Rule changes are usually done in conjunction with rate revisions. Rules may also consider characteristics that are already addressed by rates—magnifying the impact of the rates. The critical flaw in the underwriting process is that selection rules for most companies have never been validated against loss results. It is quite possible that the very rules that insurers rely on to protect their results are having the opposite effect.

Beginning in the early 1990s insurers began to develop expert systems that were intended to automate the underwriting process. Such systems were designed to apply existing selection rules in the same manner that the underwriter would. For insurers who adopted this approach, the number of cases requiring an underwriter's attention was significantly decreased. Nevertheless, their promise of consistency and accuracy did not significantly improve loss ratios.

In more recent times, the use of credit scores and more specialized insurance scores has grown in popularity. A strong correlation between credit score and loss cost for personal lines insurance exists. Industry insiders have clearly demonstrated the effectiveness of credit scoring for insurance underwriting and pricing and have also shown that credit scores are not unfairly discriminatory. Because of recent negative press, some insurers and vendors have begun to develop insurance scores that are targeted directly at loss results, rather than credit. This type of underwriting scoring model has great promise as a means of more accurately predicting the future loss potential of individual risks.

Another modeling opportunity in underwriting revolves around the prediction of "probable maximum loss" associated with catastrophic events such as hurricanes, earthquakes and other natural or unnatural disasters that affect a wide geographic area. There are relatively few specialty firms that analyze a company's exposures and provide PML estimates. The creation of this type of model generally requires knowledge of the insurance products, weather, geology and geography, as well as predictive modeling.

Claims Analytics

The processing of claims is where insurers fulfill their promises. Insureds would like to receive rapid and accurate payouts without hassles. Negative experiences with claims processing have a significant detrimental effect on customer retention. Claims payments represent the most significant revenue outflows for any insurer and present the greatest opportunity for fraud and leakage.

When a claim occurs, the insurer establishes a reserve that represents the expected ultimate payout for that loss. For many types of claims, reserves are set up based on simple averages of past losses of the same type. Only when an adjuster has investigated the claim more thoroughly the reserve gets adjusted to reflect a more accurate prediction of the potential payout. Claim payment patterns vary by geography, type of loss, and the economic climate in which the loss occurred. For example, the cost to reconstruct a single home that was destroyed by fire may be significantly less than the cost to rebuild the same home if most of the homes in the neighborhood were destroyed by a larger catastrophe such as a brush fire, hurricane or earthquake. Insurers have not done an effective job of modeling case reserves and would benefit from the application of predictive modeling techniques to incorporate more characteristics.

For many lines of business, the insured is insulated from the claims adjudication process. For example, when an automobile accident happens people typically file claims with their respective insurers who indemnify their clients for their loss. Behind the scenes, however, insurance companies take steps to recover their payouts from the offending parties and their insurers. This process, called subrogation, involves the identification of potential recoveries and appropriate communications with insurers and defendants. The identification and prioritization of subrogation opportunities represent an excellent target for predictive modeling and text mining. By optimizing the use of their subrogation units, insurers can maximize their recoveries and avoid missed subrogation opportunities.

For some insurers, subrogation is handled by a specialized unit within the claims organization. For many insurers, it is the adjuster's responsibility to subrogate losses. Regardless of the approach taken, it is usually labor intensive and often fruitless to subrogate claims. In many cases, insurers fail to recognize opportunities for recovery, in others they pursue recovery when their chance of success is minimal.

By building predictive models that score claims based on their probability of a successful recovery as well as based on the potential magnitude of the recovery, insurers can focus their efforts on those claims that will provide the most benefit to the company. This approach enables them to prioritize and optimize their subrogation activities thereby lowering their overall loss adjustment expense as well as their claims costs.

Probably the greatest opportunity for modeling in the claims organization is in the area of claims fraud detection and prevention. Claims fraud is a massive global problem. Healthcare fraud represents the largest financial impact followed closely by P&C claims. The major problem faced by modelers attacking fraud is that they attempt to build supervised models with inaccurate data. While all companies maintain data on adjudicated claims, few companies capture whether fraud was detected. Furthermore, most companies will admit that they catch only a small portion of the frauds that occur. Consequently, the data available to the typical insurer contains a significant portion of misclassified claims if classification is even available. The more enlightened approach is to use advanced unsupervised modeling techniques that do not require a database of correctly classified outcomes. The creation of such models requires both a thorough understanding of the claims process and great statistical expertise. In spite of this obstacle, insurers who have used predictive models have reported favorable results.

Case Study—The Underwriting Challenges

The underwriter has two basic functions: to ensure rate integrity and to select risks that match the profile of the business desired. Rates are established by actuaries who must assume that the book consists of a set of homogeneous exposures. Without a consistent book, the rates recommended by actuaries have little hope of being accurate and the company's ability to achieve loss ratio goals will be jeopardized. To ensure homogeneity, underwriters usually have based their decisions on risk selection rules.

Underwriting rules may also consider characteristics that are addressed by rates. This double dipping magnifies the impact of the rates. Underwriting rules tend to address only ten to twenty risk characteristic overlooking the impact that hundreds of other characteristics may have. This leaves the door open for competitors who rely on additional characteristics for underwriting or pricing to separate the profitable risks from the unprofitable.

Another crucial flaw in the underwriting process is that selection rules for most companies have never been validated against loss results. It is quite possible that the very rules that insurers rely on to protect their results are having the opposite effect.

For example, when considering the relationship between insurance losses and age and the relationship between insurance losses and prior accidents, it is no surprise that younger drivers tend to cost more to insure and that drivers with prior accidents cost more to insure. These findings, however, don't account for the fact that a larger proportion of younger drivers tend to have prior accidents. Knowing this could make a difference in the way an insurer chooses to surcharge younger drivers for prior accidents.

Predictive modeling helps insurers define groups that are more homogeneous for rating, underwriting and marketing. An insurance company may rate the city of Mumbai and the areas surrounding the city the same. Predictive modeling may show that the risk of loss outside the city of Mumbai is considerably different from the risk of loss inside the city. A company that successfully separates the Mumbai area into more homogenous risk areas will gain a significant competitive advantage.

Further, by discovering new risk identifiers or new relationships between current risk identifiers, predictive modeling also can identify new ways to segment risks. Using credit history for generating insurance scores is a vivid example of predictive modeling. Insurance scores have been used not only for rating, but also for tiering underwriting and marketing.

Reducing Loss Ratio

Loss ratio reduction can be achieved three ways: increase earned premium, reduce losses and loss adjustment expenses, or a combination of the two. Raising rates will increase written premium, but in a competitive market, it will ultimately result in lost business - and usually the better quality business is the first to go. Therefore simply raising rates across the board is not a viable solution. Reducing loss payments is equally challenging. However opportunities exist to improve this aspect of the loss ratio equation by identifying claims leakage or overpayment of losses.

In a commoditized insurance market, many insurers use similar rating characteristics. Traditional pricing models consider common, easily obtained characteristics and rates are developed for fairly broad classes of risk based on the average past performance for similar risks. Within any pricing cell, there will be risks that perform better than the average and others that perform worse. Predictive analytics can be used to analyze hundreds of characteristics to identify those that will separate the under-priced and over-priced risks. The resulting model can then be used to score each policy. This insight enables carriers to gain competitive advantage by selecting only those risks that have the highest likelihood of profitability.

The Figure 7.10 below illustrates the situation found at most insurers as it pertains to pricing and underwriting. The solid curved line represents the optimal relationship between risk and price. Each risk is priced exactly based on the exposure that it presents. Charging more would be overpricing the risk and charging any less would result in an inadequate premium. Most insurers do not have the ability to charge an infinitely variable price either due to regulatory constraints or a lack of analytic capabilities. Consequently, insurers group their risks based on similar characteristics and charge a price that is based on the expected performance for that group. Within each of these pricing groups, a certain portion of the risks are under-priced while others are over-priced. Under-priced risks will produce unfavorable results over time while over-priced risks are likely to seek out lower priced competitors. If a significant proportion of the book is overpriced and moves to the competition, then the overall performance for that risk class will diminish as the relative proportion of under-priced business will increase.

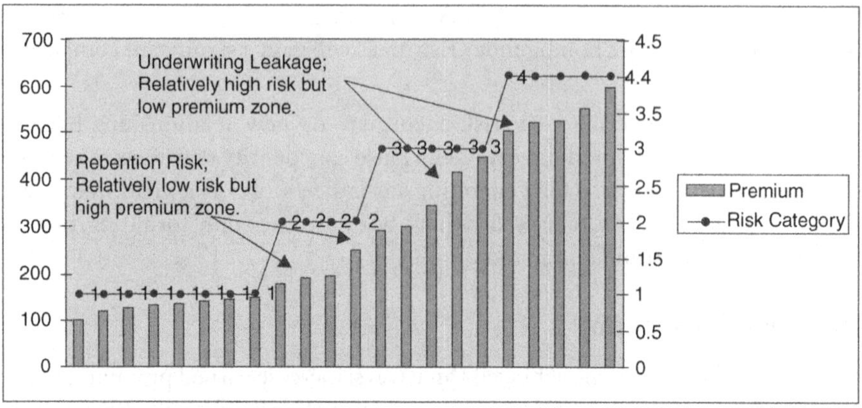

Figure 7.10 Premium and risk category analysis.

The solution to this problem is to create pricing structures and/or risk tiers of increasing granularity so that the cells formed by these structures result in a closer approximation of the optimal risk/price curve. Traditional analytic techniques do not produce structures that are sufficiently granular and they result in models that incorrectly estimate the impact of risk characteristics that are linked to each other. A simple example of this would be to examine the effects of age and gender on automobile insurance loss frequency. Simplistic models indicate that loss frequency is highest for younger drivers, diminishes through early adult ages, and then increases again in retirement years. However, the shape of the curve is different for males and females. Simply building a model that accounts for age will result in subsidization of rates from one gender to the other at certain ages. More advanced predictive modeling techniques account for the relationships between inputs and provide much more accurate models. Figure 7.11 below illustrates the impact of the increase in granularity.

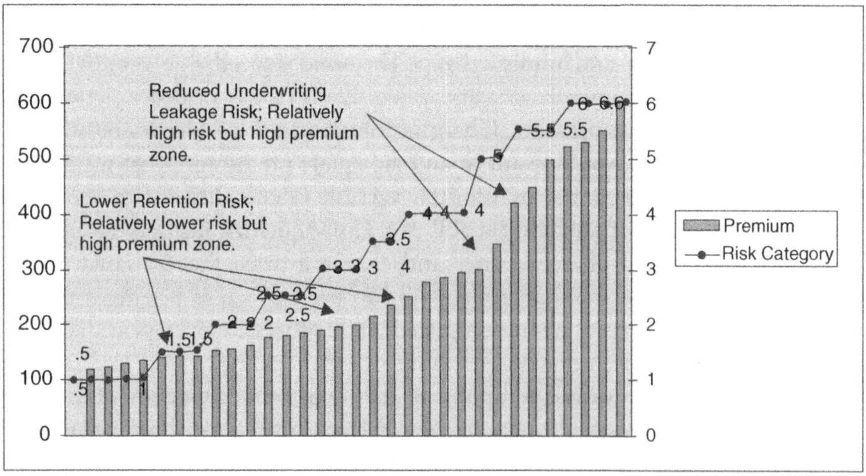

Figure 7.11 Premium and risk category analysis with further segmentations.

By using a larger number of pricing and/or underwriting classifications, the price is more closely matched to the risk that is actually presented. This increase in accuracy has multiple benefits. First, a smaller proportion of the granular company's book will be under-priced thereby ensuring profitability.

Second, less subsidization of rates will occur and consequently, fewer overpriced contracts will exist resulting in an increase in policy retention. Finally, a less intuitive, yet equally important benefit is the competitive advantage that arises from pricing granularity. The division of existing pricing cells into smaller cells will result in a price increase for some risks, but price reductions occur for other risks. In a highly competitive market, a price reduction improves competitive position of the company even if that price reduction is not as large as possible. The non-granular competitor's business that falls into the lower priced cells will tend to migrate to the granular company. When this migration happens, business that has been subsidizing the premiums for under-priced business will have migrated and a greater proportion of the non-granular book will be under-priced. Unless the non-granular company adopts a more granular strategy immediately, their loss ratio will deteriorate resulting in price increases. In addition, a portion of the granular company's book of business that receives a price increase will be attracted to the non-granular company where the business is under-priced. By adopting a granular pricing/underwriting strategy, the innovative company creates an adverse selection condition for their non-granular competitors. This underscores the need to adopt such strategies early in order to avoid being a victim of adverse selection.

Analytics in Retail Industry

Large retail chains and grocery stores store vast amounts of point-of-sale data that is information rich. In the forefront of the applications that have been adopted in retail are direct marketing applications. Almost every type of retailer, including catalogers, consumer retail chains, grocers, publishers, business-to-business marketers, and packaged goods manufacturers, uses direct marketing. Direct marketers are often concerned about customer segmentation, which is a clustering problem in data mining.

For example, one retail company with $2 billion in revenue, 300,000 UPC codes, and 129 stores in 15 states found some interesting results after analyzing its sales information. They found that people who were coming into the shop gravitated to the left-hand side of the store for promotional items and were not necessarily shopping the whole store. Such information is used to change promotional activity and provide a better understanding of how to lay out a store in order to optimize sales.

Retailers are interested in many different types of data-mining studies. In the area of marketing, retailers are interested in creating data-mining models to answer questions like:

- How much are customers likely to spend over long periods of time?

- What is the frequency of customer purchasing behavior?
- What are the best types of advertisements to reach certain segments?
- What advertising mediums are most effective at reaching customers?
- What is the optimal timing at which to send mailers?

Merchandisers are beginning to profile issues such as:

- What types of customers are buying specific products?
- What determines the best product mix to sell on a regional level?
- What are the latest product trends?
- When is a merchandise department saturated?
- What are the times when a customer is most likely to buy?
- What types of products can be sold together?

With regards to customer profitability, retailers may wish to build models to answer questions like:

- How does a retailer retain profitable customers?
- What are the significant customer segments that buy products?

Customer identification is critical to successful retail organizations, and is likely to become more so. Data mining helps model and identify the traits of profitable customers and reveal the "hidden" relationship that standard query processes have not already found.

Retail Shopping Basket Analytics

Traditional reports reveal item counts and amounts by store, region or channel. But the challenge is to take it one step further—to identify relationships between products. Plain and simple, POS data is only valuable if it can be quickly interpreted, analyzed and turned into action.

Wouldn't it be great to know the answers to these questions?

- If a customer purchases Product A, does it drive or indicate other purchases?
- If the price of a Product A goes up or down, how does it impact the sales of Product B?
- Knowing that a customer has purchased, or is in the process of purchasing, Product A, can an offer be made that will incentivise the customer to purchase additional products? Or can up-sell or cross-sell opportunities be presented?
- Each customer is unique and has different buying habits. Can an offer be customized to each customer?
- How can less-frequently-purchased items be exposed to customers?

Shopping Basket Analysis is a technique that examines customer buying habits at the product and transaction level. When each customer's real or virtual shopping basket is analyzed, insightful and often unexpected buying patterns often emerge. For example:

If man buys diapers, he is 90% likely to buy beer (but not the other way around)

- 96% of people who bought hammers also purchased AA batteries.
- 87% of customers over the age of 34 that purchased 100-watt light bulbs also purchased work gloves.

The patterns might also be obvious and reaffirm product grouping, but they can also test price elasticity:

- 97% of people who bought an electronic game also bought AA batteries
- Battery price increased 50%:95% of people who bought an electronic game also bought AA batteries
- 99% of customers who buy cookies also buy milk
- Milk prices increased 85%:57% of customers who buy cookies also buy milk.

Shopping Basket Analysis also can dynamically generate recommendations during an online shopping experience. Using this technique, when a customer calls into a call center to place an order, the call center operator can present the customer with additional products, and even present product cross-sell and up-sell opportunities:

- "People who have these same books/items in their cart also like these other books/items. Can I tell you about them?"
- "I see that you purchased Product A, Product B and Product C. Might I recommend Product D?"
- "I see that you are buying Product C. Can I offer you a 10% discount if you upgrade to Product X, if you buy it right now?"

Association Rules Algorithm is used in Market Basket Analysis to find which items or products are frequently associated or purchased together. An Association Rule Algorithm used in Market Basket Analysis analyzing the content of several shopping baskets from different customers and then creating rules that describe which items or products customers tend to buy together in one shopping transaction.

For Example, at the checkout desk in a store, each customer will have a Shopping Basket containing all the items that the customer purchased. This list of items in one shopping basket constitute a transaction. Several transactions from several customers will then be analyzed using an Association Rules Algorithm to find which items are likely to be purchased together.

'Market Basket' databases consist of a large number of transaction records. Each record lists all items bought by a customer on a single purchase transaction. Managers would be interested to know if certain groups of items are consistently purchased together. They could use this data for store layouts to place items optimally with respect to each other, they could use such information for cross-selling, for promotions, for catalog design and to identify customer segments based on buying patterns. Association rules provide information of this type in the form of "if-then" statements. These rules are computed from the data and, unlike the if-then rules of logic, association rules are probabilistic in nature. In addition to the antecedent (the "if" part) and the consequent (the "then" part) an association rule has two numbers that express the degree of uncertainty about the rule. In association analysis the antecedent and consequent are sets of items (called itemsets) that are disjoint (do not have any items in common).

- The first number is called the support for the rule. The support is simply the number of transactions that include all items in the antecedent and consequent parts of the rule. (The support is sometimes expressed as a percentage of the total number of records in the database.)
- The other number is known as the confidence of the rule. Confidence is the ratio of the number of transactions that include all items in the consequent as well as the antecedent (namely, the support) to the number of transactions that include all items in the antecedent. For example if a supermarket database has 100,000 point-of-sale transactions, out of which 2,000 include both items A and B and 800 of these include item C, the association rule "If A and B are purchased then C is purchased on the same trip" has a support of 800 transactions (alternatively 0.8% = 800/100,000) and a confidence of 40% (=800/2,000).

One way to think of support is that it is the probability that a randomly selected transaction from the database will contain all items in the antecedent and the consequent, whereas the confidence is the conditional probability that a randomly selected transaction will include all the items in the consequent given that the transaction includes all the items in the antecedent.

Example 1

The manager of the All Electronics retail store would like to know what items sell together. He has a database of transactions as shown below:

Table 7.4 - Transactions Table

Transaction Id		*Item Codes*		
1	1	2	5	
2	2	4		
3	2	3		
4	1	2	4	
5	1	3		
6	2	3		
7	1	3		
8	1	2	3	5
9	1	2	3	

There are nine transactions. Each transaction is a record of the items bought together in that transaction. Transaction 1 is a point-of-sale purchase of items 1, 2, and 5. Transaction 2 is a joint purchase of items 2 and 4, etc. Suppose that we want association rules between items for this database that have a support count of at least 2 (equivalent to a percentage support of 2/9=22%). By enumeration we can see that only the following item sets have a count of at least 2:

- {1} with support count of 6;
- {2} with support count of 7;

- {3} with support count of 6;
- {4} with support count of 2;
- {5} with support count of 2;
- {1, 2} with support count of 4;
- {1, 3} with support count of 4;
- {1, 5} with support count of 2;
- {2, 3} with support count of 4;
- {2, 4} with support count of 2;
- {2, 5} with support count of 2;
- {1, 2, 3} with support count of 2;
- {1, 2, 5} with support count of 2.

Notice that once we have created a list of all item sets that have the required support counts, we can deduce the rules that meet the desired confidence ratio by examining all subsets of each item set in the list. Since any subset of a set must occur at least as frequently as the set, each subset will also be in the list. It is then straightforward to compute the confidence as the ratio of the support for the item set to the support for each subset of the item set. We retain the corresponding association rule only if it exceeds the desired cut-off value for confidence. For example, from the item set {1,2,5} we get the following association rules:

- {1, 2} => {5} with confidence = support count of {1, 2, 5} divided by support count of {1, 2} = 2/4 = 50%;
- {1, 5} => {2} with confidence = support count of {1, 2, 5} divided by support count of {1, 5} = 2/2 = 100%;
- {2, 5} => {1} with confidence = support count of {1, 2, 5) divided by support count of {2, 5} = 2/2 = 100%;
- {1} => {2, 5} with confidence = support count of {1, 2, 5} divided by support count of {1} = 2/6 = 33%;
- {2} => {1,5} with confidence = support count of {1, 2, 5} divided by support count of {2} = 2/7 = 29%;
- {5} => {1,2} with confidence = support count of {1, 2, 5} divided by support count of {5} = 2/2 = 100%.

If the desired confidence cut-off was 70%, we would report only the second, third, and last rules. We can see from the above that the problem of generating all association rules that meet stipulated support and confidence requirements can be decomposed into two stages. First we find all item sets with the requisite support (these are called frequent or 'large' item sets) ; and then we generate, from each item set so identified, association rules that meet the confidence requirement. For most association analysis data, the computational challenge is the first stage.

The Apriori Algorithm: The key idea of the apriori algorithm is to begin by generating frequent item sets with just one item (1-item sets) and to recursively generate frequent item sets with 2 items, then frequent 3-itemsets and so on until we have generated frequent item sets of all sizes. In the example scenario explained above, without loss of generality we denote items by unique, consecutive (positive) integers and that the items in each item set are in increasing order of this item number to illustrate the algorithm.

It is easy to generate frequent 1-item sets. All we need to do is to count, for each item, how many transactions in the database include the item. These transaction counts are the supports for the 1-itemsets. We drop 1-itemsets that have support below the desired cut-off value to create a list of the frequent 1-itemsets. Based on the same approach, the general procedure to obtain k-item sets from (k – 1)-item sets for k = 2, 3, ... , is as follows: Create a candidate list of k-item sets by performing a join operation on pairs of (k–1)-item sets in the list. The join is over the first (k – 2) items, i.e., a pair is combined if the first (k–2) items are the same in both members of the pair. If this condition is met the join of pair is a k–item set that contains the common first (k–2) items and the two items that are not in common, one from each member of the pair. All frequent k–item sets must be in this candidate list since every subset of size (k–1) of a frequent k–item set must be a frequent (k–1) item set. However, some k-item sets in the candidate list may not be frequent k-item sets. We need to delete these to create the list of frequent k-item sets. To identify the k-item sets that are not frequent we examine all subsets of size (k–1) of each candidate k-item set. Notice that we need to examine only (k–1)-item sets that contain the last two items of the candidate k–item set (Why?). If any one of these subsets of size (k–1) is not present in the frequent (k–1) item set list, we know that the candidate k-item set cannot be a frequent item set. We delete such k–item sets from the candidate list. Proceeding in this manner with every item set in the candidate list we are assured that at the end of our scan the k-item set candidate list will have been pruned to become the list of frequent k–item sets. We repeat the procedure recursively by incrementing k. We stop only when the candidate list is empty.

Let us examine the output from an application of this algorithm to a small randomly generated database of 50 records shown in the example below.

A high value of confidence suggests a strong association rule. However this can be deceptive because if the antecedent and/or the consequent have a high support, we can have a high value for confidence even when they are independent! A better measure to judge the strength of an association rule is to compare the confidence of the rule with the benchmark value where we assume that the occurrence of the consequent item set in a transaction is independent of the occurrence of the antecedent for each rule. We can compute this benchmark from the frequency counts of the frequent item sets. The benchmark confidence value for a rule is the support for the consequent divided by the number of transactions in the database. This enables us to compute the lift ratio of a rule. The lift ratio is the confidence of the rule divided by the confidence assuming independence of consequent from antecedent. A lift ratio greater than 1.0 suggests that there is some usefulness to the rule. The larger the lift ratio, the greater is the strength of the association.

Table 7.5 Retail transaction analysis

Transaction ID	*Item Code*					*Transaction ID*	*Item Code*			
1	8					26	1	6	8	
2	3	4	8			27	5	8		
3	8					28	4	8	9	
4	3	9				29	9			
5	9					30	8			
6	1	8				31	1	5	8	
7	6	9				32	3	6	9	
8	3	5	7	9		33	7	9		
9	8					34	7	8	9	
10	8					35	3	4	6	8
11	1	7	9			36	1	4	8	
12	1	4	5	8	7	37	4	7	8	
13	5	7	9			38	8	9		
14	6	7	8			39	4	5	7	9
15	3	7	9			40	2	8	9	
14	1	4	9			41	2	5	9	
17	6	7	8			42	1	2	7	9
18	8					43	5	8		
19	8					44	1	7	8	
20	9					45	8			
21	2	5	6	8		46	2	7	9	
22	4	6	9			47	4	6	9	
23	4	9				48	9			
24	8	9				49	9			
25	6	8				50	6	7	8	

Rule #	*Confi-dence*	*Anlece-dent (a)*		*Course-quest (a)*	*Support (a)*	*Support (c)*	*Support (aUc)*	*Confidence If Pr (c,a= Pr (c)%*	*Lift Ratio*
1	80	2	≥	9	5	27	4	54	1.5
2	100	5.7	≥	9	3	27	3	54	1.9
3	100	6.7	≥	8	3	29	3	58	1.7
4	100	1.5	≥	8	2	29	2	56	1.7
5	100	2.7	≥	9	2	27	2	54	1.9
6	100	3.8	≥	4	2	11	2	22	4.5
7	100	0.4	≥	0	2	29	2	30	1.7
8	100	3.7	≥	9	2	27	2	54	1.9
9	100	4.5	≥	9	2	27	2	54	1.9

What does a ratio less than 1.00 mean? Can it be useful to know such rules? In our example the lift ratios highlight Rule 6 as most interesting in that it suggests purchase of item 4 is almost 5 times as likely when items 3 and 8 are purchased than if item 4 was not associated with the item set {3, 8}.

Customer Profitability

How much a customer contributes to your company's profit? Before spending a whole lot of time on customer profitability (or relationship based marketing in general for that matter) it makes a whole lot of sense to figure out who are these "customers". And believe it or not, "Customer" likely means different things to different people within a company.

For example, within a retail bank a customer might mean an account holder; the originator of a transaction, an individual, a household or a family. Depending on who in the organization you ask, you may hear very different views about who or what a customer is. There may also be complexities in the nature of the relationship between a company and its customers. Joint ownership and multiple beneficiaries of accounts (especially in business to business relationships) add complexity to the question. Intermediaries that play a bridging role between company and end customer, for example the relationship between Insurance provider and broker pose challenges to a simple notion of customer.

So, it is evident that we had best figure out what we mean by "Customer" before we get started. To offer some guidance and to make it simplistic, let's suggest this guideline: a customer should be a purchasing decision unit. What this means in the context of a business may require some careful thought.

Once we have defined who these customers are, the next issue that pops up is whether or not we can actually recognize them in the data. We need the ability to say which transactions and accounts relate to a given customer or we cannot achieve an actionable view of their behavior and it's implication for profitability of the company. This is usually achieved by establishing a customer hierarchy within the database.

Creating a customer hierarchy is a technical issue, usually resolved by building a Customer Information File (CIF) which cross references customers—however defined—to accounts and transactions. In many cases we use "House holding" algorithms to achieve a similar matching of customers to business activity. Both CIF development and House holding methods are substantial topics that we will leave to a separate discussion. Suffice it to say that it is very difficult to proceed without a reliable customer hierarchy if we want to measure customer profitability.

What is profitability? What is profit anyway? The obvious answer - it is revenue minus expenses. But which revenues and which expenses to include and when to include them is not at all clear when you take a closer look at your customers' behavior and the business.

Should revenue be recognized when it is received (cash basis) or when it is earned (accrual basis)? Should the existing customers bear the cost of money spent on soliciting new business from someone else? Which customers should bear the cost of corporate overheads? Should insurance claim experience or loan losses, or warranty claims or coupons be attributed to individuals (and when)?

These are not trivial or easy questions to answer. The decisions we make concerning the treatment of individual revenue and expense items will have profound impact on the absolute profitability measurement results and the relative profit ranking of the customers. For example using average cost per account instead of individual transaction costs could change the ranking of many of the customers by three deciles or more.

The other question we should think about as well to ensure that the measurement we are going to build will support the decisions we need to make in your business. In some businesses it is imperative to measure the profitability of customers in relation to the capital resources they consume (e.g., Return on Capital for a lending business). In others it is important to measure profitability over the duration of a cycle that is inherent in the business (e.g., lifetime of a car lease, a growing season for a farmer, a project lifetime for a building contractor, a redemption cycle for a loyalty program customer). There are a wide variety of measurements that may be used to provide insight into the profitability of customers' business. Choosing what to measure and how will profoundly affect the usefulness of the information we produce.

Why should we measure it?

Managing Sales - Sales effectiveness is best monitored through a combination of activity measurements and results measurements. Activity measurements are needed to promote productivity and identify actions that can be taken to improve individual performance. It is quite clear that acquiring profitable customers is a key to managing the margin and the bottom line of a business. Without a disciplined analysis of the profitability of existing client base it is very difficult to tell which types of customers one should be identifying for acquisition. All of the other target marketing information presently used remains valid and useful, however the difference is you learn which customers you want to acquire.

Having knowledge of customer profitability enables a company to manage and compensate the sales function for delivering value to the organization, rather than revenue or unit sales.

For example, while analyzing compensation program for a commissioned sales force it was found that the 100 or so sales people were generating a substantial negative net present value to the company. The solution developed was to retarget the sales on which commissions were paid: the rate of commission was built on a sliding scale related to the profitability of the business generated. The result was a turn-around from loss to profit to the tune several million dollars a year (NPV). At the heart of the analysis was an understanding of customer profitability.

In another example a retail bank found the discounts demanded by one customer drove their profitability so far into the negative ($40,000 on $10 million in deposits) that they were actually better off letting the customer go elsewhere. Situations like this occur across many different industries where customers negotiate prices.

Managing Service - for the sake of simplicity, let's define service as providing fulfillment of the sales promise to the customers. Each industry is different in the way it provides service to customers but it is invariably an activity that provides value to the customers and cost to the organization. One of the key issues in managing service is the allocation of costly resources to customer service rationally.

For example, an energy services company established a policy of increasing the general level of reserved service "black-out" periods to create capacity. This enabled reallocation of their trucks and technicians to more rapidly service their best customers without increasing overall cost.

Understanding customer profitability offers a myriad of opportunities for managing the effectiveness of the resource allocation decisions. Not all customers offer the same value to a company. Why then must we provide the same service to all customers? The answer may be complex in a regulated industry or one with a high public profile or public purpose, but in many for-profit corporations there is really no good reason that service differentiation cannot or should not be implemented.

Service differentiation opens up the potential to treat your best customers better and to save money by reducing the levels of service provided to customers who contribute less to the company's well being. Remember that there is a numbers game going on here: it is possible to reduce service level 10% on 80% of the customer base and increase it 40% for the remainder for the same cost.

Altering service levels can take many forms. It may involve alterations in reward and recognition program premiums; call wait periods; access to privileged locations, times or content; face time with staff; fast-track processing or just about anything else you can think of that might be valuable to the preferred customers.

The key to affecting service level decisions is knowing two things: who you are affecting and how much change you can afford. Measuring customer profitability can help us answer both of those questions with facts.

Managing Product - Product management is as necessary a discipline in a customer centric organization as it ever has been. Product managers have usually been blessed with access to some form of product profitability measurement which informs their management processes and thinking.

What the customer view brings to them is a deeper understanding of product interdependencies from a customer perspective. It is no longer appropriate to look at a pricing decision or a product add / drop decision strictly on the basis of the individual product's profitability. Management of customer value demands that we also consider which of the customers are using the products or services we are making these decisions about.

Where are the opportunities to optimize loss leaders for the preferred customers? Where can we create an opportunity for holistic relationship pricing? How much can we afford to give as discounts - and to whom? Where can we raise prices without risking our key customers?

What are the implications for new product development? These are the kind of questions the product managers need to be considering.

Managing Operations - Operations management is largely concerned with optimizing processes to achieve efficiency and effectiveness. This management challenge inevitably results in substantial change as new technologies and practices are adopted. One of the several insights that customer profitability can provide is to highlight which customers are affected by changes and the risk that the organization is taking by implementing operational changes. This is critical when evaluating risk and when making communications to customers about changes the company is implementing.

Another important way that customer profitability can be used in operations is in the evaluation of which processes and procedures are adding value to the company. For example, processes which involve few of the higher end customers have lower value than those that support large numbers of high end customers. Ultimately operations processes can and should be measured in relation to customers and customer value.

Managing Finance - I am always amused by the budget setting process. It seemed to be a tug-of-war between the conservative projections of management and the Board which always demanded a far higher return. In the end I always found the resultant plans to be somewhat dissatisfying, sort of like a cease fire called because we ran out of time for the war.

Did we have the kind of information we really needed? What would happen if the Board said the objective was to "close the gap between current value and potential value by 10% and add 5% to revenue from net new business". With customer profitability measurement this kind of objectives based business planning becomes possible. It also gives a much clearer direction to management than traditional planning measures.

In my experience customer profitability information has not yet taken on this level of strategic use in Finance. This may be because the measures are relatively new, and adoption takes time. Nonetheless we foresee that this is where business planning is inevitably going to head, because the customer really is the central measurement basis for the company. A company's present value is the sum of the present values of it's customers. A company's potential value is the sum of the potential value of it's customers plus a factor for net new business. In many business acquisitions these are now taken into account as critical factors in the valuation process. Knowing what these values are is central to understanding the real value of your business franchise.

Having understood the customer and profitability let's explore the measurement issues we are likely to encounter in the design of a customer profitability measurement "formula". We will talk about these issues in the context of business decisions, because the appropriate measurement method depends on what question we are trying to answer. Unlike public financial reporting, where accounting rules are prescribed, customer profitability measurement is management information. There are no set rules that have to be followed. The choice of accounting methods depends on the information needs of internal decision makers.

To build a model that will meet our needs, we need to understand the relationship between the types of decisions we make and the accounting choices that have to be made when building a measurement model. If we don't consider these factors we run the risk of (a) building an expensive model that doesn't help us run the business or even worse (b) making misinformed business decisions that have a direct impact on the customers.

Types of Decisions

Customer profitability can be useful to inform decision making in many contexts. Regardless of where responsibility lies within the organization, decisions are made routinely in which the value exchange between customer and company is being changed. Measuring customer profitability gives us insight into the effects of these changes and offers us the opportunity to manage them.

Some of the proactive decisions that marketing managers face every day deal with the allocation of resources, specifically things like:

- Choosing which prospective customers to acquire
- Choosing which customers you want to retain
- Choosing which customers to cross-sell (and what to sell them)
- Choosing which customers you may want to abandon
- Choosing channels of distribution
- Setting the price (or discount structure) for a product or service
- Setting sales compensation rates
- Setting reward programme entitlements
- Setting advertising and promotion budgets
- Setting service levels for customers
- Identifying customer behaviors that create or destroy value

In addition to making these proactive choices, we also want to know what kind of results we are producing. Customer profitability can provide us insight into key performance metrics like:

- Measuring the cost of lost business
- Measuring the value of new business
- Return on a campaign
- Return on an offer
- Return on a pricing change
- Return on changes in service delivery

Customer Profitability Case Study

To illustrate this process consider loan losses in a bank. You know that you will have some losses and you know some customers are more at risk than others, but you don't know how much will be lost, when or on which specific loan customers. Unfortunately it is also a big dollar item so it can't be ignored. So what do banks do?

First they recognize that the amount at risk is specific to each individual loan, depending on the amount of the loan, it's insurance status and any collateral that backs the loan up as security. This solves the problem of estimating, at the account level, how much could be lost.

The second step is to identify the probability of default. This is done using, among other things, credit risk scoring of individual customers. Other considerations like the type of property pledged as collateral and the type of loan and the payment history of the customer may also be considered. Banks mine their historical data to determine historical probability of default for their customers based on factors such as these.

The next step is to identify the periodic charge for expected loss that should be reflected on the account. This is done with reference to the life of the loan itself, to ensure that when all the periodic charges are added up it equals the amount at risk times the probability of default (the total expected loss). Since all of these factors are tied specifically to an individual customer and their account, there is a high degree of precision in the allocation of these costs to individual customers.

Loan loss estimation in a Bank is both mature science and sophisticated because of the mission critical nature of the cost. In most industries a less sophisticated analysis (using a similar framework, however) will prove adequate for measurement of indeterminate items.

An Example of Analyzing Customer Profitability in Retail

Customer value is not only determined by past revenues, but also by the customer's expected future purchasing behavior. This can be measured by customer activity and expected lifetime. Activity gauges the likelihood that a customer will purchase again, while lifetime measures how long a customer is expected to remain active. This would allow a retailer to measure the overall "health" of its customer base by determining profitability and "churn" rate. In turn, retailers could use these findings to determine customer acquisition goals needed to meet future revenue or profitability objectives.

Retail customers rarely ever tell a store that they have stopped shopping there (have become "inactive"). Therefore, it is highly advantageous for a store to know how many "active" customers reside in its customer base, how much sales revenue is expected from them, and what the customer churn or attrition rate is.

A common method of measuring churn rates is by looking at rules of thumb based on recency. For example, if a customer has not shopped for a long hiatus, say for the past year, she is considered inactive. While intuitive, this rule of thumb is overly simplistic in that it ignores differences in purchasing behavior across customer segments and individuals. For example, suppose that a customer shops twice a month. If this frequent shopper became inactive eight months ago, we may still count her as "active" because her last purchase is within the arbitrarily specified hiatus of one year. However, given her purchase habits, it is unlikely that this customer is still active. Likewise, infrequent shoppers might be incorrectly classified as inactive when in fact they are still active.

However, there is usually not enough data on individual customers to be able to adequately extract their purchasing patterns. Transactional data could be analyzed to measure the probability that any given customer is active (the activity), gauges how many active customers reside in the customer database, determine the customer-base churn or attrition rate, and forecast revenues from the currently active customers. Other useful information, such as average customer lifetime (how long customers are expected to remain active), and average repurchase rates could be derived.

For example, segmenting the customer base by activity and value can suggest marketing strategies to stimulate those customers who are marginally active, but who have high expected value. Churn rates in conjunction with revenue forecasts can be used to determine what customer acquisition rate is required to meet revenue or profitability goals. Churn rates over time can also be used to identify and counteract seasonal periods that might trigger inactivity.

Defining a Scoring System Using RFM Approach

Let's look at what each of the RFM variables means:

- *Recency* is the time that has elapsed since the customer made his most recent purchase. A customer who made his most recent purchase last month will receive a higher recency score than a customer who made his most recent purchase three years ago.
- *Frequency* is the total number of purchases that a customer has made within a designated period of time. A customer who made six purchases in the last three years would receive a higher frequency score than a customer who made one purchase in the last three years.
- *Monetary* is each customer's average purchase amount. A customer who averages a \$100 purchase amount would receive a higher monetary score than a customer who averages a \$20 purchase amount (average purchase amount = total dollars spent on purchases in last three years / total number of purchases in last three years).

The question that may have arisen in your mind is how you determine who gets what score for each variable. The simple answer is that it depends on your business model. A low-volume, high-purchase-amount business will define the parameters of the scoring system much differently than a high-volume, low-purchase-amount business. Illustratively, a car dealer may define the parameters of the scoring system as follows:

Recency

1 = Customers who made a purchase more than 48 months ago

2 = Customers who made a purchase more than 12 months ago but fewer than 48 months ago

3 = Customers who made a purchase in the last 12 months

Frequency

1 = Customers who made a single purchase in the past 60 months

2 = Customers who made two purchases in the past 60 months

3 = Customers who made three or more purchases in the past 60 months

Monetary

1 = Customers with an average purchase amount up to $20,000

2 = Customers with an average purchase amount from $20,001 to $40,000

3 = Customers with an average purchase amount greater than $40,000

Therefore, a customer receiving a score of 3 in each variable (333) made a purchase in the last 12 months, made three or more purchases in the past 60 months, and has an average purchase amount greater than $40,000. Obviously, this customer is very valuable to the car dealer. Conversely, a customer scoring a 1 in each variable (111) is less valuable to the car dealer.

The corner pharmacy may define the parameters of the scoring system as follows:

Recency

1 = Customers who made a purchase more than nine months ago

2 = Customers who made a purchase more than three months ago but fewer than nine months ago

3 = Customers who made a purchase in the last three months

Frequency

1 = Customers who made a purchase in the past 12 months

2 = Customers who made 2 to 12 purchases in the past 12 months

3 = Customers who made 13 or more purchases in the past 12 months

Monetary

1 = Customers with an average purchase amount up to $15

2 = Customers with an average purchase amount from $16 to $45

3 = Customers with an average purchase amount greater than $45

The point here is that every business is different and, therefore, you must define the parameters of the scoring system based upon your unique business model.

Building the Model

Now let's get started building a RFM model. Pull a list of every customer who has made a purchase during a reasonable purchase cycle. In the car dealer example, we assume a reasonable purchase cycle of 60 months, or five years. The logic behind that number is that if a customer hasn't purchased a second car from the dealer in five years, it is likely the customer bought a car someplace else and isn't coming back to the original car dealer anytime soon. Use similar logic to determine a reasonable purchase cycle for your business. Make sure you pull the following data for each customer record: date of most recent purchase, total purchases during the purchase cycle, and average purchase amount during the purchase cycle.

First, score the customer database for recency. Sort the customer base by date of most recent purchase, with the most recent purchase date at the top descending to least recent purchase date at the bottom. Assign a score of 3 to the top 20% of customers, a score of 2 to the middle 60% of customers, and a score of 1 to the bottom 20% of the customers. Your recency segmentation is complete. Relatively easy, isn't it? Repeat the process above for the frequency and monetary variables so that every customer is assigned a score of 1, 2, or 3 for each of the three variables.

Once completed, sort the customer list so that the customers receiving scores of 333 appear together to form a single segment, the customers receiving scores of 323 appear together to form a single segment, the customers receiving scores of 322 appear together to form a single segment, and so on (remember that the numbers are always represented in RFM order). When this is complete, you will have 27 total customer segments, one segment for each combination of the RFM variables (listed below). Identical to the car dealer example above, customers who score 333 are your most valuable customers. Customers who score 111 are your least valuable customers.

Recency	Frequency	Monetary
111	222	333
121	212	323
131	232	313
112	211	332
113	213	331
122	231	321
123	233	322
132	221	312
133	223	311

Scoring Approach:
Score 3 for top 20% of your customers
Score 2 for middle 60% of your customers
Score 1 for bottom 20% of your customers

Figure 7.12 RFM analysis

The point of transaction for a retailer is obvious. It's the point at which a customer buys -when a customer opens up the wallet and plunks down cold, hard cash in exchange for a product. For an Internet media company, the point of transaction is less obvious. It's when a site visitor either is exposed to advertising (impression-based ads) or makes a revenue-generating action (performance-based advertising). When a visitor sees a paid banner ad, a transaction occurs. When a visitor clicks on a paid search result, a transaction occurs. Defining the point of transaction is the key.

An RFM Model for Impression-Based Advertising

Let's look at building an RFM model for an Internet media company selling impression-based advertising. First, let us define the transaction cycle. In today's

Internet media environment (which fosters attention-deficit disorder by offering access to mountains of information at the click of a mouse), if a visitor has not returned in 90 days, it's reasonable to assume he is not coming back anytime soon. He didn't find what he was looking for or found better information elsewhere. Pull a list of all visitors in the past 90 days (the assumption here is that your site tracks visitors, most likely through a cookie). When pulling the list, collect the following information for each visitor:

- Date of most recent visit
- Number of visits in the past 90 days
- Average ad revenue per visit

Obtaining the third item may require some mathematical derivations. Multiply the total number of page views for each visitor in the past 90 days by the percentage of ad inventory sold (assume one ad unit per page view). This gives you a projected number of advertising impressions for each visitor in the past 90 days. Multiply this number by the average ad revenue per impression to get the projected total ad revenue generated by each visitor in the past 90 days. Divide this number by the total number of visits. You arrive at a projection for average ad revenue per visit for each visitor.

You now have the data you need to perform the RFM analysis. Start with recency. Sort the list of visitors by date of most recent visit, with the most recent visit at the top descending to the least recent. Assign a score of 3 to the top 20% of visitors, a score of 2 to the middle 60% of visitors, and a score of 1 to the bottom 20%.

Now move to frequency. Sort the list of visitors by number of visits in the past 90 days, with the highest number of visits at the top descending to the lowest number at the bottom. As before, assign 3 points to the top 20%, 2 to the middle 60%, and 1 to the bottom 20%.

Finish with monetary. Sort the list by average ad revenue per visit, with the highest at the top. Once again, use the same scoring method: 3 points for the 20%; 2 points for the middle 60%; 1 point for the bottom 20%.

As with the retail model, sort the list so visitors receiving scores of 333 (remember to always represent the numbers in RFM order) appear together to form a single segment, visitors scoring 323 appear together, visitors scoring 322 appear together, and so on. When complete, you will have 27 total segments of visitors, one segment for each combination of the RFM variables. People in the 333 segment are your most valuable visitors. Those in the 111 segment are the least valuable.

Analyze the cut-off points between the top 20% and the middle 60% and between the middle 60% and bottom 20% for each recency, frequency, and monetary. You will find it illuminating to understand how visitors fit into each of the 27 segments. For example, after performing the cut-off points analysis, you may determine that to receive a score of 333, a visitor must have visited the site in the last 15 days (recency), visited a minimum of 45 times in the past 90 days (frequency), and generated average advertising revenue per site visit of at least $2.00 (monetary). After analysis, you may also determine that to receive a score of 111, a visitor must not have visited the site in the last 50 days (recency), visited a maximum of 10 times in the last 90 days (frequency), and generated average advertising revenue per site visit of no greater than $0.05 (monetary). By translating the 333 and 111 scores into these terms, you can create successful marketing strategies targeted at each segment of site visitors.

As an illustration, following are the cut-off points—the top 20%, middle 60%, and bottom 20%:

Recency

3 = Visitors whose most recent Web site visit was in the last 15 days

2 = Visitors whose most recent Web site visit was between 15 and 50 days ago

1 = Visitors whose most recent Web site visit was 50 or more days ago

Frequency

3 = Visitors who made a minimum of 45 Web site visits in

2 = Visitors who made between 10 and 45 Web site visits in

1 = Visitors who made a maximum of 10 Web site visits in the last 90 days

Monetary

3 = Visitors who generated an average ad revenue of at least $2.00

2 = Visitors who generated an average ad revenue between $0.05 and $2.00 per site visit

1 = Visitors who generated an average ad revenue of no more than $0.05 per site visit

Now that the analysis phase is complete, we can develop marketing strategies targeting individual customer segments to maximize the value of each customer relationship. Assuming that the Web site is in business to make money (if it's not, then why is it in business?), start by focusing on the customer segments that can make the greatest impact in the shortest period of time, otherwise known as the low-hanging fruit.

Increasing Recency and Frequency

One method is to isolate customer segments that end in 3:

Table 7.6 Increasing recency and frequency

Recency	*Frequency*	*Monetary*
113	213	313
123	223	323
133	233	333

Visitors within these segments each generate ad revenue of at least $2.00 per site visit, meaning their site visits are more valuable than site visits from visitors scoring a 1 or 2 on the monetary variable. Generating more site visits from this group will have the greatest positive impact on ad revenue. The marketing campaign should attempt to move visitors from their existing customer segments toward the customer segment in the lower right-hand corner of the above nine-box matrix (333)—increasing the recency and frequency values. The marketing messages employed to reach each customer segment will differ.

Illustratively, the people in the lower left-hand corner (133) made their most recent Web site visit 50 or more days ago, made at least 45 Web site visits in the last 90 days (meaning they visited 45 times between day 50 and day 90), and generate average ad revenue of at least $2.00 per site visit. This is a group of visitors that is moving in the wrong direction. As recently as two months ago, they were in the 333 segment, the group of most valuable visitors. Develop a marketing strategy to get these visitors to come back before you slip off their radar screen entirely. As someone with a background in email marketing, I'd advise testing multiple email messages to various groups within the segment to determine which message generates the highest probability of moving visitors into the 233 segment (hopefully visitors provided email addresses and permission to send email while they were still loyalists).

The people in the upper right-hand corner (313) made their most recent Web site visit in the last 15 days, made a maximum of 10 Web site visits in the last 90 days, and generate average ad revenue of at least $2.00 per site visit. This is a group of visitors that is ripe with opportunity. They rank high on the recency and monetary variables but low on the frequency variable. The marketing strategy to target this customer segment should encourage more frequent visits to the Web site. Again, I'd advise testing multiple email messages to test groups within the segment to determine which message generates the highest probability of moving visitors into the 323 segment.

Increasing Monetary

Another method is to isolate customer segments that end in 1:

Table 7.7 Increasing monetary

Recency	*Frequency*	*Monetary*
111	211	311
121	221	321
131	231	331

Visitors within these segments each generate an average ad revenue of less than $0.05 per site visit. Why are we targeting this group? We're not going to target the whole group, just the four boxes in the lower right-hand corner (221, 231, 321, and 331).

The people in the lower right-hand corner group (331) made a Web site visit in the last 15 days, made a minimum of 45 Web site visits in the last 90 days, and generated an average ad revenue of less than $0.05 per site visit. These visitors rank high on the reach and frequency variables but, unfortunately, are not being exposed to many advertising units. Either these visitors are viewing content that has a low percentage of advertising inventory sold or they are viewing a very low number of pages on each visit to the Web site. The key then is to leverage the affinity these visitors have for the site and migrate them to areas that have a higher percentage of advertising inventory sold. This can turn a visitor from a money-losing proposition into a cash cow very quickly. Note that the same holds true for visitors in the 221, 231, and 321 segments.

RFM Cells Versus Statistics-Based Predictive Models

The Limitations of RFM Cells

Consider a relatively large direct marketer that uses the following characteristics to classify its one million active customers:

- *Recency*, or the number of months since the most recent paid order. Each customer is placed in one of four possible monthly categories: 0-6, 7-12, 13-24 or 25+ months since the last order.
- *Frequency*, or the total number of historical orders. Individuals are classified by 1, 2 or 3+ previous orders.
- *Monetary*, or historical Average Order Size. Three equally-sized customer groups are created: "Low," "Mid," and "High."

The result is 36 (i.e., 4 × 3 × 3) Recency /Frequency /Monetary permutations, or RFM Cells. With an average cell quantity of 27,778 (i.e., one million / 36), sufficient sample size is available to analyze past promotions and construct a stable selection hierarchy. Also, the 36 cells are easy to implement.

Let's examine how these 36 RFM Cells are used to determine whom to contact. First, some assumptions:

- The direct marketer is willing to promote to the breakeven of $1.25 per piece mailed.
- A re-mail is done several weeks after the initial drop, with performance that is 50% of the initial contact.

To determine which customers to promote, historical results are analyzed to develop by-cell estimates of future purchase volume. Then, a cell hierarchy is created, from highest to lowest estimated performance. Those cells that are expected to do at least $1.25 per piece mailed are contacted. Likewise, those at $2.50 or more on the initial drop are targeted a second time.

Consider the crudity of such a strategy. Of all the information contained in the database, only three of the fields are being used. And, even these three fields are not being optimally leveraged. Consider, for example, the Frequency input to this 36-cell segmentation strategy. Customers who have purchased—say—ten times, have been categorized identically to those who have bought just three times. In reality, they have been much more loyal and should be designated as such.

Recognizing this problem, the direct marketer decides to expand the number of categories for the Recency and Frequency portions of the RFM Cells:

- For Recency, each customer is placed in one of seven possible monthly categories: 0-6, 7-12,13-18,19-24, 25-36, 37-48, and 49+ months since the last order.
- For Frequency, four groups are created: 1, 2, 3-4, and 5+ previous orders.

This results in 84 (i.e., 7 × 4 × 3) cells. And, the average number of customers per cell of 11,905 (i.e., one million / 84) remains sufficiently large to analyze past promotions and construct a selection hierarchy.

The direct marketer then tries to incorporate additional key database fields into the selection process, including:

- Merchandise categories.
- Satisfaction indicators, such as returns, exchanges and allowances.
- Service measures, such as backerders and out-of-stocks.
- Payment indicators, such as cash versus credit, and phone versus mail.
- Promotion history.

Consider just the merchandise categories. Our direct marketer sells hundred of SKU's, with price points ranging from $9.99 to $995. Clearly, not all of the merchandise is created equal, and a given customer's past purchase patterns will be a strong predictor of future behavior.

Although segmentation by SKU is not practical, the direct marketer decides to create eight groupings. With this, the number of cells jumps to 672 (i.e., 7x4x3x8), with an average quantity per cell of just 1,488. This is too small to achieve a consistently valid read of response performance, even though the customer count is a relatively large one million. This problem will be exacerbated for the majority of direct marketers that have significantly smaller customer files.

Also, the account manager at the direct marketer's computer service bureau has to create over 1,000 lines of lines of Boolean logic each time the RFM strategy is implemented. After all, records must be selected, test panels created, and mail keys assigned. This, of course, increases dramatically the opportunity for error.

Recognizing the futility of the endeavor, the direct marketer begins to search for an alternate approach.

Predictive Models—A Selection Tool for Sophisticated Data Analysis

Predictive models do not have these limitations. All database fields with the potential to isolate future buyers from non-buyers can be evaluated. There are none of the sample-size issues that are inherent in RFM Cells. The result of the model is a rank ordering of customers by an individualized estimate of predicted future purchase behavior. All customers above a predetermined predicted performance will be promoted, and the balance will not.

To understand why this is true, it is important to understand how statistics-based predictive models work. Please refer to the table below as we walk through a very simple example of how two hypothetical customers, Jack and Jill, are evaluated by a model in terms of their future predicted purchase behavior from a national retail chain:

Table 7.8 Prediction model for future purchase behavior

		Jack			*Jill*		
Variable	*Coefficient*	*Value*	*Partial Score*	*Cumulative Partial Score*	*Value*	*Partial Score*	*Cumulative Partial Score*
Recency	–0.06	18	–1.08	–1.08	2	–0.12	–0.12
Frequency	0.27	4	1.08	0	2	0.54	0.42
Monetary	0.015	$30	0.45	0.45	$81	1.215	1.635
Cosmetics	1.95	1	1.95	24	0	0	1.635
Female	1.44	0	0	24	1	1.44	3.075
Distance	-0.135	2	–0.2	2.13		–0.945	213

This model contains the following independent (i.e., predictor) variables:

- The standard Recency, Frequency, and Monetary (i.e., Average Order Size) measures.
- Two supplemental measures of whether or not the following conditions exist: An order from "Cosmetics Department," and Gender = "Female."
- The distance in miles between each customer's home and the retailer's nearest store.

A predictive model works by determining each individual's value for every independent variable, and then multiplying it by a number called a Coefficient. The Coefficient can have either a positive or a negative sign. The Product is called a Partial Score. The Products of each of these multiplications are then summed to create an overall number called a Score—"The higher the Score, the more favorable the predicted future behavior".

Consider the first independent variable, Recency. Because the Coefficient has a negative sign, the longer it has been since the most recent order, the lower the Partial Score, and the more negative the impact on the overall prediction of future purchase behavior (i.e., the Score):

- Jack has not ordered for 18 months. This is multiplied by negative 0.060 to create a Partial Score of—1.080. Jack, in a sense, starts out as a not favorable person.
- Jill, on the other hand, ordered just two months ago. Therefore, with a Partial Score of negative 0.120, she starts out in a more favorable position than Jack.

The next variable is Frequency. Because the Coefficient is positive, the higher the number of previous orders, the higher the Partial Score, and the more positive the impact on the overall prediction of future purchase behavior:

- Jack has four lifetime orders. This is multiplied by 0.270 to create a Partial Score of 1.080. Now, Jack's Cumulative Partial Score is 0. His favorable Frequency profile has, in a sense, cancelled out his unfavorable Recency.

- Jill, on the other hand, has just two lifetime orders. Therefore, with a Cumulative Partial Score of 0.420, she remains "ahead" of Jack.

Jack falls further behind once his inferior Monetary Partial Score is added to the equation. However, note that Jack has previously ordered from cosmetics department. This merchandise category has a major positive impact on the overall prediction of future purchase behavior. For the first time, he is ahead of Jill, with a Cumulative Partial Score of 2.400 to 1.635.

This so-called jockeying for position continues throughout the remaining two independent variables, Female and Distance. When it is all said and done, however, Jack and Jill end up with the same Score of 2.130.

When all of the retailer's customers are rank ordered by Score, Jack and Jill end up in the identical position. Despite the fact that they display stark differences on each of the six independent variables, the two are equivalent in terms of their predicted future purchase behavior.

Consider the advantages of this predictive model versus RFM Cells:

- Formal statistical procedures were employed to systematically evaluate all available potential independent variables, and identify a subset of six that—together—optimally predict future purchase behavior.
- Each customer is evaluated individually on each of these six independent variables, thereby eliminating the cell proliferation that makes it difficult to achieve a statistically valid read of response patterns.
- All of the database information that corresponds to each of the six independent variables is being leveraged. Consider, for example, Frequency. The higher the number of previous orders, the higher the Partial Score, and the more positive the impact on the overall prediction of future purchase behavior (i.e., the Score). Contrast this to the earlier RFM example, where customers with ten previous purchases were being categorized identically to those with three.
- Because each customer has been evaluated individually, promotional decisions can be made on an individual basis. This is particularly advantageous when a pre-set quantity is available to be mailed. Consider a re-mailing where 51,000 pieces are available for the promotion. Invariably in such circumstances, the required quantity will "split" one of the cells in the hierarchy. To counteract this phenomenon, additional Boolean logic will have to be incorporated into the selection criteria.
- Proper weights (i.e., the Coefficients) are assigned to each independent variable, thereby improving the accuracy of the predictions.

In short, predictive models are more stable than RFM Cells. They are easier to implement. And, they do a substantially better job of determining future purchase behavior.

Financial Simulation

Consider a single promotion by a hypothetical direct marketer with 300,000 active customers. This promotion will be segmented first by traditional RFM Cells and then by a predictive model. Even with conservative assumptions, we will see how an investment of, say, $25,000 in a predictive model will return an incremental $9,000 in revenue and $33,900 in profit over traditional RFM Cells after just one promotional cycle; that is, a single mailing followed several weeks later by a re-mail. At $33,900 thousand per promotion, it is clear that the profitability gains over a full year will be profound.

The starting point for our financial simulation is the underlying promotion assumptions outlined in Table 7.9.

Table 7.9 Financial simulation

Size of customer file	300,000
Overall response rate assuming 300,000 are mailed	2%
Average order size	$75
Cost of goods	50%
Fulfillment of cost per order	$5
Promotion cost per mail piece	$0.50
Company overhead allocated to promotion	$45,000

Organizing these promotion assumptions into the worksheet below shows how mailing all 300,000 customers generates $450,000 in sales but $0 in profit. With nothing left over for critical functions such as customer acquisition, an indiscriminate promotional strategy results in a business with no future. What is needed to ensure long-term viability is some kind of segmentation strategy.

Table 7.10 Financial simulation

Mail quantity	300,000
Times response rate	×2%
Number of orders	= 6,000
Number of orders	6,000
Times average order size	×$75
Total sales (assuming an insignificant returns rate)	= $450,000
Total sales (assuming an insignificant returns rate)	$450,000
Less cost of goods sold @ 50%	-$225,000
Less fulfillment cost @$5 per order	-$30,000
Less promotion cost $0.50 per mail piece	-$150,000
Less company overhead allocated to promotion	-$45,000
Profit	= $0

For decades, direct marketers have understood the need for segmentation. Traditionally, they have resorted to RFM Cells. The idea behind any segmentation strategy is to identify and eliminate from a given promotion all individuals whose predicted performance is below breakeven.

With this in mind, we must first establish the breakeven response rate for our promotion. As outlined in Table 7.11 below, this works out to 1.54%, or 15.4 orders per 1,000 pieces mailed:

Table 7.11 Financial simulation

Orders per 1,000 pieces mailed @54% response rate	15.4
Average order size	×$75
Sales per 1,000 pieces mailed (assuming insignificant returns race)	= $ 1,155
Less cost of goods sold @50%	$578
Less fulfillment cost @$5 per order	–$77
Less promotion cost $0.50 per mail piece	–$500
Contribution to overhead and profit	$0

The breakeven response rate has been calculated without regard to company overhead. This is because—arguably—breakeven is a consideration only at the margin; that is, for those customers who are borderline candidates for promotion. If overhead is not comfortably exceeded by the more productive customer segments, then structural business problems exist that even segmentation will not cure.

Table 7.12 illustrates just how an RFM segmentation strategy works. Before discussing this in detail, however, some background information is necessary:

- For the sake of simplicity, only 10 RFM Cells have been created. In reality, RFM segmentation strategies range from a few simple cells to ones that number in the thousands.
- For our example, the absolute number of cells is not important. Instead, the key issue is how well they differentiate those customers who are likely to respond from those who are not. And, the measurement of this discriminatory power involves a concept called "lift."
- "Lift" as illustrated in Table 7.12 is defined as the ratio of a given RFM Cell's response rate to the overall rate of 2.00%. For the top 10% of the file, which is defined by Cell 1, the response rate of 4.00% translates into a ratio-to-average of 2.00 (i.e., 4.00% / 2.00%). The bottom 10% or Cell 10, on the other hand, has a ratio-to-average of 0.40 (i.e., 0.80% / 2.00%).

Although in the real world one never sees RFM Cells that are uniformly divided into 10% chunks of the overall universe, a "lift" of 2.00 for the cells that correspond to the approximately top 10% of customers is common.

As is evident in the Table 7.12 RFM Cells—as with any other segmentation strategy—do nothing more than re-sequence the customer file from most to least likely to respond. This is why, if all ten RFM Cells were mailed, the total revenue would remain at $450,000 and the total profit at $0.

Notice that the Contribution to Overhead and Profit for Cells 8, 9 and 10 is negative $1,350, negative $4,275, and negative $7,200, respectively. This is not surprising, given that their corresponding response rates of 1.40%, 1.10%, and 0.80% are below the 1.54% breakeven.

Segmentation Strategy #1 — RFM Cells

Table 7.12 Segmentation strategy

Cell	*Mail Quantity*	*Response Rate*	*Ratio to Average*	*Cumulative Ratio in Average*	*Revenue @ $75 Average Order Size*	*Contribution to Overhead and Profit*
1	30,000	4%	2	2	$90,000	$4,000
2	30,000	2.9%	1.45	1.73	$65,250	$13,275
3	30,000	2.3%	1.15	1.23	$51,750	$425
4	30,000	2.1%	1.05	1.41	$47,250	$5,475
5	30,000	2%	1.0	1.33	$45,000	$1,500
6	30,000	2.8%	0.9	1.26	$40,500	$2,550
7	30,000	2.6%	0.8	119	$36,000	$600
8	30,000	2.4%	0.7	1.13	$31,500	–$1,350
9	30,000	1.1%	0.5	1.07	$24,750	–$4,275
10	30,000	0.3%	0.4	1.00	$18,000	–$7,200
Total	**300,000**	**2%**			**$450,000**	**$15,000**
Overhead						**–$45,000**
Contributions						**$0**
% Revenue						**0%**

Although these cells are generating incremental revenue, overall profitability is lowered in the process. We would be better off sacrificing this additional revenue for the sake of the bottom line.

Table 7.13 illustrates the effect of mailing only the seven profitable RFM Cells. Although revenue is down almost $75,000, to $375,750, we now have a mailing that is $12,825 or 3.41% of total sales. Although not outstanding performance, it is a significant improvement over indiscriminately mailing the entire file.

Table 7.13 Effect of mailing profitable RFM cells

Cell	*Mail Quantity*	*Response Rate*	*Ratio to Average*	*Cumulative Ratio to Average*	*Revenue @ $75 Average Order Size*	*Contribution to Overhead and Profit*
1	30,000	4%	2	2	$90,000	£4,000
1	30,000	2.9%	1.45	1.73	$65,250	$13,275
3	30,000	2.3%	1.15	1.23	$51,750	$7,425
4	30,000	2.1%	1.05	1.41	$47,250	$3,475
5	30,000	2%	1.0	1.33	$45,000	$1,500
6	30,000	2.8%	0.9	1.16	$40,500	$5,550
7	30,000	2.6%	0.8	1.19	$36,000	$600
Total	**210,00**	**2.39%**			**$375,750**	**$57,825**
Overhead						**–$45,000**
Contribution						**$12,825**
% Revenue						**3.41%**

Let's now replace the RFM Cells with 10 segments generated by a statistics-based predictive model. Again, the concept of lift will be used to illustrate the segmentation power of the model. As is seen in table below, Segment 1's response rate of 6.80% has a ratio-to-average of 3.40 versus the overall response rate of 2.00%. This level of lift is often seen in models built off databases with a wealth of detailed and accurate transaction history.

Segmentation Strategy #2 — Predictive Model

Table 7.14 Segmentation strategy with predictive modeling

Cell	*Mail Quantity*	*Response Rate*	*Ratio to Average*	*Cumulative Ratio to Average*	*Revenue @ $75 Average Order Size*	*Contribution to Overhead and Profit*
1	30,000	0.8%	3.40	3.40	$153,000	$ 1,300
2	30,000	3.00%	1.30	2.45	$67,300	$ 4,250
3	30,000	2.20%	1.10	2.00	$49,500	$ 4,500
4	30,000	2.00%	1.00	1.73	$45,000	$ 4,500
5	30,000	2.70%	0.85	1.27	$38,250	$ 1,575
6	30,000	2.40%	0.70	1.53	$31,500	–$ 1,350
7	30,000	2.10%	0.55	1.30	$24,750	–$ 4,275
8	30,000	0.80%	0.40	1.19	$18,000	–$7,200
9	30,000	0.60%	0.30	1.09	$13,500	–$9,150
10	30,000	0.40%	0.20	1.00	$9,000	–$11,100
Total	**300,000**	**2%**			**$450,000**	**$45,000**
Overhead						**–$45,000**
Contribution						**$0**
% Revenue						**0%**

Notice also that the bottom segments have much lower response rates and lifts than their RFM counterparts. Segment 10, for example, has a response rate of 0.40% and a ratio-to-average of 0.20 versus RFM Cell 10's 0.80% and 0.40. This is because the predictive model is doing a much better job of concentrating high-probability responders in the top segments and low-probability responders in the bottom segments. (Under ideal circumstances, top-10%-to-average lifts of over 4.00 are attainable, as are bottom-10%-to-average lifts of about 0.15.)

Because our predictive model is doing such an efficient job of concentrating high-probability responders in the top segments, Segments 6 and 7 join Segments 8 through 10 in qualifying for elimination. As is apparent in Table 7.15, mailing only the five above-breakeven segments generates $353,250 in revenue, which is even less than with the RFM strategy. However, profitability is up significantly to $33,075, or 9.36% of sales. Again, revenue has been sacrificed for profitability.

Some readers might be concerned with a predictive modeling strategy that sacrifices revenue for the sake of an improved bottom line. Fortunately, this effect is counteracted in the form of improved re-mail performance.

Re-mailings generally result in a response rate decline, and often at about 50% compared with the initial mailing. With this assumption, the re-mail strategy for our hypothetical direct marketer will be targeted only to segments that are sufficiently responsive to remain above breakeven with a 50% response rate decline.

Table 7.15 Profitability vs revenue

Cell	*Mail Quantity*	*Response Rate*	*Ratio to Average*	*Cumulative Ratio to Average*	*Revenue @ $75 Average Order Size*	*Contribution to Overhead and Profit*
1	30,000	8.8%	3.40	3.40	$153,000	$31,300
2	30,000	2.00%	1.30	2.05	$67,500	$14,250
3	30,000	1.20%	1.10	2.00	$49,500	$4,500
4	30,000	2.00%	1.00	1.75	$15,000	$1,500
5	30,000	1.70%	0.85	1.17	$38,250	$1,575
Total	**150,000**	**3.14%**			**$353,250**	**$38,075**
Overhead						**–545,000**
Contribution						**$83,075**
% Revenue						**9.3$ %**

As is seen in Table 7.16 and Table 7.17 below, only RFM Cell 1 and Predictive Model Segment 1 meet this criterion. (This is a conservative assumption because a predictive model often generates a larger number of profitable re-mail segments than does an RFM approach.) Predictive Model Segment 1, because of its superior concentration of high-probability responders, performs much better than RFM Cell 1: $76,500 versus $45,000 in revenue, and $18,150 versus $4,500 in profit.

Table 7.16 Re-mail performance RFM model

Cell	*Maill Quantity*	*Response Rate*	*Re-mail @ 50 ft*	*Revenue @$75 Average Order Size*	*Contribution to Overhead and Profit*
1	30,300	4%	2.00%	$45,000	$4,300
2	30,300	2.9%	1.45%		
3	30,300	2.3%	1.15%		
4	30,300	2.1%	1.03%		
5	30,300	1%	1.00%		
6	30,300	15%	0.90%		
7	30,300	1.6%	0.80%		

Table 7.17 Re-mail performance predictive model

Cell	*Maill Quantity*	*Response Rate*	*Remail @ 50 ft*	*Revenue @$75 Average Order Size*	*Contribution to Overhead and Profit*
1	30,000	6.8%	3.40%	$76,500	$13,150
2	30,000	3.0%			
3	30,000	2.20%			
4	30,000	2.00%			
5	30,000	1.70%			

Summarizing the results (Table 7.18), the predictive model has a small, $9,000 revenue advantage over the RFM Cells. On the profit side, however, the model has a substantial, $33,900 advantage. In short, the model has enhanced profitability significantly while increasing revenue modestly.

Table 7.18 Comparison between RFM Model vs. predictive model

	RFM Cells	*Predictive Model*	*Advantage*
Revenue Model			
Original Mailings	$375,030	$353, 200	-$22,500
Remailings	$45,003	$76,500	$31,500
Overall	$420,750	$429,750	$9,000
Profit Model			
Original Mailings	$12, 825	$33,075	$20,250
Remailings	$4,500	$18,130	$13,650
Overall	$17,325	$51,225	$33,900
% of revenue	4.12%	11.92%	

If RFM is inferior, then why is it so popular? One reason is fear of the unknown. Many direct marketers are suspicious of statistics-based predictive modeling techniques because they do not understand them. If they have difficulty comprehending what lies behind "Regression Segments 6 through 10," for example, it will be a challenge to explain to the CEO why they should not be mailed.

For all of its shortcomings, RFM is understandable. Every direct marketer can explain why a customer with, say, just one previous order, five years ago, for $5, should not be contacted.

Let us look at few other alternatives. One such approach is "CHAID" (Chi-Square Automatic Interaction Detection). Another is "CART" (Classification and Regression Trees). Tree analysis is similar to RFM in that each node (i.e., cell) is defined by. easy-to-interpret Boolean statements. The technique methodically divides universes into multiple groups with response rates that are significantly different from each other. Below is an example of a simple hypothetical tree:

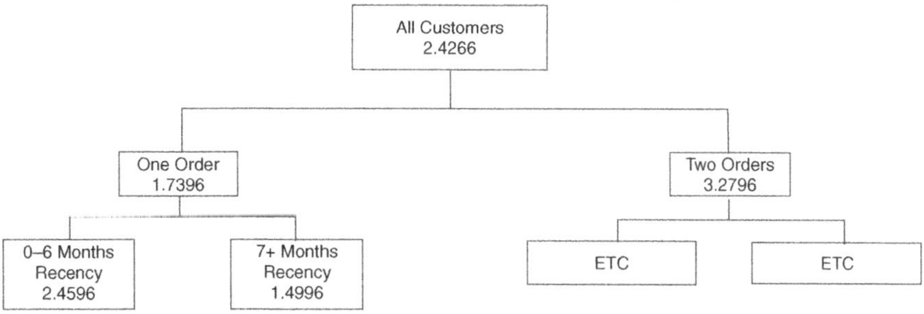

Figure 7.13 Customer universe and classification example.

From a customer universe with an overall performance of 2.42%, the tree determined that Frequency is the primary differentiator of response. Customers with at least two previous orders at the time of a promotion did 3.27%. This is an improvement of 89% versus the 1.73% for those with just one order.

Within the one-order cell, the tree identified Recency as the most important driver of response. Customers whose single order was within the past six months did 2.45%, a slight improvement over the entire customer universe of 2.42%.

However, the subset whose order was at least seven months ago responded at just 1.49%.

Analytics in Telecommunication

In recent years, the telecommunications industry has undergone one of the most dramatic makeovers as compared to any other industry. With the hyper-competitive nature of this industry, a strong need to understand customers, to keep them, and to model effective ways to market new products/services to these customers is driving a demand for analytics in telecommunications industry.

Telecommunication companies face significant business challenges as they expand services. Integration of voice, VOIP, Internet, IFTV (Internet Protocol TV) and mobile services increases data volumes and broadens the need for analytics to predict subscriber usage. Call Detail Records (CDR) often range between 500 million and 2 billion rows a day just for voice data.

More so, there is a greater need to analyze CDR Records to reduce customer churn in the face of strong competition. Customer retention reduces the investment required to win new subscribers and increases network efficiency. Churn increases exposure to fraud and bad debt and reduces investor confidence. Churn analysis is increasing in complexity as business and residential subscribers split their business between several network operators.

Following are few other pertinent questions that a telecom company seeks answers to:

- What characteristics make a customer likely to be profitable or unprofitable?
- How does one retain customers and keep them loyal when competitors offer special offers and reduced rates?
- What are the factors that influence customers to call more at certain times?
- What products and services yield the highest amount of profit?
- What characteristics differentiate our products from those of our competitors?
- What set of characteristics indicates companies or customers who will increase their line usage?
- How does one predict whether customers will buy additional products like cellular service, call waiting, or basic services?
- How does one recognize and predict when cellular fraud occurs?
- What characteristics indicate high-risk investments, such as investing in new fiber optic lines?

Below is a conceptual architecture of data management and analytics solution for a telecom company.

As markets become more mature, competitive and undifferentiated, many companies find themselves struggling with high customer attrition (churn). Companies try to recover from churn impact by acquiring new customers by means

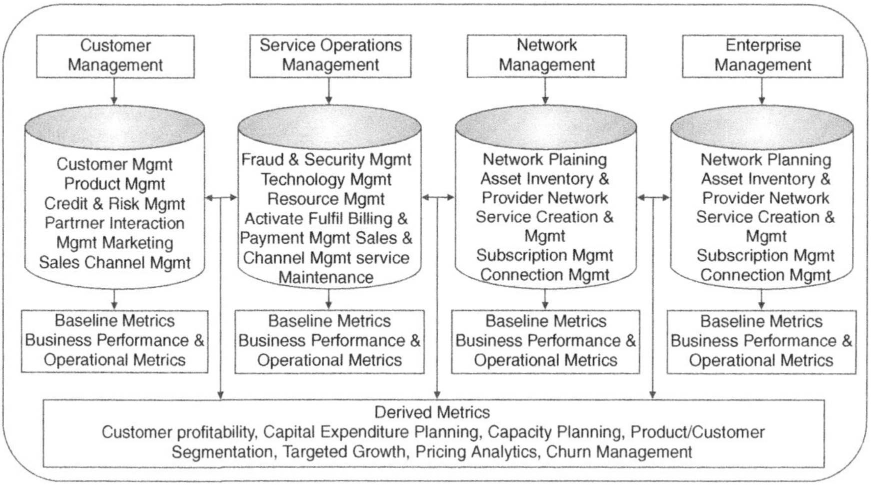

Figure 7.14 Telco analytics framework.

of attractive acquisition offers, which many cases, encourages churn behavior as competitors adopt similar acquisition strategies. In order to address the root cause of customer attrition, it is vital for companies to identify the dissatisfiers. The dissatisfiers may result from several factors; for e.g., poor products, service, lack of trust, company policies, perception/ brand issues or dissatisfied segments and in most cases, a combination of all of these.

Since the dissatisfiers can exist on several factors, analysis of historical data can provide invaluable insights. However, the real challenge of churn related data analytics does not lie in the execution of the analysis, but rather in the generation of insightful interpretation with an actionable remediation plan. For instance, churn denotes that a customer moves from one provider to another. Churn prediction is a prediction of subscribers' churn probability.

When a classification technique is used in churn prediction, the input variables are always the predictors derived from subscriber's demographic information, service contractual information, transaction records and billing details and so on. And the decision outcomes are always the values implying the status of the subscriber in the prediction period—"churner" or "non churner".

Churn Heat Map is a useful technique that enables companies to identify churn drivers in an efficient and reliable way. The technique is used to analyze historical customer attrition data to generate a color coded heat map of churn rate modulated by the severity of churn and volume on a grid of churn drivers and customer segments. The churn drivers and customer segments are chosen from standard attributes in order to address specific needs of a problem. The rules for color coding are also customizable (e.g., red color may indicate above industry churn for a segment). The Churn heat map is useful in customer attrition remediation initiatives and is applicable to a variety of industries—telecommunications, financial services (credit cards, banking, brokerage etc.), media, and many more industries plagued by churn/attrition problems.

A sample application of such a technique when applied to a telecom churn data analytics is shown below:

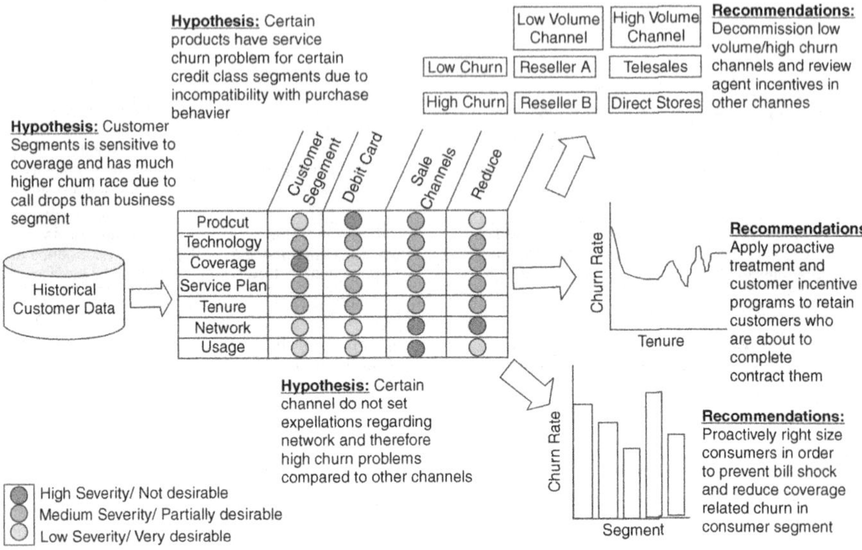

Figure 7.15 Sample churn heatmap.

Figure 7.15 shows the logical flow of transformation of historical customer data into a churn heat map, which can then be readily leveraged to generate hypotheses, which once validated can yield actionable recommendations leading to early wins in a churn remediation initiatives.

Competition in the wireless telecommunications industry is rampant. As many as seven competing carriers operate in each market. The industry is extremely dynamic, with new services, technologies, and carriers constantly altering the landscape. Carriers announce new rates and incentives weekly, hoping to entice new subscribers and to lure subscribers away from the competition. The extent of rivalry is reflected in the deluge of advertisements for wireless service in the daily newspaper and other mass media.

Typically, carriers attempt to control churn with a welcome call after subscribers have been on board for one or two months. Churn rates among subscribers at this point are about 10%. Thus, carriers have concluded that it is profitable to operate a call center that contacts nine satisfied subscribers for every one dissatisfied subscriber. Until very recently, there was seldom if ever been a systematic attempt to proactively contact subscribers outside of the initial few months of service, although many carriers have a win-back group that tries to talk subscribers out of leaving after the subscriber calls to disconnect. Some carriers have begun to look at their churn data, typically examining a small number of variables and searching for dependencies using traditional statistical models.

Below we will evaluate the benefits of predicting churn using techniques from analytics. We will design models that predict the probability of a subscriber churning within a short time window, and evaluate how well these predictions could be used for decision making by estimating potential cost savings to the wireless carrier under a variety of assumptions concerning subscriber behavior.

Figure 7.16 shows a framework for churn prediction and profitability maximization. Data from a subscriber is fed into four components which estimate: the likelihood that the subscriber will churn, the reason for subscriber dissatisfaction given the likelihood of churn, the profitability (expected monthly revenue) of the subscriber, and the subscriber's credit risk, which influences profitability. The profitability determines how valuable the subscriber is to the carrier, and hence influences how much the carrier should be willing to spend to retain the subscriber. Based on the predicted quantities, a decision making component determines an intervention strategy—whether a subscriber should be contacted, and if so, what incentives should be offered to appease them and at what cost.

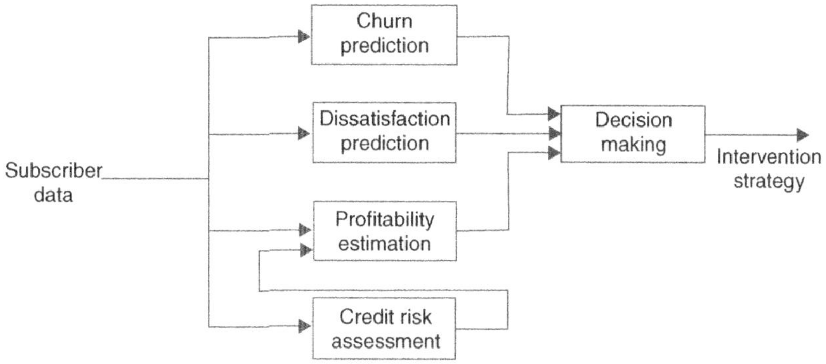

Figure 7.16 Churn analytics and decision making.

We adopt a decision-theoretic approach which aims to maximize the expected profit to the carrier. In this section we focus on churn prediction and utilize simple measures of subscriber profitability and credit risk. Additionally, it is also valuable to model the likelihood of success of an intervention for a particular subscriber, in order to assess the benefit of intervention.

DATA SET

For the purpose of our discussion we focus on subscriber data of a major wireless carrier. The data consists of subscribers, all of whom had multiple services. (Each service corresponds to a cellular telephone or to some other service, such as voice messaging or beeper capability.) All subscribers are from the same region, about 20% in major metropolitan areas and 80% more geographically distributed. The total revenue for all subscribers is $14 million and the average revenue per subscriber was $234. We choose to focus on multi-service subscribers, because they provide significantly more revenue than do typical single-service subscribers.

When subscribers are on extended contracts, churn prediction is relatively easy: it seldom occurs during the contract period, and often occurs when the contract comes to an end. Consequently, all subscribers in our data base were month-to-month, requiring the use of more subtle features than contract termination date to anticipate churn.

The subscriber data was extracted from the time interval October through December. Based on these data, the task was to predict whether a subscriber would churn in January or February next year.

INPUT FEATURES

Ultimately, churn occurs because subscribers are dissatisfied with the price or quality of service, usually as compared to a competing carrier. The main reasons for subscriber dissatisfaction vary by region and over time. Table 7.19 lists important factors that influence subscriber satisfaction, as well as the relative importance of the factors.

Table 7.19 Subscriber satisfaction and influence factors

Factor	*Importance*	*Nature of data required for prediction*
Call quality	21%	Network
Pricing options	18%	Market, Billing
Corporate capability	17%	Customer Service
Credibility/Customer	10%	Market, Customer Service
Communications		
Roaming/Coverage	7%	Network
Handset	4%	Application
Billing	3%	Billing
Cost of roaming	3%	Market, Billing

In the third column, we list the type of information required for determining whether a particular factor is likely to be influencing a subscriber. We categorize the types of information as follows.

- *Network* - Call detail records (date, time, duration, and location of all calls), dropped calls (calls lost due to lack of coverage or available bandwidth), and quality of service data (interference, poor coverage).
- *Billing* - Financial information appearing on a subscriber's bill (monthly fee, additional charges for roaming and additional minutes beyond monthly prepaid limit).
- *Application for Service* - Information from the initial application for service, including contract details, rate plan, handset type, and credit report.
- *Market* - Details of rate plans offered by carrier and its competitors, recent entry of competitors into market, advertising campaigns, etc.
- *Demographics* - Geographic and population data of a given region.

As you can see, the data contains thousands of fields, from which we will have to identify variables associated with each subscriber which might be linked to churn. For the purpose of our discussion, the following variables are selected: subscriber location, credit classification, customer classification (e.g., corporate versus retail), number of active services of various types, beginning and termination dates of various services, avenue through which services were activated, monthly charges and usage, number, dates and nature of customer service calls, number of calls made, and number of abnormally terminated calls.

Case Study—Churn Prediction

Across the world, churn is measured in a number of different ways by different telecom operators. Exactly which definition is used is not as important as choosing one definition and using it consistently. However, different definitions highlight slightly different aspects of churn and so it is sensible not to be prescriptive about the choice, but to choose the definition that best suits Telecom company's specific business issues.

In general, there are three important questions to answer with regard to the definition of churn:

- Is churn counted only for permanent disconnections (PDs) or also for temporary disconnections (TDs), voice redirections (VRs), reactivations and migrations?
- What exact computation is used to define the churn percentage?
- Over what period of time should churn be measured?

To understand who should qualify as a "churner", we need to understand why churn is so important to Telecom Companies. When a subscriber lifetime comes to an end, the Telecom Company has either recovered the cost that they expended to acquire and retain that subscription or they have not. If they have not, then the loss made on that subscription must be shouldered either by other subscriptions or as a loss by the company.

The most important point in the subscriber lifetime with relation to churn, therefore, is when that subscriber will not use the service any more and never generate additional revenue for the Telecom Company.

Few technicalities we also need to keep in mind while analyzing churn:

- A temporarily disconnected subscriber will generate only the monthly service fee.
- A permanently disconnected subscriber will generate no further revenue unless they are subsequently reactivated.

In addition, there are two other important customer events that should be recognized. One is rate plan migration and the other is "rotation".

- Rate plan migration is where a subscription changes from one rate plan to another. These subscribers simply remain within the stock of active subscribers.

- "Rotation" is more complex. This occurs when a subscription of a particular customer is terminated (either voluntarily or involuntarily), and this customer then purchases another subscription to the same service without making this known to the operator as a reactivation.

Although rate plan migration is easy to understand, rotation may seem a curious customer event to highlight. Rotation is important to try and measure, and prevent, due to the two primary situations in which it occurs:

- A subscriber who has been involuntarily terminated due to, for example, non-payment of bills, may try to purchase another subscription. The subscriber may be successful either because he or she successfully disguises his or her identity, or the blacklisting processes are not robust. Clearly this subscriber presents a risk based on past behavior.
- A subscriber who wishes to replace his or her handset may voluntarily disconnect and then purchase another subscription in order to avail of a particularly attractive offer on a new handset. This occurs as very few operators offer a structured handset replacement program for existing users. In this case the operator will pay an additional acquisition cost for an existing subscriber. In a number of European countries this is becoming an important and costly phenomenon, sometimes encouraged by the dealers who gain extra commission through this method.

How exactly churn should be computed?

Over any period of time there is a situation where there is an opening balance of subscribers (A), new additions (B), losses (C) and a closing balance (D). Below Table includes four popular ways of computing churn. As the formulas are different, a number of different measurements can be produced as demonstrated by the simple example.

Table 7.20 Churn computation example

Churn Definition	*Formula*	*Example Churn Rate*
The number of subscribers lost in the period over the starting number	C/A	10%
The number of subscribers lost in the period over the average number of subscribers for the period	C/((A+D)/2)	9.5%
The number of subscribers lost in the period over the ending number	C/D	9.1%
The number of subscribers lost in the period over the starting number plus the new additions	C/(A+B)	8.3%

Churn measurement requires both a long-term and a short-term focus.

- Annual churn measured month-by-month as the churn rate over the previous twelve months.
- Monthly churn measured as the churn rate over the previous month.

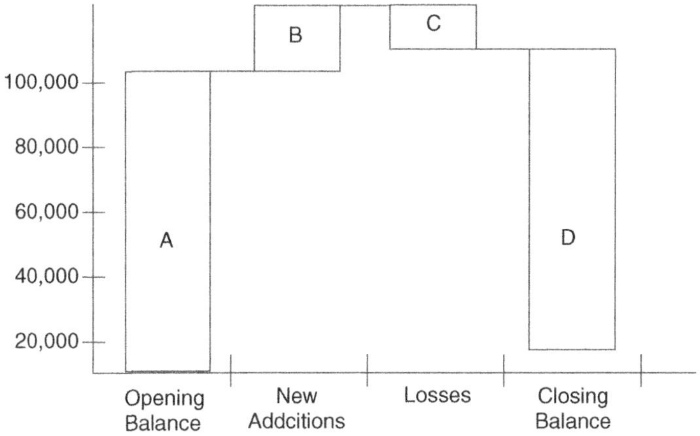

Figure 7.17 Indicative subscribers for churn computations.

The annual churn provides the long-term trend but will overstate current churn if the subscriber base is growing rapidly or terminations are happening frequently. The monthly churn provides a more current view of the churn rate but is subject to large fluctuations and less suitable for analyzing a trend. Taken together, these measures provide a complete view of long-term trend and the most current information available.

It is useful to separate churn into a number of different categories .as each category needs to be treated differently, and the goals of the Telecom Company with regard to each should be different. Starting with all permanent disconnections (not including reactivations and rotation) the first level separates "involuntary" from "voluntary" churn.

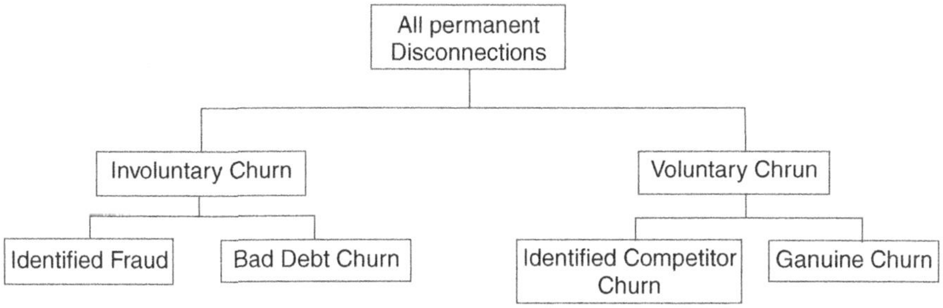

Figure 7.18 Churn classification example.

Involuntary churn is churn initiated by the Telecom Company rather than by the customer. Within this there are two further classifications that are useful:

- Disconnection by the Telecom Company of subscriptions that are positively identified as resulting from fraudulent activities by customers, sales channels (dealers, agents, etc.), employees or other sources.
- Disconnection by the Telecom Company of subscriptions who are unable to settle past accounts. In general this is caused either by bad

customer selection at point of acquisition, or process failures in billing and collection on a regular basis.

The target for involuntary churn should be to reduce it to zero by eliminating opportunities for and acceptance of fraudulent applications, by not bringing onto the network customers who are unable to pay, and by ensuring no accumulation of more than a single month balance for a customer through efficient and effective billing and collection processes.

Voluntary churn is churn initiated by the customer rather than by the Telecom Company. Again, two subdivisions are useful:

- Customers who can be positively identified to have switched to competitors.
- Customers who terminate themselves and do not take another mobile service. In general this is either because they cannot manage the ongoing financial burden of the service, or they find no further value for the service due to a lifestyle/life stage progression (e.g., change of job, moving from city to province, leaving the country) or the increase in a substitute product (e.g., available land lines).

The target for voluntary churn should be to reduce it to the "natural" level. This level is the number of subscribers who are good customers that genuinely have no further need for the service. This means, again, not bringing onto the network those with the likely inability to pay, ensuring that customers who are planning a switch to the competition are retained, and impressing on customers that the service has value above and beyond fixed wire substitutes.

Although these churn classifications are simple in principle, there are three main difficulties to overcome. One is the accurate measurement of permanent disconnections, second is the identification of fraud, and third is the accuracy of customer responses.

In relation to the accurate measurement of permanent disconnections, the major problem is that the number gets overstated by counting reactivations and rotation. Without a defined method for distinguishing a reactivation from a new activation would mean that both permanent disconnections and activations are overstated by the number of reactivations that are made unless a manual correction is made.

In relation to fraud, the problem is not so much with correctly classifying basic fraud events such as falsified, tampered or misrepresented documents, but in more subtle cases. The two most important are the "can't pay / won't pay" distinction and dealer incentive-inspired fraud:

- The "can't pay / won't pay" distinction refers to a subscriber involuntarily terminated for outstanding payment. Strictly, fraud should be defined by intent to defraud; the difficult question to ascertain is whether a particular subscriber had a genuine intention to pay, or always had the intent to defraud. This has the effect of understating identified fraud and overstating bad debt churn.

➤ Dealer incentive-inspired fraud occurs where it is profitable for the dealer to pretend to be a real customer, acquire the service, maintain for a minimum period with no real use, and then terminate. This can only occur where the incentives are substantially greater than the minimum monthly payment and termination fees are not strictly enforced. This has the effect of understating fraud and overstating voluntary churn.

Observe that throughout this section, the term "subscription" rather than "customer" has been used. Individual customers may have many subscriptions and the cancellation of one subscription does not necessarily imply the end of a customer relationship. From a customer-behavior point of view it could be argued that it is better to measure churn by the end of a customer relationship (e.g., all subscriptions) rather than by individual subscriptions. There are two reasons why this is not appropriate:

➤ Most of the acquisition costs are per subscription rather than per customer.

➤ As there are segments of the Telecom company's customer base - particularly corporate accounts - that may have a three-level hierarchy (e.g., subscriptions within customers within accounts), counting of churn has to done carefully.

Let us look at the following details in order to understand the churn analysis better.

Table 7.21 Customer activation details for churn analysis

	12 Months (1996)	*9 Months (1997)*
Opening balance of active subscribers	42,491	49,741
New activations	+ 40,769	+ 65,957
Permanently disconnected accounts	−33,519	−15,482
Closing balance	49,741	100,216
Chum rate	79%	31%

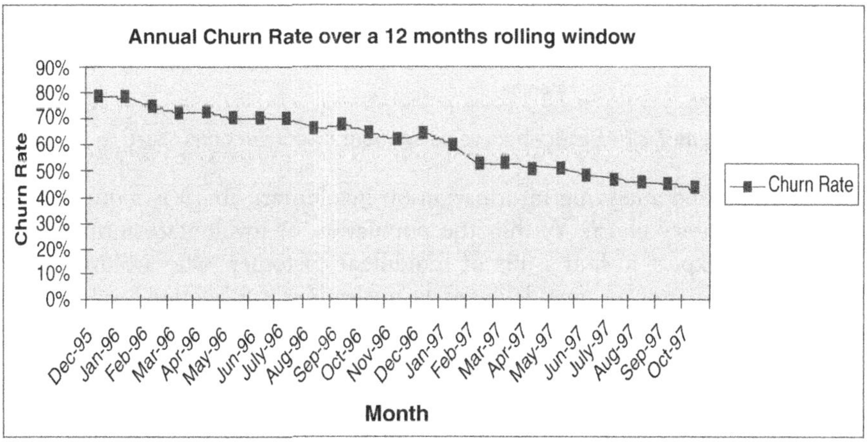

Figure 7.19 Annual churn rate example.

The long-term trend in overall churn is clearly downwards. The annual churn over the previous twelve months has fallen steadily from 79% at the end of December 1995 to 43% at the end of October 1997.

As a hypothesis, the fall in churn from 1995 to 1997 could be attributed to a large reduction in the number of permanent disconnections. However, it would be wrong for the Telecom Company to unduly congratulate itself on this apparent control of churn. Analysis of the number of terminations and number of subscribers since February 1997 shows that the former is flat while the latter is growing rapidly. As churn is a ratio it can be affected both by the numerator (number of terminations) and denominator (number of subscribers). Only major changes in the numerator can be used as evidence of proactive control of churn. Illustration below shows that in the last 6 months the denominator has had a more powerful effect than the numerator.

- The dramatic fall in the level of terminations since last year is reflective of the major "clean-up" of accounts during 1996. Since early 1997 the number of terminations per month has been static.
- The fall in monthly churn rate since February 1997 can be attributed mainly to denominator changes with the rapidly increasing number of subscribers since the launch of Plan 100.

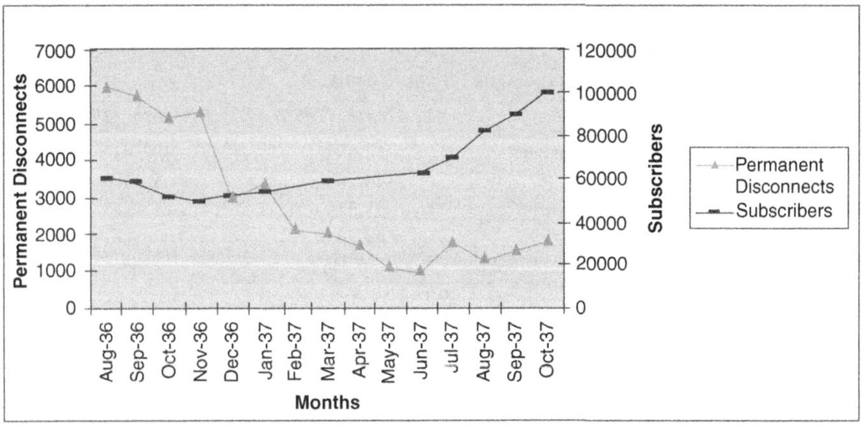

Figure 7.20 Subscribers vs permanent disconnections chart.

Collecting and analyzing information on involuntary churn is more difficult than for voluntary churn. Within the population of involuntary terminations you can also expect to find a mix of fraudulent customers who are unlikely to give any information or give deliberately misleading information, and genuine customers who have been terminated. These genuine customers are more likely to give unbiased information than the fraudulent ones, but are generally not as forthcoming as the voluntarily terminating subscribers.

There are many reasons given by the customer for having arrived at a point where they have been involuntarily terminated. Over 55% of reasons fell into just two categories -"financial difficulty" (36%) and "no bills received" (20%) as can be seen in figure below. A further 9% were associated with some type of customer relocation ("out of town" and "went abroad") and another 4% on "late bills". The remaining 31% is split amongst a number of other reasons.

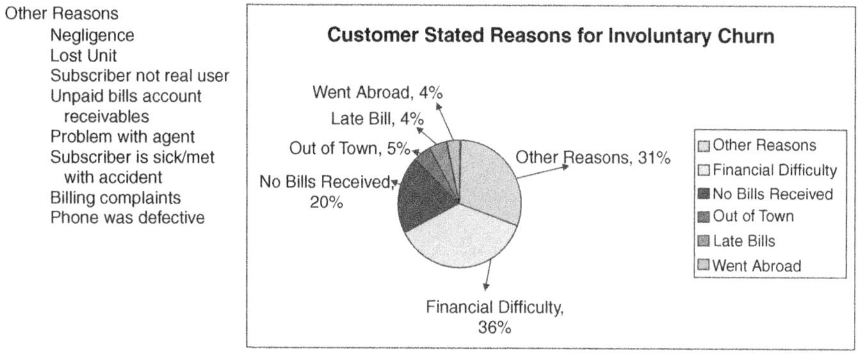

Figure 7.21 Customer stated reasons for involuntary churn.

These figures immediately suggest that the presumption of fault being primarily with billing is not correct. Although 24% report billing as the source of their payment problems, the other 76% do not. Experience suggests that consumers are quick to use the billing problems of the past as an excuse. These prime causes are likely to stem from two sources -poor customer selection or deliberately fraudulent usage.

The information above is also not revealing anything useful on customer selection due to the lack of demographic information. Detecting deliberately fraudulent usage (e.g., never any intention to pay) is more difficult, but analyzing the data from the point of view of payment history suggests that deliberately fraudulent usage is significant (see figure below). Payment history records that 77% were terminated for "no single payment", 13% for "poor paying habits" throughout their lifetime, 6% for customers "stopped payment" after a period of paying bills, and the final 4% split amongst other reasons

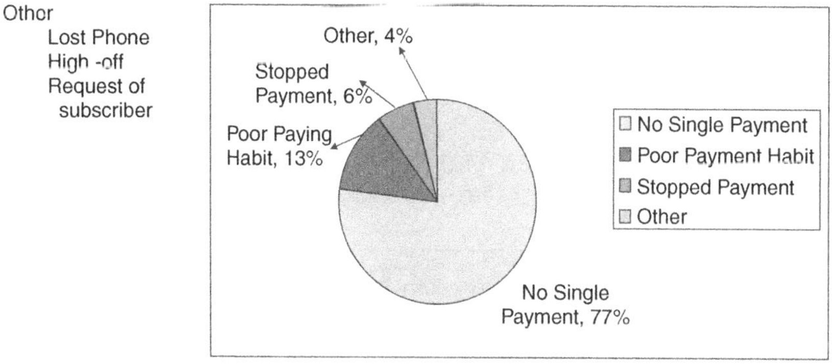

Figure 7.22 Payment habits classification.

These figures are surprising when compared with the customer stated reasons. Table below shows the expected association between the customer reason and the payment history.

Table 7.22 Customer non payment reason and payment history

	Payment History	*No Single Payment*	*Poor Paying Habit*	*Stopped Payment*	*Other*
Customer Reason		77%	13%	6%	4%
Financial Difficulty	36%	Yes	Yes	Yes	Yes
No Bills Received	20%	Yes			Yes
Out of Town/Went Abroad	9%			Yes	Yes
Late Bills	4%		Yes		Yes
Other Reasons	31%	Yes	Yes	Yes	Yes

In order to match the 77% who made no single payment, we have to add-up all of the "no bills received" and "financial difficulty" and almost all of the "other reasons" category. Obviously it is legitimate to pay no bills if none are received, but the other observation—that almost 100% of the people claiming "financial difficulty" as the reason for non-payment had, in fact, not paid a single bill—is a reason for concern. This suggests one of two hypothesis:

- They were the victim of large "bill shock" on the first bill which was serious enough to discourage making any payment whatsoever.
- The term "financial difficulty" is hiding a large number of people who never had the intention to pay.

Voluntary Churn

Across the entire customer base the reasons for voluntary termination fall into five categories. Thirty percent cite some form of problem with the service, 23% that the phone is no longer needed, 19% for a lifestyle/life stage progression reason, 14% for financial difficulty and 12% for other reasons. The number citing switching to a competitor is only 2%.

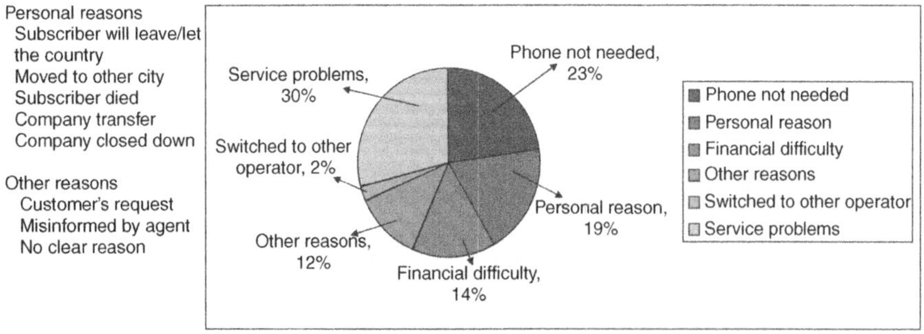

Figure 7.23 Voluntary churn and classification example.

Taking the service problems alone, the network attracts the most citings - 36% of all service problems (18% on quality, 14% on coverage, and 4% on other), followed by 29% citing overall service dissatisfaction, 18% on customer service issues, problems and 7% on billing problems.

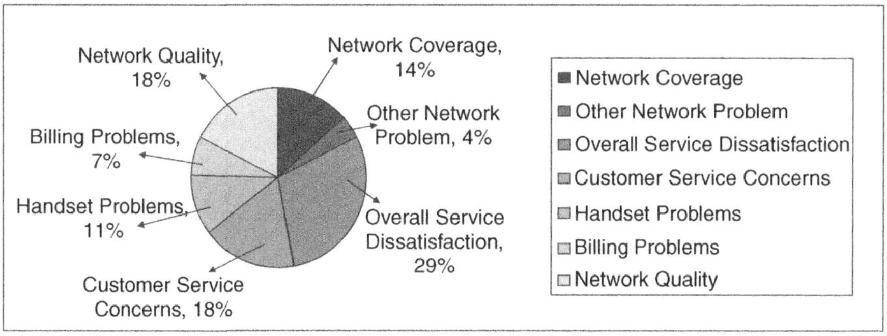

Figure 7.24 Voluntary churn reasons.

Given that reasons associated with lifestyle/life stage progression changes are counted elsewhere, the 23% citing "phone not needed" is high, especially if one considers the number of genuine reasons for this type of change:

- Mobile phone used as land line substitute and no longer needed.
- After a period of time, user cannot find any use for the service any longer.

It is worthwhile considering how many subscribers fall into the second category. The experiences in markets is that once a subscriber has a mobile phone and is able to pay for it on a regular basis, very few decide to give up this facility. There are at least three other possibilities for the source of these "phone not needed" subscribers:

- They have been given or inherited another telephone and prefer to use this instead, either on the same network (a rotation) or on another network (a switch).
- They are deliberately terminating in order to gain a new handset from a dealer (a rotation).
- They are switching to another operator but do not wish to make this known to the Telecom Company (a switch).

A further analysis of this information suggests that the reasons above are more likely to be the real reasons for "phone not needed" rather than the legitimate reasons that could be given.

How would we analyze these scenarios:

- Comparison of retention rates of subscribers as measured by the level of temporary disconnects by rate plan, channel and lifetime.
- Analysis of reasons for voluntary churn by searching for statistically significant differences in reason by rate plan, channel, and lifetime.
- Analysis of reasons for involuntary churn by searching for statistically significant differences in reason by rate plan, channel, and lifetime.

The first two pieces of analysis listed above yielded very valuable information about the nature of churn and customer quality.

Differences by Rate Plan

The retention rates by rate plan form a pattern that would be expected, retention rates are generally higher for the higher-value rate plans. Executive plans have the highest retention rates while Personal have the lowest.

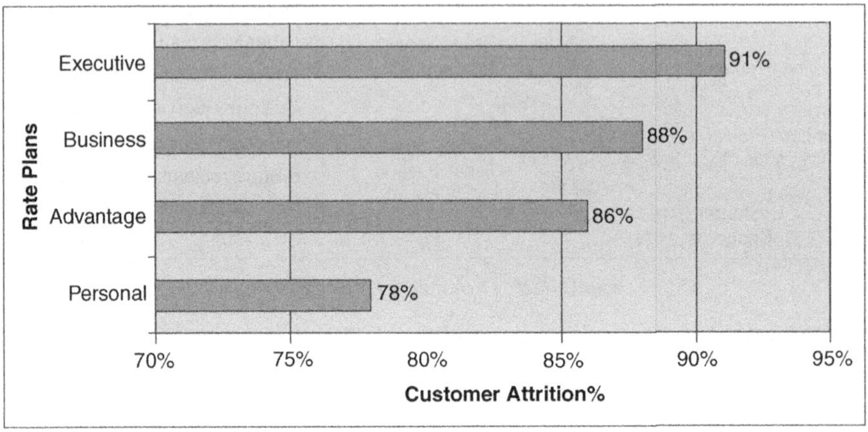

Figure 7.25 Customer attrition and rate plan impact.

In addition to the numbers, there are significant differences in customer reasons for voluntary terminations as discussed in Table 7.23.

Table 7.23 Terminate reason and likely rationale

Termination Reason	*Major Difference by Rate Plan*	*Likely Rationale*
Financial difficulty	o Executive plan holders rarely cite reason o It is above average for both personal and advantage	o A reflection of the cost of the service in relation to disposable income of the subscriber o Some executive plans are paid for by a company than the user o Executive plan users are more aware of the costs at the point of purchase
Technical service dissatisfaction	o Above average on advantage and personal o Below average on business	o Higher quality handsets used by business plan holders over advantage and personal o Better service explanation to business subscribers
Customer service dissatisfaction	o Above average on executive and business o Lower than average on personal	o Higher expectations and more exacting service standards from higher usage customers
Overall service dissatisfaction	o Above average on executive and business	Same as above

It is also worth looking at some of the niche plans. In fact, the retention rates for these niche product types (fax, data and rental) are the highest amongst all of the rate plans. This is to be expected and a reflection of the fact that users for these services are unlikely to be "casual" users and have a real need for the service.

Differences by Channel

The retention rates by channel form a pattern that confirms expectations on channel quality. The in-house channels of Corporate Sales and Business Centers have significantly higher retention rates than the dealer channel - whether they be Metro channels or Provincial channels.

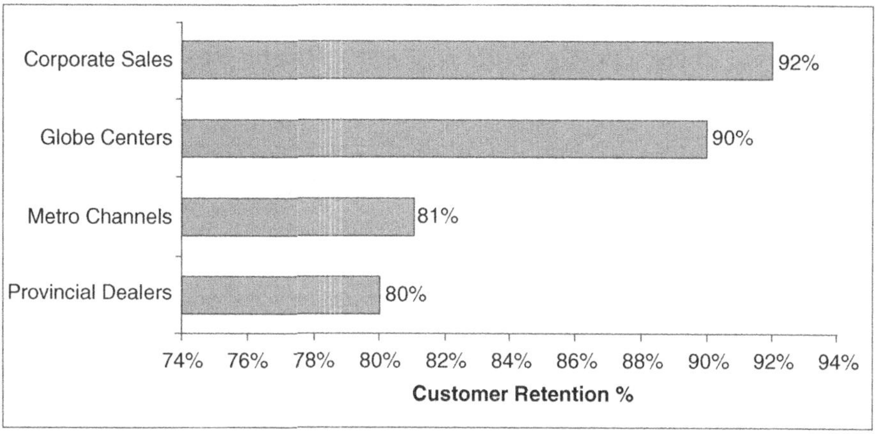

Figure 7.26 Customer retention by sales channel.

In addition to the numbers, there are significant differences in customer reasons for involuntary and voluntary terminations as discussed in Table 7.24.

Table 7.24 Channel type and likely rationale

Corporate sales channel	o Much lower technical service dissatisfaction	o Superior setting of customer expectations o One-to-One training and hand holding over the first few weeks
Globe centers	o Below average instances of "financial difficulty"	o Higher handset costs prevents marginal customers from buying o Superior service explanation o Existing relationship with customer leads to more success in persuading a "phone not needed" customer to downgrade, transfer ownership, etc
Dealers	o No significant differences	o Is majority of sample so reflects the average
Small retailers	o Above average instances of "financial difficulty" o Above average reporting of "no bills received" by involuntary churners o For phones on financing, only 70% returned	o Poor service cost explanation o "Hard sell" on customers not able to afford service o Higher instance of fraudulent customers from this channel

This information confirms the hypothesis that the in-house channels of the Telecom Company have traditionally produced higher quality customers - albeit at much lower volumes than the other channels. This provides one of the main rationales for diversification of the sales channels, at least partially away from a dependence on dealers.

Differences by Lifetime

Viewing the churn rates by lifetime provides insight into the nature and causes of churn for voluntary terminations (e.g., is the subscriber just as likely to churn at 3 months than at 16 months?). This hypothesis can be tested by analyzing the percentage of subscribers remaining on the network at a particular time from activation date as this should follow a straight line if the churn rate is constant.

However, looking at the data over 16 months from the launch of the network presents problems as the large number of involuntary and fraudulent churners during 1996 and 1997 distorts the data and is much larger than any effect on voluntary termination. However, analysis of the retention rates by channel and rate plan reveals that those who purchased through Corporate Sales were not significantly impacted by the events of 1996 and 1997. For these subscribers the retention rates do follow a straight-line relationship with time but also have a distinctive curve around this line. The rate of churn changes over the course of the average customer lifetime.

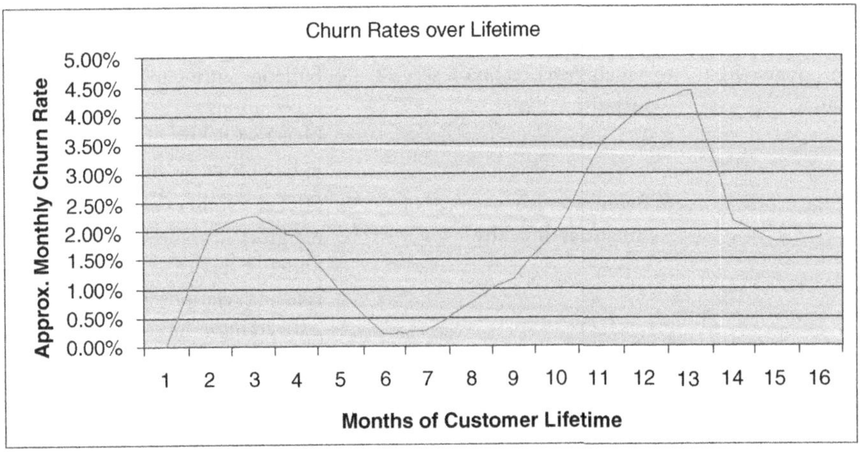

Figure 7.27 Churn rate across customer lifetime.

These times correspond to different reasons for voluntary termination being significant which allows building a hypothesis of shifting customer concerns over the lifetime discussed in the table below.

Table. 7.25 Churn rate—customer lifetime and likely rationale

Life Time	*Churn Rates*	*Major Difference in Reason*	*Likely Rationale*
0–5 months 20% of total	o Very low in first two months o Building to early peak between 2-3 months o Falling to a low by 4-5 months	o Many service related, concerns (network, overall service and handset problems) are above average o Very few report phone not needed or financial difficulty	o Terminations driven primarily by difficulties in using the service (handset, network quality), coverage not as expected, or overall expectations not being met o Little bill shock experienced by these customers
5–8 months 9% of total	o Churn rate gradually rises over the period, but on average is lowest over all lifetime	o Financial difficulty and other reasons are above average o Very few report phone not needed	o After passing the initial hurdle of service reality vs. expectations, users settle into a steady usage pattern o Some users start to accumulate charges and get into difficulty
8–12 months 52% of total	o Churn rates build to peak at 10-11 months	o Phone not needed emerges as the single most important reasons	
12–15 months 19% of total	o Churn rates seem to fall off again to more average levels	o Phone not needed remains a very important reason o Few subscribers get into financial difficulty	

The most extreme differences are noticeable by comparing the 1–3 month group and the 10–11 month group. An estimation of the different reasons for voluntary churn as illustrated below.

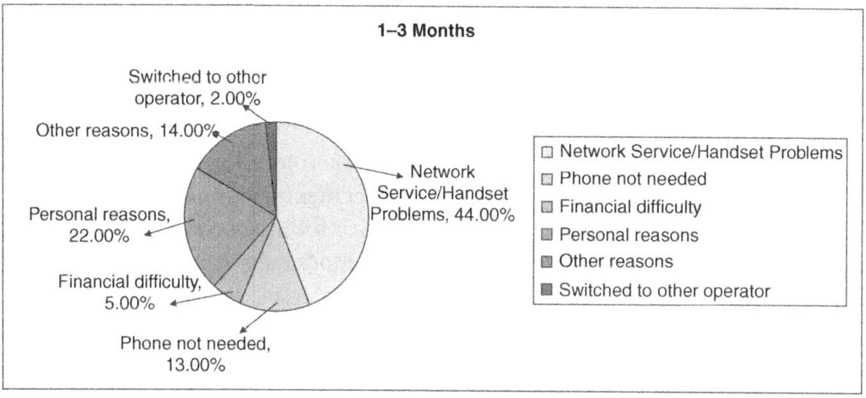

Figure 7.28 Customer attrition reasons for voluntary churns in first 3 months.

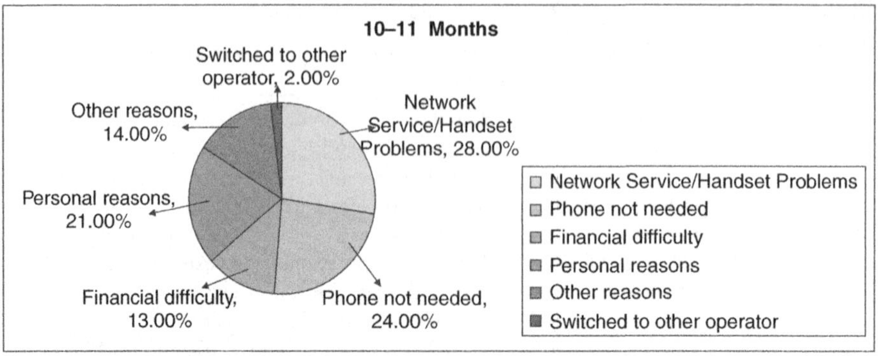

Figure 7.29 Customer attrition reasons for voluntary churns in 10–11 months.

The churn rates and significant reasons for termination over the first 8 months make intuitive sense, that if users are to terminate due to dissatisfaction with handsets, network or overall service then this will be in the first few months on the network. After this hurdle is passed, the churn rates fall.

The peak at around 10–11 months is more curious for two reasons:

- It is not correlated with the termination clause which has a one year time scale.
- It is associated very strongly with a "phone not needed" reason (as is 12 months plus).

The first of these points merely confirms that the termination clause is not a particularly effective churn device. The "phone not needed" reason is more complicated to understand. There is no reason why "phone not needed" should be more significant at one lifetime than another assuming the consumer is genuine in the reporting of this reason (e.g., there is no reason why this should happen more at 10–11 months than at 3 months or 8 months).

The period of 8 months + probably marks the period when a user would seriously consider switching their handset. Given the large number of new models appearing in the marketplace and the associated advertising, it is not surprising that subscribers would wish to upgrade. This is still a serious decision as any switch to a new operator or a "rotation" would involve a change in telephone numbers which is a great inconvenience. What may drive subscribers to do this anyway is the number of promotional deals in the marketplace for new activations vs. the non-existence of structured handset replacement programs from operators. Faced with the choice between paying full price for a new handset, or taking a discounted handset and changing telephone number, subscribers may opt for the latter.

Let us look at the following pattern:

- 0–5 Months : a combination of better setting of customer expectations on service, good customer training, and more hand-holding over the first nine months will reduce the churn due to service dissatisfaction.

- 8 Months+ : a structured handset replacement program for selected users will reduce churn and activation costs simultaneously.

Interpreting this pattern to the whole subscriber base is obviously prone to error. However, the following points suggest that the analysis is of value as a starting hypothesis:

- It is consistent with experiences seen in the market for customer development over the customer lifetime.
- The data for end 1996 and early 1997 covering the first 5 months of more recent customer lifetimes for all plans except Personal show a similar pattern to data from the Corporate Sales and Executive Plan data from covering the first 5 months of these customers. All of these plans show a peak in churn at approximately 3 months as shown by the lower than average retention rate of customers.
- The best fit line for the Corporate Sales given a monthly churn rate of 1.9% is consistent with the churn rates for all plans which is averaging at 1.8%.

Differences by Activation Date

With the hypothesis of churn rates over the customer lifetime, and the number of activations made in each month, the expected and actual number of subscribers on the network from each month of activation can be analyzed. Customers joining in the first few months of the service have a slightly higher retention rate than expected. This is explained as below:

- customers usually exhibit higher retention rates than later customers as they are attracted to, and remain loyal to, the technological features of the product despite service problems. Until the next generation technology arrives, or another company offers similar technology at better service levels, these customers are likely to stay.

The Cost of Churn and Customer Profitability

The cost of churn to the Telecom Company is a useful number to estimate because it indicates the size of potential savings that could be achieved by reducing churn levels. There are a number of ways to estimate this. In addition, there is also a need to understand the cost of churn in the overall context of customer profitability.

To keep it illustrative and simple, let us analyze customer profitability as a one-off exercise using revenue data from one particular month along with actual and budgeted marketing, sales and retention costs and budget costs. Conducting an analysis of customer profitability and the cost of churn requires a number of basic inputs. These inputs can be grouped as revenue, acquisition costs, retention costs, and other one-off costs.

Measuring Revenues

For the purpose of our analysis, let us look at revenues provided by billing for the month of June 1997 and grouped in two ways—by rate plan and by billing group. The billing groups were defined as 0-500, 501-1000,1001-1500, etc. These represent monthly billable traffic (e.g., they are exclusive of the monthly service fees and free minutes, but inclusive of VAT and interconnect payout). Table 7.26 shows how these figures need to be augmented to reflect true revenue per subscriber for calculating customer profitability.

Table. 7.26 Elements for revenue calculation

	Elements	*Used for Calculation*
Revenue per subscriber	Monthly Service Fee Traffic Tax Interconnect Payout	Monthly Service Fee Billable Traffic Revenue Less 10% VAT on Traffic Interconnect estimated at historical average of 25% of Billable Traffic

Revenue Distribution

Analyzing the billable traffic by rate plan and billing group shows some expected and unexpected results. The distribution of the different plans by revenue group is shown below.

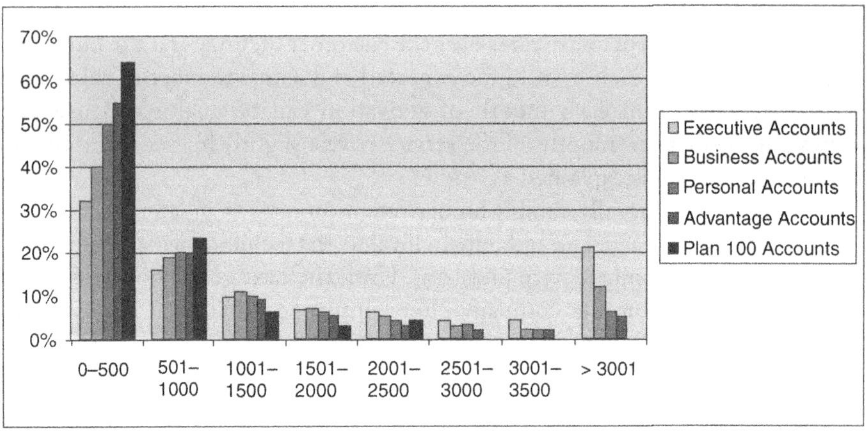

Figure 7.30 Customer accounts by rate plans.

All rate plans show an approximate exponential decline in the number of subscribers in each category of usage (0–500, 501–1000, etc.) as the category increases. Two issues are immediately apparent:

- All of the plans exhibit a rough 80:40 rule or 60:20 rule. That is, 80% of the revenues come from around 40% of the subscribers, or, 20% of the subscribers generate around 60% of the revenues.
- All plans have a large number of users in the 0–500 billing category. This rises from 32% of subscribers on Executive plan to 64% on Plan 100.

The low billing category equates to a low average number of minutes per day for the plans. The implication of a 0–500 tollable revenue on each plan given approximate call charges is shown in Table 7.27.

Table 7.27 Rate plans details

	Free Mins.	*Rate Plan Elements*								*Approx. Mins. of use for 0-500 Billable Traffic*	
		A	*B*	*C*	*D*	*E*	*F*	*G*	*H*	*Per Month*	*Per Day*
Executive	180	3.5	2	3.5	2	4.5	3	4.5	3	0–330	1–11
Business	100	5.4	4	3.5	2	6.5	5	4.5	3	0–220	0–7
Personal	40	5.4	4	3.5	2	6.5	5	4.5	3	0–160	0–7
Advantage	20	7	7	7	7	8	8	8	8	0–90	0–3
Plan 100	10	7	7	7	7	8	8	8	8	0–70	0–2

Where A = Peak, First Minute, Mobile to Mobile; E = Peak, First Minute, Mobile to Land Line; B = Peak, Succeeding Minute, Mobile to Mobile; F = Peak, Succeeding Minute, Mobile to Land Line; C = Off Peak, First Minute, Mobile to Mobile; G = Off Peak, First Minute, Mobile to Land Line; D = Off Peak, Succeeding Minute, Mobile to Mobile; H = Off Peak, Succeeding Min, Mobile to Land Line.

Low minutes of usage on any plan simply indicates that these customers have not found significant value in the service for some reason. At this rate, it is unlikely that most subscribers have the mobile phone switched on unless they are a particular customer segment that receives calls rather than makes calls. However, anecdotal evidence on network utilization suggests the former rather than the latter. At present the reasons for this low usage are not well known, but two points are clear:

- The implication that over 40% of current users find little value in the service is a major concern.
- In looking for ways to increase revenue per subscriber, this group of customers is an obvious place to start.

Average Revenue per Subscriber

Using the information above and the number of subscribers on the network the revenue per subscriber can be generated as required.

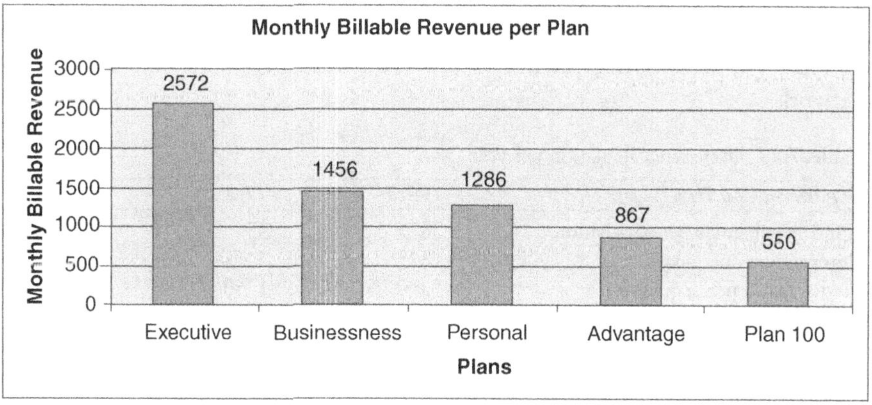

Figure 7.31 Monthly billable revenue per plan.

Information from the Financial Statements also can be used to determine if there are any exceptional trends. Three points are notable:

- Seasonal variations are evident in the data - for example, May and August appear to be "low" months across all rate plans.
- There is no evidence of a general decline in Net Revenue per subscriber across the year by plan.
- Plan 100 appears to have had a steeper decline than other plans in August. However, since a large number of new Plan 100 subscribers are arriving on the network, this steep decline may be an impact of billing of subscribers who have not been on the network for a full month.

Acquisition Costs, Retention Costs and One-Off Costs

If possible all directly attributable costs for acquiring and retaining a customer should be included in calculating customer profitability and the cost of churn. This would normally include all marketing, channel, customer service and billing costs. Network costs would not usually be included at this stage.

Table 7.28 Acquisition and retention elements

	Elements	*Used for This Calculation*
Acquisitions costs per subscriber	Commission Handset subsidies Media costs Channel costs	Average commissions per subscriber Average handset subsidies per subscriber Allocated media costs Allocated 100% of marketing department operating expenses and 100% dealer sales support operating expenses Allocated 50% of corporate sales operating expenses
Retention	Customer Service	Allocated 60% of business center operating expenses Allocated 100% of customer service Allocated 40% of business center operating expenses

To simplify, let us exclude the cost of billing and other information technology support costs. Acquisition costs are spread over all activated subscriptions in that period (e.g., gross) while retention costs are spread over all subscribers on the network.

Table. 7.29 Revenue calculation per year

Acquisition Cost Item	*1997*	*1998*
Handset subsidies per acquisition	2875	350
Commissions per acquisition	1895	2475
Media spend per acquisition	2390	1750
Marketing, Sales and Channel cost	1560	1560
Total	8720	6135
Retention Cost Item	1997	1998
Customer Service OpEx	668	532
50% Business Center OpEx	210	200
Total	878	732

There are two important features of these costs which are immediately apparent:

- The large size of the acquisition cost in absolute terms.
- The large size of the acquisition cost relative to the retention cost.

Calculation of Customer Profitability

The methodology used to estimate customer profitability is presented below. For any individual customer, their profitability is defined as illustrated below:

- Customer Profitability = Total Lifetime Revenues - Total Lifetime Costs
- Total Lifetime Revenues = Lifetime * (Monthly Service Fees + Net Monthly Billable Traffic)
- Net Monthly Billable Traffic = Monthly Billable Traffic - Interconnect Payout
- Total Lifetime Costs = Acquisition Cost + (Lifetime * Monthly Retention Cost)

The calculation of customer profitability is done per rate plan and results are shown in the table below.

Table 7.30 Customer profitability (with respect to plan)

	1997	*With 1998 Acquisition Cost*
Executive	o 100% of customers payback within 6 months o Top 20% payback within 2 months	o All within 4 months
Business	o 100% of customers payback within 8 months o Top 20% payback within 3 months	o All within 5 months o Top 20% within 2 months
Personal	o 100% of customer payback in just over a year o Profitability builds more slowly, it takes 9 months to bring 50% through the payback period	o All within 8 months o Top 20% within 4 months
Advantage	o 100% of customers payback within 19 months o Again profitability builds slowly within 14 months to bring 50% through the payback period	o All within 13 months o Top 20% within 8 months
Plan 100	o Although the top 25% of customers are profitable within 15 months, it takes 28 months to get 50% of the base profitable o The remaining customers will take over 5 years to payback	o 25% within 11 months o 50% within 20 months o Just under 4 years for remaining customers

In summary, as we looked across various dimensions of churn management in telecom industry, we realize that, at the core remains the data and analytics. The better quality and better detailed data you have, the better and insightful your analytics outcome will be.

Analytics in Airlines Industry

While competition is increasing, there is a need to better understand customers, and to quickly respond to their individual needs and wants. Thus, the objective is to increase the share of wallet for each individual customer and save costs by focusing on more targeted promotions. In the airline industry this development is rather at a starting point. Nevertheless, due to frequent flyer programs there is a wealth of data available, which allows the companies to get a better understanding of customer types and customer behavior. Most airlines have introduced a frequent flyer program in order to increase and award loyalty of their customers. The key program features are mileage accrual (members can earn miles for air travel, but also for activities like hotel stays, car rental and credit card usage) and mileage redemption (members can spend miles for air travel, hotel stays etc.). Thus, the currency of such a program is miles. Moreover, the program is also used to identify high value customers and provide them with special services and benefits (like lounge access and upgrades) by the means of a top tier program.

However, since these data are collected only for administrative usage, features like monetary measures, which are relevant yet missing. A second issue, which has to be noticed, using this data source, only part of the current customers are considered, since there are also many customers of an airline, which are non-members of the frequent flyer program.

Business Goals and Business Requirements

At a broad level the business goal of an airlines industry would be to enrich the knowledge about individual customers leading to new strategic customer segments. These segmentation results are mainly needed for marketing concerns (e.g., promotions, targeted campaigns). Additionally, the new knowledge can also improve the customer service (e.g., makes the information available for the customer call centers).

There are several other business requirements, which have to be taken into account. The segmentation must be explainable and the added value must be evident. One key issue is to assign a monetary value to each passenger, which can be used to calculate profitability based on segmentation results and also allows the company to identify core customers.

In this context, there are few important data components, which need to be reflected in strategic customer segments in order to be considered within marketing campaigns.

- Region: The needs of the customers can be satisfied more successfully, if the geographical preferences of customers are well known.
- Market: Based on a sales view, there are distinct markets that have to be served with their own means. There has to be an insight into home market, third market serving connecting passengers, third market serving stopping passengers and other markets.
- Travel preferences: To be able to give customers the right offer, it is necessary to know which travel conditions they prefer.

- Travel behavior: One important information about customers is to know which types of tickets are purchased regularly. The type of ticket is highly correlated with the purpose of the journey, e.g., leisure or business concerns.

Analytics goals

The current customer value of a passenger is based on individual mileage, but it is known that mileage is a rather rough measure for customer profitability. Thus, the first data mining goal is to combine distinct data sources and to derive a forecasting model that yield a reliable revenue value for each customer, based on flight activities and the booking history.

The strategic customer segmentation is a classical unsupervised learning problem. In order to provide segments, which can be explained to marketing experts, let us focus on data preparation and exploratory data analysis. This allows us to identify few but substantial attributes as input for the analytics modeling phase.

We will make separate customer segmentations, to ensure that all distinct requirements are taken into account. The result of this approach is an assignment of all members to a segment in each of the views. Since we will be treating the segmentations separately, we will be able to discover more homogenous segments and the information given by each segment is more appropriate. Moreover, using the results from multiple segmentation views, a more detailed characterization of the customers is possible and one has the flexibility to design marketing actions based on each segmentation view. Nevertheless, the multiple view segmentation can still be summarized into few 'grouped' segments.

The following list gives some ideas about how the input of the distinct segmentation views looks like:

- *Region:* Customers can be separated according to their favorite origins and destinations of their journeys.
- *Market:* Customers can be separated according to the market, they are using, and the place, they are living.
- *Travel preferences:* Customers can be segmented according to the ratio of long-haul (intercontinental) flights to short-haul flights, according to the ratio of high to low fare tickets and according to the preferred combination of both.
- *Travel behavior:* Since the level of the ticket price is mainly based on rules concerning time and booking restriction, some evidence can be obtained by investigating the temporal pattern of a journey. Moreover, this information often reveals the travel purpose.

Data understanding

Given the analytics goals, we have to investigate which data are available and might be useful for achieving the goals.

- Our primary source of data is the frequent flyer program database. In focusing on this group of customers, we have a selection bias compared to all airline customers. For each member, data about demographic figures as well as the current state within the program are collected.
- We will also need information about all single past flight legs, which contains departure and arrival airports, some booking information as well as the member id.
- Supplier activities like credit card usage, etc.
- In order to complete the flight activities in the frequent flyer database with revenue data, we have to assign the corresponding values to the individual flight segments from a sales information database, where revenue information about individual bookings is available.

The target population contains not all customers, but the members of the frequent flyer program of an airline. We assume for this population, the data quality is reliable and the data about flight activities are rather complete. We draw a random sample out of all members of the frequent flyer program database (n =70,000). For these members, we extract all flight activities (about 700,000) as well as all supplier activities (about 300,000) for a 24-month period. We restrict the database to members of certain program countries and members which had at least one flight activity in the period given (about 60 % of all members in the sample). The final sample size is about 40,000 customers.

For the segmentation, we will keep one quarter of the target population for training sub-sample; another quarter for validation sub-sample. In an explanatory data analysis, we investigate the content of the distinct data sources. It turns out that the most valuable information (with respect to the observed variation between customer groups, and correlation to customer value measures) is given by the historical flight activities. However, data transformations and aggregation are needed.

An important issue is to derive a monetary customer value. We extract sales information concerning the flight activities observed within the sample and try to assign a revenue value to each flight activity.

Data Preparation, Data Transformation, and Aggregation

Here we will focus on two examples of the data preparation task. Valuable information about the business can often only be revealed, if subsequent observations are combined. Especially, this is important in our case, where we have to derive key measures about behavioral data aggregated on member level. The success of modeling can only be measured, if the customer value in terms of revenue is available for all flight activities, i.e., we have to decide how to impute missing values.

Considering single flight segments gives little indication on the type of customer and the travel purpose. Particularly, one cannot decide whether a passenger flying the segment Mumbai to Frankfurt arrives at the final destination or at the first stop of a multi-segment journey like Mumbai–Frankfurt–New York, nor whether the flight segment is part of a round trip. However, patching together single flight segments, which are likely to belong to the same itinerary, enables one to get information about the routing and the duration of a journey. Using this kind of information yield an improved estimate of the prices, paid for the tickets, as well as gives an impression about the travel purpose of the customer. This more specific information is even more important, since we have to aggregate data.

The main driver for a successful targeted marketing is knowledge about customer value. Financial measures attributed to each customer are better suited to estimate customer value than miles. This becomes clear from the following example. The price range for an economy round trip Mumbai–New York is 1,20,00 INR, but each passenger receives the same mileage reward of 3,919 miles per leg. The price range for economy round trip Mumbai–Helsinki ranges from 45,000 INR. Once again, the same mileage reward of 1,105 for each leg is awarded. Passengers, who fly business class, will receive 1658 miles per leg while paying 70,000 INR. In the mileage scheme, a passenger flying to New York is always worthier (in terms of miles) than a passenger flying to Helsinki even if the latter flies business class.

Combing subsequent flight segments allows to reveal similar behavioral patterns of customers and allows to derive further key figures describing this itinerary. We can develop an algorithm to identify 'trips': any logical sequence of flight segments belonging to the same itinerary. The member's travel purpose (e.g., leisure or business or mixed) is revealed by the properties of their 'trips'. The fact of returning within the week or stay over the weekend is highly correlated to the ticket price and gives an indication for the purpose. The definition of a 'trip' consists of three major steps:

- Ordering sequence of segments: For each customer, the flight segments are sorted by date and departure time. If departure time is missing, then the algorithm still provides a sensible ordering of the flight segments.
- Rules for sequential segments within one country: Often flights within a certain area (e.g., country) are connecting flights. Thus, all segments sequentially flown within one country are gathered, except certain rules are not valid.
- Trips are only allowed to have following country patterns (A/B/C/D): Most itineraries can be described with rather simple patterns. We only consider following sequences:
    - 1 country - return: A(R)
    - 1 country - no return: A
    - 2 country - return: AB(R) ABA (B with/without R)
    - 2 country - no return: AB
    - 3 countries - return: ABC(R) ABCA ABCB ABCBA (C with/without R)
    - 3 countries - no return: ABC
    - 4 countries - no return: ABCD

A new trip starts if either the rules are violated or some local and temporal conditions are exceeded. The restrictions are necessary in order to avoid collecting too many segments to one itinerary. For each trip, the following attributes are derived:

- RET_WW return trip & trip within 1 week & no weekend
- RET_WE return trip & trip within 1 week & includes weekend
- RET_LS return trip & trip takes more than 1 week (long stay)

Revenue values on a certain flight segment result from several fares, which are published for this flight segment and are usually constant within a certain period. For this reason, it is more accurate to base a model on observed values for a given flight (and further strengthen the aggregation level), rather to develop a model which try to explain all flights. Since fares are no random values, it is better to use observed values within a subgroup than to build a model based on main effects.

To introduce a suitable customer valuation, we developed the following procedure:

- Merge sales information to flight activities: The revenue data is attributed to those flight activities, where a unique match is possible.
- Applying a 'Trip Builder' algorithm to differentiate between local and connecting Flights: The revenue of a flight largely differs for local and connecting flights. Thus, it is necessary to reconstruct the trip made by a customer to identify whether a flight was local or connecting.
- Development a model to prepare appropriate look-up tables: The forecasting model essentially calculates mean revenue values for a flight activity by using historical data of similar flight segments. The results of the model are various look-up tables by which revenue values are matched to flight activities with unknown revenue. An entry of such a look-up table is the average revenue of a certain subpqpulation, determined by attributes like airport pair, season, booking class, connecting flag and round trip flag. The matching procedure is applied in several steps, while the matching criteria are sequentially relaxed.

Model building and evaluation

The main objective is to derive strategic customer segments. We apply a clustering algorithm in order to identify groups which are different from each other according to their product mix as well as to their value, but whose members are very similar to each other. Clustering algorithms are appropriate, if there is no predefined segmentation. We illustrate our model building and model evaluation approach in more details by means of an example, the travel behavior of customers.

Airline customers can be characterized by their travel purpose (i.e., business or leisure travel) and by the type of tickets they purchase regularly. As mentioned above, the newly derived attributes, which describe the trips of customers and are aggregated on member level, give a good indication for this view. Further potential attributes are properties, which are given by the booking process. The objective of the segmentation is to identify typical customer groups, which are similar with respect to the frequency of the product usage as well as with respect to the product mix, but which significantly differ between the groups.

One important requirement for the segmentation is that the derived segments can be explained to marketing experts: If they can understand what has been discovered, they will trust it and put it into use.

The second criterion is the validity of results: the results are only valuable, if they are representative for the complete database and the rules are robust. Moreover, the results are only relevant to the business problem, if they differ between high and low potential customer groups. An alternative way of confirmation is to perform plausibility checks based on additional important variables.

The input variables of the final models are number of trips and segments, the number/proportion of return trips and the number/proportion of within week, weekend, and long stay return trips. Few other pertinent information (if available) like the time period between booking and departure , late business tickets, late sales offers and flag of promotional offers, can make the model more robust.

Finally, the segmentation based on travel behavior leads to six customers segments, which are described in Table 7.31.

Table 7.31 Travel segments

Segment	*Description*	*Percentage*
LS_LOW	Few long stay returns	26.50%
LSWE_MED	Medium amount of trips, both weekend and long stay returns	20%
NO_RET	Few segments, no return flights	5%
WE_LOW	Few weekend flights	8%
WW_HIGH	High within week returns, no other returns	19%
WWLS_TOP	High amount of trips, mainly within weeks, but also long stays as well as weekend flights	21.50%

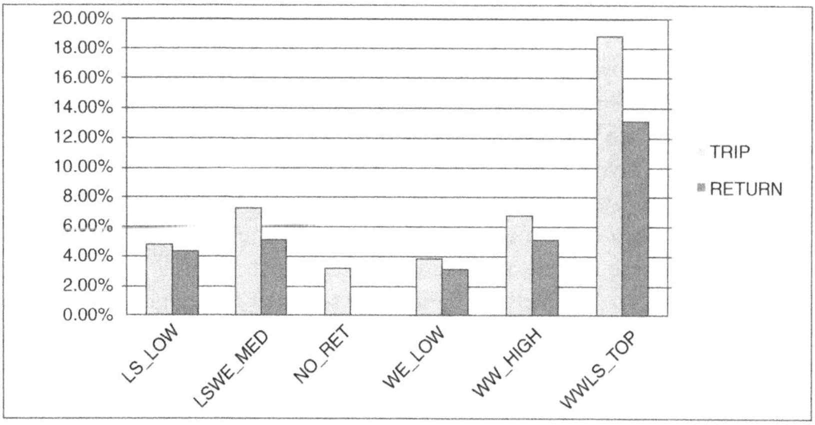

Figure 7.32 Customer travel patterns.

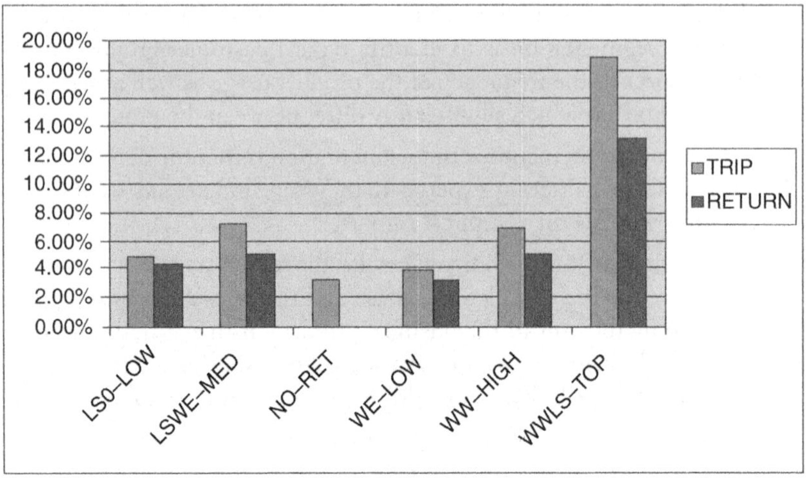

Figure 7.33 Customer travel pattern.

The above two figures describe activities within each segment: Number of trips and return trips and return trips resolved into sub-types (RETLS: long stays, RETWE: journey which contains a weekend, RETWW: within week journey).

The segmentation leads to sensible clusters concerning the business problem. There is a clear separation between the 'No_Return' segment and the other segments, which have comparable rates of return trips. There are 3 classes of frequencies: low (LS_low, WE_low), medium and high (LSWE_med, WW_high) and top (WWLS_top). The behavior is rather homogeneous within the segments. The customers of LS_low are mainly leisure holiday travelers, whereas WE_low are customers, which are exclusively traveling on weekends. WW_high contains the pure business customers. LSWE_med and WWLS_top use all types of return trips, but the number of flight activities can distinguish them. The WWLS_top class is the high value core customer segment and the LSWE_med are the low value core customers.

There is no actual quantitative definition of a good segmentation, thus assessing the groups by investigating their revenue distribution (customer value) is worthwhile. From a revenue point of view, the dominating group is WWLSJTOP. But the segments LSWE_MED and WW_HIGH are also of interest. If we take the criterion revenue per mile then WW_HIGH and WWLSJTOP are highest. As expected, the segments having within week trips (WWLS_TOP and WW_HIGH) have a different fare level usage. Members falling in the segment 'No_Return' purchase more expensive fares than the remaining segments. These are customers, which are likely to fly a flight segment by chance. This segment is clearly an interesting prospect population, since their fare level is higher than average.

If we take a look on the distribution of the type of fares: There is significantly higher portion of high fares (Business class: FCH, FCM, and economy full fare

FYH) in the segments WWW_HIGH and WWLSJTOP. We also compare the distribution of further key attributes (e.g., average mileage).

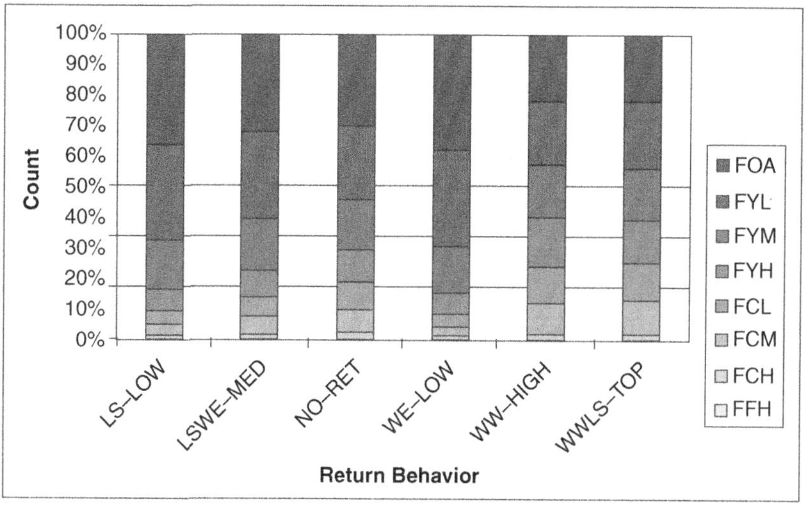

Figure 7.34 Customer travel patterns with return behavior.

Above diagram gives a description of segmentation view 'Return behavior' with Preferred Fare Level (FFH: first class, FCH: business class high, FCM: business class medium, FCL: business class low, FYH: economy class high, FYM: economy class medium, FYL: economy class low, FOA: other fares).

By means of classification trees, we can derive a simple rule set to uniquely classify the data into six segments. The most important quantities that are used in the rule set are the proportion of return trips to all trips and the percentage of within week return flights, trips over the weekend and long stays.

Note: In this case study we have looked at members of the frequent flyer program, which are only one part of airlines customer base. A further task is to find strategies to bundle information about flight activities of all customers. The gained information can also be used to identify future potential customers beyond prospects. A further focus of future work is to develop a monitoring system, which is able to identify trends within customer segments, to discover outliers and to control the quality of the segmentation model. This is necessary, since customer behavior is strongly influence by exogenous factors (e.g., competitors' offer, new travel policies of companies).

END POINTS

Information is only getting more complex. In addition to its sheer volume, its velocity is accelerating, the variety of its forms are increasing every day, and it is approaching quantum levels of granularity. A substantial portion of enterprises worldwide understand the challenge posed by this extreme information environment. More importantly, some are seizing the opportunity to use advanced information analytics, previously the domain of academic research, for business advantage. These enterprises are no longer relying on intuition to fill information gaps. Instead they are combining the analytics techniques with expertise in business process management to make decisions in an entirely different way. They are able to extract the precise information they need - highly relevant and contextualized - and predict the most likely outcomes of key decisions and events. By embracing advanced analytics across the enterprise, enterprises optimize their various business functions. From the various industry specific business analytics examples we discussed above, it is self evident that there are six key characteristics that an analytics driven enterprises employ:

Aware - The enterprise is aware, meaning that it gathers and uses structured and unstructured information from every aspect of the enterprise thereby gaining insights from previously unquantifiable and unusable data.

- ➤ What if an investor could mine every broker's e-communication, each consumer's public facebook post, and multiple companies' annual reports at the same instant?

Linked - The enterprise connects internal and external functions front to back across geographies, departments, business units and teams in a way that aligns to the desired business outcomes. It is able to bring disparate groups together to share and leverage information for mutual benefit.

- ➤ What if an oil rig could constantly "speak" to its production supervisors in the control room, which is connected to the supply chain planning systems, which are connected to the oil markets, which are connected to the pump? Each change in the actual petroleum supply could inform the entire value chain.
- ➤ What if retailers used loyalty card information to identify shoppers while still in the store, and inform them of new meat and poultry products that meet their personal requirements for humane husbandry practices?

Precise - The enterprise uses only the most relevant information to support timely decisions and actions closer to the point of impact and consequence. Information is delivered contextually, providing the ability to act swiftly.

- ➤ What if repairmen servicing thousands of different types of grids had the instrumentation to sense breakdowns and inefficiencies? They would be automatically alerted and deployed based on their skill, location and availability and fed all the metrics, history and solutions they need. Schematics are beamed to screens on their wireless devices. Then their actions and data are added to the collective repair history of the entire grid.
- ➤ What if a large fleet owner could know the exact maintenance requirements of vehicles based on their unique history, thereby keeping them all on the road longer without impacting safety? And at the same time, it was able to use real-time GPS information, past and present,

to consolidate maintenance resources, locations and equipment without reducing service levels?

Questioning - The enterprise challenges the status quo while creating new opportunities. Assignments are rarely taken at face value, but instead reveal opportunity: How can this be done faster, at a lower cost, and with higher quality? How can we make this customer happier? How can we make this safer?

- What if an auto manufacturer could monitor driving behavior via dashboard-embedded computers - and analyze the patterns it discerned to understand what new features would be most appreciated?
- What if a procurement specialist could initiate comparative audits of suppliers' quotes when sensing that their proposals are "too good to be true" and then, based on audit results, provide new guidelines for responsible pricing levels in specific geographic regions?

Empowering - The enterprise enables and extends employees' insight and reach, as well as the authority to decide and act. As automation takes care of more and more routine decision making, employees are trusted with the authority to make higher-value decisions and act on them.

- What if a service agent knew how to, and was able to, go above and beyond the norm to delight a top customer who had two bad experiences in the last week?
- What if large, multidisciplinary teams of sales people could close the next big multimillion dollar deal in hours instead of months because they can reconfigure complicated schedules of prices and resources over years of contract length?

Anticipating - The enterprise predicts and prepares for the future. Instead of just reacting to or correcting actions, it also steers and evaluates trade-offs. The future is modeled and simulated based on a rich history of past events and external insights.

- What if an international trade operation could orchestrate and dynamically reroute shipments based on its ability to model and predict global weather patterns?
- What if human resource managers had the insight and capability to hire and train entire work forces in enough time to meet sudden waves of demand, but not a second earlier?

REFERENCES

Olivia Parr Rud: "*Data Mining Cookbook: Modeling data for Marketing, Risk and Customer Relationship Management*" Wiley.

Larry E Rosenberger, John Nash, Ann Graham: *The Deciding Factor: The Power of Analytics to Make Every Decision a Winner.* Jossey-Bass.

CHAPTER 8

PUTTING IT TOGETHER—INTEGRATED VIEW OF CUSTOMERS

Taking customers to a higher level of responsiveness and profitability by rendering a truly integrated view of each and every relationship requires more than a CRM and Data Warehousing solution; it requires to be driven by analytics.

INTRODUCTION

Over the years companies have invested in enterprise scale CRM applications and also implemented enterprise data warehouses. The objective behind these massive undertakings was to ensure the business and decision makers have a single source of truth enabling their marketing, sales and customer service strategies; but the central problem remains: neither operational CRM databases nor data warehouses meet the needs of a holistic marketing, sales or customer service agenda. Most CRM database implementations are channel-specific; most data warehouses are not channel-centric, and they are not customer-centric either. No CRM database integrates everything you need to know about your customers – their interactions, the products and services they've purchased and the channels they've used—at the exact moment when you need to know it.

The result? Unused data and lost opportunities. The missing link is an Integrated View of Customers (IVoC) which would serve as the touch point for all interactions a company has with its customers. This capability is essential for companies to realize better value from their existing CRM and Data Warehousing investments.

Integrated View of Customer is an enabling business capability that supplies the missing link for CRM implementations—the connection between customer interaction channels and customer strategy. IVoC brings together demographic, behavioral, and contact data for analysis and customer scoring. It also makes those customers and their scores available to, for example, the brokerage's website and email system for outbound campaign execution.

Equally important, as companies feel their way through initiatives meant to extend CRM value across channels and product lines, they loose focus on a key ingredient – the context. Defined as the intent or purpose of the customer interaction, context determines how all of these interactions work together to shape a customer's overall experience with a company. For example, call centers gain access to email addresses captured on the Web, and the website gains access to customer service contact data stored in the call center system. This seamless integration and sharing of data across various customer interaction channels is a key to optimized customer interaction strategy and hence context is required to translate customer strategy into action. To achieve an IVoC, a company's customer contact channels should be connected together to ensure that contact history, transaction history, demographic data, and preferences are available as needed across all channels. In addition, key information required to generate customer insight needs to be captured and made available to customer insight functions, such as analytics and campaign management, in a timely manner. Finally, campaigns and offers intended to shape customer interactions need to be delivered back to contact channels such as the sales force, call centers, and the Web.

An IVoC capability that will provide this context is composed of:

- Customer contact and marketing processes that are linked to ensure that customer insight can be generated and leveraged by the customer contact channels.
- Technologies that deliver the required data to the right business function on a continual, real-time basis.
- An organization and governance model, enabled by technology that can apply the customer strategy across business units and contact channels.

An IVoC capability is essential to ensure that the right data is delivered to the right business functions at the right time to help shape subsequent customer interactions. Not all customer data need to be accessible to all processes at all times—only meaningful data, delivered just in time. This is a far cry from the traditional data warehousing approaches. In fact, the IVoC capability is the third stage in the evolution of data warehousing.

The first stage, which came into being in the 1980s, highlighted virtual information access. It provided for online access to business information contained in systems of record. However, this approach was characterized by poor performance and inadequate data availability. Systems typically were locked down and inaccessible, except for night time batch reporting. Online query and reporting software was limited. No architecture was available to support the concept, and no methodology or process existed for building such a system. Finally, no solution could be found to the problem of inconsistent data across multiple systems.

In an attempt to correct these deficiencies, a data warehousing methodology emerged in the 1990s. Like any evolutionary process, this step solved previous problems but created new side effects. Data warehousing methodology insisted that companies define specific business problems in the form of KPIs/Reports etc. upfront. This approach helped guarantee business value, performance and availability for known questions. However, due to the time-intensive and capital-intensive nature of this approach, flexibility to deal with day-to-day issues and answering business problems, real time became a larger challenge. The primary reason was that data were delivered as snapshots—one point in time, they were processed through a lengthy batch cycle, reports were refreshed consuming some more time. Thus the overall solution, in the form of delivered answers to known business questions, created a time lag between the event happening and decision making. As businesses took new directions and users changed their minds about what types of questions they wished to ask, data warehouses were slow to respond and required ever-larger development efforts.

The ultimate example of business users changing their minds occurs when they become customer-centric. This represented a huge process shift for businesses and often invalidated existing data warehouses that were built to be product-centric. Moreover, this process change brought with it two new requirements that traditional data warehouses were ill equipped to satisfy—value and speed. Data warehouses must be constructed more quickly, with less investment, and be flexible as businesses' customer-centric needs change. Analytical results must be fed back into interaction systems so they can deliver value by shaping the customer experience. A real-time feedback loop was never a requirement before, but it became a necessity now.

As the next stage of evolution, IVoC as a business capability looked into three vital components that would produce the business value and speed that a customer-centric business strategy required:

- *Data* – includes the information required about the customer to extend CRM solutions across contact channels or product lines within the enterprise.
- *Rules* - are the instructions for using the data to shape the next interaction with the customer. Rules define what you do with the information after it is warehoused.
- *Context* - is the translation of company's customer strategy into rules meant to deliver that strategy.

Let's look at the significance of these three components:

Data—A wide variety of data is required to drive CRM value and provide an IVoC. More is not necessarily better, however. What you really want your IVoC capability to enable is delivery of the right data to ensure the desired customer experience across channels. For instance, if preliminary analysis shows that an e-mail address plays no part in customer segmentation or is not used in any channel other than the Web, then it is unlikely that you will want to store that attribute in your IVoC data architecture. You also should consider how the data could best be organized. Information required to drive customer interactions, such as demographic updates, will require an interactive data architecture. The data required for generating customer insight also will need to be accessed by data mining and analytic tools. In addition, the quality of data and privacy issues must be considered. Bad data draw wrong inferences. Hence it is extremely important for the IVoC data architecture to ensure high data quality.

Timing is another important consideration. For example, some businesses would find significant value in receiving real-time updates as customers log complaints. Complaint data would help drive real-time analytics and effect customer treatments applied in real time at the point of interaction. Another example: information shared between two customer contact channels is very often required in near real time, as a customer may use both a call center or a Web site within minutes of each other.

Rules—The rules required for an IVoC capability come in two primary forms—personalization and data transformation. Importantly, their development should be considered a business function and not simply delegated to IT department. Why? Most rules are manifestation of business objectives, decisions and requirements rather than technical implications of those requirements. At a broad level there are two types of rules:

- Personalisation rules shape each customer interaction. They provide for consistent, timely, and relevant individualized interactions and offer across multiple customers touch points. Personalization rules govern what information is "pushed" to customers and how customer information is collected.
- Data transformation rules, on the other hand, govern non-customer-facing activity. They provide for a similarly important business function: integrating customer data from disparate source systems, enriching in-house data with external data, data de-duplication—if there are multiple occurrences of the same data, then which one to keep as the survivor and which ones to drop, etc.

Both forms of rules—personalization and data transformation—are most effective when they address the broadest possible set of scenarios.

Context—Context is the most critical component of IVoC. You can ensure you have got all the required data. You can also work with business to create an exhaustive set of business rules. However if you do not have the context associated with the data and/or business rules, your customer interactions will be lacking insight. Two facets of context are especially important:

- A holistic understanding of all the potential customer interactions within an organization, the events that make up those interactions, and how the outcome of each interaction affects subsequent interactions or the overall customer relationship.
- The reason why a rule is being implemented or a decision is being made. To better understand the critical importance of context, let us look at a brokerage example. Automated stock alerts sent by a brokerage to PDAs—cell phones or pagers may have the unintended effect of driving trading requests to a call center if convenient Web connections are not available at the time customers receive the trading message. The call center, not anticipating such peaks, may experience reduced service levels at the very moment their customers desire and expect immediate attention. After

all, it was the brokerage that notified them, not the other way around. It is at this touch point that context becomes real and urgent.

In addition, the purpose of each rule needs to be determined. As more and more rules governing interactions and data transformation are implemented across the enterprise, it is important to understand the intended effect. Which rules are meant to contribute to which dimension of the customer strategy—acquisition, cross-selling or retention? As the strategy is defined, rules should be defined for each of the dimensions. For instance, an up-selling rule implemented as part of a direct mail campaign for an automotive manufacturer may actually cannibalize a retention program currently in place at the customer service center. The company's IVoC capability should provide awareness of this conundrum and the ultimate long-term strategy. This goal is the manifestation of context, which governs which of these rules should take precedence at any given time.

BUILDING A CUSTOMER INTELLIGENCE SOLUTION

Let us look at few more examples, before we dive deep into how to build a customer intelligence solution and IVoC Capabilities.

Jason just finished his graduation and is planning to buy a new car. If you knew Jason's life stage and likely next service need, and made that information available across channels, the call center rep he calls with questions about his credit card account could talk with him about auto loans. His statements, the site, and ATMs could reinforce this message.

James has been a very profitable customer for years. However due to unforeseen circumstances he has been delinquent in few of his credit payments. From your records you can also see James has setup a new business initiative which has a great potential to capture an emerging market. Hence he needs a relaxed payment option for coming 3 months. If you knew which of your customers were profitable, and which were likely to become profitable in response to marketing triggers, you could make customized pricing decisions rationally and communicate them consistently to customers like James.

Lynda has several stock options from her company and the options are about to vest. She is not a pro in this area. She has visited your investment advisory cite multiple times over the last few weeks and has not made any decision yet. Clearly she needs help to make the right investment decisions. If you understood Lynda's value and your share of that value, you could proactively engage with her to make sure that she knows about your investment expertise and alternatives. Bankers and brokers could reach out to her with relevant offerings, and qualified service representatives could help to deepen her relationship as she interacts with the organization. As she used your online options calculator, you could serve her updated information about your offerings.

Richard has received a bonus of $5000. His savings account is at a steady state. It seems he has surplus fund. His life style is not that extravagant, and recently he contacted your relationship manager, and has been asking questions about investment options. If you knew Richard's value to your company, and understood that he was highly likely to move his money to the competition, you could make him a priority for targeted retention efforts. Knowing his likely next service need, you would understand what to offer, to make you more valuable to him, and him more valuable to you.

The above examples are clearly indicating the need for an integrated view of customer across channels. Now let us look at the following questions:

- Customer Relationship
    - Can you consistently identify a customer on any channel?
    - Can you share customer contacts across channels?
    - Can you share a customer's business transactions across channels?
    - Can Customer Service Representatives (CSRs) view a customer's entire book of business?
    - Can Marketing analyze a customer's entire book of business?
    - Can Marketing analyze complete and consistent attitudinal and behavioral data for a customer?
    - Can you run an integrated multi-channel campaign in real time?
    - Can you provide a differentiated level of service based on who is calling?
    - How many callers can a CSR accurately identify?
    - How many times does a CSR have to enter in the customer number?
    - Do your CSRs know the customers' Web preferences?
    - How many of your customers use two or more channels to interact with you?
    - How much revenue is generated from a cross-sell by a CSR?
    - Can you cross-sell and up-sell on the Web?
- Customer Data
    - Do you have the right kind of data? Is there enough information and is it rich enough? Could it move a metric, such as revenue per call?
    - Where does all your customer data reside? Is information in the right places?
    - What information is duplicated in multiple databases? How many databases?
    - Is information easy to access for CSRs, marketers and others who need to use it?
    - Of the shared information available, how much is being used? For example, are CSRs using the data available?
    - When the shared information is used, how are revenues affected?
- Rules

(Instructions for using the data to shape the next customer interaction)

- Are the rules consistent across multiple channels?

- Can you deliver a consistent message across all your customer interaction channels?
- How many systems store rules that govern customer interactions?
- How many systems store rules that unify customer data?

➤ Context

(Translating your customer strategy)

- Are you meeting the goals set forth in your customer strategy?
- Are you experiencing undesirable side effects from your campaigns?

If you do not have answers to the above questions, it is high time that you need to focus on building a customer intelligence solution and IVoC capabilities. In the sections below, we will look at the various aspects of building a customer intelligence solution.

Business Requirements

Let us discuss the common considerations and factors which go into IVoC-specific business requirements. At a broad level these requirements drive the technical solution development, which we will discuss later in this section.

Figure 8.1 provides a holistic view of customer across channels and also recommends what are the next steps. Ideally, this is what a business requirement should look like. However, every business will have its own peculiarity, and hence it is prudent to outline some of the commonly seen business requirements.

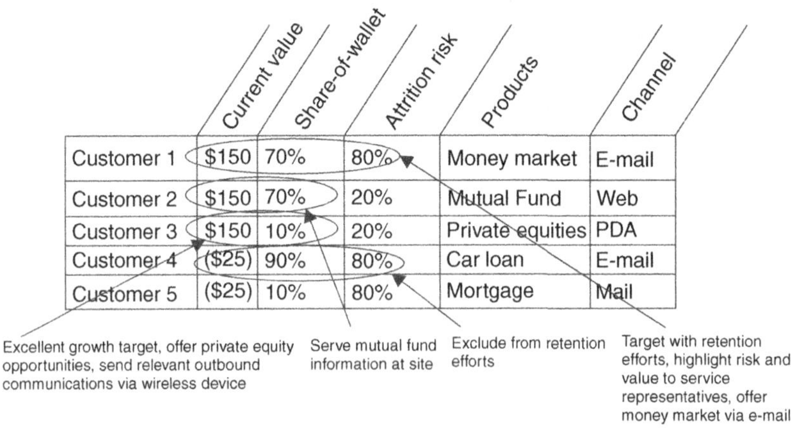

Figure 8.1 Customer-centric view across several portfolios.

IVoC solutions typically begin within a specific quadrant. As the business requirements expand, the core capability is then extended into other solution models.

As you can see from Fig. 8.2, data requirements are at the core of developing a customer intelligence solution. Below, let us look at some of the specifics of data related requirements. A key driver to designing the Customer Intelligence

Type of data / Currency of data	Customer channel (Profile/transaction data)	Customer insight (Derived data)
Near Real Time	Near real time cross channel integration	Near real time insight generation
Batch	Batch, cross channel integration	Batch insight generation

Figure 8.2 Currency of data and type of data requirement for customer insight.

solution and IVoC capabilities is the type of customer data that needs to be shared and/or integrated.

Type of customer data—What type of data needs to be shared/integrated?

- Channel customer data (e.g., profile and transaction data)
- Customer unique identification
- Householding
- Customer profile
- Customer transaction data, e.g., account transactions, product purchases,
- Customer contacts, e.g., promotions, call center, surveys, etc.
- Customer insight data (derived data such as segments, scores, etc.)
- Customer segmentation
- Propensity to churn
- Propensity to respond
- Propensity to purchase
- Lifetime value
- Demographics
- Credit
- Lifestyle/lifestage

While the above-mentioned type of data provides a comprehensive view of customer as he/she interacts across several channels, another key consideration is data latency. Data latency is dependant on business requirements and usages of customer data. Near real-time data integration may be required for specific business reasons. Because of the costs involved, the value of each customer data sharing opportunity needs to be clearly identified. How immediately does the data need to be shared/integrated? Let us look at some of the latency-specific requirements.

- Near-real-time integration (within seconds)
    - Integration of customer identification and profile across channels—Examples could be: Provide sales representatives with confirmation that customer is unique when creating a new customer; Provide sales or customer service representatives (CSRs) immediate access to customer profile after web registration; Provide CSRs immediate access to profile updates made by the customer on the web; Provide customers personalized marketing messages

  - Integration of transaction data across channels—Examples could be: Provide sales representatives immediate access to customer orders entered via web; Provide CSRs immediate access to customer account updates entered via web; Provide a customer immediate web or VRU access to orders/account updates completed via phone by a CSR
  - Prevent/restrict a business event—Examples could be: Prevent an airline customer from checking in on the Web if a ticket was canceled through the travel agency; Prevent a customer from requesting service once product return has been initiated
  - Execution of decisioning tools or recommendation engines—Examples could be: Provide a customer recommendations for additional products/services when ordering via the web or phone; Offer a monitor, memory or hard disk upgrade with a PC purchase; Offer a customer automatic overdraft protection when they contact a financial services company via phone
  - Evaluate customer information to drive real-time analytical scoring —Examples could be: Prospect scoring; Credit scoring; churn predictability
- Batch (from minutes to days)—Many data integration issues are better addressed in a batch mode because of the quantity of data, the significant analytical processing, or need to integrate third party data.
  - Analytics and Descriptive modeling to generate customer segmentation—Examples could be: Execution of decisioning tools or recommendation engines; RFM, customer profitability, customer lifetime value analysis; Appending third party demographic data used for modeling and House-holding of consumer customers; Predictive analysis of response rates for a customer offer
  - Generating email or direct mail offers to a customer or prospect —Examples could be : Capturing email or direct mail campaign responses
  - Supporting customer privacy and contact management—Examples could be: Historical customer purchase, sales, contact analysis, opt-outs
  - Integration of service applications across channels—Examples could be: CSR or automated response to customer emails; Automated response based on data triggers (e.g., lease expire, warranty expiration, product upgrades)

Another key consideration when designing an IVoC solution is where the data is needed. This includes what data is required by interaction, analytical and legacy applications. Where does the data need to be delivered? Examples could be: Customer Interaction Channels; Web; Call Center; Sales Force Application; Mail, email, Fax; Analytical Applications; Query and Reporting; Campaign Optimization; Campaign Management; Client-specific (e.g., Billing, ERP, Accounting, Claims)

Customer Intelligence Application Requirements

The whole purpose of building a customer intelligence application and IVoC capabilities is to share and use relevant customer information across customer touch points. Thus the customer interaction application requirements are primarily focused on insight-driven interactions—how well do we understand the customer? How can we interact with the customer in a mutually beneficial way? At a broad level following are some of the business requirements for customer intelligence applications:

- Share and use appropriate customer information cross-channel
  - Ability to update the information consistently
  - Access to appropriate information at the right time
  - Ability to provide actionable information
- Personalize/tailor customer experience and interaction
  - Tailored sales and/or customer service process
  - Personalized content and messaging on the web
  - Call routing based on customer data
- Deliver personalized/targeted marketing
  - Communications and product/service offers
  - Two-way dialog
  - Single channel and integrated cross-channel
  - Contact/communicate with customers based on their preferences
  - Channel and frequency
  - "Opt-in/Opt-out" subscriptions
  - Do not contact

Customer Intelligence Architecture Requirements

In a typical enterprise the various customer touch point applications are managed by different business functions such as marketing, sales, services, etc. It is also quite common the data related to these applications are also maintained and governed in silos. In order to truly achieve customer intelligence capabilities, it is critical that the customer interaction architecture has an integrated view of the customer across all these applications and siloed data sources. Following are the customer interaction architecture requirements.

Data and Integration Processes

- Integration of data cross-channel and cross-business unit to create 360° view of the customer
- Seamlessly data access of customer information regardless of application source
- Retrieve/update individual customer data near real-time
- Provide a single logical instance of a customer — 360° view
- Collect and provide appropriate customer information cross-channel/ business-unit

  - Profile and preferences
  - Demographic and psychographic
  - Derived insight data
  - History of detail interaction and transaction records (e.g., contacts, offers, purchases, cases/issues)
- Uniquely identify a customer and create a universal customer ID (e.g., real-time customer de-duplicationhouse-holding process)
- Access rules and case-base reasoning responses
- Purchase and integrate external third party data
  - Prospect lists
  - Customer/household demographics
  - Psychographics and attitudinal data
- Capture internal data (e.g., profile, contacts, offers, purchases, cases/issues)
- Integrate external and internal data sources
- Support both batch and online execution architectures
- Develop repeatable ETL processes to populate target data sources
- Perform standard transformations and merge data sources
- Support Complex data cleansing (Standardize and cleanse names, addresses, and other data)
- Perform customer matching and house-holding services (Universal Customer ID {central vs. distributed})
- Provide error handling procedures that log specific reason codes
- Provide statistics, load counts, reject counts, and reject files to review bad data

Rules

- Access and execution of common rules:
  - Common business functions (e.g., profile update)
  - Common customer functions (e.g., unique customer identification)
  - Edits & validations
- Access and execution of real-time, dynamic rules:
  - Personalization to tailor messages and offers
  - Model execution/scoring
  - Customer interaction aids (e.g., customer services scripts, case based reasoning)
  - Privacy/contact restrictions (e.g., opt-in)

Performance

- Provide replication services (if necessary)
- Highly available (mission critical 7 × 24)
- Support high transaction volumes (CSRs, web hits, etc.)
- Support sufficient data storage capacity

Meta Data

- Develop common definitions of data (e.g., customer, prospect, inactive customer)
- Reconcile conflicting calculations of data across groups (e.g., profit, revenue, high-value)
- Provide real-time access to business descriptions of attributes, rules, etc.

Customer Intelligence Analytics Requirements

Analytical requirements are primarily focused on analyzing customers and deriving insights to maximize the next customer interaction. Analytics provides insights from the raw transactional data. Following are some of the customer interaction analytics requirements:

Data

- Provide a time series view of customer
- Track customers' multiple relationships within and across business units (e.g., customer by multiple dimensions)
- Include sufficient, appropriate customer data to drive segmentation, predictive modeling, analysis and campaign management usages
- Support functional specific usages via data marts
- Push results of analytical processes into the interaction channels

Customer Decision Analytics

- Use descriptive analysis to profile and classify prospects/customers
- Segment customers based on Demographics/Psychographics; Behaviors/ Attitudes; Life stage/Preferences
- Use predictive analysis to identify responders and non-responders; Propensity to purchase/cross-sell; Propensity to churn
- Perform regression analysis to support quantitative consumer research
- Define targeted communications and product/service offers to customers
- Measure costs and response rates for offers
- Track targeted communications to customers by segment, channel, etc.
- Capture and analyze customer contacts
    - Capture and analyze customer surveys
    - Perform click-stream analysis on web sites

Performance

- Sufficient data storage capacity
- May or may not be mission critical (7 × 24)

Customer Intelligence Solution Design Approach

There could be several approaches to design customer intelligence solution and IVoC capabilities. However, as a best practice it is always advisable to first conduct interviews and/or workshops with business function owners to determine key business capabilities that are important and meaningful for the business. Following is an illustration of the design approach:

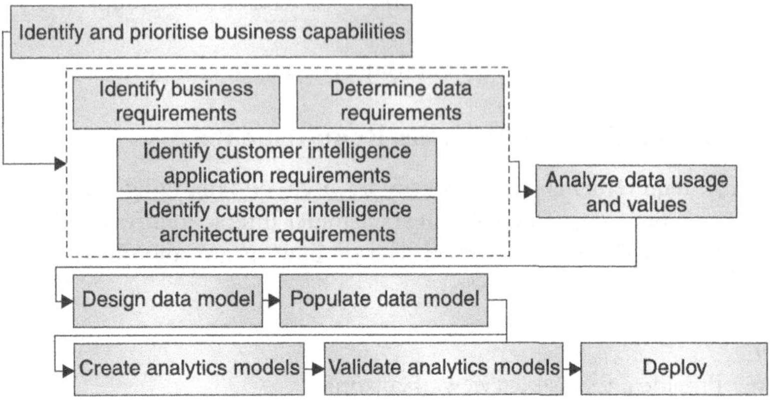

Figure 8.3 Customer insight implementation methodology.

For example, from a marketing function perspective, there could be several key business capabilities considered. At a broad level, the marketing function could be interested in attaining comprehensive customer understanding by—

- Customer/Market Research
- Customer Analysis and Profiling
- Customer Segmentation
- Customer Behavior Analysis
- Customer Valuation and Predictive Modeling
- Analyze Customer Purchase History
- Analyze Customer Support History

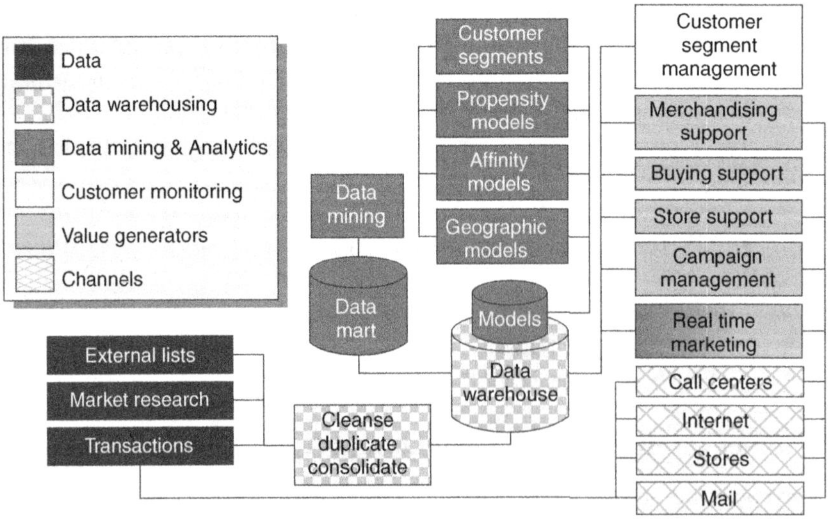

Figure 8.4 Customer insight implementation business architecture.

However, not all of these business capabilities could be achieved at once and there are several dependencies between them. Hence it is advisable to align these business capability requirements to initiatives, for example,

- Targeted campaign management based on products owned, profile/segmentation, behavior, demographics, life stage needs, etc.
- Life stage marketing programs based on integrated cross channel and cross product campaigns, etc.
- Differentiated sales processes, support services based on customer profile, their transaction history and preferences, etc.

Once the business capabilities are prioritized, the customer interaction activities and means to achieve the same are carved out, for example,

- Customer driven communication content and frequency based on personalization of content (web and non-web), etc.
- Product offers/recommendations based on profile/segmentation, behavior, demographics, life stage needs, etc.
- Campaign response captures and performance evaluation based on sales leads follow-up, knowledge based diagnostics, e-support (faqs, emails, search engines, etc.), integration of e-support with call center applications, etc.

Some of the examples of prioritized business capabilities are given in Fig. 8.5:

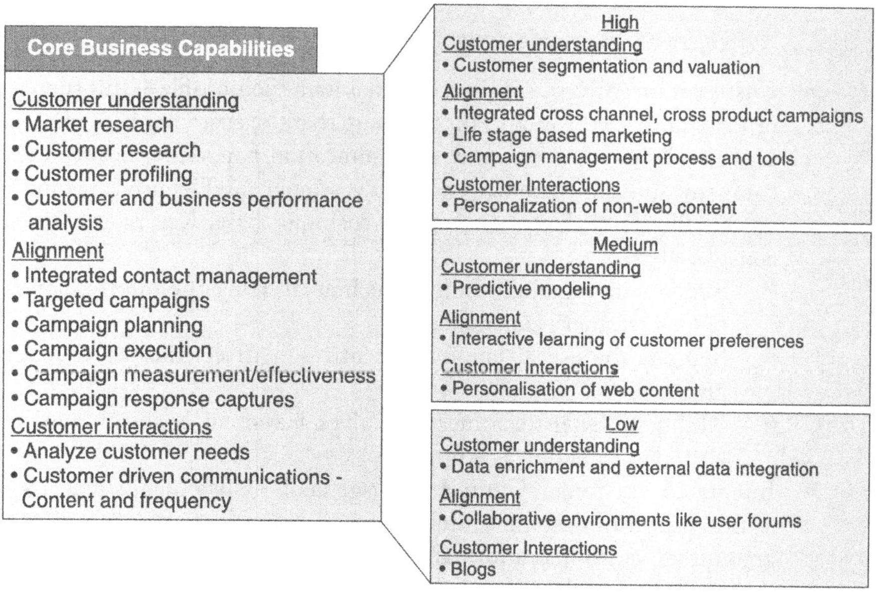

Figure 8.5 Customer insight prioritized marketing capabilities.

In addition to business functions, support capabilities are critical to keep the various customer intelligence initiatives sustainable. Typical business requirements are:

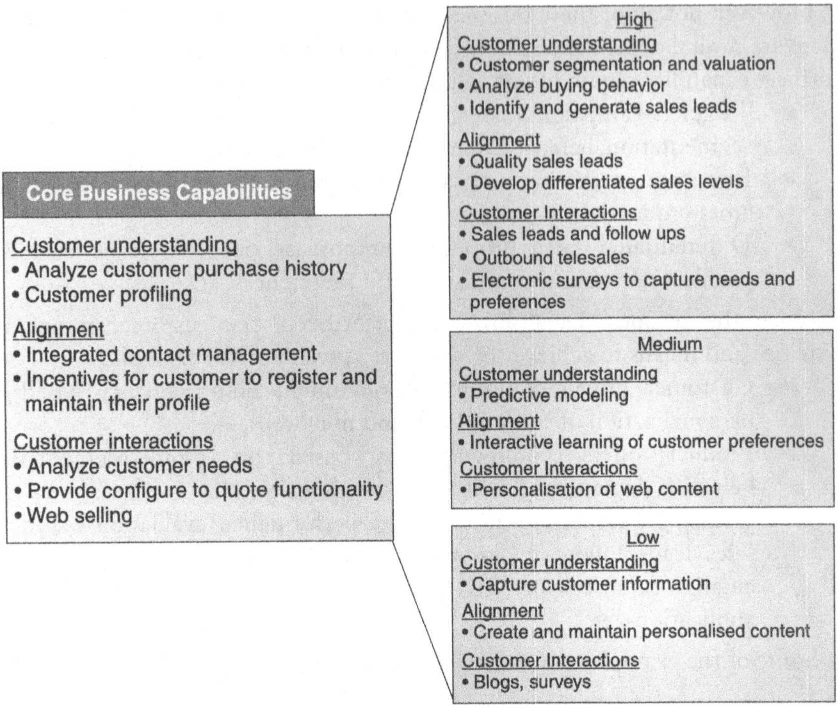

Figure 8.6 Customer insight prioritized sales capabilities.

- Customer incentives to register and maintain their profile—This support functionality is very important to ensure that the customer base remains active and there is a two way communication happening between the company and the customer base. All customer intelligence capabilities are heavily dependent on an active customer base. Key aspects to be considered are:
  - Support intangible incentives such as utilizing the information to tailor customer's experience
  - Support the use of tangible incentives—gift certificates, coupons, giveaways
  - Ability to offer customer incentives based on business rules by customer valuation and profile
- Integrated Customer Contact Management—Customer contact is a critical aspect of customer intelligence solution. You can collect a huge amount of customer information. However if the customer contact aspects are not well managed and the data collected is of bad quality the entire initiative will be a failure. Key aspects to be considered are:
  - Capture integrated customer contacts over time
  - Capture summary of inbound and outbound contacts across channels
  - Capture contact date, type, and status

- Customer Driven Content (customization) and Frequency—Understanding customer preferences and interacting with them accordingly is a powerful medium. It is common to see a vast range of messages/content reaching customers; how much of those are really effective if it does not match customer's preferences? Content customization and frequency if not done properly can put the entire customer intelligence solution outcomes in jeopardy. Key aspects to be considered are:
  - Ability to capture customer's content preferences
  - Ability to allow customer to select/customize content based on categories
  - Ability to capture preference of communication frequency
  - Capture customer channel preferences for communications
- Campaign Response Capture—It is also important to measure the performance of the customer intelligence solution. One example could be to capture and track how the campaigns are performing; did the sales pickup? What was customer's response to campaigns? How many enquiries were made over web channels versus non-web channels? etc. Key aspects to be considered are:
  - Ability to capture customer's response to marketing messages
  - Use responses to determine campaign effectiveness
  - Ability to apply unique identifiers (key codes) to campaigns
  - Ability to capture end result of response interaction

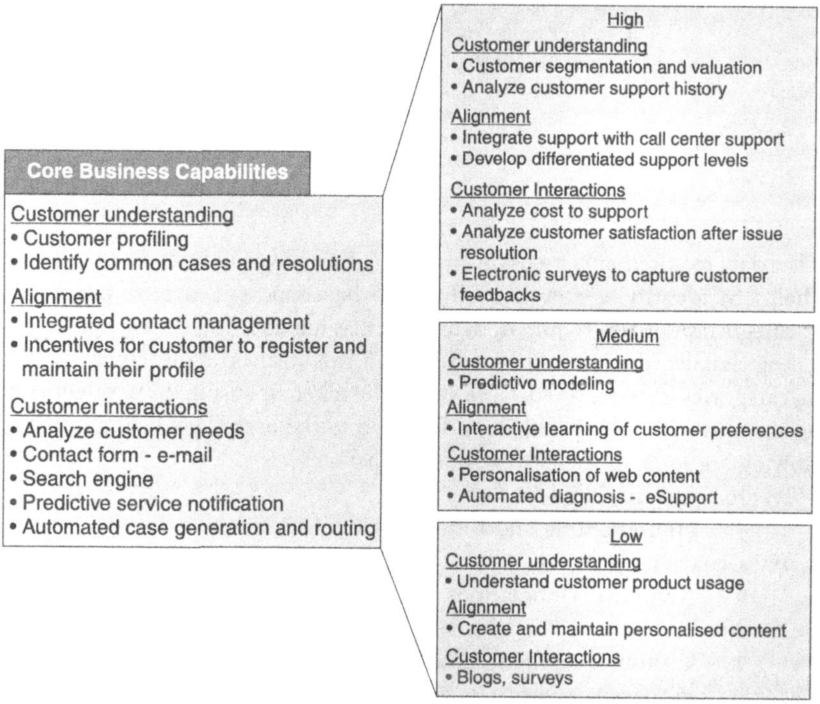

Figure 8.7 Customer insight prioritized support capabilities.

Once the capabilities are identified and prioritized, the next step is to determine key performance metrics.

Table 8.1 Customer insight KPIs

Priority	*Key Measures Name*	*Definition*	*Calculation Components*	*Analysis Dimensions*
H	Customer Registration	• # of Customers who have registered their profiles • Used to determine effectiveness of registration incentives • Used to identify new customers available as marketing contacts	• # of registered customers • % with "OK" to contact • % with e-mail address • % with valid phone number • % with valid zip codes	• Customer type • Customer segment • Product line • Geography • Time • Registration channel • Registration Incentive
H	Profile analysis of customers	• # of customer with specific attributes • Used to analyze and profile customer base • Used to define marketing campaigns	• # of customers • % of customers within segment like platinum, gold, silver, bronze	• Customer type • Customer segment • Product line • Geography • Time
H	E-mail campaign effectiveness	• Responses (inquiries, sales) per e-mail campaigns • Used to evaluate the effectiveness of an e-mail campaign	• # of responses • $ cost of campaign • $ revenue of campaign • # of subscribers	• Customer type • Customer segment • Product line • Geography • Time • Customer event (Returned as undeliverable, URL click, Inquiry)

The data requirements focus on answering the above-mentioned key questions. It helps in identifying key capabilities to be supported, determines different key categories/entities required, determines value and usage, and also helps in creating detailed data definitions. Based on the business requirements, a list of data categories is determined. Care should be taken to ensure these categories are relevant to the business problem and aligned to the overall goal. At a broad level following are some of the key considerations:

- ➤ Identification Fields
    - ♦ Householding and Individual identification
- ➤ Behavior Fields
    - ♦ Accounts, Transactions and Products
- ➤ Model Scores
    - ♦ Customer segmentation
    - ♦ Propensity scores

- Customer Profiling Data
  - Demographic append and lifestyle/lifestage
- Contact History
  - Promotions and call center

Figure 8.8 is an illustration of how data requirements and data architecture enable the company to achieve customer intelligence:

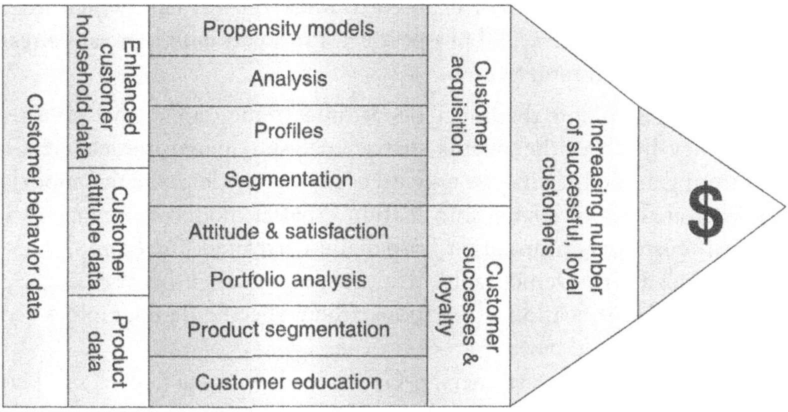

Figure 8.8 Data requirements and data architecture enabling customer intelligence.

In Fig. 8.8, you can clearly see a layered approach to achieving business benefits by utilizing available customer data, applying various analytics models and then devising strategies to increase customer base and/or retaining loyal customers. To start with, customer behavior data serve as the key input. It consists of asset level, account type, credit usage, transactions, seasonal transaction information, etc. The customer data could also be enriched by appending lifestyle and lifestage data, attitudinal data from surveys and census data. The product data provides the links to product price, yield history, market indicators, event triggers, etc.

Propensity models are then used to create prospect lists that could be used for cross-sell campaigns or even direct marketing programs. Propensity models are usually created by data mining tools like decision trees, neural networks,

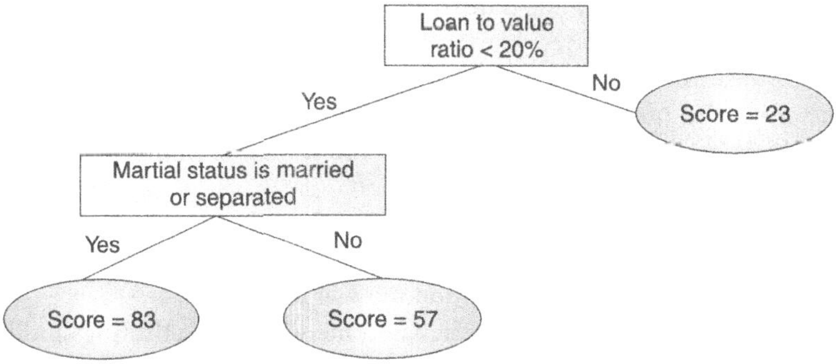

Figure 8.9 Decision tree model enabling customer intelligence.

Propensity models predict by a score that indicates the similarity of each prospect to existing customers who exhibit similar behavior.

The model is trained using data with a known outcome; for example, customers who have mutual funds compared to customers without mutual funds. The score is an indicator as to how much the customers with that particular score resemble customers who have mutual funds. Once the scored are determined by the model, the model is further exposed to score on test data which was kept separate and could be the actual prospect list. Prospects with highest scores then become the campaign targets.

It is interesting to note that much of customer demographic analysis is related to where they live, in other words spatial analysis. Spatial models are usually derived from geographic analysis and are used to provide predictive models and higher level analysis of spatial information. Spatial models use maps as input data. Much customer information is spatially correlated, for example, Income, Lifestyle, Education, Demography, Cultural and Language use, etc. Spatial analysis allows identification of locations where specific demographics tend to cluster. Examples could be:

- Where are your customers?—Geocode all your customers and perform spatial statistics to identify concentrations of customers by analyzing behavioral demographics, lifestyle, lifestage characteristics.
- Where your company has penetration?—Spatially analyze your customers and product usage showing areas where potentially good customers live, but penetration is low and vice versa.
- Where are the special target groups for example Hispanic, Chinese, etc.—Spatial statistics on non-customers by demographic profiles, non-English speaking areas, so that in your stores you can employ sales representatives and customer service representatives who speak those languages or for your campaigns you can prepare fliers in those languages to be distributed in those areas.

Profiles are nothing but enhancing customer data with external demographic, lifestyle and credit data and provides an opportunity to evaluate the customer base from a myriad of dimensions. Profiles are usually created by statistical tools and usually illustrate the internal and external customer attributes using quantifiable measures like mean, median, mode, standard deviation, etc. These quantifiable measures are evaluated in terms of business sense and opportunity. The profile is created by analyzing customer records delivering value by validating business opportunities and improving marketing strategies. Examples could be:

- A report summarizing the breadth of demographic, credit and lifestyle data associated with each customer record. This report serves as a reference for insight generation moving forward.
- A spatial analysis of the designated market areas reflecting similarities, differences, unique geographic patterns contained in the customer data. Working in unison with the segmentation results, the profile data and

findings overlay the segmentation and provide a clearer picture of each segmentation.

Segmentation is important for understanding the behaviors of your customers — but you also need to know how your customers stack up against the universe.

By analyzing Fig. 8.10, a company can develop profiles of the entire population (customers and non-customers) by segment and then develop acquisition models targeting segments that are low or under represented.

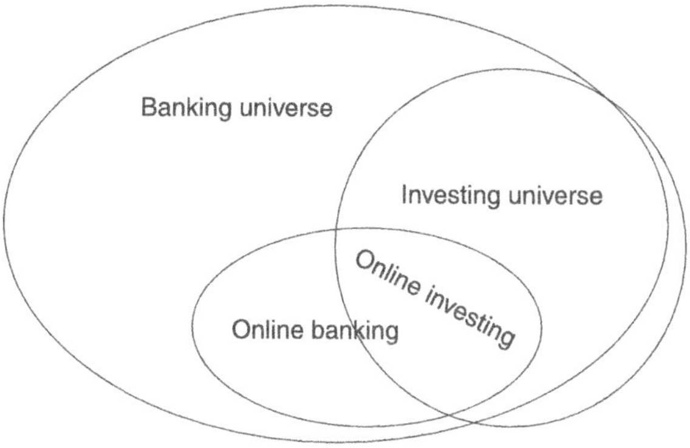

Figure 8.10 Segmentation as compared to universe example.

CUSTOMER ANALYTIC RECORD (CAR)

We have been discussing about analytics and models, but how does an analytic record look like? What are the attributes? What is the importance of each of these attributes? How do they help in getting insight? Let us consider an investment banking company example and understand what would be the constituents of the customer analytic record.

The analytic record is a virtual record describing each customer. The records are defined as views in the modeling database that are based on tables and views. Depending on line length factors, the analytic records may consist of one or more virtual records per customer.

For analytics purpose, the data set needs to be flat containing one record per entity. The data set should also contain all data transformations and extra variables needed to develop the model.

ID Fields	Behaviour Fields	Demographic Fields	Model Scores	Contact History

Figure 8.11 Customer analytic record example.

The customer analytic record contains the following information:

- *Identification section* - IDs, name, address, etc. Behavior section — behavior summary information
- *Demographic section* - Lifestyle/Lifestage information

- *Model scores* - the scores for all models are appended to the customer analytic record and retained permanently
- *Contact history* - How many times the customer has been contacted, what interactions happened, what were the outcomes, etc.

The customer analytic record is split into three core areas, information about the customer, customer's behaviors and customer values.

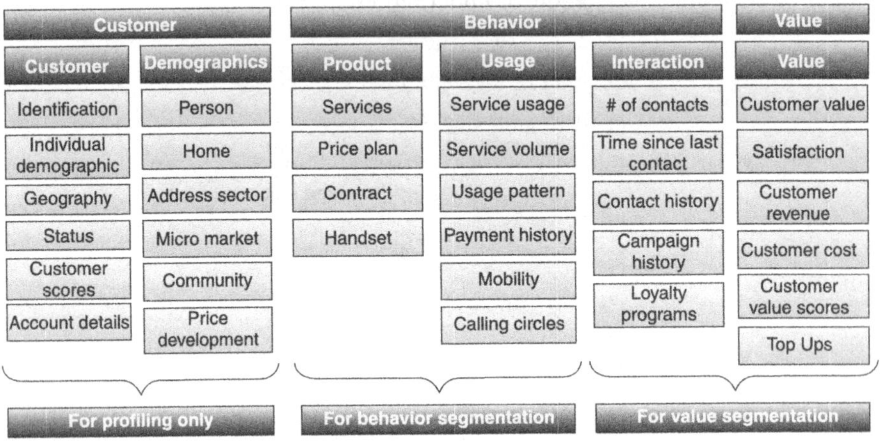

Figure 8.12 Customer analytic record constituents.

Some of the key considerations to be followed while designing the customer analytic record are given here:

Customer Information

- Depending on the customer type only certain attributes get populated (e.g., individual at a business will have job title and job responsibility populated).
- Historical record of changes to customer information kept through effective dating.

Contact Methods/Preferences

- All customer contact channel information such as email, addresses, and phone numbers are captured.
- Customers can have multiple contact channels of the same type (e.g., customer may have two email addresses or have a day phone # listed for communications during the day time and home phone # listed for communications during off hours).
- Flexibility to add new contact channel types and/or preferences without modifying the underlying data model needs to be considered.
- Historical record of changes to contact methods/preferences kept through effective dating the information.

Customer Needs

- Should support the capture of customer's purchase intentions.

- Should have the flexibility to capture customer psychographics such as attitudes and preferences. Purchase intentions and psychographics may be purchased from external data vendors to be populated.

Customer Products

- Should support the capture of customer product ownership relationship at time of sales transaction.
- Should have the ability to identify customers who have purchased but not yet registered.
- Should have the ability to capture of additional customer product ownership information at the time of registration.
- Should have the ability to link to product master for all the product details.
- Should have the flexibility to capture information about other products customer is using which are not offered/serviced by the client company.
- Should have the flexibility to access Warranty Commencement Date based on purchase date, born-on data (service id), or installation date of the products.

Household

- Should have the ability to capture household information at family level as well as independent level. Household may be comprised many customers, Family is a "super-household" and is technically made of independent economic buying units that have a different demographic profiles.

Campaign

- Should have the ability to capture campaign information at a program level as individual initiatives level so that various metrics can be looked at holistically. Campaign program is an overall marketing strategy that can have many campaigns. Individual campaigns are initiatives that target a particular product or set of products. Campaign may have many cells that identify the set of households/customers that have been selected. Cell identifies which individuals get particular treatments such as a rebate, brochure, or discount. Overall campaign metrics needs to be captured, calculated, and fed back into marketing process for future program planning and analysis.
- Should have the ability to associate a customer response with a specific campaign when the customer was not originally selected/assigned to the campaign. Typical metrics are: Capture # of customers selected for campaign, Capture # actually delivered/sent.

Contact History

- Should have the ability to capture contact information that contains entries for each inbound or outbound contact. Examples include:
    - Inbound sales transaction from the customer
    - Outbound survey mailed to customer

- Inbound survey response from the customer
- Outbound email campaign mailed to customer
- Contact subject area—marketing, sales, support
- Capture contact type—email campaign, support case, etc.
- The organization that contacted the customer
- Channel that was used for the contact
- Contact history for the past one year (archive contact history older than one year)
- Customer Valuation Model Scores

Table 8.2 Customer Analytic Record detailed variable list

Category	*Attribute*
Demographics	House Hold Relationship Code
	Customer ID
	Name
	Home Address
	Secondary Address
	Phone #
	Alternate Phone #
	Email Id
	SSN #
	Date of Birth
	Gender
	Age
	Marital Status
	Income Range
	Occupation
	Ethnic Background
Psychographics	Interests/Hobbies
	Media Consumption
	Spending Behavior
	Activities
	Automobiles
	Home Owner
	2nd Home Owner
	PC Owner
	# of PCs
	Cell Phone Owner
	# of Cell Phones
	PDA Owner
	Pets
	Education Level
	Religion
	College Attended
	Internet Savvy
	Health Care Membership
	Frequent Flier Memberships
	Vacations

Category	*Attribute*
Household Attributes	Household Indicator
	Household Size
	Household Income
	Customer living in Household Indicator
	Non-Customers living in Household Indicator
Preference and Privacy Attributes	Preferred Contact Channel
	Website Preferences
	Survey Participation Preference
	Opt-In Subscriptions
	Registered Website User
	Website User ID
	Partner Website Identifier
	OK to contact Indicator
	OK to call Indicator
	OK to send email Indicator
	OK to send direct mail Indicator
	Preferred Language
Prediction Attributes	Segmentation Name
	Segmentation #
	Life Stage Name
	Propensity to convert to customer
	Propensity to re-purchase
	Propensity to buy Product A, Product B, etc
	Propensity to Defect
	Risk Level
	Buying Behavior Attribute
Contact Attributes	Service ID
	CSR ID
	Inquiry Open Date
	Inquiry Close Date
	# of Inquires made in a month rolling upto 12 months
	Inquiry Status
	Inquiry Reason Code
	Inquiry Channel
	Inquiry Description
	Inquiry Resolution Code
Communication Attributes	Communication Channel
	Communication Type
	Communication Media
	Communication Date
	Communication Identifier
	Communication Content Code
Channel Usage Attributes	Call Center Usage Indicator
	VRU Usage Indicator
	VRU Navigation
	Web Usage Indicator
	Web Navigation
	Topics Selected

Category	*Attribute*
	Banners Clicked 1st Topic Selected Last Topic Selected Site Arrived From Site Departed To Time Spent in Major Categories Time Spent in Each Page Email Usage Indicator
Campaign Attributes	Campaign # Campaign Type Campaign Channel Campaign Start Date Campaign End Date Offer Response Response Date
Product Attributes	Product ID Product Type/Line Product Name Channel Purchased Date Ordered Date Shipped Quantity Product Price Shipping Method

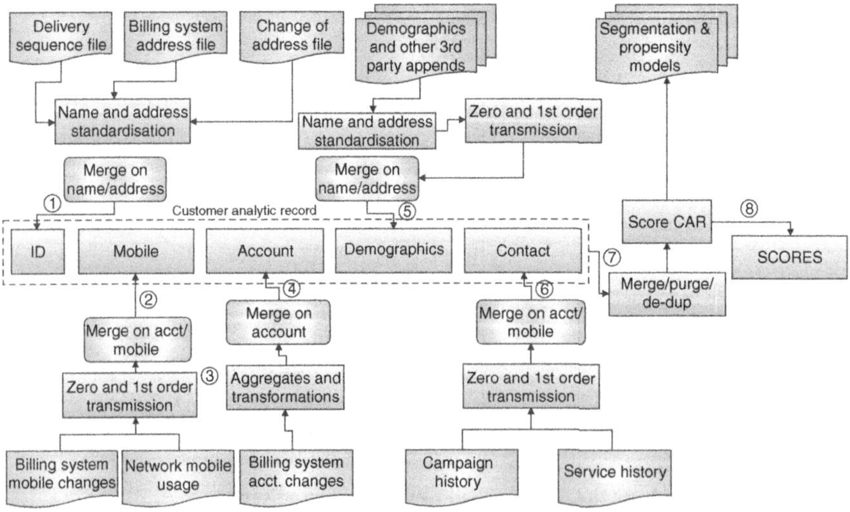

Figure 8.13 Customer analytic record schematic process flow for a wireless carrier.

Figure 8.13 gives a schematic processes flow to develop a CAR for wireless telecommunication industry and segmentation models. Please note Harris Surveys are also taken as a critical input to the segmentation process. Segmentation and modeling each have a broad range of applications that could be leveraged within any customer-centric organization. Let us look at some of the examples below:

We have taken two service offerings—pre-paid (denoted as PR) and post-paid (denoted as PO) for our example scenarios. Profiling and segmentation was done on customer base subscribing to these two offerings. Several key variables like ARPU (Average Revenue Per User), MoU (Minutes of Use) attributes, Behavior attributes, Demographics and Lifestyle attributes were instrumental in determining various segments. Since ARPU and MoU are important factors for our segmentation example, let's discuss what actually they mean and how they are calculated.

MoU (minutes of use) is a measurement usually in minutes as unit of time that show how long each user (in average) consumes a product/service in a month. This measurement often used in telecommunication industries or other industries in which the product/service consumption is calculated in time unit (i.e., they follow time based pricing). Examples of such companies are: electric/power companies, gas companies, sterilized water companies, etc.

Just like MoU, ARPU (Average Revenue Per User) is also one of performance indicators in running one business. This is the measurement usually in currency unit that shows how much money each user spends to consume one or more products or services.

Both of MoU and ARPU are business performance indicators that could be related to the revenue as its end result. For example: a service company has 3,000 customers with MoU value as 120 minutes per month. If the unit price of its service is US $ 1.5 per minute (in average), we can conclude that the monthly revenue of that company is = 3,000 × 120 × 1.5 = US $ 540,000. Assumed if the next coming month the MoU increase to 150 minutes at the constant unit price. We can easily calculate the revenue based on the previous month revenue. We just do the simple mathematics operation as follow: 150/120 × 540,000 = US $ 675,000.

Just like MoU, almost the same simple mathematics operation works in ARPU calculation, but a little simpler. For example: if the ARPU of a company is US $ 180 and the number of customers is 3,000 users then the revenue of that month is = 3,000 × 180 = US $ 540,000. Imagine if in the next coming month the value of ARPU increase from US $ 180 to US $ 225. The revenue will be increase also to: 225/180 × 540,000 = US $ 675,000. ARPU method is used when there are multiple variables involved and multiple products/channels involved. For example a telecommunication operator that provides voice call (pricing in US $ per minutes), data internet (pricing in US $ per Mbyte), and also mailbox feature (pricing in US $ per month). We should use ARPU method for analysis. For getting the ARPU value, we have to calculate the average of invoice of all customers we have. But if in case internet service provider which used flat rate time based charging method, we could use MoU method for analysis in order to evaluate the business performance.

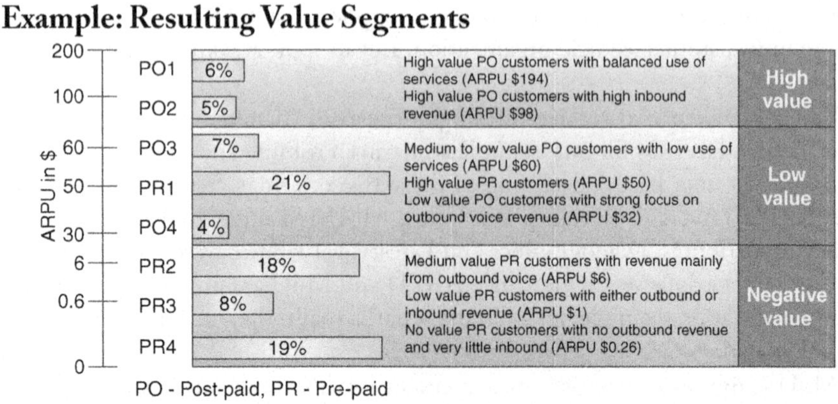

Figure 8.14 Customer behavior segments.

Usage	Low airtime	Low data	Avg. airtime	High airtime	High text	High data	High all
Contacts	1	2	5	3	4	4	8
Services (Post-paid)	$32-4 Serv.	$44-5 Serv.	$40-5 Serv.	$74-9 Serv.	$44-5 Serv.	$52-9 Serv.	$80-9 Serv.
Top ups (Pre-paid)	$8	$28	$8	$24	$42	$46	$57
Demographics	20% known	27% known	52% known	51% known	74% known	61% known	56% known

Pre-paid behavior segments	
Secondary SIM card users	Do not make calls or CS contacts any more, possible churners
Hardly callers or texters	Unknown segments with medium to high airtime and data usage. Do not call CS
Potential leavers	Customers under risk with low overall usage, but quite frequent CS calls
Price sensitive	Very loyal customers with old price plans, high roaming usage
High potential	Very loyal, discount sensitive customers with highest roaming and high CS calls
Heavy users	Discount shoppers with highest airtime and data usage and high CS contact rate

Post-paid behavior segments	
Use different SIM cards	Very loyal and well off customers with low usage and CS contacts often to accept offers
Only when on the road	Price sensitive contracts with tendency to over use.
Call always all friends	They like to text more than average.
Spare time users	Make long calls after hours and on weekends, but do not text a lot, regular contacts with CS
Good basic services users	Medium to low income families with high usage (voice, text and data), more than one contract
Advanced services users	Youngest segment with extreme text usage. They also like entertainment, often contact CS
Technology lovers	Small with very high data usage, with strong focus on 'internet on your phone' very low voice usage high usage technical geeks with highest mobility, entertainment and airtime use and high dem and on CS

Figure 8.15 Customer segmentation, profiling and insights.

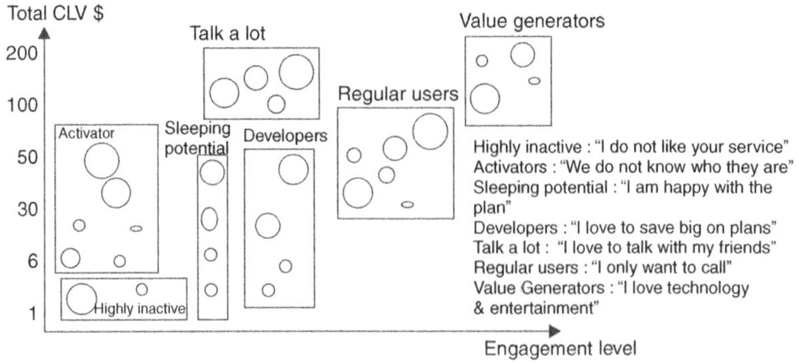

Figure 8.16 Customer segmentation and classification example.

The above three segmentation examples provide deep insights into type of customer, their contribution to ARPU and leading to profitability.

Retail Segmentation Case Study

Perhaps the best way to illustrate the integrated use of segmentation and modeling is through the use of a hypothetical example. In the situation depicted below, a national retailer (retail store and online channels) has developed eight customer segments. Customers are separated along the following key shopping dimensions: Recency of last visit, Frequency of visits and Monetary amount.

Four of the customer segments are highlighted. Frequent Shoppers are the retailer's best customers, shopping regularly and spending a large amount per visit. The Slow and Steady segment contains active customers; however, they spend significantly less per shopping occasion. At Risk customers have not shopped with this retailer recently and have never fully engaged with this national retailer. Sleeping Potential are the customers, who stay inactive for longer duration; however whenever they shop they spend a lot of money.

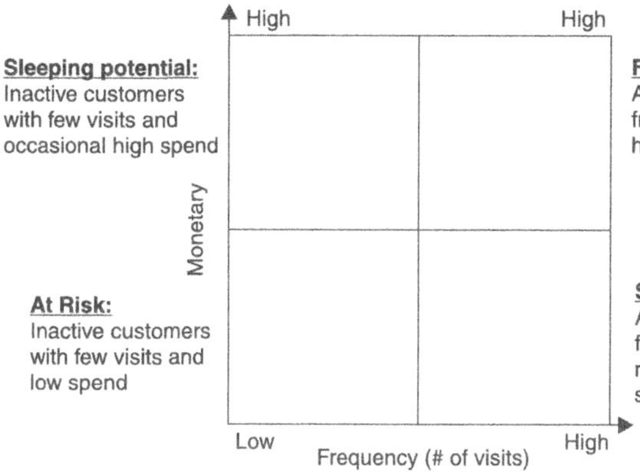

Figure 8.17 Customer Universe and Classification Example.

Each of these customer segments is further explored to provide examples of how predictive models can be used in conjunction with the segmentation solution to identify growth opportunities and support the development of extremely targeted programs.

Frequent Shopper Segment

Primary Objective: Recognize and Defend

Customers in this segment generate the most profit for the organization. It is critical that the national retailer maximize retention of these best customers. Furthermore, the company needs to fully comprehend why these customers prefer to shop with them and leverage this knowledge in an effort to influence customers in lower performing segments to migrate to the Frequent Shopper segment.

Predictive models can be developed to forecast customer's retention probability. In this case, two types of retention are important to understand: customer retention and revenue or spend retention. A decline in either of these rates would weaken the profitability of the organization. Customer behaviors that are likely be useful in predicting a potential decline in retention are: a decrease in the length of time between shopping occasions, purchasing in fewer product categories, reduced utilization of one or both of the primary channels (online or store).

Implementing a retention model would give the retailer a way to proactively detect any Frequent Shoppers that may be a retention risk. Armed with this knowledge, the organization can quickly communicate with these customers and attempt to offset this anticipated decline in shopping behavior with targeted offers or incentives.

Slow and Steady Segment

Primary Objective: Cross-Sell and Stimulate Incremental Activity

These customers shop fairly regularly but do not provide the same level of revenue to the organization as the Frequent Shoppers. This is because they purchase from a smaller number of product categories and typically only use the in-store channel. Two sets of models could help marketers at this organization identify opportunities to increase the spend behavior of these customers: product purchase propensity models and online shopping propensity model.

The objective of the product purchase models would be to identify the best cross-sell opportunities and convince more Slow and Steady customers to purchase across a broader set of product categories. The online purchase propensity model would be designed to identify Slow and Steady customers with the greatest likelihood of using the online channel. Once identified, incentives can be used to entice Slow and Steady customers to begin to use the online channel in addition to the retail outlets, creating the potential for more shopping occasions.

At Risk Segment

Primary Objective: Selectively Engage and Cross-Sell

Either the current value proposition or awareness of the value proposition appears to fall short for this group of customers. Customers in this group have spent very little with the national retailer and have not shopped online or at any of their retail locations for a long time. Conducting research to gain a deeper understanding of why these customers do not regularly shop at the national retailer would be very useful. These insights could lead to a refinement of the value proposition that causes At Risk customers to favorably change their shopping behaviors.

Incentives or offers may be required to get these customers to become more engaged. Because this group has not contributed significant profits to the company in the past, it would be inappropriate to provide offers that only lead to one additional visit. The goal would be to develop an offer optimization engine, informed by predictive models, that identifies the best offer sets for distinct groups of At Risk customers and leads to sustainable and profitable shopping behavior.

This ensures that the offer investment is distributed in a way that maximizes the expected return. In addition, the development of a long-term customer value model would help determine the amount the national retailer should be willing to invest in certain At Risk customers. Having visibility into the longer-term value of each customer allows the national retailer to only target At Risk customers with an expected ROI equal to or above acceptable corporate standards.

Segmentation without modeling or modeling without segmentation should be considered an incomplete analytic solution. Segmentation provides a robust foundation for designing, testing, measuring and rolling out tailored marketing programs. However, an exhaustive understanding of all expected customer behaviors cannot and should not be built into the segmentation solution. Instead, predictive models, developed outside of the segmentation solution, should be viewed as a set of companion tools that help expose additional opportunities and provide the means to achieve an even greater level of targeting precision.

It is common practice to begin the journey into marketing analytics with the development of a segmentation scheme or a single predictive model. However, the analytic roadmap needs to provide the vision for how and when the complete suite of analytic tools can be drawn upon to fully exploit the benefits of data-driven customer marketing. The roadmap will help the organization pace itself, integrating tools in a way that supports the company's ability to act on the insight these powerful tools provide, and building on each success.

Sleeping Potential

Primary Objective: Find Less Costly Channels to Engage and Entice

Customers in this group have been dormant for a larger part; but whenever they shop then spend a lot. The spending behavior of these customers needs to be analyzed further to understand any external influencers for such behaviors like seasonal patterns, lifestage patterns, householding patterns, etc. These insights could lead to a refinement of the value proposition that causes these customers to favorably change their shopping behaviors.

On other hand, careful considerations should be made to optimize the amount of money spent in chasing these customers. Incentives or offers may be required to get these customers to become more engaged, but through low cost channels such as online advertisements, etc. Because this group has not shown any predictability and has not contributed significant profits to the company in the past, it would be inappropriate to provide offers that only lead to one additional visit.

Best Practices for IVoC

Relationship Marketing Process

- Segment customers by "value" or "worth" and identify most valuable customers and least valuable customers.
- Identify customers that are not profitable (to invest in, collaborate with, or cater to) and treat appropriately. Understand and predict customer needs.
- Understand the importance of each customer touch point on buyer values.
- Implement Best Customer Profiling/Cloning programs.
- Develop one-to-one marketing that allows the creation of individualized/targeted incentives and promotions.
- Establish a two-way, interactive marketing communication with customers.
- Develop a marketing process that is integrated with sales and customer service.
- Provide incentives for customers to respond to research and provide feedback.
- Share marketing data internally within the organization and externally with strategic business partners.
- Develop joint promotions with strategic business partners.

Comprehensive and Integrated Customer Information

- Capture customer information at all touch points (e.g., across all product lines and channels).
- Develop consistent data views of "a customer" across all applications and functional areas.
- Share and integrate customer information with strategic business partners.
- Maintain up-to-date customer repositories that contain accurate information from all appropriate data sources.
- Capture complete customer contact and transaction activity and maintain it for relevant time periods.
- Develop a comprehensive customer profile from internal and external data sources.
- Create a shared base of customer information that is available for inquiry and update by all appropriate parties.

Integrated Technical Architecture

- Develop an overall data architecture implementation plan and modify it based on business and market changes.
- Implement periodic validation and/or update processes for strategic data entities which are propagated to all appropriate data stores.

- Optimize data structures for the platform, software and specific use.
- Develop and maintain strategic data stores to support analysis associated with unique business needs.
- Implement processes to identify and eliminate duplication for all strategic data stores (e.g., customer, householding).
- Capture and store operational data consistently across the organization.
- Appropriately protect strategic information resources from inadvertent access or misuse.

Integrated Delivery Channels

- Provide users with applications that are integrated across functional areas and channels in order to provide accurate and comprehensive information.
- Enable users to make real-time decisions by integrating decision models into applications.
- Provide staff access to comprehensive customer profile including appropriate transactional information at the point of contact.
- Develop channel treatment strategies based on the customer segments, insights, profitability, and transaction history.

Range of Analysis Tools and Techniques

- Utilize the appropriate mix of modeling tools and data analysis techniques to solve the business problem and support a course of action.
- Maximize the value added by performing analysis across all of the pertaining information.
- Capture and maintain insights, measures, and metrics (e.g., scores, behavioral values, categorical classifications) developed through analytical processes for appropriate time periods.
- Develop an integrated business process which drives and prioritizes all data analysis efforts and activities for high-end quantitative problems.
- Establish data analysis processes to enable defining, measuring, and disseminating key financial, process, and customer performance measurements.

END POINTS

It would be interesting to see how the concepts we discussed in this chapter are applied to the popular online registration based gaming industry. In this industry there are customers, there are services offered by the gaming companies, and there are also competing companies offering similar type of products and services. Thus for these companies it is essential to know how to make money, how much they can expect to make, and the market size.

The Life Time Value (LTV) is a key metric for profitability: the LTV of all paying customers must be greater than the cost to acquire those customers, plus the cost of servicing all free and paying customers.

The lifetime value is driven by three metrics:

- Conversion of free players to paying players
- Spend per paying player
- Length of active membership

Its important to monitor and optimize these three metrics, as we'll see later, small changes can make big differences.

Average Revenue Per User

We start by taking the conversion from free to paying and the average spend to calculate the Average Revenue Per User (ARPU).

ARPU = % Converted × Ave Spend

Let's plug some numbers into our hypothetical world. We'll assume that 10% of our users will signup for a $4 monthly subscriptions. The ARPU is:

$4 × 10% = $0.40 ARPU

If the world also includes micro payments, perhaps through mobile or credit cards, we can extend the model:

ARPU = (% Subscribing × Subscription) + (% Micro paying × Ave Spend)

If we assume that 15% buy through micro payments, and spend an average of $2–$4 per month, then the ARPU is:

($4 × 10%) + ($2 × 15%) = $0.70 ARPU

Churn

Churn is a measure for the number of players that leave your world every month and is typically calculated as a percentage of the total active user base. For example, a 33% churn means that on average 1 in 3 players leave the world every month.

We can calculate the lifetime of our average player with the formula:

LT = 1 / % Churn

So, for our 33% churn our player lifetime is:

1 / 33% = 3 Months

Lifetime Value

The ARPU calculation gave us the revenue per user per month and the churn rate allowed us to calculate the average user lifetime. We combine these two numbers to get our lifetime value:

LTV = ARPU × LT

So, in our hypothetical world we have a LTV value:

$0.70 × 3 Months = $2.10

Let's revisit churn, remember that the player lifetime is calculated as 1/% Churn. This means that if we can half our churn we double our revenues. This becomes an increasingly big lever as we start to approach low churn rates.

For example, with a 20% churn:

LTV = $0.70 × (1 / 20%) = $3.50

If we cut the churn down to 10%:

LTV = $0.70 × (1 / 10%) = $7.00

User Acquisition

At this point it would seem reasonable to assume that to acquire a new customer we can afford to spend up to the LTV less the cost of servicing that player. In other words:

Max Acquisition Cost = Lifetime Value – Servicing Cost

However, this does not take into account any viral effects.

While some of your world traffic will come through your own marketing activity, such as ad networks, and search advertising, another portion will come through your players telling their friends. It's this second portion that gives you significant growth options.

When we talk about viral growth we often think of exponential viral growth, the kind of growth that Facebook has seen. To see exponential growth you need each of your players to invite and convert more than 1 new player. That is, for every player who joins, they bring another 2 new players with them.

Because the cost to acquire these viral players is effectively zero it can be tempting to optimize for achieving exponential viral growth. However, achieving long lasting exponential viral growth is difficult, and may not be the best strategy.

With a solid conversion to subscription and micro payments you can afford to spend money on advertising or other marketing activity. In contrast, social networks have to focus on low cost viral growth because their ARPUs are significantly lower.

Continuing our hypothetical virtual world, if we have a viral growth where on average 20% of our new players invite 4 people then we have a viral factor = 20% × 4 = 0.8.

This means that on average each player invites 0.8 other players, who invite another 0.8 players, who invite another 0.8 players, and so on. This geometric series can be simplified to:

1 / (1 – 0.8) = 5 Players

So, for every player that we acquire through our paid marketing activity we get 4 for 'free' through viral effects.

Getting to the bottom line, we can calculate the total value of acquiring one customer as:

Total Value = LTV × (1 / Viral Factor)

For our hypothetical model we see:

$2.10 × 1 / (1 – 0.8) = $10.50

In other words, we could afford to spend up to \$10.50, less servicing costs, to acquire one new player. Although, it's unlikely you would need to spend over \$10 acquiring one new player!

By paying attention to understand your customer base, by having an integrated view of customers across channels and service lines and by having a well managed metrics analysis program it is possible to optimize the various levers to achieve a profitable growth.

REFERENCES

Rud, Olivia Parr. *Data Mining Cookbook: Modeling Data for Marketing, Risk and Customer Relationship Management:* Wiley, November 2000.

Rosenberger, Larry E. John Nash, and Ann Graham: *The Deciding Factor: The Power of Analytics to Make Every Decision a Winner:* Jossey-Bass , March 2009.

CHAPTER 9

TAMING THE UNSTRUCTURED—TEXT MINING

An alert reader will make connections between seemingly unrelated facts to generate new ideas or hypotheses. However, the burgeoning growth of published text means that even the most avid reader cannot hope to keep up with all the reading in a particular area, let alone other related areas. Nuggets of insight or new knowledge is at risk of languishing undiscovered in the literature.

INTRODUCTION

We now have electronic books, documents, web pages, emails, blogs, news, chats, memos, research papers, etc. All of this information is accessible, thanks to databases and information retrieval (IR). Let us take the example of Biotech Industry:

- 80% of biological knowledge is only in research papers.
- If you read 60 research papers in a week, and 10% of those are interesting, you will manage to analyze 6 research papers per week or 300 research papers in a year.
- While you were analyzing 300 research papers in a year, MEDLINE® (MEDLINE is the National Library of Medicine's premier bibliographic database covering the fields of medicine, nursing, dentistry, veterinary medicine, the health care system, and the preclinical sciences) added more than 10,000 abstracts in a month and Chemical Abstracts Registry (CAG) registered 4000 entries each day.

The main purpose of text mining is to process unstructured (textual) information, extract meaningful numeric indices from the text and derive summaries for the words contained in the documents or to compute summaries for the documents based on the words contained in them. Thus, enabling us to analyze words, clusters of words used in documents, etc. A key element is the linking together of the extracted information to form new facts or new hypotheses to be explored further by more conventional means of experimentation.

TEXT MINING

Text mining is different from what we're familiar with in web search. In search, the user is typically looking for something that is already known and has been written by someone else. The problem is pushing aside all the material that currently isn't relevant to your needs in order to find the relevant information. In text mining, the goal is to discover heretofore unknown information, something that no one yet knows and so could not have yet written down.

Text mining is a variation of data mining that tries to find interesting patterns from large databases. The difference between data mining and text mining is that in text mining the patterns are extracted from natural language text rather than from structured databases of facts. Databases are designed for programs to process automatically; text is written for people to read. We do not have programs that can "read" text and will not have any such for the foreseeable future. Many researchers think it will require a full simulation of how the mind works before we can write programs that read the way people do.

However, there is a field called computational linguistics (also known as natural language processing) which is making a lot of progress in doing small subtasks in text analysis. For example, it is relatively easy to write a program to extract phrases from an article or book that, when shown to a human reader, seem to summarize its contents. (The most frequent words and phrases in this chapter, minus the really common words like "the" are: text mining, information, programs, and example, which is not a bad five-word summary of its contents.)

There are programs that can, with reasonable accuracy, extract information from text with somewhat regularized structure. For example, programs that read in resumes and extract out people's names, addresses, job skills, and so on, can get accuracies in the high 80%s. I don't consider this to be text mining; rather it falls into an area called information extraction. However, I am a bit of a purist when it comes to defining what text mining is. I distinguish between what I call "real" text mining that discovers new pieces of knowledge, from approaches that find overall trends in textual data.

An analogy I like to use comes from the realm of crime fighting. I think discovering new knowledge vs. showing trends is like the difference between detective following clues to find the criminal vs. analysts looking at crime statistics to assess overall trends in car theft. People are using the output of such programs to try to link together information in interesting ways. For example, one can extract all the names of people and companies that occur in news text surrounding the topic of wireless technology to try to infer who the players are in that field. There are a number of companies that are investigating this kind of application.

One problem with these approaches is that it is difficult to recognize which of the many relations that are shown are truly interesting. You'll immediately see who the big players are, but anyone who knows the business will already be aware of this. You'll also see many weak links between various players, hundreds or thousands of such links, and you can't tell which are the really interesting ones that you should pay attention to.

The most active and I think promising, application area for text mining is in the biosciences. As another example, one of the current big questions in genomics is which proteins interact with which other proteins. There has been notable success in looking at which words co-occur in articles that discuss the proteins in order to predict such interactions. The key is to not look for direct mentions of pairs, but to look for articles that mention individual protein names, keep track of which other words occur in those articles, and then look for other articles containing the same sets of words. This very simple method can yield surprisingly good results, even though the meanings of the texts are not being discerned by the programs. Rather, the text is treated like a "bag of words". To get farther though we need more sophisticated language analysis.

Essentially, when we look at text, we start working on statistical techniques that try to assign semantics, or meaning, to parts of the text. We break off pieces of the problem of analysis, targeted towards particular applications, rather than trying to "read" the articles as a whole. This approach is especially promising in the biosciences due to the nature of the text itself.

TEXT MINING—TECHNOLOGY FOUNDATIONS

Figure 9.1 depicts a generic process model for a text mining application. Starting with a collection of documents, a text mining tool would retrieve a particular document and pre-process it by checking format and character sets. Then it would go through a text analysis phase, sometimes repeating techniques until information is extracted. Three text analysis techniques are shown in the example, but many other combinations of techniques could be used depending on the goals of the organization. The resulting information can be placed in a management information system, yielding an abundant amount of knowledge for the user of that system.

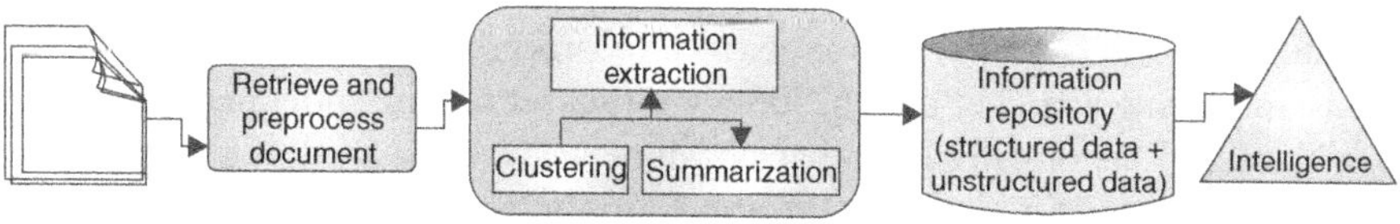

Figure 9.1 Text mining process and components.

Although the differences in human and computer languages are expansive, there have been technological advances which have begun to close the gap. The field of natural language processing has produced technologies that teach computers natural language so that they may analyze, understand, and even generate text. Some of the technologies that have been developed and can be used in the text mining process are information extraction, topic tracking, summarization, categorization, clustering, concept linkage, information visualization, and question answering. In the following sections we will discuss each of these technologies and the role that they play in text mining. We will also illustrate the type of situations where each technology may be useful in order to help readers identify tools of interest to themselves or their organizations.

Information Retrieval

Information Retrieval (IR) is most commonly referred to as the "search problem". The problem is simple: given a collection of documents and a user query, find a subset in the collection that is relevant to the user query. The problem sounds easy but there are many subtleties. Both the documents and the query are often ambiguous and lack well-defined semantics. Unlike the rigid structures found in traditional relational databases, text has barely any structure. A search for "football" is ambiguous across different cultures. Does the user actually mean "soccer?" Furthermore, what if the word "football" never actually appears in a document that is about football? Should the article be discarded as being non-relevant? The judgment for relevance is even hard for human beings. Different backgrounds can result in vastly different judgments.

The presentation of the results is another problem as well. Studies have shown that most users prefer a ranked list of the relevant documents with the more relevant ones higher up. The comparison of document A and B in regards to relevance has no answers other than empirical testing.

Information Extraction

A starting point for computers to analyze unstructured text is to use information extraction. *Information extraction process identifies key phrases and relationships within text.* It does this by looking for pre-defined sequences in text, a process called pattern matching. For example, given the sentence "set a stiff target of 303 to win, Pakistan made early inroads into India's famous batting line up by claiming wickets of Sachin Tendulkar and Gautam Gambhir; ICC Championship Trophy has not been a happy hunting ground for India from a historical context", information extraction process should identify India and Pakistan playing a cricket match, 303 is a target set to win, India has already lost 2 wickets and historically India has not done well in this kind of a tournament. Information extraction infers the relationships between all the identified people, places, activities and time to provide the user with meaningful information. This technology can be very useful when dealing with large volumes of text. Almost all text mining software uses information extraction since it is the basis for many of the other technologies discussed below.

Topic Tracking

A topic tracking system works by keeping user profiles, and based on the documents the user views, predicts other documents of interest to the user. Yahoo offers a free topic tracking tool (www.alerts.yahoo.com) that allows users to choose keywords and notifies them when news relating to those topics becomes available. Topic tracking technology does have limitations, however. For example, if a user sets up an alert for "text mining", he/she will receive several news stories on mining for minerals, and very few that are actually on text mining. Some of the better text mining tools let users select particular categories of interest or the application automatically can even infer the user's interests based on his/her reading history and click-through information.

There are many areas where topic tracking can be applied in industry. It can be used to alert companies anytime a competitor is in the news. This allows them to keep up with competitive products or changes in the market. Similarly, businesses might want to track news on their own company and products. It could also be used in the medical industry by doctors and other people looking for new treatments for illnesses and who wish to keep up on the latest advancements. Individuals in the field of education could also use topic tracking to be sure they have the latest references for research in their area of interest.

Summarization

Text summarization is immensely helpful for trying to figure out whether or not a lengthy document meets the user's needs and is worth reading for further information. With large texts, text summarization processes and summarizes the entire document in the time it would take the user to read the first paragraph. The key to summarization is to reduce the length and detail of a document while retaining its main points and overall meaning. The challenge is that, although computers are able to identify people, places, and time, it is still difficult to teach software to analyze semantics and to interpret meaning. Generally, when we summarize text, we read the entire selection to develop a full understanding, and then write a summary highlighting its main points.

One of the strategies most widely used by text summarization tools, sentence extraction, extracts important sentences from an article by statistically weighting the sentences. Further heuristics such as position information are also used for summarization. For example, summarization tools may extract the sentences which follow the key phrase "in conclusion", after which typically lie the main points of the document. Summarization tools may also search for headings and other markers of subtopics in order to identify the key points of a document. Microsoft Word's Auto Summarize function is a simple example of text summarization. Many text summarization tools allow the user to choose the percentage of the total text they want extracted as a summary.

Summarization can work with topic tracking tools or categorization tools in order to summarize the documents that are retrieved on a particular topic. If organizations, medical personnel, or other researchers were given hundreds of documents that addressed their topic of interest, then summarization tools could be used to reduce the time spent sorting through the material. Individuals would be able to more quickly assess the relevance of the information to the topic they are interested in.

Categorization

Categorization involves identifying the main themes of a document by placing the document into a pre-defined set of topics. When categorizing a document, a text mining application will often treat the document as a "bag of words". It does not attempt to process the actual information as information extraction does. Rather, categorization only counts words that appear and, from the counts, identifies the main topics that the document covers. Categorization often relies on a thesaurus for which topics are predefined, and relationships are identified by looking for broad terms, narrower terms, synonyms, and related terms. Categorization tools normally have a method for ranking the documents in order of which documents have the most content on a particular topic.

As with summarization, categorization can be used with topic tracking to further specify the relevance of a document to a person seeking information on a topic. The documents returned from topic tracking could be ranked by content weights, so that individuals could give priority to the most relevant documents first. Categorization can be used in a number of application domains. Many businesses and industries provide customer support or have to answer questions on a variety of topics from their customers. If they can use categorization schemes to classify the documents by topic, then customers or end-users will be able to access the information they seek much more readily.

Clustering

Clustering is a technique used to group similar documents, but it differs from categorization in that documents are clustered on the fly instead of through the use of predefined topics. Another benefit of clustering is that documents can appear in multiple subtopics, thus ensuring that a useful document will not be omitted from search results.

A basic clustering algorithm creates a vector of topics for each document and measures the weights of how well the document fits into each cluster. If someone goes to www.clusty.com, and type in "Saturn" in the search field, the returned topics include planet, photo, car and performance. This clustering tool allows the user to quickly narrow down the documents by identifying which topics are relevant to the search and which are not. Clustering technology can be useful in organizing thousands of documents.

Concept Linkage

Concept linkage tools connect related documents by identifying the commonly shared concepts and help users find information that they perhaps wouldn't have found using traditional searching methods. It promotes browsing for information rather than searching for it.

Concept linkage is a valuable concept in text mining, especially in the biomedical fields where so much research has been done that it is impossible for researchers to read all the material and make associations to other research. Concept linking comes in very handy, while identifying links between diseases and treatments. For example, a text mining application may easily identify a link between topics X and Y, and Y and Z, which are well-known relations and also provide useful information detecting a potential link between X and Z, something that a human researcher has not come across yet because of the large volume of information she would have to sort through to make the connection.

A well known example of this is Dan Swanson's research in the 1980's that identified magnesium deficiency as a contributor to migraine headaches. Swanson looked at articles with titles containing the keyword "migraine" from those identified keywords that appeared often within the documents. One such term was "spreading depression." He then looked for titles containing "spreading depression" and repeated the process with those documents. Then, he identified "magnesium deficiency" as a key term, and hypothesized that magnesium deficiency was a factor contributing to migraine headaches. There were no direct links between the two, and no previous research had been done suggested the two were related. The hypothesis was only made from linking related documents from migraines, to spreading depression, to magnesium deficiency. The direct link between magnesium deficiency and migraine headaches was later proved accurate by actual scientific experiments, showing that Swanson's linkage methods could be a valuable process in future medical research. Experiments similar to Swanson's have been replicated through the use of automated tools that can be applied to text mining.

Information Visualization

Information visualization puts large textual sources in a visual hierarchy or map and provides browsing capabilities, in addition to simple searching. There are tools that can show mappings of large amounts of text, allowing the user to visually analyze the content. The user can interact with the document map by zooming, scaling, and creating sub-maps. Information visualization is useful when a user needs to narrow down a broad range of documents and explore related topics.

Information visualization can be extended to both data as well as text, and is often referred to as "duo-mining". Vendors have begun recommending duo-mining to their customers as a way of giving them the edge on consolidated information for better decision making. This process combination has proven to be especially useful to banking and credit card companies. Instead of only being able to analyze the structured data they collect from transactions, they can add call logs from customer services and further analyze customers and spending patterns from the text mining side. These new developments in text mining technology that go beyond simple searching methods are the key to information discovery and have a promising outlook for application in all areas of work.

APPLICATIONS OF TEXT MINING

Unstructured text is very common, and in fact may represent the majority of information available to a particular research or analytics project. There are several applications of text mining in industry. Advent and popularization of Internet has further necessitated the cause of widespread adoption of text mining.

Text Mining as Document Search

The automatic search of large numbers of documents based on key words or key phrases is also often referred to as an application of text mining. This is the domain of, for example, the popular internet search engines that have been developed over the last decade to provide efficient access to Web pages with certain content. This is obviously an important type of application with many uses in any organization that needs to search very large document repositories based on varying criteria.

Automatic Processing of Messages, Emails, etc.

Another common application for text mining is to aid in the automatic classification of texts. For example, it is possible to "filter" out automatically most undesirable "junk email" based on certain terms or words that are not likely to appear in legitimate messages, but instead identify undesirable electronic mail. In this manner, such messages can automatically be discarded. Such automatic systems for classifying electronic messages can also be useful in applications where messages need to be routed (automatically) to the most appropriate department or agency.

Analyzing Open-Ended Survey Responses

In survey research (e.g., marketing), it is not uncommon to include various open-ended questions pertaining to the topic under investigation. The idea is to permit respondents to express their "views" or opinions without constraining them to particular dimensions or a particular response format. This may yield insights into customers' views and opinions that might otherwise not be discovered when relying solely on structured questionnaires designed by "experts."

Sentiment Analysis

Determining the degree to which a sentiment is positive, negative, or neutral for the entire content or a segment of the content is described as one of the reasons for conducting sentiment analysis. A gamut of online sites including communities, weblogs and discussion boards are being analyzed for gaining an insight into customer opinion and market perception. Brand owners are increasingly making use of analytics engine that instantaneously filters and analyses a plethora of consumer conversations taking place on the web.

It is said that sentiment is typically a localised phenomenon that is more appropriately computed at the paragraph, sentence, or entity level. Sentiment analysis is not simply the problem of determining whether a document, a paragraph or even a sentence expresses a positive or negative sentiment or opinion. It is also about entities. Without such information, any sentiment is of little practical use. So one should not only talk about sentiment analysis of documents, paragraphs, or sentences, but also about the entities that sentiments have been expressed upon. Here an entity can be a product, service, person, organization, event, or topic.

Furthermore, in many cases, only looking at entities may not be sufficient because one may want to know sentiments on components and attributes of entities. Second, we should realise that localisation is also important in terms of the text content. For example, it does not make much sense studying sentiment analysis of a document as a whole if the document talks about multiple entities.

In the next chapter, we will discuss Sentiment Analysis at length.

Analyzing Warranty or Insurance Claims, Diagnostic Interviews, etc.

In some business domains, the majority of information is collected in open-ended, textual form. For example, warranty claims or initial medical (patient) interviews can be summarized in brief narratives; or when we take our cars to a service station for repairs, typically, the attendant will write some notes about the problems that we report and what we believe needs to be fixed. Increasingly, those notes are collected electronically. So those types of narratives are readily available for input into text mining algorithms. This information can then be usefully exploited to, for example, identify common clusters of problems and complaints on certain automobiles, etc. Likewise, in the medical field, open-ended descriptions by patients of their own symptoms might yield useful clues for the actual medical diagnosis.

Investigating Competitors by Crawling Their Websites

Another type of potentially very useful application is to automatically process the contents of Web pages in a particular domain. For example, you could go to a Web page, and begin "crawling" the links you find there to process all Web pages that are referenced. In this manner, you could automatically derive a list of terms and documents available at that site, and hence quickly determine the most important terms and features that are described. It is easy to see how these capabilities could efficiently deliver valuable business intelligence about the activities of competitors.

APPROACHES TO TEXT MINING

To reiterate, text mining can be summarized as a process of "numericizing" text. At the simplest level, all words found in the input documents will be indexed and counted in order to compute a table of documents and words, i.e., a matrix of frequencies that enumerates the number of times that each word occurs in each document. This basic process can be further refined to exclude certain common words such as "the" and "a" (stop word lists) and to combine different grammatical forms of the same words such as "traveling," "traveled," "travel," etc. (stemming). However, once a table of (unique) words (terms) by documents has been derived, all standard statistical and analytics techniques can be applied to derive dimensions or clusters of words or documents, or to identify "important" words or terms that best predict another outcome variable of interest.

Note: Try the various automated translation services available via the Web that can translate entire paragraphs of text from one language into another. Then translate some text, even simple text, from your native language to some other language and back, and review the results. Almost every time, the attempt to translate even short sentences to other languages and back while retaining the original meaning of the sentence produces humorous rather than accurate results. This illustrates the difficulty of automatically interpreting the meaning of text.

Issues and Considerations for "Numericizing" Text

Large Numbers of Small Documents vs. Small Numbers of Large Documents

Examples of scenarios using large numbers of small or moderate sized documents were given earlier (e.g., analyzing warranty or insurance claims, diagnostic interviews, etc.). On the other hand, if your intent is to extract "concepts" from only a few documents that are very large (e.g., two lengthy books), then statistical analyses are generally less powerful because the "number of cases" (documents) in this case is very small while the "number of variables" (extracted words) is very large.

Excluding Certain Characters, Short Words, Numbers, etc

Excluding numbers, certain characters, or sequences of characters, or words that are shorter or longer than a certain number of letters can be done before the indexing of the input documents starts. You may also want to exclude "rare words," defined as those that only occur in a small percentage of the processed documents.

Include Lists, Exclude Lists (Stop-words)

Specific list of words to be indexed can be defined; this is useful when you want to search explicitly for particular words, and classify the input documents based on the frequencies with which those words occur. Also, "stop-words", i.e., terms that are to be excluded from the indexing can be defined. Typically, a default list of English stop words includes "the", "a", "of", "since", etc., i.e., words that are used in the respective language very frequently, but communicate very little unique information about the contents of the document.

Synonyms and Phrases

Synonyms, such as "sick" or "ill", or words that are used in particular phrases where they denote unique meaning can be combined for indexing. For example, "Microsoft Windows" might be such a phrase, which is a specific reference to the computer operating system, but has nothing to do with the common use of the term "Windows" as it might, for example, be used in descriptions of home improvement projects.

Stemming Algorithms

An important pre-processing step before indexing of input documents begins, is the stemming of words. The term "stemming" refers to the reduction of words to their roots so that, for example, different grammatical forms or declinations of verbs are identified and indexed (counted) as the same word. For example, stemming will ensure that both "traveling" and "traveled" will be recognized by the text mining program as the same word.

Support for Different Languages

Stemming, synonyms, the letters that are permitted in words, etc. are highly language dependent operations. Therefore, support for different languages is important.

Transforming the Word Frequencies

Once the input documents have been indexed and the initial word frequencies (by document) computed, a number of additional transformations needs to be performed to summarize and aggregate the information that was extracted.

Log-frequencies

First, various transformations of the frequency counts need to be performed. The raw word or term frequencies generally reflect on how salient or important a word is in each document. Specifically, words that occur with greater frequency in a document are better descriptors of the contents of that document. However, it is not reasonable to assume that the word counts themselves are proportional to their importance as descriptors of the documents. For example, if a word occurs 1 time in document A, but 3 times in document B, then it is not necessarily reasonable to conclude that this word is 3 times as important a descriptor of document B as compared to document A. Likewise, an even simpler transformation can be used that enumerates whether a term is used in a document. The resulting documents-by-words matrix will contain only 1s and 0s to indicate the presence or absence of the respective words.

Inverse Document Frequencies

Another issue that you may want to consider more carefully and reflect in the indices used in further analyses are the relative document frequencies of different words. For example, a term such as "guess" may occur frequently in all documents, while another term such as "software" may only occur in a few. The reason is that one might make "guesses" in various contexts, regardless of the specific topic, while "software" is a more semantically focused term that is only likely to occur in documents that deal with computer software. A common and very useful transformation that reflects both the specificity of words (document frequencies) as well as the overall frequencies of their occurrences (word frequencies) is the so-called inverse document frequency (for the *i*'th word and *j*'th document).

Latent Semantic Indexing

As described above, the most basic result of the initial indexing of words found in the input documents is a frequency table with simple counts, i.e., the number of times that different words occur in each input document. Usually, one would transform those raw counts to indices that better reflect the (relative) "importance" of words and/or their semantic specificity in the context of the set of input documents.

A common analytic tool for interpreting the "meaning" or "semantic space" described by the words that were extracted, is to create a mapping of the word and documents into a common space, computed from the word frequencies or transformed word frequencies (e.g., inverse document frequencies).

In general, here is how it works: Suppose you indexed a collection of customer reviews of their new automobiles (e.g., for different makes and models). You may find that every time a review includes the word "gas-mileage," it also includes the term "economy." Further, when reports include the word "reliability" they also include the term "defects" (e.g., make reference to "no defects"). However, there is no consistent pattern regarding the use of the terms "economy" and "reliability," i.e., some documents include either one or both. In other words, these four words "gas-mileage" and "economy," and "reliability" and "defects," describe two independent dimensions—the first having to do with the overall operating cost of the vehicle, the other with the quality and workmanship.

The idea of latent semantic indexing is to identify such underlying dimensions (of "meaning"), into which the words and documents can be mapped. As a result, we may identify the underlying (latent) themes described or discussed in the input documents, and also identify the documents that mostly deal with economy, reliability, or both. Hence, we want to map the extracted words or terms and input documents into a common latent semantic space.

In general, the purpose of this technique is to reduce the overall dimensionality of the input matrix (number of input documents by number of extracted words) to a lower-dimensional space, where each consecutive dimension represents the largest degree of variability (between words and documents) possible. Ideally, you might identify the two or three most salient dimensions, accounting for most of the variability (differences) between the words and documents and, hence, identify the latent semantic space that organizes the words and documents in the analysis. In some way, once such dimensions can be identified, you have extracted the underlying "meaning" of what is contained (discussed, described) in the documents.

INCORPORATING TEXT MINING RESULTS INTO THE ANALYTICS PROJECT

After significant (e.g., frequent) words have been extracted from a set of input documents, and/or after latent semantic indexing has been applied to extract salient semantic dimensions, typically the next and most important step is to use the extracted information in an analytics project.

Graphics and Visualization Methods

Depending on the purpose of the analyses, in some instances the extraction of semantic dimensions alone can be a useful outcome if it clarifies the underlying structure of what is contained in the input documents. For example, a study of new car owners' comments about their vehicles may uncover the salient dimensions in the minds of those drivers when they think about or consider their automobile (or how they "feel" about it). For marketing research purposes, that in itself can be a useful and significant result.

Clustering and Factoring

You can use cluster analysis methods to identify groups of documents (e.g., vehicle owners who described their new cars), to identify groups of similar input texts. This type of analysis also could be extremely useful in the context of market research studies, for example, of new car owners.

Automated Classification of Text

Classification of text records is an example of supervised learning that seeks to build a probabilistic model of a function and maps documents to classifications. In supervised learning of text, where an entire record represents one example to be classified, a learning algorithm is presented with a set of already classified, or labelled, examples. This set is called the training set. A number of classified records from the training set are removed prior to model building to be used for testing the performance of the model. This set is known as the testing set.

To better measure the classification accuracy of a model, often several models are built from different partitions of the examples to training and testing sets. The classification error is then averaged over each model.

Once a model has been constructed, it can be used to predict the classification of unlabeled records. The accuracy of such models is largely dependent on the "representativeness" of the training data with respect to newly acquired data to be classified. In general, the more representative the training data, the better the performance. A larger number of training examples is often better, because a larger sample is likely to be more reflective of the actual distribution of the data as a whole.

TEXT TRANSFORMATION STEPS

Classification algorithms operate on numerical quantities as inputs. Hence integer counts of the attribute values are all that is required. The conversion of text records to numeric attributes is a multi-staged process of feature construction, which employs several key transformations. There are many approaches to this process—one of the most common is to treat each text record as a "bag of words." Each unique word constitutes an attribute. The number of occurrences of a word in a record (frequency of occurrence) is the value of the attribute for that document. Records are therefore represented as numeric attributes where each attribute value is the frequency of occurrence of a distinct term.

For even modest sized text collections the number of distinct terms across the entire collection can be quite large—often in the tens of thousands. For any single record, however, the number of distinct terms is often quite small in comparison. As a result, the majority of attribute values in a representation of record will be set to zero (conceptually empty) because those terms do not appear in the record.

Note: *Attributes whose values are predominantly empty is commonly referred to as sparse. Because of the nature of sparse tables a special table implementation is used that only stores the non-empty data values thereby saving a large amount of memory space and greatly reducing the runtime for many algorithms that access the data. In most instances, if this special implementation were not used, the table would be too large to store in conventional memory.*

Often, simply extracting out all unique terms, or tokens, is not the most effective way to acquire attributes for text mining. Many tokens may not be words at all—possibly constituting noise in the process that should be filtered out. Furthermore, some types of words, or series of words, may be preferable for learning. For example, often nouns or noun phrases are preferred. Part-of-speech identification algorithms and lexical/semantic dictionaries are typically used to provide additional information about terms. Also, very common words like "and" and "the" are often filtered out to improve performance. All of these transformations are performed before any learning takes place. The number of steps involved in this pre-processing can be quite numerous and often constitutes the bulk of the overall model building process. Following are the steps often followed in text transformation.

Sentence Splitting and Tokenization

Identifying sentence boundaries in a document is not as trivial a process as it may seem. Using rules or statistical models (or both), they need to be split to individual words or sometimes word parts needs to be labelled. This is important because many down stream components need the tokens to be clearly identified for analysis.

Part-of-Speech (PoS) Tagging

Such components typically assign a pos tag to a token. Other data such as synonyms (to name a very few) may also be identified at this stage.

Stop Word Filtering

Very common words like "and" and "the" are often filtered out to improve performance. This process is called stop word removal. One basic approach is to remove all words that appear on a list of common words. Another approach is to remove words that occur in large number across most documents — these types of terms create "noise" that makes text records less distinguishable.

PoS Filtering

This component reads a document object as input and filters the tokens for that document based on part of speech tag information. A document object is taken as input. The token list is retrieved from the document and only those tokens with part of speech tags that match at least one value in the selected tag list are retained.

Note: Some components use regular expressions of pos tags to identify "chunks" of tokens (perhaps all noun phrases for example). This process is sometimes called chunking.

UNSUPERVISED TEXT MINING

Clustering

Unsupervised approaches do not rely on a training set of labelled examples for building a model. Instead, these approaches use a similarity or difference heuristic that is a function of only the content of text records. The heuristic function is used to construct classifications of clusters that are said to be emergent from the data.

Cluster formation techniques vary depending on the type and number of cases being analyzed. One of the most prevalent approaches uses a group of methods known as hierarchical clustering algorithms. In the most basic applications, these methods form a tree of classifications whose root is the set of N objects and whose leaves are the individual objects. The intervening levels of the tree define various hierarchical partitions of the set of N objects. The classification process can be a top-down, "divide and conquer" approach or, alternatively, a bottom-up, agglomerative process. The heuristic for grouping (or partitioning) is based on some similar function applied to the values of the p variables for each individual object.

Hierarchical Agglomerative Clustering (HAC)

Hierarchical agglomerative (bottom-up) technique (HAC) models individual text items as points in vector space. Not all words in a document are considered terms. Terms are primarily nouns and/or noun phrases. Common words that have little semantic content, such as prepositions and conjunctions, are routinely discarded, as are most verbs. For each term, a weight value is computed as the normalized frequency of occurrence of that term. Terms are further weighted based on their uniqueness for that document using the following formula:

term weight = normalized term freq*log (inverse document freq)

The agglomerative process starts by placing each individual response in its own cluster and computing the similarity values for all possible cluster pairings. The two most similar clusters will then be combined and the process repeated until either a finite number of clusters are formed or the similarity between any two clusters does not rise above some threshold value.

Case Study – Text Mining and Claims Analytics

Table 9.1 Structured data claims

Claim No	*Accident Date*	*Status*	*Attorney*	*Paid*	*Outstanding*	*Incurred ALAE*	*Incurred Loss*	*State*
200916	01/01/2009	C	YES	37,230	0	11,021	37,230	NY
200943	01/16/2009	C	NO	0	0	0	0	NY
200861	09/09/2008	O	NO	195	0	3	195	CA
200879	10/18/2008	C	YES	99,852	0	31,807	99,852	NJ
200884	12/11/2008	C	NO	286	0	72	286	IL

Table 9.2 Sample claims file—text data

Injury Description
Broken ankle and sprained wrist
Foot contusion
Unknown
Mouth and knee
Head and arm lacerations
Foot puncture
Lower back and legs
Back strain
Knee

The examples above illustrate simulated data from a general liability claims file. The data contain both structured and unstructured data (one free form text field: injury description). The sample data also contains other insurance related information in the form of structured data: incurred losses, incurred loss adjustment expenses, accident year, status (open/closed) and whether or not an attorney is involved in the claim. In the text data simple, there is no injury or body part code in the data and the only information about the nature of the injury is the free form text description. The injury description is a very brief description, generally containing only a few words. The data are representative of which might be available from a small self insured exposure. While many claims databases contain larger accident and claim description fields, these data serve as a simple example for us to demonstrate of how text mining works.

Term Extraction

During term extraction, character text is first parsed into words. The term extraction process also strips away words that convey no meaning such as "a" or "the". An additional part of the process involves finding words that belong together such as "John Smith".

When data are parsed, string functions are used to extract the words from the character string composing the text data. To do this, spaces, commas and other delimiters must be used to separate words. The result of parsing is data organized in a rectangular matrix containing indicator variables for the words extracted from the text field.

Table 9.3 Examples of terms created

Injury description	Broken	Ankle	AND	Sprained	Wrist	Foot	Contusion	Unknown	Neck	Back	Mouth	Knee	Head	Arm	Lacerations	Puncture	Lower	Legs	Strain
Broken ankle and sprained wrist	1	1	1	1	1	0	0	0	0	0	0	0	0	0	0	0	0	0	0
Foot contusion	0	0	0	0	0	1	1	0	0	0	0	0	0	0	0	0	0	0	0
Mouth and knee	0	0	1	0	0	0	0	0	0	0	1	1	0	0	0	0	0	0	0
Unknown	0	0	0	0	0	0	0	1	0	0	0	0	0	0	0	0	0	0	0
Neck and back strain	0	0	1	0	0	0	0	0	1	1	0	0	0	0	0	0	0	0	1
Head and arm lacerations	0	0	1	0	0	0	0	0	0	0	0	1	1	1	0	0	0	0	0
Foot puncture	0	0	0	0	0	1	0	0	0	0	0	0	0	0	0	1	0	0	0
Lower back and legs	0	0	1	0	0	0	0	0	0	1	0	0	0	0	0	0	1	1	0
Back strain	0	0	0	0	0	0	0	0	0	1	0	0	0	0	0	0	0	0	1
Knee	0	0	0	0	0	0	0	0	0	0	0	1	0	0	0	0	0	0	0

Table 9.3 displays data that could be created from an injury description text field. Each claim description is treated as a "bag of words". The matrices resulting from parsing text data are typically sparse. That is, for most of the terms, most of the records contain a zero for that term and only a few records have a one.

The example shown is a relatively simple one. The claim description field is relatively short and contains no delimiters other than a blank space. However, other delimiters such as the comma and period occur frequently and need to be identified also. Some delimiters, such as a single apostrophe (as in I'll) and period (as in etc.) may be part of the words; so the complex rules for finding and using such delimiters must be coded into the program that parses the data.

Certain words occur very frequently in text data. Examples include "the" and "a". These words are referred to as "stop words". The stop words are words removed from the term collection because they have no meaningful content. By creating a list of such stop words and eliminating them, the number of indicator variables created is reduced. Table 9.4 displays a sample of stop words used in this analysis. Many of these stop words do not appear in the claim description data, but appear frequently in text data.

Table 9.4 Example stop words

Stop Words
A
And
Able
About
Above
Across
Aforementioned
After
Again

Table 9.5 presents a collection of words obtained from parsing the injury description data into single words and removing stop words.

Table 9.5 Example of parsed words

Parsed Words			
Head	Laceration	Knee	Injury
Unknown	L	Leg	None
Arm	R	Foot	Bruised
Hand	Ankle	Hip	Twisted
Shoulder	Left	Cut	Lower
Wrist	Neck	Fracture	Broken
Finger	Injuries	Lip	Right
Knees	Face	Pain	FX

There are other issues affecting the usefulness of the parsed data. One issue is multiple versions and spellings of words. Table 9.5 illustrates this. Both L and LEFT are used to denote left, R and RIGHT are used to denote right and the table above has both the singular and plural versions of KNEE. In addition, it can be seen from the table that certain "words" stand for the same injury. For example, as a result of abbreviations used, FX and FRACTURE as well as BROKEN all denote the same injury. The process referred to as stemming is used to substitute one word, referred to as a stem (because in the example of knee and knees, both words have the same stem) for all versions of the term.

Once the words have been parsed, stop words removed and stemming performed, the sparse matrix of term indicators is ready for the next step: feature creation. During the feature creation step, words and sequences of words are classified into groups that contain similar information.

In some text mining applications, especially those that attempt to understand the content contained in large documents, other analysis such as grammatical analysis is performed before progressing to the feature creation step. Such analysis will not be described here as it is not relevant to the example in this section.

Feature Creation

Term extraction is the first step in deriving meaning or content from free form text. The next step is feature creation. Thus far, each line of text has been parsed into a "bag of words". The data can be represented as a rectangular array that has indicator variables for each term in the injury description. When we analyze the terms more carefully, we may find that some words such as "back strain" and "neck strain" denote similar injuries and are unlike "head trauma". Thus, occurrence or non-occurrence of specific words may tell us something useful about the nature and severity of the injury.

One of the most common techniques used to group records with similar values on the terms together is known as cluster analysis. Cluster analysis is an example of dimension reduction. Before describing cluster analysis, let us discuss the concepts of dimension and of dimension reduction.

Dimension Reduction

Table 9.6 displays the two views of dimensionality for a sample claims database. Each column of data can be viewed as a separate dimension.

Each column contains information about the claimants and is a potential variable in an actuarial or modeling analysis. Each column is a separate dimension. Often in a large database containing hundreds or even thousands of variables, many variables are highly correlated with each other and contain redundant information. The large number of variables can be reduced to a smaller number of components or factors using a technique such as factor analysis. For instance, figure below displays three of the dimensions related to financial information in

Table 9.6 Dimensions example

Claim No	*Date of Loss*	*Status*	*Incurred Loss*
1998001	09/09/1998	C	457.98
1998002	09/21/1998	C	871
1998003	10/09/1998	C	1459
1998004	10/11/1998	C	265.76
1998005	11/04/1998	C	8945
1998006	11/18/1998	C	297.98
1998007	11/30/1998	C	1276.01
1998008	12/17/1998	C	7000

the sample claims data; ultimate incurred loss, ultimate allocated loss adjustment expense (ALAE) and ultimate incurred loss plus ALAE. It can be seen from the graph that the three dimensions are correlated, which one would expect, particularly when one of the variables is the sum of the other two. It is common in actuarial analysis (particularly with small databases) to work with only one of these variables; ultimate loss and ALAE. Thus the number of "dimensions" used in the analysis is reduced to one.

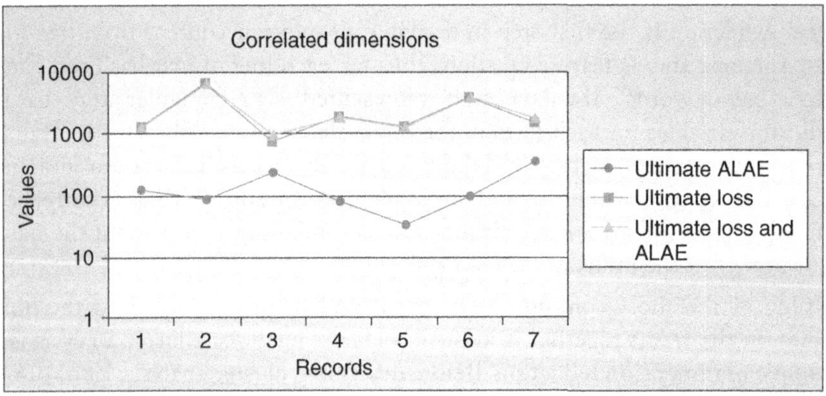

Figure 9.2 Correlated dimensions.

Each record in the data is also a dimension. When data are aggregated by accident year and development age in order to construct a loss development triangle, row-wise dimension reduction is taking place. The number of dimensions is reduced from the total number of records in the database to the number of cells in the loss development triangle.

K-means Clustering

In statistics, a formal procedure known as clustering is often used to perform dimension reduction. The objective of this technique is to group like records together. A common application of this method in property and casualty insurance is territory development. Policyholders are grouped into territories according to where they live and the territories are used in ratemaking. Both geographic information such as longitude and latitude and demographic information such as population density can be used for the territorial clustering. Cluster analysis is an unsupervised learning method; there is no dependent variable. Rather, records with similar values on the variables used for clustering are grouped together. In the territory example, policyholders living in high population density zip codes in the south eastern part of a state might be grouped together into one territory. In text mining, clustering is used to group together records with similar words or words with similar meanings.

Many different techniques for clustering exist. One of the most common methods is K-means clustering. When using K-means clustering the analyst specifies the number of clusters she wants. A statistical measure of dissimilarity between records is used to separate records that are the most dissimilar and group together records that are the most similar. Different measures of dissimilarity are used for numeric data as opposed to categorical data. Text data are generally viewed as categorical. However, when terms are coded as binary indicator variables, it is possible to apply the techniques that are used on numeric data. Moreover, text mining is commonly applied to documents containing large collections of words, such as academic papers and e-mail messages. Some words appear multiple times in such text data, and the number of times a word appears may be recorded and used for text analysis instead of a binary indicator variable.

Table 9.7 displays a calculation of both measures using two sample records. The first record has injury "broken ankle and sprained wrist" and the second record has injury "contusion to back of leg". Binary variables indicating the presence or absence of words after the parsing of text are the variables used in the measure.

A major objective of text mining is to create new information that has predictive value. The simple illustration in this chapter mined an injury description field and assigned each claim to one of seven duster groups based on the words in the injury description. The cluster group is a new independent variable that can be used to predict a dependent variable of interest to the analyst. Potential variables of interest in a claims database include financial variables such as losses and loss adjustment expenses, whether or not there has been subrogation or recovery on the claim, and whether or not the claim is likely a fraud or abuse claim. The data used in this exercise is representative of what might be available in cases where a third party claims adjuster supplied data to a self insured entity. It is therefore smaller and less rich than what one would find in a large insurance company database.

Let us look at the new injury feature added by the text mining procedure to predict the likelihood that a claim will be a serious claim. One application of analytics is to develop models to score claims early in the life of the claim. The objective is to identify claims that are likely to be the costliest to the company and apply more resources to those claims. For this analysis, a serious claim is defined

Table 9.7 K-means clustering

Variable	*Record 1 Broken Ankle and Sprained Wrist*	*Record 2 Contusion to Back of Leg*	*Squared Difference*	*Absolute Difference*
Back	0.0	1.0	1.0	1.0
Contusion	0.0	1.0	1.0	1.0
Head	0.0	0.0	0.0	0.0
Knee	0.0	0.0	0.0	0.0
Strain	0.0	0.0	0.0	0.0
Unknown	0.0	0.0	0.0	0.0
Laceration	0.0	0.0	0.0	0.0
Leg	0.0	1.0	1.0	1.0
Arm	0.0	0.0	0.0	0.0
Foot	0.0	0.0	0.0	0.0
Hand	0.0	0.0	0.0	0.0
Ankle	1.0	0.0	1.0	1.0
Shoulder	0.0	0.0	0.0	0.0
Hip	0.0	0.0	0.0	0.0
Left	0.0	0.0	0.0	0.0
Neck	0.0	0.0	0.0	0.0
Wrist	1.0	0.0	1.0	1.0
Cut	0.0	0.0	0.0	0.0
Fracture	0.0	0.0	0.0	0.0
Surgery	0.0	0.0	0.0	0.0
Finger	0.0	0.0	0.0	0.0
None	0.0	0.0	0.0	0.0
Broken	1.0	0.0	1.0	1.0
Trauma	0.0	0.0	0.0	0.0
Lower	0.0	0.0	0.0	0.0
Right	0.0	0.0	0.0	0.0
Total Distance			7	7
Measure			2.65	7

as a claim whose total losses plus allocated loss adjustment expenses exceeds \$1,000. There are several claims in the data exceed this threshold.

A histogram of claim severities is shown in Fig. 9.3. The histogram indicates that the severity distribution is right skewed and heavy tailed. Approximately 98% of loss dollars are due to claims defined as serious.

The injury group used in the model is the injury grouping of seven clusters created by the text mining analysis. The attorney variable denotes whether an attorney is involved in the claim. The table below shows the average model probability of a serious claim for both the serious and non-serious claims. It can be seen that the model predicts a much higher probability, on average, for the serious groups of claims than the non-serious group of claims.

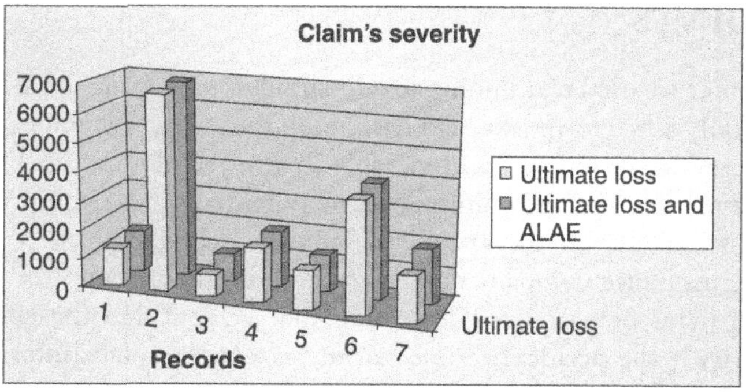

Figure 9.3 Claims severity.

Table 9.7 Mean probability of serious claim vs. actual value

Average Probability	*Actual Value*
1	0
0.31	0.01

One other application of the text variable is illustrated above. A simple analysis of variance (ANOVA) was used to predict ultimate losses and ALAE. An ANOVA is a linear model where the dependent variable is numeric and the independent variables are categorical.

Note this model includes the interaction term attorney * injury group. In this regression, both attorney involvement and injury group as well as the interaction between attorney and injury are significant. As an alternative to the classification procedure illustrated in the example, such a regression could be used to identify serious claims (i.e., the claims with high predicted values for the ultimate losses and ALAE). Another application of models that predict ultimate losses and ALAE is estimating reserves for insurance exposures. There are two components to using claim data to estimate ultimate losses for a reserving application:

- Estimate ultimate losses for claims already reported using the individual information for each claim's independent variables. Historic information on more mature claims is used to develop a model for less mature claims.
- Estimate ultimate losses for claims that have occurred, but because of a long reporting lag, have not yet been reported. In order to estimate ultimate values for unreported claims the actuary needs:
    - An estimate of unreported claims (perhaps derived from a claim development triangle).
    - An estimate of the proportion of claims in each category of the key predictor variables (i.e., an estimate of the proportion within each attorney/injury type combination). Recent historical patterns could be used to derive such estimates.

END POINTS

In this chapter we used text mining to add an injury type code to a database that contained only a free form text field describing the injury. The injury description was then used as an independent variable in two simple predictive models. In more realistic situations text mining has the potential to add significantly to the information available to the analyst in large modeling projects. For instance, many large insurance company databases contain one or more free form claim description fields or narratives describing the accident and the circumstances associated with the accident. These narratives often contain information not contained in injury, cause of loss or other coding.

This may be particularly true when new types of claims or new patterns of claiming behaviour are beginning to emerge. For example, while analyzing rising homeowner claims and suspicious and possibly fraudulent auto claims at a large insurance company; analytical approaches using only structured information coded into the company's database were unsuccessful in explaining the patterns.

Following hypothetical example of text from a claim description field:

"The claimant is anxious to settle; mentioned his attorney is willing to negotiate. Also willing to work with us on loss adjustment expenses (LAE) and calculating actual cash value. Unusually familiar with insurance industry terms. Claimant provided unusual level of details about accident, road conditions, weather, etc. Need more detail to calculate the LAE."

Certain terms in the text such as "anxious", "settle" and "familiar" may provide clues to suspicious" claims that cannot be found in the structured data in the claims database. Mining the text data for such terms significantly improved the ability to model the patterns in the data.

REFERENCE

Weiss, Sholom. Indurkhya, Nitin, Fred Dameru, and Tong Zhang: *Text Mining—Predictive Methods for Analyzing Unstructured Information:* Springer, 2005.

CHAPTER 10

SENTIMENT ANALYSIS AND OPINION MINING

An important part of our information-gathering behavior has always been to find out what other people think. With the growing availability and popularity of opinion-rich resources such as online review sites and personal blogs, new opportunities and challenges arise as people now can, and do, actively use information technologies to seek out and understand the opinions of others.

INTRODUCTION

"What other people think" has always been an important piece of information for most of us during the decision-making process. Long before awareness of the World Wide Web became widespread, many of us asked our friends to recommend an auto mechanic or to explain which model of TV is a good buy (both from a price and value perspective), requested reference letters regarding job applicants from colleagues, or consulted Consumer Reports to decide what dishwasher to buy. But the Internet and the Web have now (among other things) made it possible to find out about the opinions and experiences of those in the vast pool of people that are neither our personal acquaintances nor well-known professional critics — that is, people we have never heard of. And conversely, more and more people are making their opinions available to strangers via the Internet.

Let us see some of the interesting figures supporting this phenomenon:

- 81% of Internet users have done online research on a product at least once;
- 20% do so on a typical day;
- Among readers of online reviews of restaurants, hotels, and various services (e.g., travel agencies or doctors), between 73% and 87% report that reviews had a significant influence on their purchase;
- Consumers report being willing to pay from 20% to 99% more for a 5-star-rated item than a 4-star-rated item (the variance stems from what type of item or service is considered);

- 32% have provided a rating on a product, service, or person via an online ratings system, and 30% (including 18% of online senior citizens) have posted an online comment or review regarding a product or service.

The user views for and reliance upon online advice and recommendations that the data above reveal is a strong reason behind the surge of interest in new type of analysis—sentiment analysis and opinion mining.

With the explosion of Web 2.0 platforms such as blogs, discussion forums, peer-to-peer networks, and various other types of social media, consumers have at their disposal a soapbox of unprecedented reach and power by which to share their brand experiences and opinions, positive or negative, regarding any product or service.

Major companies are increasingly coming to realize, these consumer voices can wield enormous influence in shaping the opinions of other consumers and ultimately, their brand loyalties, their purchase decisions, and their own brand advocacy. Companies can respond to the consumer insights they generate through social media monitoring and analysis by modifying their marketing messages, brand positioning, product development, and other activities accordingly.

Today, vendors, practitioners, and the media alike call this still-nascent arena everything from 'brand monitoring', 'buzz monitoring' and 'online anthropology', to 'market influence analytics', 'conversation mining' and 'online consumer intelligence', etc. The field of "social media monitoring and analysis" deals with the computational treatment of (in alphabetical order) opinion, sentiment, and subjectivity in text. Such work has come to be known as opinion mining, sentiment analysis, and/or subjectivity analysis. The phrases review mining and appraisal extraction have been used, too, and there are some connections to affective computing, where the goals include enabling computers to recognize and express emotions.

OPINION MINING

Opinion mining in a broad sense means processing a set of search results for a given item, generating a list of product attributes (quality, features, etc.) and aggregating opinions about each of them (poor, mixed, good).

Sentiment analysis parallels that of opinion mining in certain respects. The term sentiment used in reference to the automatic analysis of evaluative text and tracking of the predictive judgments as to their polarity (either positive or negative).

To see that the distinctions in common usage of opinions and sentiments can be subtle, consider how interrelated the following sets of definitions are:

Synonyms: opinion, view, belief, conviction, persuasion, sentiment mean a judgment one holds as true.

- Opinion implies a conclusion thought out, yet open to dispute; example —each expert seemed to have a different opinion.

- View suggests a subjective opinion; example—very assertive in stating his views.
- Belief implies often deliberate acceptance and intellectual assent; example—a firm belief in her party's platform.
- Conviction applies to a firmly and seriously held belief; example—the conviction that animal life is as sacred as human.
- Persuasion suggests a belief grounded on assurance (as by evidence) of its truth; example—was of the persuasion that everything changes.
- Sentiment suggests a settled opinion reflective of one's feelings; example—her feminist sentiments are well-known.

FUNDAMENTALS OF OPINION MINING AND SENTIMENT ANALYSIS

In general, opinions can be expressed on anything, e.g., a product, a service, a topic, an individual, an organization, or an event. The general term *object* is used to denote the entity that has been commented on. An object has a set of *components* (or *parts*) and a set of *attributes*. Each component may also have its sub-components and its set of attributes, and so on. Thus, the object can be hierarchically decomposed based on the *part-of* relationship.

Definition (object): An *object O* is an entity which can be a product, topic, person, event, or organization. It is associated with a pair, *O*: (*T*, *A*), where *T* is a hierarchy or taxonomy of *components* (or *parts*) and *sub-components* of *O*, and *A* is a set of *attributes* of *O*. Each component has its own set of sub-components and attributes.

In this hierarchy or tree, the root is the object itself. Each non-root node is a component or subcomponent of the object. Each link is a part of relationship. Each node is associated with a set of attributes. An opinion can be expressed on any node and any attribute of the node. However, for an ordinary user, it is probably too complex to use a hierarchical representation. To simplify it, the tree is flattened. The word "*features*" is used to represent both components and attributes. Using features for objects (especially products) is quite common in practice. Note that in this definition the object itself is also a feature, which is the root of the tree.

For example, a document *d*, which contains a product review, a forum post or a blog that evaluates a particular object *O*. In the most general case, *d* consists of a sequence of sentences d = {*s1*, *s2*, …,*sm*}.

Definition (opinion passage on a feature): The *opinion passage* on a feature *f* of the object *O* evaluated in *d* is a group of consecutive sentences in *d* that expresses a positive or negative opinion on *f*. This means that it is possible that a sequence of sentences (at least one) together expresses an opinion on an object or a feature of the object. It is also possible that a single sentence expresses opinions on more than one feature, e.g., "The picture quality of this camera is good, but the battery life is short".

Definition (opinion holder): The *holder* of a particular opinion is a person or an organization that holds the opinion. In the case of product reviews, forum postings and blogs, opinion holders are usually the authors of the posts. Opinion holders are important in news articles because they often explicitly state the person or organization that holds a particular opinion. For example, the opinion holder in the sentence "John expressed his disagreement on the treaty" is "John".

Definition (semantic orientation of an opinion): The *semantic orientation* of an opinion on a feature *f* states whether the opinion is positive, negative or neutral. Putting things together, a *model* for an object and a set of opinions on the features of the object can be defined, which is called the *feature-based opinion mining model.*

Model of Feature-Based Opinion Mining

An object *O* is represented with a finite set of features, *F* = {*f*1, *f*2, ..., *fn*}, which includes the object itself. Each feature *fi* in *F* can be expressed with a finite set of words or phrases *Wi*, which are *synonyms*. That is, there is a set of corresponding synonym sets *W* = {*W*1, *W*2, ..., *Wn*} for the *n* features. In an evaluative document *d* which evaluates object *O*, an opinion holder *j* comments on a subset of the features *Sj* in *F*. For each feature *fk* in *Sj* that opinion holder *j* comments on, he/she chooses a word or phrase from *Wk* to describe the feature, and then expresses a positive, negative or neutral opinion on *fk*. The opinion mining task is to discover all these hidden pieces of information from a given evaluative document *d*.

Mining output: Given an evaluative document *d*, the mining result is a set of quadruples. Each quadruple is denoted by (*H*, *O*, *f*, *SO*), where *H* is the opinion holder, *O* is the object, *f* is a feature of the object and *SO* is the semantic orientation of the opinion expressed on feature *f* in a sentence of *d*. Neutral opinions are ignored in the output as they are not usually useful. Given a collection of evaluative documents *D* containing opinions on an object, three main technical problems can be identified (clearly there are more):

Problem 1: Extracting object features that have been commented on in each document.

Problem 2: Determining whether the opinions on the features are positive, negative or neutral.

Problem 3: Grouping synonyms of features (as different opinion holders may use different words or phrase to express the same feature).

Opinion Summary

There are many ways to use the mining results. One simple way is to produce a *feature-based summary* of opinions on the object. An example is used to illustrate what that means.

Table 10.1 Example of a feature based summary of opinions

Digital Camera	*Object*
Camera	
Positive: 125	<Individual review sentences>
Negative: 7	<Individual review sentences>
Feature: Picture Quality	
Positive: 123	<Individual review sentences>
Negative: 6	<Individual review sentences>
Feature: Size	
Positive: 82	<Individual review sentences>
Negative: 10	<Individual review sentences>
...	...

Table 10.1 summarizes the opinions in a set of reviews of a particular digital camera. The opinion holders are omitted. In Table 10.1, "CAMERA" represents the camera itself (the root node of the object hierarchy). 125 reviews expressed positive opinions about the camera and 7 reviews expressed negative opinions about the camera. "picture quality" and "size" are two product features. 123 reviews expressed positive opinions about the picture quality, and only 6 reviews expressed negative opinions. The <individual review sentences> points to the specific sentences and/or the whole reviews that give the positive or negative comments about the feature. With such a summary, the user can easily see how existing customers feel about the digital camera. If he/she is very interested in a particular feature, he/she can drill down by following the <individual review sentences> link to see why existing customers like it and/or dislike it.

Sentiment Classification

Sentiment classification has been widely studied in the natural language processing (NLP) community. It is defined as follows: Given a set of evaluative documents *D*, it determines whether each document *d* in *D* expresses a positive or negative opinion (or sentiment) on an object. For example, given a set of movie reviews, the system classifies them into positive reviews and negative reviews.

This is clearly a classification learning problem. It is similar but also different from the classic topic based text classification, which classifies documents into predefined topic classes, e.g., politics, sciences, and sports. In topic-based classification, topic related words are important. However, in sentiment classification, topic-related words are unimportant. Instead, opinion words that indicate positive or negative opinions are important, e.g., great, excellent, amazing, horrible, bad, worst, etc. Sentiment classification is done at the document level as it treats each document as the basic information unit. Sentiment classification thus makes the following assumption: Each evaluative document (e.g., a review) focuses on a single object *O* and contains opinions of a single opinion holder.

Since in the above, opinion mining model an object *O* itself is also a feature (the root node of the object hierarchy), sentiment classification basically determines

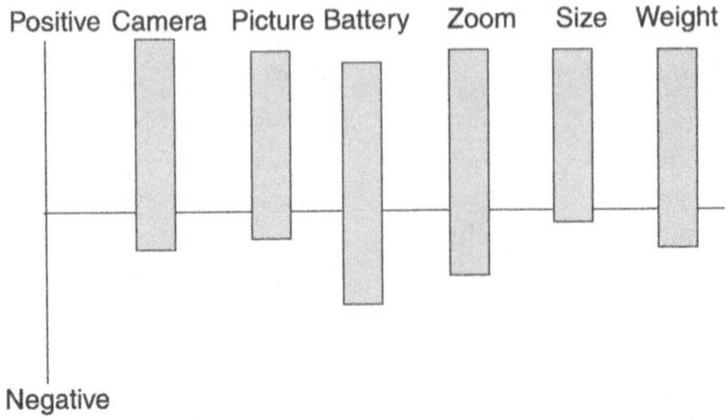

Figure 10.1 Feature based summary of opinions of a digital camera.

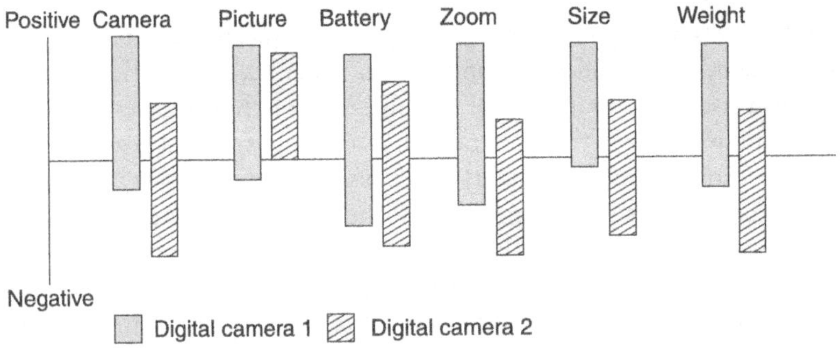

Figure 10.2 Opinion comparison of two digital cameras.

the semantic orientation of the opinion expressed on *O* in each evaluative document that satisfies the above assumption.

Apart from the document-level sentiment classification, semantic classification can be also extended to *sentence-level*, i.e., classifying each sentence as a subjective or objective sentence and/or as expressing a positive or negative opinion. Like the document-level classification, the sentence-level sentiment classification does not consider object features that have been commented on in a sentence. Compound sentences are also an issue. Such a sentence often expresses more than one opinion, e.g., "The picture quality of this camera is amazing and so is the battery life, but the viewfinder is too small".

Feature-Based Opinion Mining

Classifying evaluative texts at the document level or the sentence level does not tell what the opinion holder likes and dislikes. A positive document on an object does not mean that the opinion holder has positive opinions on all aspects or features of the object. Likewise, a negative document does not mean that the opinion holder dislikes everything about the object. In an evaluative document (e.g., a product review), the opinion holder typically writes both positive and negative aspects of the object, although the general sentiment on the object may be positive or negative. To obtain such detailed aspects, going to the feature level is needed. Based on the model presented earlier, three key mining tasks are:

- *Identifying object features* - For instance, in the sentence, "The picture quality of this camera is amazing", the object feature is "picture quality". This is an example of a supervised pattern mining method. In an unsupervised method the technique basically finds frequent nouns and noun phrases as features, which are usually genuine features. Clearly, many information extraction techniques are also applicable, e.g., conditional random fields (CRF), hidden Markov models (HMM), and many others.
- *Determining opinion orientations* - This task determines whether the opinions on the features are positive, negative or neutral. In the above sentence, the opinion on the feature "picture quality" is positive. Again, many approaches are possible. A lexicon-based approach has been seen to perform quite well. The lexicon-based approach basically uses opinion words and phrases in a sentence to determine the orientation of an opinion on a feature.
- *Grouping synonyms* - As the same object features can be expressed with different words or phrases, this task groups those synonyms together. Not much research has been done on this topic.

Mining Comparative and Superlative Sentences

Directly expressing positive or negative opinions on an object or its features is only one form of evaluation. Comparing the object with some other similar objects is another. Comparisons are related to but are also different from direct opinions. For example, a typical opinion sentence is, "The picture quality of camera x is great." A typical comparison sentence is, "The picture quality of camera x is better than that of camera y". In general, a comparative sentence expresses a relation based on similarities or differences of more than one object. In English, comparisons are usually conveyed using the *comparative* or the *superlative* forms of adjectives or adverbs. The structure of a comparative normally consists of the stem of an adjective or adverb, plus the suffix *-er*, or the modifier "more" or "less" before the adjective or adverb. The structure of a superlative normally consists of the stem of an adjective or adverb, plus the suffix *-est*, or the modifier "most" or "least" before the adjective or adverb. Mining of comparative sentences basically consists of identifying what features and objects are compared and which objects are preferred by their authors (opinion holders).

WHAT ARE THE INDUSTRY APPLICATIONS OF OPINION MINING AND SENTIMENT ANALYSIS?

When broad interpretations are applied, "sentiment analysis" and "opinion mining" denote the same field of study (which itself can be considered a sub-area of subjectivity analysis). Following are examples of industry applications.

Applications to Review-Related Websites

Clearly, the same capabilities that a review-oriented search engine would have, could also serve very well as the basis for the creation and automated upkeep of review- and opinion-aggregation websites. Topics need not be restricted to product reviews, but could include opinions about candidates running for office, political issues, and so forth. There are also applications of the technologies we discuss to more traditional review solicitation sites, as well. Summarizing user reviews is an important problem. One could also imagine that errors in user ratings could be fixed: there are cases where users have clearly accidentally selected a low rating when their review indicates a positive evaluation. Moreover, as discussed later in this chapter, there are also common examples that user ratings can be biased or otherwise in need of correction, and automated classifiers could provide such updates.

Applications as a Sub-Component Technology

Sentiment-analysis and opinion-mining systems also have an important potential role as enabling technologies for other systems. One possibility is as an augmentation to recommendation systems, since it might become an important input to such a system not to recommend items that receive a lot of negative feedback. Detection of "flames" (overly heated or antagonistic language) in email or other types of communication is another possible use of subjectivity detection and classification. In online systems that display ads as sidebars, it is helpful to detect web pages that contain sensitive content inappropriate for ads placement; for more sophisticated systems, it could be useful to bring up product ads when relevant positive sentiments are detected, and perhaps more importantly, nix the ads when relevant negative statements are discovered.

Information extraction can be improved by discarding information found in subjective sentences. Question answering is another area where sentiment analysis can prove useful. For example, opinion-oriented questions may require different treatment. Alternatively, for definitional questions, providing an answer that includes more information about how an entity is viewed may better inform the user.

Applications in Business Intelligence

Summarization may also benefit from accounting for multiple viewpoints. Consider, for instance, the following scenario. A major computer manufacturer, disappointed with unexpectedly low sales, finds itself confronted with the question: "Why aren't consumers buying our laptop?" While data such as the weight of the laptop or the price of a model of competitor, are obviously relevant, answering this question requires focusing more on people's personal views of such objective characteristics. Moreover, subjective judgments regarding intangible qualities like "the design is tacky" or "customer service was condescending" or even misperceptions like "updated device drivers are not available" when such device drivers do in fact exist must be taken into account as well.

It would be difficult to try to directly survey laptop purchasers who have not bought the company's product. Rather, we could employ a system that (a) finds reviews or other expressions of opinion on the Web—newsgroups, individual blogs, and aggregation sites are likely to be productive sources and then (b) creates condensed versions of individual reviews or a digest of overall consensus points. This would save an analyst from having to read potentially dozens or even hundreds of versions of the same complaints.

Note: *Internet sources can vary wildly in form, tenor, and even grammaticality; this fact underscores the need for robust techniques even when only one language (e.g., English) is considered.*

Besides reputation management and public relations, one might perhaps hope that by tracking public viewpoints, one could perform trend prediction in sales or other relevant data.

Applications Across Different Domains

One exciting turn of events has been the confluence of interest in opinions and sentiment within computer science with interest in opinions and sentiment in other fields. As is well known, opinions matter a great deal in politics. What voters are thinking about politicians and their positions on various areas of national interest, etc. Sentiment analysis can be proposed as a key technology enabling the automatic analysis of the opinions that people submit about pending policy or government regulation proposals.

How Is It Different from Standard Fact-Based Textual Analysis?

The increasing interest in opinion mining and sentiment analysis is partly due to its potential applications, which we have just discussed. Equally important are the new intellectual challenges that the field presents to the research community. So what makes the treatment of evaluative text different from text mining and fact-based analysis?

Traditionally, text categorization seeks to classify documents by topic. There can be many possible categories, the definitions of which might be user- and application dependent; and for a given task, we might be dealing with as few as two classes (binary classification) or as many as thousands of classes (e.g., classifying documents with respect to a complex taxonomy).

In contrast, with sentiment classification we often have relatively few classes (e.g., "positive" or "3 stars") that generalize across many domains and users. The regression-like nature of strength of feeling, degree of positivity, and so on seems rather unique to sentiment categorization.

In the next section, we will see a few examples of what makes these problems difficult compared to traditional fact-based text analysis.

Factors That Make Opinion Mining Difficult

Let us begin with a *sentiment polarity* text-classification example. Suppose we wish to classify an opinionated text as either positive or negative, according to the overall sentiment expressed by the author within it. Is this a difficult task?

To answer this question, first consider the following example, consisting of only one sentence (by Mark Twain): "Jane Austen's books madden me so that I can't conceal my frenzy from the reader". Just as the topic of this text segment can be identified by the phrase "Jane Austen," the presence of words like "madden" and "frenzy" suggests negative sentiment. So one might think this is an easy task, and hypothesize that the polarity of opinions can generally be identified by a set of keywords.

Similarly, if we look at the movie reviews that appear in newspapers, coming up with the right set of keywords might be less trivial than one might initially think. Compared to topic, sentiment can often be expressed in a more subtle manner, making it difficult to be identified by any of a sentence or document's terms when considered in isolation. To better understand the difficulty of the document level sentiment polarity classification problem, let us look at the following examples:

- "If you are reading this because it is your darling fragrance, please wear it at home exclusively, and tape the windows shut." This was a review comment on "Givenchy Perfume". No ostensibly negative words occur, and it does not explicitly say whether this perfume is good or bad!
- "This has all the elements of a hit movie however none of the ravishing enthusiasm of artistry was evident". There is no clear view whether it is a good movie or bad movie coming out of the statement. No ostensibly negative words occur.

Note the fine line between facts and opinions: while "This has all the elements" can be considered to be a fact, "none of the ravishing enthusiasm of artistry" should probably be considered as an opinion, even though the two phrases (arguably) convey similar information.

Thus, not only can we not easily identify simple keywords for subjectivity, but we also find that objectives like "no sentiment" apparently do not guarantee the absence of opinions, either. In general, sentiment and subjectivity are quite context-sensitive, and, at a coarser granularity, quite domain dependent (in spite of the fact that the general notion of positive and negative opinions is fairly consistent across different domains).

Note that although domain dependency is in part a consequence of changes in vocabulary, even the exact same expression can indicate different sentiment in different domains.

For example, "go read the book" most likely indicates positive sentiment for book reviews, but negative sentiment for movie reviews. It does not take a seasoned writer or a professional journalist to produce texts that are difficult for machines to analyze. The writings of Web users can be just as challenging, if not as subtle, in their own way—see Table 10.2 for an example.

Table 10.2 Example of movie reviews produced by web users

It sucks By all movie lovers Oct 5, 2009	Overall Rating F	Great Movie By the Director Oct 5, 2009	Overall Rating A+
3 out of 12 people found this review helpful		1 out of 12 people found this review helpful	
I loved this movie when I was little. Now I hate it! I think I have grown out of it. I might like it again, eventually.		I loved this movie. It was really good. Everyone should. see this	

While the overall topic of a document should be what the majority of the content is focusing on regardless of the order in which potentially different subjects are presented, for opinions, the order in which different opinions are presented can result in a completely opposite overall sentiment polarity. In fact, somewhat in contrast with topic-based text categorization, order effects can completely overwhelm frequency effects.

Consider the following excerpt, again from a movie review:

This film should be *brilliant*. It sounds like a *great* plot, the actors are *first grade*, and the supporting cast is *good* as well, and Stallone is attempting to deliver a *good* performance. However, it can't hold up.

As indicated by the (inserted) emphasis, words that are positive in orientation dominate this excerpt, and yet the overall sentiment is negative because of the crucial last sentence; whereas in traditional text classification, if a document mentions "cars" relatively frequently, then the document is most likely at least somewhat related to cars. Order dependence also manifests itself at more fine-grained levels of analysis: "A is better than B" conveys the exact opposite opinion from "B is better than A." In general, modeling sequential information and discourse structure seems more crucial in sentiment analysis.

CLASSIFICATION AND EXTRACTION

A fundamental technology in many current opinion-mining and sentiment-analysis applications is *classification*. The reason that classification is so important is that many problems of interest can be formulated as applying classification/regression/ranking to given textual units. Examples of the same include making a decision for a particular phrase or document ("how positive is it?"), ordering a set of texts ("rank these reviews by how positive they are"), giving a single label to an entire document collection ("where on the scale between liberal and conservative do the writings of this author lie?"), and categorizing the relationship between two entities based on textual evidence ("does A approve of B's actions?"). This section is centered on approaches to these kinds of problems.

First, extraction problems (e.g., retrieving opinions on various features of a laptop) are often solved by casting many sub-problems as classification problems (e.g., given a text span, determine whether it expresses any opinion at all). Second, extraction is often a means to the further goal of providing effective summaries of the extracted information to users.

Sentiment Polarity and Degrees of Positivity

One set of problems share the following general characteristic: given an opinionated piece of text, wherein it is assumed that the overall opinion in it is about one single issue or item, classify the opinion as falling under one of two opposing sentiment polarities, or locate its position on the continuum between these two polarities. A large portion of work in sentiment-related classification/regression/ranking falls within this category. The polarity or positivity labels so assigned may be used simply for summarizing the content of opinionated text units on a topic, whether they be positive or negative, or for only retrieving items of a given sentiment orientation (say, positive).

The binary classification task of labeling an opinionated document as expressing either an overall positive or an overall negative opinion is called *sentiment polarity classification* or *polarity classification*. Much work on sentiment polarity classification has been conducted in the context of reviews (e.g., "thumbs up" or "thumbs down" for movie reviews). While in this context "positive" and "negative" opinions are often evaluative (e.g., "like" vs. "dislike"), there are other problems where the interpretation of "positive" and "negative" is subtly different. One example is determining whether a political speech is in support of or in opposition to the issue under debate; a related task is classifying predictive opinions in election forums into "likely to win" and "unlikely to win".

The input to a sentiment classifier is not necessarily always strictly opinionated. Classifying a news article into good or bad news has been considered a sentiment classification task. But a piece of news can be good or bad news without being subjective (i.e., without being expressive of the private states of the author): for instance, "the stock price rose" is objective information that is generally considered to be good news in appropriate contexts. It is useful to point out that (a) in determining the sentiment polarity of opinionated texts where the authors do explicitly express their sentiment through statements like "this laptop is great", (arguably) objective information such as "long battery life" is often used to help determine the overall sentiment; (b) the task of determining whether a piece of *objective* information is good or bad is still not quite the same as classifying it into one of several topic-based classes, and hence inherits the challenges involved in sentiment analysis; and (c) as we will discuss in more detail later, the distinction between subjective and objective information can be subtle. Is "long battery life" objective? Also consider the difference between "the battery lasts 2 hours" vs. "the battery lasts only 2 hours."

Note: While it is of utter importance that the problem itself should be well-defined, it is of less, if any, importance to decide which tasks should be labeled as "polarity classification" problems. Whether this should be considered as an objective statement may be up for debate: one can imagine another reviewer retorting, "You call that long battery life?"

An alternative way of summarizing reviews is to extract information on why the reviewers liked or disliked the product. Such "pro and con" expressions can differ from positive and negative opinion expressions, although the two concepts—opinion ("I think this laptop is terrific") and reason for opinion ("This laptop only costs $399")—are for the purposes of analyzing evaluative text strongly related.

Additional problems related to the determination of degree of positivity surround the analysis of comparative sentences. The main idea is that sentences such as "The new model is more expensive than the old one" or "I prefer the new model to the old model" are important sources of information regarding the author's evaluations.

Categorisation and Rating Inference

The more general problem of rating inference, where one must determine the author's evaluation with respect to a multi-point scale (e.g., one to five "stars" for a review) can be viewed simply as a multi-class text categorization problem. Predicting degree of positivity provides more fine-grained rating information; at the same time, it is an interesting learning problem in itself. For instance, if we are classifying an author's evaluation into one of the positive, neutral, and negative classes, an overall neutral opinion could be a mixture of positive and negative language, or it could be identified with signature words such as "mediocre". This presents us with interesting opportunities to explore the relationships between classes.

Note it is possible to feel quite strongly (high on the "strength" scale) that something is mediocre (middling on the "evaluation" scale). Also, note that the label "neutral" is sometimes used as a label for the objective class ("lack of opinion").

Interestingly, neutral comments in feedback systems are not necessarily perceived by users as lying at the exact mid-point between positive and negative comments; rather, "the information contained in a neutral rating is perceived by users to be much closer to negative feedback than positive."

The opposing nature of polarity classes also gives rise to exploration of *agreement detection*; e.g., given a pair of texts, deciding whether they should receive the same or differing sentiment-related labels based on the relationship between the elements of the pair. This is often not defined as a standalone problem but considered as a subtask whose result is used to improve the labeling of the opinions held by the entities involved. In addition to classification based on emotion, another related area of classification that addresses non-topic-based categorization is that of determining the genre of texts. Since subjective genres, such as "editorial," are often one of the possible categories, such work can be viewed as closely related to subjectivity detection.

FEATURES AND PARTS OF SPEECH

Converting a piece of text into a feature vector or other representation that makes its most salient and important features available is an important part of data-driven approaches to text processing.

Information Retrieval (IR) techniques represent a piece of text as a feature vector wherein the entries correspond to individual terms. Term frequencies have traditionally been important in standard IR, at the same time *presence* rather than frequency also is valuable in numerous instances. A binary-valued feature vector in which the entries merely indicate whether a term occurs (value 1) or not (value 0) formed a more effective basis for determining the document category (for example legal document, research document, etc.). Whereas in a real-valued feature vector in which entry values increase with the occurrence frequency of the corresponding term would tend to define the polarity expressed (for example brilliant, terrific, astounding, etc if used in a statement certainly says there is something really good about the object).

This indicates an interesting difference between typical topic-based text categorization and polarity classification: while a topic is more likely to be emphasized by frequent occurrences of certain keywords, overall sentiment may not usually be highlighted through repeated use of the same terms.

Position information finds its way into features from time to time. The position of a token within a textual unit (e.g., in the middle vs. near the end of a document) can potentially have important effects on how much that token affects the overall sentiment or subjectivity status of the enclosing textual unit.

Part-of-speech (PoS) information is commonly exploited in sentiment analysis and opinion mining. Subjectivity detection reveals a high correlation between the presence of adjectives and sentence subjectivity. Certain adjectives are good indicators of sentiment, and sometimes have been used to guide feature selection for sentiment classification, in that a number of approaches focus on the presence or polarity of adjectives when trying to decide the subjectivity or polarity status of textual units.

The fact that adjectives are good predictors of a sentence being subjective does not, however, imply that other parts of speech do not contribute to expressions of opinion or sentiment. In fact, nouns (e.g., "gem") and verbs (e.g., "love") can be strong indicators for sentiment.

Handling negation can be an important concern in opinion- and sentiment-related analysis. While the bag-of-words representations of "I like this book" and "I don't like this book" are considered to be very similar by most commonly-used similarity measures, the only differing token, the negation term, forces the two sentences into opposite classes. However, not all appearances of explicit negation terms reverse the polarity of the enclosing sentence. For instance, "No wonder this is considered one of the best." conveys a strong positive opinion about the object.

DOMAIN ADAPTATION AND SEMANTIC ANALYSIS

The accuracy of sentiment classification can be influenced by the domain of the items to which it is applied. One reason is that the same phrase can indicate different sentiment in different domains: "unpredictable" is a positive description for a movie plot but a negative description for the steering abilities of a car.

Difference in vocabularies across different domains also adds to the difficulty when applying classifiers. Even when one is handling documents in the same domain, it is also possible for a document to contain multiple topics. For instance, a review can be a comparison of two products. Or, even when a single item is discussed in a document, one can consider features or aspects of the product to represent multiple (sub-) topics. In such cases it is more common to try to identify the topics and then determine the opinions regarding each of these topics separately.

Unsupervised Approaches

Quite a number of unsupervised learning approaches take the tack of first creating a *sentiment lexicon* in an unsupervised manner, and then determining the degree of positivity (or subjectivity) of a text unit via some function based on the positive and negative (or simply subjective) indicators.

A crucial component to applying this type of technique is, of course, the creation of the lexicon via the unsupervised labeling of words or phrases with their sentiment polarity or subjectivity status. An approach based on linguistic heuristics built on polarity classification where the two classes of interest represent opposites. Specifically, constraints between pairs of adjectives where the two words are linked by conjunctions such as "but" (evidence for opposing orientations: "elegant but over-priced") or "and" (evidence for the same orientation: "clever and informative"). The task is then to develop a clustering.

Once the clustering has been completed, the labels of "positive orientation" and "negative orientation" need to be assigned; for example, simply give the "positive orientation" label to the class whose members have the highest average frequency. Although reviews are not explicitly marked up with respect to their semantics, they do contain explicit rating and aspect indicators. For example, from such data, we learn that one way to express the concept "weather conditions" is "nice and comfortable".

Classifications Based on Relationships and Opinion Oriented Extraction

One interesting characteristic of document-level sentiment analysis is the fact that a document can consist of sub-document units (paragraphs or sentences) with different, sometimes opposing labels, where the overall sentiment label for the document is a function of the set or sequence of labels at the sub-document level. Modeling the relationships between these sub-document units may lead to better sub-document labeling as well. An opinionated piece of text can often consist of evaluative portions (those that contribute to the overall sentiment of the document, e.g., "this is a great movie") and non-evaluative portions (e.g., "Spiderman learned that with great power comes great responsibility"). The overlap between the vocabulary used for evaluative portions and non-evaluative portions makes it particularly important to model the context in which these text segments occur.

Many applications, such as summarization or question answering, require working with pieces of information that need to be pulled from one or more textual units. For example, a *multi-perspective question-answering* (*MPQA*) system might need to respond to opinion-oriented questions such as "Was the most recent presidential election in Zimbabwe regarded as a fair election?"; the answer may be encoded in a particular sentence of a particular document, or may need to be stitched together from pieces of evidence found in multiple documents.

It is important to understand the similarities and differences between opinion-oriented IE and standard fact-oriented IE. They share some sub-tasks in common, such as entity recognition. What truly sets the problem apart from standard IE is the specific types of entities and relations that are considered important. For instance, although identification of product features is in some sense a standard entity recognition problem, an opinion extraction system would be mostly interested in features for which associated opinions exist; similarly, an opinion holder is not just any named entity in a news article, but one that expresses opinions.

One may often want to present the output of opinion extraction in summarized form; conversely, some forms of sentiment summarization rely on the output of opinion extraction.

In the context of review mining, two important extraction-related sub-tasks are:

- The identification of product features, and
- The extraction of opinions associated with these features

While the key features or aspects are known in some cases, many systems start from the identification of product features. Identification of product features is in some sense a standard information extraction task with little to distinguish it from other non-sentiment-related problems. After all, the notion of the features that a given product has seems fairly objective.

Identifying product features discussed in reviews often relies on the simple linguistic heuristic that (explicit) features are usually expressed as nouns or noun phrases. This narrows down the candidate words or phrases to be considered, but obviously not all nouns or noun phrases are product features. A common approach is to identify frequent features through association mining, and then apply pruning aimed at removing (a) multi-word candidates in which the words do not appear together in a certain order, and (b) single-word candidates for which super-strings have been collected (the idea is to concentrate on more specific concepts, so that, for example, "life" is discarded in favor of "battery life").

In contrast, consider product features to be concepts forming certain relationships with the product (for example, for a scanner, its size is one of its properties, whereas its cover is one of its parts) and seek to identify the features connected with the product name through corresponding taxonomy. To identify expressions of opinions associated with features, a simple heuristic is to simply extract adjectives that appear in the same sentence as the features. Deeper analyses can make use of parse information and manually or semi-automatically developed rules or sentiment-relevant lexicons.

In the context of analysis of newswire and related genres, we need to identify text spans corresponding both to opinion holders and to expressions of the opinions held by them. As is true with other segmentation tasks, identifying opinion holders can be viewed as a sequence labeling problem.

SUMMARIZATION

So far, we have discussed about *analyzing and extracting* opinion information from individual documents. The focus of this section is on *aggregating and representing* sentiment information drawn from an individual document or from a collection of documents. For example, a user might desire an at-a-glance presentation of the main points made in a single review; thus creating a single-document sentiment summary.

Single-Document Opinion-Oriented Summarization

There is clearly an obvious connection between extraction of topic-based information from a single document and topic-based summarization of that document, since the information that is pulled out can serve as a summary. In terms of creating longer summaries, by tracking the sentiment flow within a document—i.e., how sentiment orientation changes from one sentence to the next, one can create sentiment summaries by choosing the paragraphs and sentences positioning in the flow (the first and last sentence). An interesting feature of this approach is that by incorporating a document's flow, the technique takes into account the entire document in a holistic way.

Indeed, one interesting aspect of the problem of extracting sentiment information from a single document is that sometimes graph-based output seems much more appropriate or useful than text-based output. For example, graph-based summaries are very suitable when the information that is most important is the set of entities described and the opinions that some of these entities hold about each other.

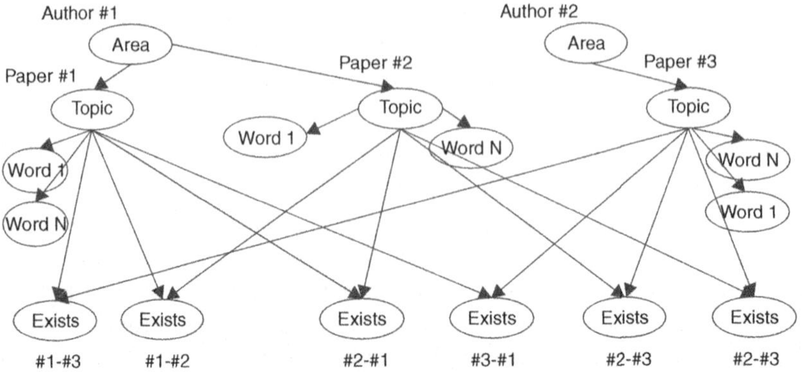

Figure 10.3 Summary of opinion shown in a graphical way.

Figure 10.3 shows an example of a summary in the form of a graph depicting various opinions expressed by authors. Note that the inclusion of text snippets on the arrows to support the inference of related words/opinions; in general, providing some sense of the evidence from which opinions are inferred, is likely to be helpful to the user.

Multi-Document Opinion-Oriented Summarization

Language is itself the collective art of expression, a summary of thousands upon thousands of individual intuitions. The individual gets lost in the collective creation, but his personal expression has left some trace in a certain give and flexibility that are inherent in all collective works of the human spirit.

We briefly discuss here some points regarding multi-document sentiment summarization, although to a certain degree, work in sentiment summarization has not yet reached a level where these problems have come to the fore. Determining which documents or portions of documents express the same opinion is not always an easy task; but, clearly it is one that needs to be addressed in the summarization area, since readers of sentiment summaries surely are interested in the overall sentiment in the documents—which means the system must determine shared sentiments within the document collection at hand.

For instance, some documents may have polarity labels, whereas others may contain ratings on a 1-to-5 scale. Consider the following from Rotten Tomatoes' frequently-asked questions page (http://www.rottentomatoes.com/pages/faq#judge): *"On the Blade 2 reviews page, you have a negative review from James Berardinelli (2.5/4 stars), and a positive review from Eric Lurio (2.5/5 stars)."*

You're seeing this discrepancy because star systems are not consistent between critics. For critics like Roger Ebert and James Berardinelli, 2.5 stars or lower out of 4 stars is always negative. For other critics, 2.5 stars can either be positive or negative. Even though Eric Lurio uses a 5 star system, his grading is very relaxed. So, 2 stars can be positive. Also, there's always the possibility of the webmaster or critic putting the wrong rating on a review.

As another example, in reconciling reviews of conference submissions, program-committee members must often take into account the fact that certain reviewers always tend to assign low scores to papers, while others have the opposite tendency. This calibration issue may be the reason why reviews should come not only with a "number of stars" annotation, but also a "thumbs up/thumbs down" indicator, in order to clarify whether, regardless of the rating assigned, the review author actually intends to make a positive recommendation or not.

An additional observation to take note of is the fact that when two reviewers agree on a rating, they may have different reasons for doing so, and it may be important to indicate these reasons in the summary. A related point is that when a reviewer assigns a balanced rating, it may be because he or she thinks that most aspects of the item under discussion are so-so, but it may also be because s/he sees both strong positives and strong negatives. Reviewers could also have the same opinions about individual item features, but weight these individual factors differently, leading to a different overall sentiment. Indeed, Rotten Tomatoes summarizes a set of reviews both with the Tomatometer—percentage of reviews judged to be positive—and an average rating on a 1-to-10 scale.

The Average Rating measures the overall quality of a product based on an average of individual critic scores. The Tomatometer simply measures the percentage of critics who recommend a certain product. For example, while "Men in Black" scored 90% on the Tomatometer, the average rating is only 7.5/10. That means that while you're likely to enjoy MIB, it probably wasn't a contender for Best Picture at the Oscars.

In contrast, "Toy Story 2" received a perfect 100% on the Tomatometer with an average rating of 9.6/10. That means, not only you are certain to enjoy it, you'll also be impressed with the direction, story, cinematography, and all the other things that make truly great films great.

The problem of deciding whether two sentences or text passages have the same semantic content is one that is faced not just by opinion-oriented multi-document summarizers, but by topic-based multi-document summarizers as well. While in traditional summarisation redundant information is often discarded, in opinion summarization one wants to track and report the degree of "redundancy," since in the opinion-oriented setting the user is typically interested in the (relative) number of times a given sentiment is expressed in the documents.

TEXTUAL SUMMARIES

In standard topic-based multi-document summarization, creating textual summaries has been a main focus of effort. Hence, despite the differences in topic- and opinion-based summarization mentioned in this chapter, several researchers have developed systems that create textual summaries of opinion-oriented information.

Instead of using size or extent to depict summary statistics, as is done with thermometer representations, one can use color shading. For instance, using color codes to represent the general assessment of (automatically determined) product features. In Fig. 10.2, you see that each of many features or topics, such as "Gas Mileage" or "service", is represented by a colored box. The colors for any given box range from red to yellow to green, indicating gradations of the average sentiment toward that topic, moving from negative to neutral (or objective) to positive, respectively. One can quickly learn from such a display what was liked and what was disliked about the product under discussion, despite the large number of topics under evaluation. For example, people like driving this car but dislike the service.

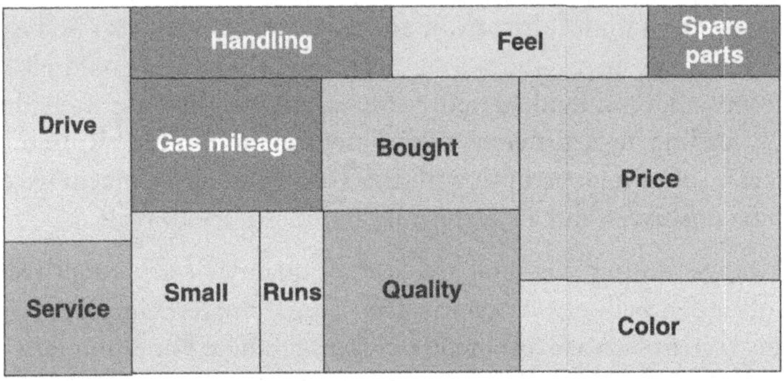

Option 1 - I bought a VW car, really liked the service, the test drive was very satisfactory, the dealer gave in a good deal on warranty, 2 year and 25,000 miles

Option 2 - The VW is nothing but all hypes. Although the feel is good and customer service is good, there was a long wait for the desired color, it is small, does not give the desired gas mileage as often quoted by the company.

Option 3 - Spare parts availability of VW is a major concern. However, I liked the way it runs smooth, there is definitely quality in the car and price is right.

Figure 10.4 Summarization depicted by heatmap.

Sentiment summaries tend to include data on the average rating, the distribution of ratings, and/or the number of ratings. For instance, as of the time of this writing, Amazon displays an average rating as a number of stars with the number of reviews next to it; mousing over the stars brings up a histogram of reviewer ratings annotated with counts for the 5-star reviews, 4-star reviews, etc. (Further mousing over the bars of the histogram brings up the percentage of reviews that each of those counts represent.)

So far, the summaries we have considered do not explicitly incorporate any temporal dimension. However, time is often an important consideration. First, users may wish to view individual reviews in reverse chronological order, i.e., newest first. Second, in many applications, analysts and other users are interested in tracking changes in sentiment about a product, political candidate, company, or issue over time. Clearly, one can create a sentiment timeline simply by plotting the value of a chosen summary statistic at different times; the chosen statistic can reflect the prevailing polarity or simply the number of mentions, in which case what is being measured is perhaps not so much public opinion, but rather public awareness.

Helpful, Useful Summarization

When creating summaries of reviews or opinionated text, an important type of information that deserves careful consideration is whether or not individual reviews are *helpful or useful*. For example, a system could use all reviews, but provide helpfulness indicators for individual reviews as a summary of their expected utility. Amazon.com annotates reviews with comments like "120 of 140 people found the following review helpful," meaning that of the 140 people who pressed one of the "yes" or "no" buttons in response to the question "Was this review helpful to you".

END POINTS

Economic Impact of Opinion Mining and Sentiment Analysis—Many readers of online reviews say that these reviews significantly influence their purchasing decisions. However, while these readers may have believed that they were "significantly influenced," perception and reality can differ. A key reason to understand the real economic impact of reviews is that the results of such an analysis have important implications for how much effort companies might or should want to expend on online reputation monitoring and management.

Given the rise of online commerce, it is not surprising many practitioners and vendors are keenly contesting the question of whether the polarity and/or volume of reviews available online have a measurable, significant influence on actual consumer purchasing. Economists have looked at the value of maintaining a good reputation as a means to overcome these problems, among other strategies. One way to acquire a good reputation is, of course, by receiving many positive reviews of oneself as a merchant; another is for the products one offers to receive many positive reviews.

Specific economic functions that have been widely exposed to opinion mining and sentiment analysis include revenue (box-office take, sales rank on Amazon, etc.), revenue growth, stock trading volume, and measures that auction sites like eBay make available, such as bid price or probability of a bid or sale being made. The type of product considered varies (although, understandably, those offered by eBay and Amazon have received more attention): examples include books, collectible coins, movies, craft beer, stocks, and used cars. It is important to note that some conclusions drawn from one domain often do not carry over to another; for instance, reviews seem to be influential for big-ticket items but less so for cheaper items. But there are also conflicting findings within the same domain. Moreover, different sub-segments of the consumer population may react differently: for example, people who are more highly motivated to purchase may take ratings more seriously. Additionally, in some studies, positive ratings have an effect but negative ones do not, and in other studies the opposite effect is seen; the timing of such feedback and various characteristics of the merchant or of the feedback itself (e.g., volume) may also be a factor.

Nonetheless, to gloss over many details for the sake of brevity: if one allows any effect then many studies find that review polarity has a significant economic effect. But there are a few studies that conclude emphatically that review positivity or negativity has no significant economic effect. For example—Consumers are rational in inferring movie quality from online user reviews without being unduly influenced by the rating, thus presenting a challenge to businesses that try to influence sales through 'planting' online word-of-mouth."

Some noteworthy best practices around opinion mining and summarization we discussed in this chapter are as follows:

- Sentiment summaries can be gathered by treating the review snippets like Rotten Tomatoes furnishes as one-sentence summaries.
- Subjective vs. non-subjective texts on the same topic can be gathered by selecting editorials versus non-editorial newswire or by selecting movie reviews versus plot summaries.
- If sentiment-oriented search engines already exist, then one can issue topical queries to such search engines and harvest the results to get sentiment-bearing sentences more or less guaranteed to be on-topic.
- Text polarity may be inferred from correlations with stock market behavior or other economic indicators.
- Negative opinions can be gathered by taking into account indications of "shouting," such as text rendered all in capital letters.

One important aspect to keep in mind with regards to sites where users rate the contributions of other users is a potential bias toward positive scores. In some cases, this comes about because of sociological effects. For example, , in a study of a music-oriented site called ACIDplanet, it can be found that various forces tend to cause users to give high ratings to each other's music. The users themselves refer to this phenomenon as "R=R" (review me and I will review you).

REFERENCE

Davenport, Thomas H. and Harris, Jeanne G., *Competing on Analytics*, Harvard Business School Press, March 2007.

CHAPTER 11

ONLINE BUSINESS CHANNEL AND WEB ANALYTICS

> *Internet as a business medium is no longer independent in its role within the corporation; it is now a viable source of revenue and customer relationship management. And, as such, it must be viewed as any other component of the business model—one that must be measured and validated in its worth. It is within this framework that Web analytics provides its greatest benefit.*

INTRODUCTION

The web is now seen as a key revenue driver and a reliable way of attracting and retaining customers. Web data are often analyzed to push and pull the three general levers available to businesses on the internet: marketing, merchandising, and site design. Marketers often use these data to determine how well (or poorly) their hard-earned marketing dollars are spent. By identifying every inbound marketing campaign, marketers are able to make apples-to-apples comparisons regarding how well each type of acquisition vehicle performs, usually by examining some type of conversion rate. Merchandisers and content managers analyze web data to better understand which products or content encourage visitors to click more deeply into the site and stay engaged. Designers use web analytics to better understand impediments to success on sites by examining the flow of traffic around the site. Perhaps the most common use of web analytics data is fall-out reporting—looking at specific valuable paths on the site (for example, the checkout process) in an attempt to understand why visitors abandon the process prior to completion.

Occasionally, we incorrectly conflate the terms "web analytics" and "web metrics", but the terms are worth differentiating. "Web (data) metrics" is the act of collecting the data against a predefined set of KPIs, whereas "web analytics" is the process of actually interpreting the data, ideally to improve your online business.

For example, hits and session counts, while interesting, provide little, if any, value when analyzing the productivity and efficiency of a website. However insights like the ability to monitor users' paths through the sites, ability to see what content is attracting them, and even from a visual perspective ability to determine which sections of landscape on web pages are attracting people's eyes most effectively, ability to measure how modifying a few words/links, or moving a picture will impact final conversion events such as product sales or user registration, ability to understand which pages people are getting hung up on, and even which fields in a form people are getting bored or frustrated about, and abandoning the process, would help an online business channel to improve their business significantly.

WEB CHANNEL PERFORMANCE MANAGEMENT

Web analytics solutions today produce an abundance of information on website usage. It is important for web site managers not to be content with simply using the Web statistics to generate a multitude of reports reflecting what has happened. If a metric in a report does not correspond with the strategic goals of the site, it is worthless and can in fact distract from what is truly important. No matter how much data are collected, and no matter what collection method is used, "all of this is useless unless it's actionable—and that means (1) the business goals must be clear, (2) technology, analytics, and the business must be aligned, and (3) the feedback loop must be complete".

WEB METRICS

Metrics or KPIs are quantifiable measures that help decision makers define and measure progress toward organizational goals. Metrics translate complex measures into a simple indicator that allows decision makers to assess the current situation and act quickly. To identify the most relevant metrics for a website, it is important to understand what type of site it is. Many websites have multiple purposes, which can make it difficult to identify how to measure the success of the site. For example a software company's website may include an e-commerce element to support direct sales of software to consumers. It may also contain content relating to the partners. It may generate leads to be followed up by the sales force. In addition, there may be an on-line knowledge base that allows customers to get answers to support issues. Most websites can be classified in one or more of the following site types:

Commerce

In this model, the goal is to get customers to buy some goods or services directly on-line. Examples of these sites are Discovery Channel Store Online, Amazon, eBay, and Expedia.

Online retail sites have always been interested in the bottom line—how much revenue does the site generated. Revenue is usually the primary objective of the site. The metrics for a commerce site should include the following:

- *Conversion rates:* there are multiple ways to measure conversions. The most common is order conversion rate—the ratio of visitors to orders. Equally important is checkout conversion rates—the ratio of people that start checkout to orders. One of the goals of advertising and marketing is to drive traffic to the site. It is important to benefit from this traffic by actualizing real revenue. When tracked at the individual marketing promotion or campaign level it is possible to see which promotions are working and which are not.
- *Average order value:* this is the ratio of revenue to orders. This is greatly dependant on the product mix of the site and the merchandising that encourages customers to buy certain things or to buy more than one item. The AOV has an impact on profit margin. Therefore it is important to entice customers to buy more expensive items and to buy more than one item at a time.
- *Visit value:* this is the ratio of all visits to revenue. This is also an important benchmark in measuring the effectiveness in driving qualified traffic to the site.
- *Customer loyalty:* the ratio of new to previously acquired customers.
- *Stickiness:* the ratio of visitors that arrive on a key landing page, such as the homepage or a promotional page, to those that stay on the site (go to a subsequent page) or make a purchase.
- *Search engine referrals:* the ratio of referrals to the site from search engines such as Google and Yahoo compared to industry average. It is also possible to track referrals and conversion rates for paid search terms.

Lead Generation

In this model, the goal of the site is to get visitors to submit their contact information so that the company's sales representative can follow up with them later. These companies focus on sales of specialized products and services that are not purchased directly online.

The metrics for a lead generating site can be somewhat similar to a commerce site. Both are conversion driven and as such they have some metrics in common. The objective of a lead generating site is to get visitors to provide their information so they can be solicited at some later date. Some useful metrics are:

Conversion rate: the ratio of site visitors to leads generated. Leads may be captured in the form of direct requests for a follow up sales contact or via requests for content downloads, signing up for mailings, and subscribing to newsletters. This is especially important to track at the campaign level to see which promotions work and which do not.

Cost per lead (CPL): the ratio of marketing/promotional costs incurred to leads generated. This is important in measuring the success of promotions.

Single access ratio: the ratio of single access pages to entry pages. This measures the effectiveness of getting people past the entry pages.

Traffic concentration: the ratio of visitors to a page or content area to overall site visitors. This is a good indicator of which areas of the site are generating the most interest.

Content/Media

Content sites are generally based on the on-line advertising business model. Alternatively, the purpose of content sites is to build affinity with the off-line content (TV or print), which results in more off-line ad sales. Examples of such sites include ESPN.com, Discovery.com, WebMD, NewYorkTimes.com, and Fox.com. The goal is to keep visitors coming back and to stay longer on the site. Content should be engaging and be updated frequently.

Since the objective of content sites is to increase readership (to bring in more ad revenue) the level of interest in the site and the length of stay is of most importance. Some of the most relevant metrics are as follows:

Depth of visit: It measures the ratio of page views to visits. This measures the level of interest in the content provided. The more engaged visitors are the more page views consumed—directly affecting ad revenue.

Returning visitors: The ratio of visits to unique visitors. This measures the effectiveness of the site at bringing visitors back to the site. This is also one factor in determining customer loyalty.

New visitor percentage: The ratio of new visitors to unique visitors, which measures the success of the site in attracting new viewers. This can mean different things depending on whether the site is new or attempting to attract large number of new visitors or is more established and is focused on retention.

Page/content depth: The ratio of page views to visitors at the page or content level. Key site content should be measured separately to measure interest in content areas over time. This can also be critical in determining the navigational effectiveness of a single page or content area.

Support/Self-Service

The support or the self-service model has a goal of providing customers with the ability to find the answers they need regarding their products or services. There are two business goals—to increase customer satisfaction and decrease call center costs. Some of the metrics that can help measure the success of the site in meeting these goals are as follows:

Customer satisfaction metrics: these are collected through use of actual online surveys or can be collected by allowing users to rate support content.

Length of visit and content depth: in contrast to media sites the goal should be to make it as quick and easy for a user to find the information they are looking for or to perform the self-service task.

Percent of visits under 90 seconds: the site should be efficient but not difficult to use. A high percentage here may indicate that users get frustrated and cannot find what they are looking for.

Top internal search phrases: not a traditional metric but important in identifying areas that may require better navigation or more content to meet customer demands.

Tactical Uses of Web Analytics

There are a number of practical ways to use Web analytics to get a better understanding of the website and how to optimize it further. The following is a summary of a number of these specific tactical approaches. In later parts of this chapter we will discuss each one of these topics at length.

Visitor Segmentation and Clustering

Segmentation isolates the behavior of certain types of important online visitors. This can help in the analysis and understanding of how important groups of people use the site by looking at the page-by-page activity of the group without being distracted by activity from other types of users. This method can be used to identify who is buying, browsing, staying the longest, coming back the most often, visiting particular parts of the site, viewing certain content, or using certain features. It can also isolate the behavior of visitors based on how they get to the site, be it a special marketing campaign, a search engine, or a partner site. Segmentation can also be performed based on demographics such as geographic location, gender, age group, and whether the user has broadband connectivity (some of which depends on the collection process for this information).

Cross-Sell/Up-Sell and Merchandising Optimization

Web analytics can help in identifying the optimal merchandising offers for product pages, the shopping cart as well as email offers. It is relatively straightforward to determine which products people most often purchase together. It is also possible to measure the performance of merchandising choices to determine which site design and navigation scheme contribute the most to maximizing merchandising offers.

For content sites it is possible to do similar analysis to determine which content areas have the most affinity with others. It is generally a good idea that if people move from one content area to another to make it easier for them to do so. This will keep visitors on the site longer.

Fall-out (Funnel) Analysis

For many sites, most particularly ecommerce sites, one of the areas of most concern are getting people to "convert". For retail sites this means getting visitors to add to the cart then proceed through each step of checkout until the purchase is complete. Conversion can be described more generically as measuring and analyzing the rate at which visitors go from page A to page B. For non-retail type sites there are many areas where conversion is worth analyzing. For example, in analyzing the behavior of people that use an internal search tool the ratio of people that search to people that click on a results page would be valuable. Another example would be analyzing the ratio of people that click on a link to register to people that complete the registration. Any "success event" that adds value to the business can be analyzed by looking at the steps it takes to get to that success event and how many people fall out at each step along the way.

Some important ways to do this is through Fall-Out or Funnel analysis and reporting. All leading Web analytics packages offer this capability. Pick the entry page for the process you want to analyze (or start with all site visitors). Then pick the intermediate steps along the way and include the final success page or event. The fall-out report will graphically represent the rates at which people are dropping out of the process at each step along the way. By keeping a close eye on this it is possible to determine what impact any changes you make have on the conversion rates for your key processes.

A/B Testing

A/B or split-run testing got its start with direct mail marketing. It is very easy to send two slightly different marketing pieces—coupons, trial offers, catalogs—to randomly selected samples of customers and track how the two marketing pieces perform in relationship to each other. By using slight variations it is possible to determine which minor differences make the biggest difference. A/B testing is a natural fit for the web since small variations are easy and it is possible to randomly present the variations to visitors and measure the results. Any part of the website can be A/B tested to determine the effectiveness of changes—the homepage, landing pages, product pages, merchandising campaigns and promotional offers.

Search Engine Optimization (SEO)

For many websites the largest amount of traffic may be coming from search engines such as Google, Yahoo, and MSN. Some studies have shown that more than 70% of Web traffic comes straight from these search engines. Referrals may be either from paid advertising placements on these sites or from so-called organic search. The top ten search engines are responsible for 90% of all search referrals. Also it has been shown that half of all search engine users will only click on the top ten results.

There are two basic approaches to increasing the referral rate from search engines. The first is to use marketing dollars effectively to buy the keywords that will generate the most qualified traffic to the site via paid search. The second is to optimise the site for organic search by ensuring the site gets indexed and highly ranked by the search engines—if the site does not get indexed or appear on page ten of the results there will be few referrals. Web analytics tools can be used to manage and measure the success of your efforts. There are vendors that specialize in helping sites get the most out of search engines referrals—just be sure to check references to ensure that these vendors are able to add real value.

Optimizing Homepage and Landing Pages

As important as it is to get people to come to your site, is the need to ensure that the key landing pages of the website draw people into the rest of the site. It has been shown that only 20% visitors coming from search engines will click through to the next page. Consequently, much analysis is required of the homepage and any of the other top entry pages into the site. Web analytics can be used to measure and analyze where people are coming from, which pages are the top landing pages and where people go after they get there, including those that go no further. By optimizing these landing pages there is the possibility for a huge return on investment. Some ways to optimize landing pages are making it clear that what the person was searching for can be found at the site. Sometimes this is not so obvious to a visitor. By calling out in bold ways the content that the person was looking for the visitor is more likely to go deeper into the site with the potential of either completing a purchase or generating more page views and ad revenue.

Online Marketing Performance Management

Any money spent on ads on external affiliate or partner sites can result in a much greater return on investment by closely measuring and analyzing the effectiveness of which banners generate the most value, which sites and campaigns produce the most revenue, and on the reverse side which do not. It does not make sense to blindly spend money on advertising without knowing what the return on investment is. Most Web analytics packages have very effective tools for tracking all campaigns and referrals to determine which ones work and which do not. The goal for each campaign should be that it generates more revenue than it costs—the campaigns that do not meet this criteria should be abandoned, those that do create additional value for the business are candidates for additional marketing effort. Without adequate measurements and tracking, this is impossible.

Performance Dashboards

One of the causes for ineffective use of Web analytics is the fact that many managers do not review reports on a regular basis. The benefit of a dashboard is that it is possible to assess the performance of the online business by having all metrics and reports in a single location. Most Web analytics packages allow a user to graphically view the site's critical visitor, sales, conversion, and other key performance metrics on a single page. It may also be able to include other information such as monthly targets and projections. The dashboard can be quickly accessed and may also be emailed and shared with other individuals interested in the performance of the online site.

Where are My Visitors Coming From?

One of the most common questions raised by marketing managers and business owners is, "Where are my customers coming from?" In the online business channel world it is all the more important to know how your visitors found you.

In the traditional media, promotions and referral programs are used to try to track which ads or resources bring in customers. Customer surveys are also used to ask the customers themselves. All of these can provide some information, but the data are fraught with inconsistencies and subjectivity. Fortunately, with the web, we get these information for almost every hit. Whenever you click on a link on a website, your browser sends a 'referrer' to the new site telling it where the link was that brought you there. Using web analytics, we can collect, summarize and, in places, evaluate these data for deeper significance.

Referrer information is collected by your web server when a visitor clicks on a link that brings them to a page on your site. Because referrer data are sent for every click, even pages on your own site send you referrer information. In this section we will discuss referrers from outside your site. Referrer information internal to your site is useful mainly for path analysis and finding broken links, covered separately in later sections.

Links on other websites are termed 'static referrers' and are the easiest to comprehend. You can find out which sites and which pages are sending traffic and can follow the links in reverse to see those pages, because the pages are still on the web. Dynamic referrers are links from content that may no longer exist by the time you see the report. This could be a news story (that only exists on the news site for a day or a week), an email campaign, or a search engine listing.

Finally, it is possible for users to find your site without providing referrer information, either by following a bookmark or favorites listing or by typing the URL into their browsers. While these hits contain no referrer information they are still valuable and you can use some tricks, covered in the final section of this chapter, to gather more information about them.

Referring Domains and Pages

Table 11.1 The list of websites with pages that link to your site

Hits	*Pages*	*Downloads*	*Referring Domain*
6037	6037	0	Widgetsource.com
1685	1664	0	Google.com
1196	1196	0	Cooltools.co.uk
440	440	0	Yahoo.com
192	192	0	Lycos.com
303	301	0	Altavista.com

Referring domains are a good place to start when you are trying to analyze who is linking to your site. By starting at the domains level (rather than looking at specific pages) you can figure out which sites are sending you the most traffic. Some of these you may have link agreements or other business relationships with. Many are likely to be search engines and portal sites. Often you may discover a significant amount of your traffic comes from sites you didn't even know about. By learning this information you can cultivate new relationships with these sites to help ensure that they bring more and better traffic to your site. Or you may decide that you don't want to be affiliated with a referring domain and ask the site to remove any links.

Table 11.1 shows the number of Hits, Pages and Downloads for the top domains. In this context these counts are for the item that was requested from your website. Usually this is a page, so Hits and Pages are often about the same. When other sites have direct links to downloads on your site, then the 'visitor' who downloaded the item will register a Download hit, rather than a Page hit. Sometimes, you will have a few hits in your report that are neither Downloads nor Pages. This often means that another site is including graphics from your site in their pages. The 'visitor' may not even know that the graphics are from your site.

Qualifying Domains on Recent Hits

Table 11.2 Recent hits data by referring domains

% of Current Hits	*Current Hits/Week*	*Hits*	*Referring Domain*
44.00	888	6037	Widgetsource.com
12.00	252	1685	Google.com
5.00	110	1196	Cooltools.co.uk
2.5	52	440	Yahoo.com
2.43	49	192	Lycos.com
2.13	43	303	Altavista.com

It is a common practice to look at statistics for the entire period derived from log files. If you have two years of data, then the Referring Domain with the most hits could still be one that was popular a year ago. In Table 11.2, you can see that some domains would be ranked higher in total historical hits than they are when sorted by Recent Hits. The Recent Hits value is usually a count of hits in the past two to three weeks. By comparing this short period to the historical total, you can see changes in trends as they are happening. This can be invaluable in helping you stay on top of changes in your traffic and allowing you to respond quickly to a fluctuating market place.

Qualifying Domains on Other Metrics

Table 11.3 Quality of visits

Pages	*Downloads*	*Avg. Steps*	*Goals = % of Hits*	*Goals*	*Referring Domain*
6037	0	6.0	19.7	1188	Widgetsource.com
1664	0	4.4	18.1	305	Google.com
1196	0	6.3	1.0	12	Startrektrivia.co.uk
440	0	7.1	61.4	270	Yahoo.com
192	0	3.3	58.3	112	Lycos.com
301	0	2.7	7.3	22	Altavista.com

The number of hits generated by a referrer may be interesting, but may not be the most important thing you want a referrer to produce. One of the simplest qualities might be Pages, rather than hits, especially if your website is content driven or funded by advertising. If you are publishing software or other downloadable content, Downloads are an important metric to follow. Table 11.3 introduces additional quantities that could help determine the quality of a referrer. Average Steps tells you, on average, how many non-graphic hits each visitor from that referring domain had as they navigated through your site. This can be especially important when you are delivering advertising, as it tells you how many potential impressions each visit from a given referrer had.

Sometimes you may have goals that are specific to your site, such as visitors who make it to the checkout page. For example, assume the site in Table 11.4 sells widgets. The referring domain data show that widgetsource.com sends a lot of visitors. Now, perhaps the site has been designed to look like the computer screens from Star Trek. You will see that the site also receives a lot of hits from the startrektrivia.co.uk site. However, if you track the receipt page from the checkout system as a data point, then the widgetsource.com site shows many goals were reached within their referrers' visits, while startrektrivia.com shows very few. Using qualities like these can vastly improve the value of your metrics.

Table 11.4 Individual pages that send visitors to your site

Hits	*Pages*	*Downloads*	*Referrer*
4655	4655	0	http://www.widgetsource.com/recommendations.html
1475	1469	0	http://www.google.com/search
391	391	0	http://ww.widgetsource.com/intro.html
492	492	0	http://www.cooltools.co.uk/products/index.html
408	408	0	http://www.cooltools.co.uk/widgetmanager/about.html
273	273	0	http://www.widgetsource.com/

Static and Dynamic Referrers

Static referrers are pages on other websites that link to your site. They are termed 'static' because they will continue to exist for a relatively long time; that is, when you read the report, you can follow the links to see the pages that sent you visitors. The static referrers themselves can be valued by the various metrics discussed in the last section: Hits, Recent Hits, Pages, Downloads, Average Steps, Value, Goals, etc. Because of their semi-permanent nature, static referrers are easy to investigate. Often, looking at the pages and analyzing the content can lead to more information than you can get from just the link.

Not all referrers are available on the web by the time you get to reading your reports. This is especially true when looking at historical data, but can even be the case for pages or links that are a day or week old. In such instances, you must either stay on top of your reports to find the resource while it is still around, or analyze the link itself for the information you want.

News Listings

Some dynamic referrers are just web pages that change rapidly. The most common example of this is a news story that links to your site. For example, a trade magazine may run a story on its home page about your site. For the day, your site gets hits from the trade magazine's home page. But they post new stories on the home page every day so the next day your story and link are no longer there.

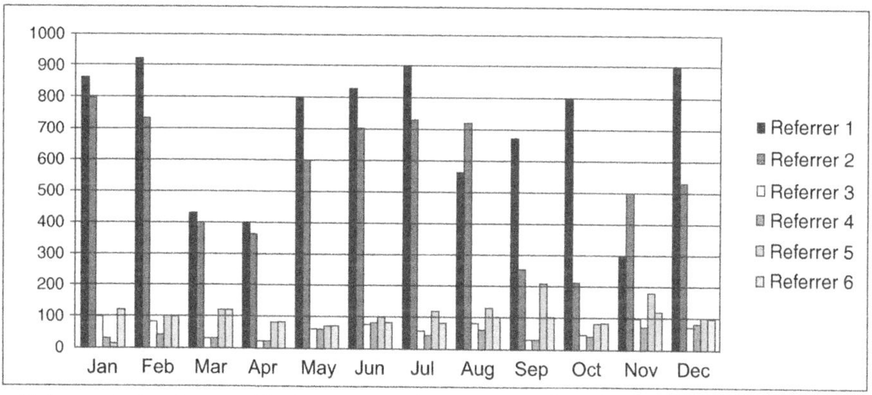

Referrer 1 - http//www.widgetsource.com/recommendations.html
Referrer 2 - http//ww.googlc.com/search
Referrer 3 - http//www.widgetnews.net/index.html
Referrer 4 - http//www.cootools.co.uk/products/Index.html
Referrer 5 - http//www.widgetsource.com/intro.html
Referrer 6 - http//www.cootools.co.uk/widgetmanagerabout.html

Figure 11.1 Hits over time trend with respect to referrer.

Usually the best solution for this is to recognize news sites and view or even save the page when it is posted. By looking for spikes on this graph you can further investigate when these events occurred that caused a large amount of traffic to be sent to your site. You can't always stay on top of these referrers and there will be times when the resource is gone before you even see the report. In this case you can often search most news sites for archives of stories. If you do find the archive, view it and, possibly, save it for later reference. If the archived story still has a link to your site, then you can click the link to register a referrer in your logs from the archive for future reference.

Search Engines

When visitors follow a link from a search engine to your site, it's very unlikely that you'll ever see the page they saw that linked to your site. This is because search engine indexes get changed regularly and because the logic the engines use gets altered as well. However, if you know the terms the visitor searched for you will often be able to see your listing. More importantly, knowing what terms users are finding your site with, can help you better understand what they are looking for, and improve your site to make it easier for them to find the right content (or for search engines to list you under the appropriate keywords.)

Table 11.5 Search phrase and search engine hits

Search Phrase	*Search Engine*	*Hits*
Analytics	Google	**91700000**
	MSN	2490
	Yahoo	26700000
Analytics Best Practices	Google	**2100000**
	MSN	7269
	Yahoo	25000000

Fortunately, almost all search engines include the search phrase in the referrer information when a user follows a link to your site. Using web analytics we can analyze the phrase and individual words. Table 11.5 is the Search Engine by Search Phrases data, which details which phrases were used to find your site and at which engines those searches were performed.

In addition to knowing what your visitors are looking for and acting on that, you also want to make sure potential visitors can find your site when searching for relevant topics. Finding the right keywords, making your site search-engine friendly, and improving your ranking incorporate a whole separate science of web analytics called Search Engine Optimization (SEO).

Visits without Referrer Data

Not all visitors arriving at your site provide referrer information. Usually these non-referred visits are from users who selected a bookmark or favorites entry in their browser or who typed in your URL directly. Perhaps you have advertisements hosted on another site that are delivered through a system producing dynamic content to include your ad. In such a case, each referrer is a unique page, so you cannot look at what pages are sending you visitors. Or, you might have an e-mail marketing campaign with a link in it to bring visitors into your site. But e-mail clients do not include any referrer, so you cannot know from the referrer data where your visitors found out about you. Or maybe your visitors are getting your URL from advertisements or marketing materials in other media.

You can work around such problems by using special URLs. Like traditional campaigns where you offer a special or incentive in response to an advertisement to track responses, you can use specific web pages on your site, such as—<http://www.mysite.com/ad001.html> or <http://ww.mysite.com/special> to track responses to advertisements or other campaigns you launch on the Internet. However, these URLs can often be harder for users to remember (especially the first kind) and don't provide the consistency that is often necessary to get people to recognize your brand.

Another cause of visits without referring URLs is spiders or robots. These are automated programs that follow website links to gather information. They may be used to index your site for a search engine, to find email addresses for unsolicited email lists, or to copy your site for off-line storage. In most cases robots won't bother providing referrer information. You can configure Summary to exclude robot visits from your statistics if you want to remove this kind of traffic.

DETERMINING VISITOR BEHAVIOUR PATTERNS

Where Visitors Spend their Time

It is important to understand how visitors use your website. This includes not only how they got there, but also where they went in the site, which pages are attracting attention, where they left from, and, if possible, where they went to.

Knowing where visitors spend their time on your site can help you improve the effectiveness of content or advertising or can indicate problems in the layout or size of pages. Table 11.6 shows the Average View Time data, which lists which files, on average, have the longest viewing time. If you have download-able files, then these will probably rank near the top (the 'view time' includes the transfer time, which is long in the case of downloads). The Total View Time data give a slightly different perspective on visitor viewing: It tells, approximately, the total amount of time that each page was in front of viewer eyeballs (there is a matter of subjectivity in this approach, user can just open the page and then doing something else for a lot of time thus giving a false impression that the user is really engage with the content and spending a lot of time). If you are only interested in maximizing the exposure of advertising, for example, this might be a better report to use. If you want to maximize exposure in individual visits, then the Average View Time data are applicable.

Table 11.6 Average view time data for pages

View Time	*Hits*	*Request*
10.12	39	/sample/intro.html
6:31	31	/sample/help.html
6:10	34	/sample/menu.html
3:46	2100	/docs/advanced.html
3:42	193	/docs/tips.html

When you know what pages visitors are spending the most time on, whether total view time or average view time, you can use the Referred From data to find out which referrers are sending visitors to those specific pages.

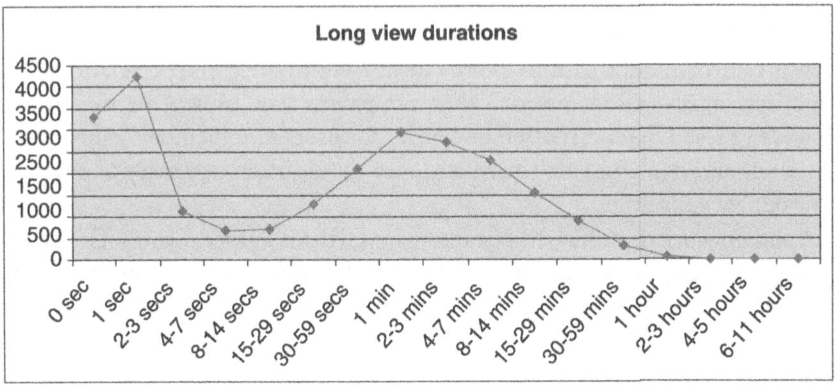

Figure 11.2 How long visitors stay on your site.

A long view duration can be a sign of good design when it indicates that your site benefits the user. This is generally only the case when the page is long, in-depth and covers the material the user is looking for. For example, documentation pages, essays and discussions, and other information that a user has decided to take time to review. However, there are reasons you should inspect long-viewed pages because they may indicate design problems in your site:

- A long load time (including referenced graphics, scripts, stylesheets, etc.)
- Slow to load because of back-end bottleneck (for dynamic or database-driven pages)
- Confusing content or layout

Visitors may spend a short amount of time on a page, indicating a problem:

- Useless—does not cover the material they expect it to
- Confusing—rather than try to figure it out they leave
- Boring—after a few paragraphs they are on to something better

On the other hand, a short view time could also indicate that a visitor found the page to be exactly what he is looking for, that it is terse and well-directed. Because it solves the problem immediately he is off to the next page or project.

In any case you will need to analyze the content of each long- or short-viewed page to determine whether you think it is a benefit or detriment to the site.

Path Analysis

Between the entry and exit points visitors will often view many other pages on your site. Web analytics can collect the entire path each visitor takes to allow you to understand how visitors use your site (which may be surprisingly different than you had intended in the design.) For example, you might be very interested in where users go next after they look at their basket in your online store. Do they check out? Leave the site? Return to browse or search for more items? Path analysis helps you find out where users are going after they get to a specific page. Conversely, you may have a particular page on your site that is important and want to know how visitors get there.

Table 11.7 Path analysis data showing visit path patterns

Source	*Destination*	*Hits*	*Hits % of Parent*
/ (main page)	/MakeYourOwnProduct Composition.html	25000	
	/AdditionalOffers.html	13000	52%
	/Checkout.html	230	0.92%
/ (main page)	/StandardOffers.html	23250	
	/Checkout.html	1800	77.4%

Using the Visit Paths data, you may be able to see common paths followed by visitors to your site. For small sites, the Visit Path report will often contain one or two very common paths with the rest being insignificant. On large sites, you will notice that there are generally so many routes to so many destinations that none of them stand out in particular. In such cases you can further segment the data to look at a portion of the traffic and analyze paths of those visitors.

Some visitors will only see a single page. They enter at a point and exit from the same page. If you are delivering content in individual pages to your visitors, then this might be a good thing. Your users will be happy to find the content they need in one step and will remember to use your site in the future. On the other hand, if you have multiple pages that takes the user through a guided navigation path and you see a lot of one page hits, you are losing visitors' attention, this could be indicative of problems in design, content or search engine listings.

Monitoring and Adapting to Patterns

When you have identified patterns your visitors follow, you will want to make changes to your site to improve it for the user experience or to capitalize on aspects of visitors' behavior. From our discussions so far, several such actions can be readily identified.

- Use the Referred data to find out which referrers are sending visitors to pages with long view times or to exit pages.
- Use the Referring Domains by Step data to find referrers that send visitors with more steps through the site.
- Analyze the content of long- and short-view pages and entry and exit points to see if they are indicative of problems.
- Install a click tracking script to see where visitors leave to.

However, remember that the design and analysis process is iterative. When you make changes, visitors will change their behavior and you have to keep on top of the data and continue to analyze every time you make a change.

Note: It is often tempting to come to conclusions about visitor patterns and make a lot of changes to the site at once. Not only can this confuse your users, but it will make it hard to determine which changes correlated with which results. A better approach is to make small changes one at a time and see how visitors react to the change. By using a controlled environment, where only one element of design, marketing or content is changed at a time you can test your customer response much more effectively and correlate specific actions to particular elements in your site.

Examining Subsets of Traffic

Once you begin to become familiar with the particular behaviors of your website traffic you will want to know more about certain groups of visits. For example, if your browser report includes a large number of hits from users browsing with mobile phones, you would want to know which particular pages on your site are most important to those visitors so you can build custom wireless versions to make access by mobile users easier and more efficient.

By defining segments to look at subsets of your site traffic you can deep dive into your area of interest like pages in your `/products/` pages or for only those hits to your online store. Segmentation can also be applied to remove subsets of traffic rather than isolate them. You would use this technique to remove traffic generated by your own employees from the data.

As with most information, the more you discover about your visitors' traffic patterns, the more questions will arise. By carefully applying segmentation and other filtering approaches you can get into specific questions that you or other people in your organization may have.

Note: While website analysis reports contain various types of data, they are all derived from a simple set of basic data elements that exist in your log files. When applying segmentation or filtering approaches, you filter one of these basic data types: Referrers (that start visits), Browsers (or other user agents), Requested page or file, Authenticated Users (if your site requires a login), Host (including domains, and country of origin of the visitor), or a Cookie that the visitor carries.

Let us look at some examples below to understand what insights can be gained:

By Referrer—Referrer filtering can be used to see where traffic from a particular search engine, advertisement or other link goes on your site. For example, perhaps the marketing manager of our widgetmanager.com site sees a peak in traffic one day and, using the Referrer Report, finds it comes from a particular news story at widgetnews.net. The manager wants to know whether they should place an advertisement on widgetnews.net to attract more visitors on a regular basis. She sets up a filter to look at just the traffic generated by that story. By looking at the Exit Point data she realizes that the significant majority of those visitors ended at a links resource page on widgetmanager.com that provides links to widget manufacturers. As widgetmanager.com sells a tool to manage widgets (not widgets themselves) she does not think this will be a lucrative lead source—these visitors are likely first-time buyers and not yet in the market for a widget manager.

By Browser—Browsers (or user agents) can be filtered to analyze traffic from particular types of users based on the software or hardware they used. As previously mentioned, looking at traffic patterns of wireless users can help you decide whether to launch a wireless-specific version of your site, and where to focus the efforts in that design or to improve the effectiveness of a wireless interface to your website. Any user agent can become an important subset of your traffic. Another example could be—Widgetmanager.com distributes a custom software tool that customers can run on their own computers to help in managing their widgets. The program connects to the widgetmanager.com site for registration, to check for updated versions of itself and to download and install updates when they are available. By focusing on just the traffic generated by this software program (a particular user agent), the developers can look at the number of hits to 'register.html,' which happens once for each copy, and 'update_check.html', which is requested each time the software is run, to see how often, on average, each copy of the software has been run. If the number of update checks is 17632 and number of registrations is 4408, then a simple math will tell us an average of four update runs results in a copy sold. The CFO can also compare the registration hits to the sales records, according to the financials, and see if there have been a significant number of pirated copies or other inconsistencies in the registration system.

By Authenticated Users—If your website has a login-required section, you can filter by authenticated user name to see how members travel around the site. If your user names include some organizational data, you can use wildcards to collect traffic reports of particular groups of users, based on their user name. For example, the widgetmanager.com site requires a login to purchase and download the widget manager software tool, submit bug reports or get technical support. The Website Manager notices an excessive number of hits by two particular users, 'Goofy' and 'Cindy'. By creating a filter for only these two users a pattern is observed that these "users" have downloaded a large number of copies of the software tool. The Website Manager suspects that the user names and passwords have been shared or leaked to public lists where people download pirated software. The CFO confirms that the registration count on the website exceeds the actual revenue. As a preventive action, the Website Manager removes the two offending accounts from the system and sends a note to customer support to contact the original registrants (if they provided legitimate contact data) and discuss the issue with those individuals.

By Host—Host filtering, like request filtering, is usually done with wildcard patterns. The only time you would want to look at a single host would be to examine unusual access patterns, generally of troublemakers. Host information includes domain and country information, so you can find patters of specific users from particular companies, Internet access providers or countries (with some limitation—many international ISP's use `.com` or `.net` domains now rather than country specific ones like `.uk` or `.jp`.). For example, by looking at just the traffic from `*.aol.com` hosts, you get details about how AOL users use your site. If you have a section of your site that is dependent on visual information, this can be especially relevant. AOL will "compress" graphics from your site beyond the compression you have already applied, reducing the quality of the images that visitors see. If your usage reports show that AOL users are frequenting your product images, for example, you may want to add a note to the site instructing them how to disable this "compression" so they see your product shots as they were meant to be seen.

Filtering by Cookie—Cookies can be very useful when you want to track user information, especially across sessions. By adding cookie filters, you can see traffic patterns of almost any subset of users you choose to follow. Let us assume widgetmanager.com runs a Christmas special offering 10% off on one of their products. They have a special web page that they send users to who click on one of their web advertisements or that users can type in when they see the ad in print media. Every user who goes to that page gets a cookie that tags them as having responded to the promotion. Now the sales manager sets up a filter showing traffic patterns of visitors who have the promotion cookie. Looking at the Weekly Report for the last six months she discovers that while the majority of hits from the promotion was the week before Christmas, there was also a significant spike in traffic for the week including the 14th of February. Apparently this particular widget manager product is not just a popular Christmas gift, but also a romantic Valentine's gift. It looks like widget managers (at least for existing customers) seem to signify true love! This information allows her to capitalize on this pattern the following year, by sending a Valentine's promotion to customers who purchased the Christmas special.

INCORPORATING BUSINESS GOALS

Web analytics is primarily concerned with measuring online behavior. Web analytics can tell you exactly what people do on your website as well as how often they do it. However, it cannot tell you why they act as they do and what they think or feel while browsing your site.

The classical example of this limitation in web analytics is the ambiguous meaning of popular metrics such as "Page Views per Visit" or "Average Visit Duration". High values for these metrics are often seen as signs of satisfaction. In principle, however, they could just as well mean that it was hard for the visitors to find what they were looking for.

Imagine a stubborn visitor who repeatedly tries to complete a check-out procedure. Such a visitor may produce many page views and spend a lot of time on your site even though he or she never completes the task. When you think about it, any given web metric or KPI based purely on behavioral data can always be interpreted positively or negatively.

Hence it is extremely important to design web metrics aligned to business goals.

Goals and Desirable Outcomes

What do you want your visitors to accomplish when they come to your site? Whatever that may be, it is valuable to track how many visitors actually do what you want them to do. In a retail model, you would want them to purchase something, or, to put it in website terms, you want them to reach the "Thanks for your order" page. In a health services model, you would want your visitors to find the information they need as quickly and easily as possible. You may even have more than one desirable outcome, depending on the type of customer that reaches the site.

You can define 'Goals' that allows you to qualify visits based on whether they got to a given page on your site. Then you can track this goal across several aspects, for example qualifying referrers or search terms, or evaluate monthly metrics based on how many visitors reached your defined goals.

Target Groups

Often you will have different goals for different types of customers. By segmenting your customers into particular categories, you can better market to each group and develop a stronger customer relationship with them. To illustrate this, let us say a health services site has identified two distinct services it provides: An online survey for anonymous self-evaluation of health related matters and an encyclopedia of health related terms, concerns, problems and solutions. The site developer wants to make sure that the survey is being used. It is several pages long so he defines a goal to track the final page of the survey. Using this, he can see what percent of the visitors are actually completing the survey by tracking the Goals % of Visits metric.

On the other hand, the content author for this site is concerned that visitors to the encyclopedia may be having trouble finding the information they need. The encyclopedia is very large and contains too many pages to include as goals. If all pages were included she would not know whether the visitors were finding the right page. Instead she looks at the search word data to see what the most common search terms on the encyclopedia are.

Then she sets up a goal to track the encyclopedia pages related to the primary search term. By comparing the Percent of Hits for the first search term in the search word data to the total percent of hits for all the encyclopedia pages, she can determine the effectiveness, for example most of the users searching for 'flu' are finding the right pages in their visit or not.

One of the most common uses for Goals is modeling e-commerce. When you are running a website from which you intend to make money, you want to know who your buyers are, where they come from, and how to make your site more profitable. By counting your visitors who make purchases and comparing this to the rest of your traffic you can find particular traffic patterns among the purchasers and use this to improve your site or marketing.

Tracking Buyers

If you have an online store, you can configure a Goal to track visitors who made purchases. At some point the visitor must get to a receipt page or some page that says "Thank you for your order". This is the page (or pages, if more than one is possible) that you want to define as the Goal. Tracking visitors who reach your store or even the "checkout" page does not indicate that they made a purchase. You want to make sure that the goal page you set up is the one they see after they have paid for their goods.

If you use an outside service to collect payment, such as PayPal or a merchant service provider, you will not have log information about purchases. The best you can do in this case is set the goal as the page users see just before they go to your payment services site. If you have "checkout" links at several places, you might want to redesign the site to include a single page just before, so you can track visitors who are on their way to checkout.

Window Shoppers

Not everyone who gets to your store will make a purchase. Sometimes visitors will shop around, filling a basket with items and then leave. They never check out or they never finish the checkout process. This is sometimes referred to as "abandoned baskets". Knowing the ratio of 'shoppers' to 'buyers' can be indicative of problems in your shopping cart software, checkout procedure, or other business factors. For example, if you have an online store and physical stores, some visitors may use your shopping basket to make a shopping list, and then take the list to shop at a physical store. Or you may have visitors who fill shopping baskets at competing sites and choose the one with the lowest price for the entire purchase.

Note: By tracking only requests to your store pages you get what percent of shoppers became buyers. Subtract this from 100 to get the percent of abandoned baskets.

Conversion Rates

In most sales metrics, a commonly used ratio is the Conversion Rate. Simply, this is the ratio of leads to sales. If ten customers come into your store and only two make a purchase, then your conversion rate is 20%. Conversion rates can be used in non-commerce business too. If you have other desired outcomes or qualities that you want visitors to have, you can divide the total number of visitors by the number of visitors who reach that goal to get your conversion rate.

Cluster Analysis

Target groups can sometimes be hard to identify. If you have designed your site for specific tasks, then usually these are a good choice. If your site seems to be all interconnected or you have several distinct goals for all visitors, you may want to consider using a cluster analysis technique to decide how to divide your visitors into meaningful groups. Cluster analysis is an advanced statistics tool for aggregating similar objects into distinct taxonomies. You may have already determined what the goals of your site are, but want to know what the customers' goals are and whether they are distinct from the design. Using cluster analysis you can analyze your visitors based on patterns or values and perhaps discover distinct groupings for marketing or further analysis.

To illustrate the application of cluster analysis, consider a typical e-commerce site using cluster analysis to group search engines that are sending qualified visitors. Earlier we discussed qualifying search engines based on how many visitors they send who reach a defined goal or based on the number of Average Steps visitors from each engine took. In this example, we want to look at both. Average Steps per visit indicates the value of the visitor for advertising—the more pages each visitor sees, the more effective the advertising. The Goal is defined as a desirable outcome, such as making a purchase at the online store. In both cases a higher the value indicates a more profitable lead from the engine.

By inputting Average Steps and Goals from the Search Engines report into a statistics program, the software can find distinct groups of engines. Figure 11.3 shows a sample distribution of search engines based on these two quantities. While the grouping seems obvious for most engines in this set of data, notice that Wise. Nut is hard to define. The clustering analysis, however, can tell, as the grey lines indicate, that it belongs in the lower left group.

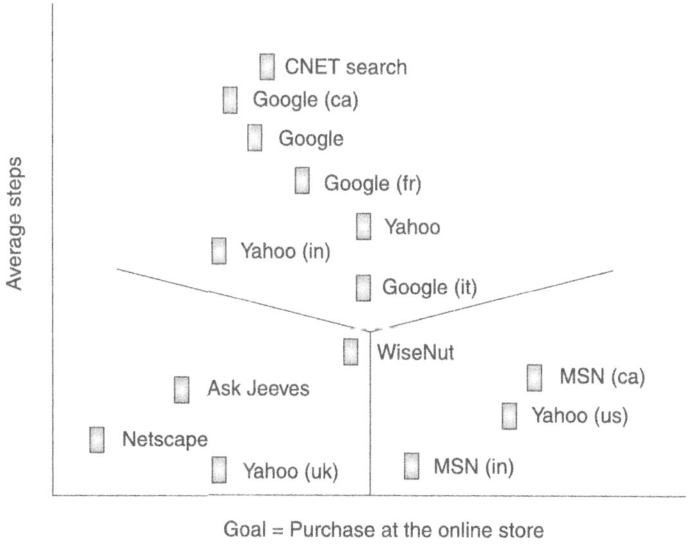

Figure 11.3 Sample distribution of search engines aligned to a business goal.

By analyzing these engines on two quantities (and in most cluster applications, you would use more than two), we can interpret the value of each engine in ways that could not be seen before. The group at the top is good for generating advertising leads. Visitors from those engines seem to spend more time on the site and, therefore, see more ads. Pages on the site that carry advertisements, could be optimized and re-submitted to make them more prominent on these engines. The group on the lower right does not spend a lot of time on the site, but makes more purchases. Pages in the online store could then be optimized to make the store more efficient, if possible, and to make them list directly in these search engines to make purchases easier for these visitors. The group on the bottom left does not have much value in either instance. Perhaps listings in those engines should be removed.

HOSTED ASP WEB ANALYTICS

Until recently Web statistics have been generated by parsing raw Web logs. There are several disadvantages to this approach.

Time and resources consumption—On a larger website, the amount of sheer processing power required to analyze log files necessitates an additional server simply for that purpose. And depending on the processing schedule, these stats can be anywhere from a day to a week behind.

Unreliability—Log files track users by their IP addresses. In today's world, where ISPs pool IP addresses and proxy servers cache data to serve to multiple users, this is simply unacceptable. Trending algorithms can only guess at users' paths and sessions by a text trail of IP logs. And a thousand people may be viewing your website from a cache on the proxy, leaving you with information on only one hit from the proxy server itself.

Partiality—There is really only so much information that a server can detect and record from a visitor. A few minor browser details can be seen, and the pages that are viewed. Nothing can be detected from the client's perspective that tells what he or she does while on a particular page.

Coming of age however, is the on-demand, hosted ASP Web analytics technology platform. Not only does this technology answer the limitations of log file solutions, but it also provides with a far more advanced, insightful perspective of Web users. Generally all of the major vendors take the same approach. You license their technology for use on your website, the cost varying based on monthly count numbers. Then all you need to do is install a small piece of JavaScript code on each page of your website, and you're off to the races. If your site is maintained by a Content Management System, this could be an implementation time of only a few hours, perhaps less!

Don't be too concerned by the use of JavaScript, as it's only a very small percentage of visitors that disable it. What will happen for approximately 97 percent of your visitors (the ones with JavaScript), is that the code will pull as much information from the user's browser as possible—which is quite a bit—and return that information to the ASP's server. This is usually accomplished by making a call for a dynamic, transparent, 1×1 pixel gif image, with the compiled information encrypted into the request. The moment this information is logged at the ASP's data store, it is immediately accessible.

A side benefit to this method is that search engine and spider traffic is not counted as valid hits to your site, only real people! And the amount of information exchanged is so insignificant that it will not disturb the user's visit to your site.

So, what sorts of unique advantages does this model provide for analytics and Web Masters?

Path Analysis

With log file solutions, path analysis was at best not very good. It was in no way a proven science, but actually observed and applied trending techniques. This is because an analysis solution would have to process an enormous text log, try to identify a series of hits from the same IP address, and try to map them together.

If the user hit the back button, the path was thrown off. If the session timed out, the user was granted a different IP from his ISP, then the path all but disappeared. It's also important to note that even if a true path could be obtained, it was by the filenames of the pages viewed, which are incredibly unreadable and useless in a large, managed website.

With on-demand analytics, the path analysis is incredibly accurate. You can very easily see a snapshot of the top 10 most common paths by visitors, and plan your Web strategy and e-marketing based on that. For example, assume a common path is the following: Home > Product > DVD Players > Orange DVD Player.

Now you have the insight that the Orange DVD Player should perhaps have some place on the home page, because it's quite clearly the most popular and such a move will very easily increase conversion on you site. Also, if you have pages that you desire to get some attention, yet they're buried in a 10-deep click-path, you'll be able to see that and find some way to shorten the path—and get more visitors to that page!

These are pages where users are ending their visit to your site, either by closing the browser window or moving on to another website. With log file solutions, these could only be assumed by an end to the IP trail. But based on how unreliable we've established this to be, it's very difficult to trust these stats.

With ASP solutions, it's quite reliable. While at first this may seem like just another statistic, it's very important for two reasons:

It enables us to examine the pages where people are dropping off, and change them. Are we not providing clear direction or navigation from that page to the rest of the site? Is the content boring or confusing? Making modifications where necessary will decrease drop-off.

Conversion Funnels

A conversion funnel is basically a representation of the following: how many visitors, originating at point X, end up completing conversion event Y. Very importantly, it also tells us how many drop out along the way, and at which stage.

You could very easily set a certain paid keyword as the point of origin, and depending on how many people come to your site and eventually buy DVD players after clicking on that keyword, you could determine the value of each click. This will help you strategically decide in which keywords to invest the most.

You could make comparisons between channels (email, direct mail), see which are generating the highest conversion rates, and determine where to invest marketing time and money.

When you look at the funnel, you can examine where in the process people are dropping off, and make necessary modifications to keep them from leaving. Are instructions too lengthy, or form error messages too frustrating? A conversion funnel will enable you to have this kind of insight. In fact, some of the more advanced offerings even enable you to see which fields in a form people are getting to before abandoning the process.

A very powerful tool that many vendors provide is a visual mapping or overlay for your site, that clearly identifies hot zones on each page—indicators that visually display which links were clicked on, and how many times. This is a very powerful way to understand which pieces of content, which action words, and which sections of landscape are attracting peoples' eyes, and generating clicks. This enables you to know where to strategically place campaign related links, so that they'll receive the most click-throughs. It will also identify underperforming links, so that they may be moved or removed, leaving more attention for performing links.

Pay Per Click (PPC) Tracking

Most of the top solutions are incorporating pay-per-click campaign tracking suites into their applications. In a situation where you're bidding on keywords from multiple search providers, these suites would allow you to consolidate the information from all campaigns, permitting you to monitor the performance of your keywords, and make suggestions as to which keywords to juggle to generate the best returns.

Exit Pages

It's one thing to know which pages are the so-called "drop-off" pages, but it's entirely separate and infinitely more insightful to know exactly where they're going to. The more advanced solutions are able to monitor users' clicks, and identify which of those clicks are on links pointing to pages external to your site or domain. If you can identify common exit pages, you can have these open in new windows, or devise another means of allowing users to retrieve that external information while still remaining on your site.

ROLE OF SEARCH ENGINES IN WEB ANALYTICS

When we want to find something on the web we look to a search engine. Sites like Google, MSN and Yahoo! let you search for websites that contain information pertinent to topics of interest to you. Potential visitors looking for your site are going to do the same thing. This makes it imperative that your site gets ranked high enough for important keywords that visitors can find it. Knowing what keywords are important means knowing what visitors are looking for when they find your site.

Keywords and Search Phrases

Using web analytics, you can find out what engines, phrases and keywords visitors are using to reach your site and produce reports to help you improve your site content and search engines listings. Each search engine will offer links to your site for certain keywords or phrases. When a visitor types these phrases your link will be given, along with many others. It is important to know the original phrases each visitor entered when they found your site. The entire original phrase is extremely helpful in knowing exactly what a visitor is looking for. Often you will see complete sentences or fragments that give you an excellent understanding of your visitors' interest. Using these data you can tailor the content of your site to help your visitors find what is important to them and to make the site more relevant to the subjects of interest.

By breaking down the search phrase into individual words, you will know what keywords bring the most traffic. When you are listing your site with search engines, this can be very useful in determining what keywords you should include.

Qualifying Search Terms and Engines

As discussed earlier, "Hits" are not always the most important metric. Average Steps is an important data point that tells you how many steps (or non-graphics hits) there were in each visit, on average, for visitors who found your site with the given search word. If the intent of your site is to deliver as many page impressions as possible to each visitor, then the search words that rank with the highest Average Steps count are the most valuable. For example, if each page on your site can carry an advertisement and you generate revenue on advertising impressions, then you will want to make those search words that generate the most Average Steps per visit more prominent in your page content and keyword listings.

Other important metrics are Goals, Goals% of Hits, and Values. Goals allow you to define specific business goals or desired outcomes of a visit and rank visits based on whether they achieve the goal. Values can be used to assess potential revenue or costs associated with actions on your site. Revenue could be from advertising or estimated revenue per impression. Costs could be for pay-for-placement listings or bandwidth estimates.

SEARCH ENGINE RANKING

Search engines are all built on the same principles, but use different techniques and technologies to achieve their goals. For a search engine to be effective it must produce the most relevant web pages for a given topic or topics as the first few items that a user sees. Most search engines use a robot (sometimes called a 'spider') to build their index. This robot is an automated program that follows links in web pages all over the Internet. For each page, it remembers the URL and determines, by many techniques, what the relevant concepts are on that page.

The 'simplest' way to get your site ranked first in each search engine is to make it the most relevant page on the Web for your given keywords. In order to do this you need to know which keywords visitors are using to find your site. You also need to know what other sites are out there and you need to decide what makes your site more relevant than others, sometimes by understanding how individual search engines determine relevancy.

Keywords and META Tags

The Search Words data show you what keywords most visitors are using to find your site. When you are listing your site with search engines, you can use these data to decide which keywords are most important to your visitors. When choosing keywords to represent your site, you will want to make these most prominent. The Search Word data can also highlight gaps in your current keyword listings. If you would expect some keywords to be common and they are not listed, then perhaps you have not taken the necessary steps to ensure that search engine robots can find those keywords on your site.

When a search engine robot looks at the pages on your site ("crawls your site"), it looks at different elements of the HTML file to determine what topics it is relevant to. Most search engines put extra weight on the words used in the page title. Also, many search engines display the page title on their search results page, so it is imperative that your keywords are included in the title and that the title is meaningful to the visitors who are reading it in that context. You can also help most search engines by giving hints about the keywords for a given page. This is done by including an HTML tag in the header of the page. This 'META tag' is never seen by most web users, but robots read it to find your keywords. The tag is in a form like this, giving a comma- or space-separated list of words or phrases that the engine should index you page with:

```
<meta name="keywords" content="keyword, a key phrase,
another phrase">
```

Each page on your website should contain one of these tags. Some sites like to use the same keywords for each page, others like to customize the keywords to make the pages most relevant to the search. In addition to title and META tag, some robots will look at the content of the page. Usually, they only inspect the first 100 to 200 words. So you should make sure that the text that starts each page includes those same keywords and any additional information that defines the page or site.

Some search engines also include support for a description META tag. This description is used in place of the first paragraph or so of text when shown to the reader. If you can summarize your page in a few lines, it may be advantageous to add this to some pages.

Also, some search engines, such as Google, put extra weight on keywords in the description META tag. The format for this tag would be something like this:

```
<meta name="description" content="Insert a few sentences
here to describe or summarize the content of the page"
```

When choosing which keywords to include in your report, you may want to select a different metric than Hits. Table 11.8 shows the number of Average Steps, Goals, and Value for each word. Whatever metric you choose to qualify your keywords by, you should be able to select the top 10 or 15 words and use those when building your META tags and deciding what to include in your titles and first few paragraphs of content.

Table 11.8 Search word data related to goals and value

Average Steps	*Goals*	*Goals % of Hits*	*$Value*	*Word*
4.2	80	7.3	1.6	Manager
5.0	120	19.2	2.2	Model
6.0	135	26.3	2.89	Best Practice
3.8	42	27	3.8	Sample
7.2	28	5	0.17	Tool
2.2	9	24	0.78	Data

Competitive Analysis

Now that you have determined what keywords are important to your site, you will want to find out how you are ranked and how other sites are ranked with the same keywords. Using the Search Engine data, Table 11.9, looks at the top five to ten entries to start your analysis.

Table 11.9 Hits by Referring Domain

Hits	*Referring Domain*
4864	Google
864	Yahoo
2186	MSN

For each listed engine, go to the search site, type in one of the keywords or phrases you have chosen, and navigate through until you find a link to your site. If it is not in the top five pages, it is as good as not listed. In fact, very few people will even navigate to the second page of results. Do this for each keyword or phrase at each engine and see where you rank. While you are finding your listing, look at the top two or three sites for each search. These sites should give you a good idea about what kind of content the engine finds relevant to the topic and may provide insight on how to improve your page to get a higher ranking. You can also use the "View Source" or equivalent function in your web browser to see what keywords they put in their META tags.

Improving Your Ranking

Getting your listing near the top of major search engines is a complex science. There are whole books written about it and services that can provide expert advice and tools to assist you. However, with the knowledge you have gained from your search data, you can start doing some of it on your own. Now that you know what keywords are important, make sure that they are included in the title, META tags and first paragraph or two of content on each relevant page. Re-submit your site for update with the engines and monitor the results.

The other major factor in search engine listings is 'link popularity'. Popularity refers to the number of other relevant sites that link to your site. If your site is referenced by other sites with the same topic, then yours is assumed to be more relevant. This technology was pioneered by Google and is now used by most major search engines. If you can get other sites that discuss your topics to link to your site, that is a good start. Of course if your site is the most relevant site, then it is in the interest of those other sites to link to yours.

Updating My Listing

Search engines crawl your site with a robot. The paths of these robots and their traffic can be analyzed. Not all robots are from search engines, but you can usually identify them because they have the phrase "Search Indexer" in them. Using the Known Robots data, you can determine how recently your site was last indexed by each engine. When all other factors are equal (which is rare) search engines often list most recently crawled sites first, so you want your site to be crawled on a regular basis. However, because of the volume of information they have to process, search engines will punish you if you submit your site too often, especially if there has been no change to the content of the site. Sites that have recent Last Hit Dates in the Known Robots data you can safely ignore for submission purposes—they are already crawling your site regularly, so you do not need to help them find it. If there are important engines that have not recently indexed your site, then you will probably want to resubmit to their indexing queue.

There are a plethora of services available on the web to assist you in submitting your site to search engines. Some will claim they submit you to 400 search engines, some 4,000. A quick look at your Search Engine data will tell you that beyond the first ten engines, the rest are insignificant. When you filter out the engines that have recently crawled your site, you are left with a very manageable number of submissions that should not take too long to do by hand. For each search engine, go to the website and look for a submission link (usually near the bottom).

Increasing Crawl Frequency

Most robots crawl sites by following links. These links, however, are often sorted by popularity. If a site is referenced from many other pages, then the robot will promote it in the queue for crawling. So, in addition to increasing your ranking (on search engines such as Google), getting other sites to link to yours will increase your index frequency. This reduces the number of manual submissions you need to do and makes your work easier.

Pay-for-Placement

Many search engines are now offering priority placement for people who want to pay a fee. Other engines offer special fee-based listings. When evaluating the available options, be sure to read the terms carefully. For example, while Overture will get your listing into most of the top search engines, Yahoo! will not guarantee a listing, even if you pay for it. Yahoo!'s service is for priority handling of your listing request and does not guarantee a placement.

As with any marketing campaign, you will need to experiment to decide whether these are worth it. While some sites have great success with pay-for-placement, others see no change in results. You should start by submitting a few URLs, bidding a reasonable price and then carefully monitoring the results. These services will give you reports on click-throughs, but you can also use your own web analytics reports to monitor it. The easiest way is to set up specific URLs that you submit to each site for each keyword.

Note: *This entire process we have been discussing is called Search Engine Optimization (SEO) and we have only touched the tip of the iceberg. There are numerous 'tricks' to get search engines to find you, but it all boils down to the fact that if your site is the most relevant for a given topic then it is in the search engine's best interest to rank you highest.*

Advertising and Revenue Analysis

Advertising plays a major role in all marketing, and has become an indispensable tool in revenue generation and site promotion on the Web. In traditional media, advertisements are measured and analyzed with estimates—impressions, reach, and other quantities are guessed from samples. Newspapers and magazines do not really know how many readers they have; only how many copies they printed. Radio and television stations can only guess at the number of viewers at any given time.

Table 11.10 Impression by each ad

% of Hits	*Hits*	*Request*
42.00	16212	/ads/campaign1.gif
28.20	10121	/ads/campaign2.gif
23.01	8522	/ads/campaign3.gif

On the Web, we have log files and a system that tracks every hit and click, so we can know almost exactly how many impressions an advertisements has (we cannot know how many people are sitting in front of a computer and other factors). We can estimate other quantities, such as reach, more accurately, because our data are virtually complete. In the Advertising data shown in Table 11.10, each Hit is a single request for the given advertisement. This is the same thing as an impression in traditional marketing. So using the Advertising data, you can see that `/ads/campaign1.html` had maximum hits or impressions.

You can define a value for every page hit. If your site hosts advertising, then every single page may be a spot you could place an ad. By giving the cost per impression you are charging (e.g., 0.05 would be $50 CPM) as the value of a page view, you can then calculate what your potential revenue is from advertising.

If you know that every visitor to your site is a potential buyer, and that every page hit makes a visitor more likely to purchase, you may be able to determine as estimated value of a page view in terms of real income using this simple formula:

Avg. Sale * Conversion Rate/Pages per Visit = Page View Value

For example, perhaps your site merely promotes your restaurant. But you have determined that 4% of your visitors actually make it to your restaurant (Conversion Rate). Assuming your site averages 3 page views per visit and the average sale at your restaurant is $48, you can estimate the value of your page views:

$48 * .04 / 3 = $0.64.

Similarly, you can assign a value to page views as a cost to estimate your bandwidth usage costs. For example, if 12,169M bytes were transferred for 14,284 pages, this gives an average of 872 bytes per page. If you know your bandwidth charge you can use the following formula to figure your cost per page (remember to convert usage costs into dollars per byte, not dollars per megabyte or gigabyte):

Bandwidth Charge * Bytes per Page = Average Cost per Page

In a similar context, you can do cost analysis by connecting costs to particular events. For example, if you have a credit card order page on your system, you can give this a value of the cost of each credit card transaction (assuming the cost is a flat fee—if it is related to the size of the purchase, then you can use an average charge as an estimate). If you track your own advertisements that are on other sites, you can assign the impression cost to each advertisement to get an estimate of your advertising expenses.

Lost Revenue

When modeling your revenue and costs in your analysis, you will also want to consider lost revenue. Are customers leaving the site instead of buying? Are some leads less profitable than others? What can be done to alleviate this?

When visitors do not become buyers, you want to know why. One of the first places to look is the Visit Exit Point data. This data would show what the last page in a visit probably was. By analyzing the content of exit pages on your site, you may be able to come up with ways to improve the access and usability so visitors can become buyers.

Another way to determine lost revenue is by qualifying leads. Earlier in this chapter we discussed about referrers as leads and also covered how to make search engines deliver more valuable leads. In each case you can use Values to qualify the leads. When you have assigned values to revenue- or cost-generating events, you can use these data to see which leads rank best and capitalize on those. Then make efforts to remove the references at lead generators that do not produce valuable visitors.

Bandwidth Management

So far we have discussed business goals and associated web metrics. Like any other business driven by IT, online business channel also requires effective infrastructure management. In the sections below, we will discuss relevant infrastructure related metrics.

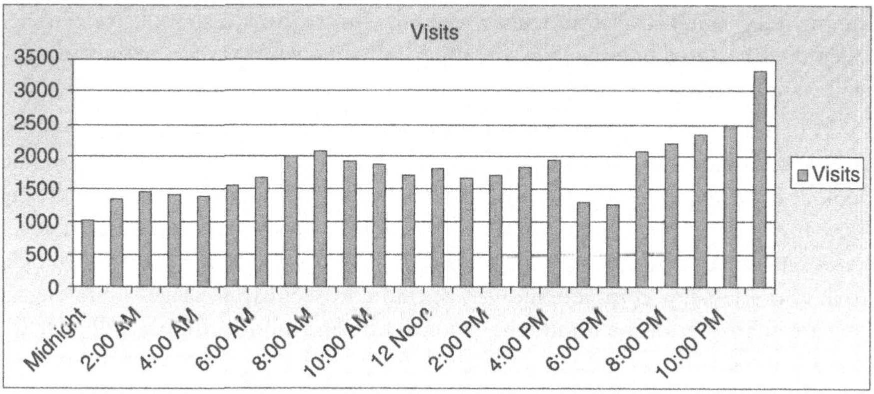

Figure 11.4 Visits data during the day.

Total Bandwidth

By tracking how many bytes you send to users over the course of any given period or for particular files you can get to know the number of bytes transferred and average transfer rate (BPS) for each month. You can also track other useful metrics regarding how much bandwidth is used, what speed connection is required to meet that volume (with adjustment for growth) and which requests are consuming the most bandwidth.

Most co-location facilities and Internet access providers limit your bandwidth usage in two ways. First, you are limited physically by the maximum available bandwidth on your Internet connection. This limitation is the peak number of bits per second (BPS) that you can transfer and affects transfer rates during your peak usage times. Second, you are generally charged on a monthly basis for the total amount of bandwidth you consumed (or the number of bytes you transferred) during that period. When someone makes a request for a page, he sends a small number of bytes over the network to your server. Then your server responds with a file or other object for the visitor. The byte counts do not include the original request or the headers that may have been sent with the response. Generally these two items are not very significant, especially if your files are large. A typical request may be 120 bytes while a response, including the file sent, is more likely to be about 15,000 bytes. When you compare your byte totals in Summary to those your access provider or co-location facility give you, theirs will generally be higher. If you have just simple web traffic you can expect about a one or two percent increase. If you use cookies, or provide other services, like email or ftp, then the actual bandwidth usage could be significantly higher.

Hence, based on the business goals, it is important to analyze your bandwidth usage and optimally determine what your connection speed should be to best serve your visitors. In order to accommodate the peak usage that your server experiences, you target a speed that is comparable to a common line speed several times the peak hourly usage you have in your logs. This allows room for momentary "burst" traffic and some room for future growth as well. You will not need the suggested line speed all the time, but when your server is really busy, you will want to have it so that your users are not waiting too long to access your site.

When determining how much bandwidth you should have, you also want to decide on a monthly contract rate. Rather than using the peak usage, you should look at how many bytes you transfer, total, each month. You can start analyzing how many bytes per month you have transferred on average and gives transfer rates for the last few months. The average is a good place to start, but you should look at the last few complete months of traffic to see if your usage is growing. If you are analyzing in the middle of a month, the last month will have a low byte-count and skew the average down slightly. Alternately, you can look at the average bytes transferred per recent day to see what your usage was in the past two to three weeks. Multiply this number by 30 to get an approximate monthly usage requirement. Depending on your provider's pricing you should probably choose the contract that offers slightly more than the greatest of all these monthly usage numbers.

While your average bandwidth usage may be low, your peak usage is often many times higher. It is important that your connection speed is large enough to accommodate the times of peak usage on your site. When many users access your site simultaneously they each get a portion of your available bandwidth. The fastest connections are slowed down by the other connections happening at the same time. When the site is very busy, the available bandwidth for the user with the fastest connection may be significantly slower and your visitors will notice this. For example, if three users come to a page at one time and each is downloading six images, that is 18 simultaneous connections. If another user is downloading at the same time, she will only get 1/19 of your available bandwidth. If your server has a 1 MBPS connection, it means each user is getting 56 kbps. That is about the same as a good analog modem. If these users all have a DSL line or a cable modem, they will be used to connections ten to twenty times faster. Imagine how much worse it would get if you have six or eight people connecting at once.

> Bandwidth speeds are measured in bits-per-second (BPS), while usage is measured in bytes. In Summary's calculations there are nine bits per byte, so when comparing the number of bytes transferred to the average BPS, you need to multiply by a factor of nine. For example, if your average bytes per day is 177 million, then your average BPS would be about 18,438: 177,000,000 / 86,400 seconds per day * 9. These units are common practice, so your reports should correspond to rates and values you get from your provider without any conversions. (The actual number of bits per byte varies depending on the transmission line so there may be a difference of exactly +/- 11%.)

In the previous section we discussed suggested bandwidth, which is based on your peak usage. Rather than increase your available bandwidth (if it is less than the recommended), you can try to manage the bandwidth usage on your site by analyzing the cause of peak usage and compensating for that.

If these peak hours or days correspond to promotions that you are running on your site, whether an email campaign, radio or television advertisement or other marketing tool, you can reduce the peak usage by carefully managing the campaign. If you spread out the campaign over a longer period of time, you can spread out the hits and reduce the load on your server for that short time. For example, if you run an email campaign for a new product release, and simultaneously announce it on several product news sites, you could run the email campaign the week before you release your announcement (perhaps as a "pre-order" special for existing customers), and even spread out the email campaign over several days.

Sometimes you cannot control the volume of requests. In that case, you may be able to control the size of them to help reduce peak usage. The Requests by Bytes data and the Directories by Bytes data can help you diagnose which files or parts of your site are consuming the most bandwidth.

Requests by Bytes shows the total number of bytes consumed by each file on your site, ranked by percent of recent bytes. So the top few items on the list are those that are currently the largest load. Where possible, you could reduce the size of these files.

Using the Directories by Bytes data, you can make similar adjustments for directories (or sections) of your site that are affecting your peak usage. If one directory is significantly higher than others, you can look at the files in that directory and try to reduce the size, where possible.

Sometimes, it is not particular files or directories that consume bandwidth but particular types of files. The Bytes by File Type can give you details of the top ranking media by byte. If you have downloadable content, such as software programs or documentation, you can expect these to rank highly. Graphics file types (gif, jpg, png, etc.) will also have a large percent of bytes. If you have audio or video content, these could be very consumptive. Often, with graphics, audio and video, you can adjust the compression level to reduce the size of the files (at the loss of some quality.)

Broken Links

Despite the best efforts of designers, even simple sites can end up with broken links in them. This looks bad and frustrates customers even resulting in loss of customers and revenues, so you would want to know which pages on your site failed and the local referrer that was associated with it. You can use these data to quickly find and fix the links.

Bad Referrers

When links on your site are broken, it is easy to fix them. However, often other sites will have links to your site that do not work, either because the link has a typo in it, or because it links to a page that existed at one point, but no longer does.

Sometimes a failed request could be because the requested file does not exist or because it is a CGI program or dynamic web page that produced an error when it was trying to run. The failed requests that are not the Bad Links or Failed Referrers are generally created by robots. This is because those reports are dependent on referrer information and most robots do not provide that. If you make changes to your site and remove pages, then robots may try to request the old pages that were previously in their indexes just to see if the pages are still there (and to see if the content has changed.) You will also likely see some typos from users who tried to type a URL to your site into their browser but accidentally typed it incorrectly.

Hijacked Graphics

The graphics that you have on your site are something you have put effort and time (and perhaps money) into developing to represent your business or service. They are indicative of your brand or service and are a valuable part of the consistent image you present to your customers. The way the Web works, however, it is not very hard for another site to simply include a reference to graphics from your site in their pages. The HTML img tag can tell a visitor's browser to retrieve graphics from anywhere else on the Web, as illustrated in

Fig. 11.5, not just the same site the page is on. When this happens, the visitors at the other site may have no idea that the graphics belong to you. This behavior is referred to as 'Graphics Hijacking'.

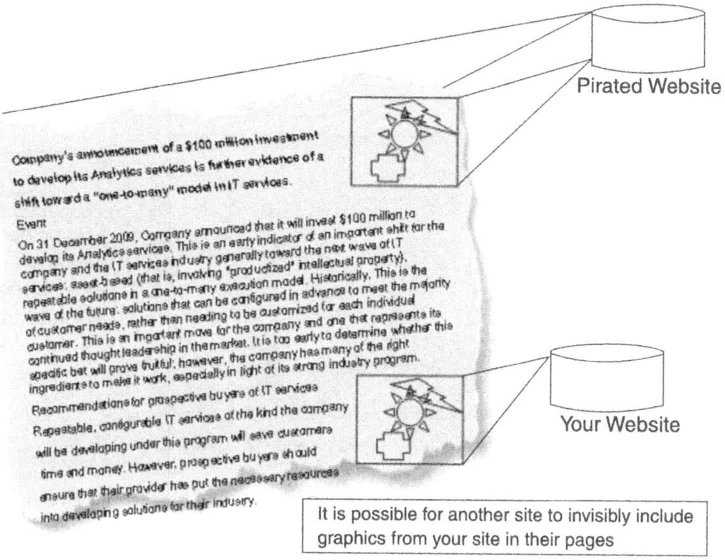

Figure 11.5 Hijacked graphics.

Table 11.11 Domain hijacking data showing which websites are using your graphics

Hijacks	*Hijacks % of Hits*	*Referring Domain*
23	0.9	Google.com
9	66.9	MyNews.com
13	1.4	Ajeeb.com

This does not necessarily mean that those domains are hijacking graphics, but it is a good indication. If you have setup an agreement with partner websites to allow them to include references to your graphics in their site (for example, linking to your logo to promote your product or linking to your advertisements to host on their sites), these instances will also show up in your data.

Another entry that you will commonly find is 'google.com' (and other Google sites). Google (and some other search engines) have image search tools. When Google users search for images they will get links to graphics on your site but not the pages. Fortunately, Google lists the page that the image is located on so visitors know where it came from.

Note: If a malicious user really wants to steal your graphics without you knowing she can simply save the image to her computer and copy it to her website. Saving an image produces the same request that viewing it in the first place does (in fact web browsers just make a copy of the image they have already cached, so you never get a request for the 'save' action if the image was already viewed.) This behavior is effectively impossible to detect. However, if the user tries to copy all the images (or a large number of images) from your site, then this can look significantly like 'mirroring' behavior.

INVESTIGATING TROUBLEMAKERS

Unusual Access Patterns

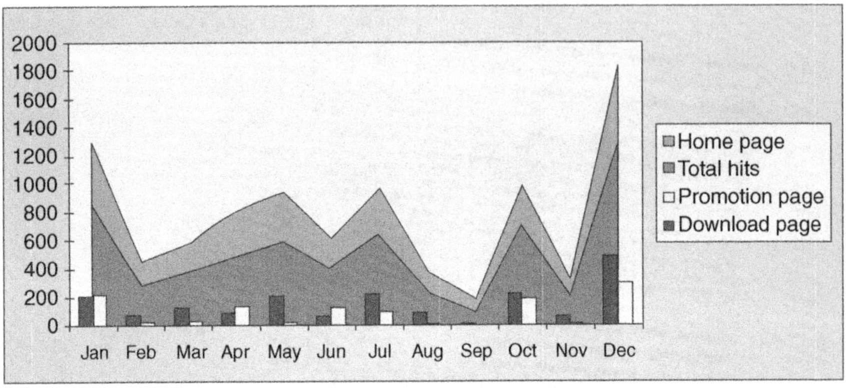

The company promotes and sells a whole lot of office and school stationary items through its online channel. At the beginning of every quarter the company puts out promotional offers, discounts, etc and runs ad campaigns in local print media as well.

Figure 11.6 Access patterns over a year.

In the course of running and managing a website or server, you may come across traffic patterns that stand out in relation to the regular traffic. Often these will be explainable, such as the `/ads/promotion.html` peak during the promotion months (Jan, Apr, Jul and Oct) in Figure 11.6. Other times you won't immediately recognize what caused the change in pattern such as May and Dec. Given the depth of data on various aspects of website usage, you generally will only notice these patterns on the higher-level reports, first, and will need to do some investigatory processing to find out what is going on.

When you dig deeper into an unusual access pattern you may realize that it was an intentional attack by a malicious visitor. People can cause all sorts of problems on your site if they want to. Most commonly, you will be dealing with some sort of Denial of Service attack, or similar brute force attack that causes excessive loads on your server (this is often when the attacks or trouble becomes apparent.) As a common example, let us assume that our site manager notices an extremely large volume of hits throughout the month in May and Dec. By digging into the details of those hits, she can find out where they came from, what period they covered, and sometimes, what the troublemaker was trying to do.

Because the site manager noticed the hit spike during particular days, she reprocesses the logs to get just that traffic. Then, looking at the host details, she can see which particular host or hosts show peak traffic for the day she has selected. The data in Table 11.12 shows that two hosts, 192.168.0.100 and 192.168.0.12, have significantly more hits than any other hosts.

Table 11.12 Hosts accessing data

Host	*% of Hits*	*Hits*
192.168.0.100	21	35966
192.168.0.12	32	40240
10.0.30.12	0.56	321
10.0.15.217	0.13	462

The site manager then filters traffic by just these hosts. She processes the logs again to build the new reports and looks at the all requests data to see which items these users were requesting.

Table 11.13 Page request data

% of Current Hits	*Request*
78.8	/members/
7.8	Home Page
7.49	/Downloads

Table 11.13 shows that the majority of hits from these two hosts went to the page `/members/` which is a secure access page to allow downloading of their commercial software tool. From this she deduces that this was a simple brute force attack to try to get into the members section of the site by someone who did not have a registration login. To verify this, she checks the authorized user access data for these particular hosts and discovers that these hits tried many different user names over the course of the day.

Based on her analysis, she can take cautionary steps to help improve the security of the site or to try to confront the individuals who were attempting to break in. For example, she might recommend to the developers that they implement a limiting algorithm on the login code so that if a given host fails to login after ten attempts, then the host will be blocked from login attempts for the next hour.

Bad Robots

Troublemakers are not always individuals. They may be automated tools that are either poorly behaved or run by users who do not understand the proper conduct for using them. Properly behaved robots abide by some self-enforced rules to make sure that they do not adversely affect your server's performance. Robots should not make large numbers of requests in a short period of time. Most robot etiquette suggests at least a second between requests. Some robots round-robin their requests across many servers so that they may have several minutes or hours between subsequent requests to your site. Well-behaved robots also adhere to the standard for robot exclusion, which states that they must read the file `/robots.txt` in the root of each website and only index content that they are allowed, through that file, to index. Unfortunately, there are some robots or spiders that do not behave according to these rules. They may not be malicious, just poorly designed or implemented. For example, some robots will crawl your site and download large files, like trial software or documents that you make available, even when the indexing tool that they are connected to cannot process those file types. If this becomes common, it can lead to excessive bandwidth usage and put a drain on your server resources. The same can be true for dynamically generated pages. If you have a database-driven section of your site that creates dynamic pages that link to more database content, robots can quickly become mired in loading the entire volume of data available for indexing. If the links that your dynamic site makes are all unique, the robot can get lost in an endless loop of loading new pages, even when they may be the same as those already loaded.

Robots generally make subsequent requests from the same host. You can use the host data to see if any hosts are making a large number of requests. You can then filter traffic from just this host and examine the request report. If there are about the same number of requests to each page on your site, it is likely that the action is caused by a robot. If the requests are in a high volume over a very short period of time (i.e., several requests per second) then you can almost guarantee that this is the behavior of a robot. You can also examine hosts that request a large number of pages (robots do not usually load graphics), or that have a large number of visits (some robots spread out their crawls over a long time such that they appear to 'visit' the site for each page they index.)

Denial of Service Attacks

Some robots are malicious. The commonest of these are ones designed to implement a Denial-of-Service (DoS) attack. DoS attacks are accomplished by flooding a server with a very large volume of requests such that the server becomes too busy to handle all traffic and the website (or other service) is no longer available for normal users. Usually, these DoS attacks will request dynamic pages or large objects from the server to consume bandwidth and processing power as effectively as possible. If your server becomes slow and unresponsive, you can use host report to see which host originated the attack. Using the all requests data you can often tell which pages or files on your site are being requested and make adjustments to reduce the load those put on your server (where possible.)

Unfortunately, there is a more complicated attack, called Distributed Denial of Service (DDos), where the flood of requests comes from a range of hosts. This makes it harder to determine who is responsible for the action (in fact most DDoS attacks are carried out by worms that have infected the systems that are hitting your server.) In addition, a Distributed Denial of Service attack is harder to detect, because you do not see the obvious traffic flood from a single host. In fact, it can often look like a large flux of regular traffic to the site. You may still notice the traffic spikes in the All Requests report, telling you that certain pages on your site are receiving much more traffic than expected. If these sites are either high-load (e.g., they require complex database queries) or are large files and not regular requests of your normal visitors, this is you clue that your site is under attack, and not just flooded with a large volume of visitor traffic.

Worms

Worms are malicious robots that look for security vulnerabilities in web (or other) servers that allow them to break in and infect the server, thus propagating themselves across the Internet. On the infected server they may implement a Distributed Denial of Service attack, as described previously, they may cripple the server, making it fail or even destroy the data stored on it, or they may open a 'back door' allowing intruders to access the system and read, change or destroy any information on it. Some of the more well known worms are Code Red and Nimda. These two achieved notoriety in 2001 by infecting most Microsoft IIS web servers on the Internet.

Table 11.14 Data showing footprint of Nimda or other worms

Hits	*Request*
8.81%	/scripts/root.exe?/c+dir
7.81%	/MSADC/root.exe ?/c+dir
7.34%	/c/winnt/system32/cmd.exe ?/c+dir
7.34%	/d/winnt/system32/cmd.exe?/c+dir

Web server worms can generally be easily detected by looking for access patterns in the All Requests report because they propagate by exploiting vulnerabilities in the web server request processing. Table 11.14 shows the footprint of Nimda worm attack as it might appear in the all requests data of an infected server.

Note that on a server that is not vulnerable to such an exploit, these request would be in the Failed Requests report, indicating that the worm did not gain access through any of these methods.

Limitations of Metrics Accuracy

Throughout this chapter it is stated that the numbers given do not necessarily correlate to any real-world values. Because of the way the web was designed and the systems installed to make it more efficient, the values that we track and metrics that we report on may not correlate to real world quantities that you want to know. When analyzing web metrics data, you should understand the definitions of the metrics and the limitations of them in regards to any expected quantities that you may want.

For example, while we can count hits or requests for advertisements on the server, this may not be the same as the number of impressions the advertisement had. The reason we cannot count the exact number of impressions is because when a visitor browses your site your server may never get a request for the content she views. HTTP protocol (which is how web browsers and web servers communicate) involves distinct requests for individual items from a server. This is why a "request" for the home page of your site, for example, can result in multiple requests (or hits) to the server (one for the page and additional requests for each graphic or other item referenced by it).

In order to improve performance, all modern browsers implement a technique called caching. The images that you get when you go to your home page are often the same ones you get on other pages of the site. The browser detects this and rather than asking for the image across the (possibly slow) Internet connection, it grabs a copy that it saved on your computer. This makes it much faster to load subsequent pages from the website. In fact, most users depend on this feature to make web surfing manageable and enjoyable. Major Internet Service Providers, to improve performance even more, add caching on their service. The affects requests from all their users, across session, as we will discuss shortly.

However, this means that your web server only sees the request for the graphic the first time it is used. A typical visit from a user may span four or five pages, and load ten graphics (rather than the forty or fifty that would be loaded without caching). The sticky part comes when a visitor navigates to a page that has already been viewed (by hitting the back button, for example). The browser loads the version of the page that is cached and you never get any indication that he viewed it again. If you are looking at counting advertising impressions or want to know how many home page views you had, you are not getting a complete count.

Visit Detection

As discussed earlier, there is no absolute way of knowing what requests comprise a single visit to your site. Each request made by a browser is an independent transaction. In order to track visits, first you need to understand what constitutes a visit. Let's see the following illustration—looking at all requests from a given host (or cluster, where appropriate) that are bounded by 30 minutes of inactivity could be a starting point. This means that if a visitor browses your site, then leaves his computer for a half hour and comes back and browses again, it will be counted as two visits. On the other hand, if the user leaves his computer for 25 minutes, it will be counted as a single visit. You can play around the number of minutes of inactivity threshold as appropriate to your business goals, but no matter what you choose there may be instances where what you count as two visits a visitor may consider one (or vice versa.)

On top of that, if you factor in the fact that some requests are never received by the server (because they are cached), it is conceivable that a visitor could "browse" your site, entirely out of his cache for a half hour or more and register two visits when he never left your site at all. It is also possible that the visitor browsed your site all day from his cache and never made a single request to your server. No visit will be registered at all in your logs. Finally, some users will keep windows open to multiple sites and switch between them. This can affect the visit because there could easily be half-hour gaps between logged requests from such 'multitasking' users.

PROXIES, CACHES AND FIREWALLS

Everyone who connects to the Internet goes through an access provider at some point. For individuals and home users, this is usually an Internet Service Provider like Airtel or Reliance, etc. These access providers also want to reduce the amount of traffic they carry and want to increase the efficiency and security of their service. In the same manner, businesses need to share Internet access and maintain the security of their internal network. To do this, these companies usually employ special servers called Web Caches, Proxies and Firewalls. Each of these servers affects the way requests to your website are seen by your server.

Caches

To reduce the network load, major Internet Service Providers implement web caching servers across their service. A web cache is similar to a browser cache except that it works for all users on the system. A browser cache recognizes files that have already been requested and gets them from the cache instead of the Internet for a single user. A web cache does this for multiple users. Imagine that a user connecting through a major provider browses your site. The same day another user (who may be in a different city or state) also navigates to your site. Every page that the first user saw is pulled from the provider's cache by the web caching server rather than from your web server. These requests are never registered on your server. You may have no record that the second visitor even saw your site.

There are different kinds of web caches, depending on what the provider has determined is most important to cache. Some caching servers will only store graphics; others only pages; some store anything. Generally the caches store items for a limited period of time, perhaps a day or a week. When the time had elapsed, the caching server will send your web server a query to see of the file has changed the next time it is requested. This query is much smaller than the original file so it uses less bandwidth.

Caches are an important part of the user experience, so while it reduces the request information that you log, it increases the performance of the site in the user's experience. However, there may be some pages that you do not want cached: live data, news pages where new material appears often, or other dynamic content.

Note: There are several ways you can tell caching servers not to cache your page or tell them when the content expires. Not all servers support it, but many of the more common ones do.

The first method involves adding HTTP 1.1 header fields to the response when a page is sent out. You can also use the 'Expires' header to tell how long the document will be valid for. (The Expires header is an HTTP 1.0 field so it may work on more systems.)

If you do not have the ability to influence the headers on a particular page, you can insert meta-tags that will take the place of them. Meta-tags are rarely read by caches (because they do not read the page, just the headers) but do influence browser caching. The meta-tag uses an 'http-equiv' attribute to indicate that it should be treated as if it were an HTTP header. For example, the following would tell supporting browsers not to cache a page:

```
<meta http-equiv= "Cache-Control" content= "no-cache">
```

Proxies

While caches will alter the amount of data you can collect for content metrics, proxy servers will significantly affect the value of data based on host counting, including visit tracking metrics. A proxy server acts as an intermediary between a group of users and the outside world. Often this takes the form of a firewall to secure a company's internal network to allow one Internet connection to work for many users (many web caches also act as proxies).

When a proxy exists between a group of users and your website, you see all requests from those users as if they came from the one host (the proxy server). Even if three different people at a company are browsing your site, it looks like they are all one host to your web server. As visit tracking depends in part on the host making the request, this can make the visit statistics much different from actual visits. Many proxies contain web caches and most web caches act as a proxy so the effects of both of these are seen at once.

Firewalls

Firewalls are computers that usually reside between a company's internal network and the Internet to secure the internal network from malicious public access. Many firewalls, because of their function and location, work like proxies. Some implement web caches. In addition to proxying visitor traffic, firewalls limit what can be sent in either direction. Often the limitation is by protocol. If all of your traffic is HTTP (i.e., a website), then that traffic should pass through. However, if your site uses Java applets that connect to your server, that would be a different protocol and probably blocked by the firewall (because it is unknown.) Some firewalls also limit or strip content as well, such as Java applets, plugins and their content (like Shockwave Flash!). Striping firewalls will even remove cookies or referrer information. Because of this it may be very hard to distinguish individual visits on the other side of the firewall and reduce the amount of referrer information you have to analyse. (For security, it is in the interest of the firewall to make requests as anonymous as possible.) The hosts will likely be the same (proxy problem), and sometimes the request will be modified so as to make them all appear to be from a single computer.

User Agents

Some user agents (or browsers) allow the user to change what they identify themselves as to your server. The Opera web browser allows the user to choose one of several more common browser that it can masquerade as. Therefore, all reports based on user agent data, are only as good as the information collected. This includes the Browsers, Browser Brands, Platforms, Known Robots and Agent reports.

Referrers

Referrer information is also easily forged. Opera (again) allows the user to configure it to not provide any referrer information. Some firewalls will strip these data from HTTP requests. Neither of these is forging, but it does affect your results and counts. There have been reports of some unscrupulous "marketers" who have used robots to fill logs with referrer information pointing back to their web site. The only reason for this would be to attract the attention of those reading the reports. This kind of traffic is easy to spot and remove with a filter. There is not much other value in faking a referrer, so it is not very commonly done.

Hosts

It is not easy to fake the host IP number that your server receives with a request. Unlike user agent and referrer information, which is included in the HTTP header (a set of text lines sent before the content), the host is included in the TCP wrapper around each packet sent over the network. In order for someone to fake her IP address, she must change her TCP stack (or TCP driver) on her computer to submit fake information. Tools to do such are certainly available and there are people in the world who have the skill to do this, but there is no commonly available software that allows this activity. On the other hand, it is simple to fake the host and domain name returned for a given IP address, but this is rarely done. You can assume that the bulk of your host-based data are accurate, especially when aggregated. However, when using the host information to identify an individual visit, especially one of malicious intent, you should be skeptical of its validity.

Validity of Reports

If you have reached thus far, I am sure you may be having growing concerns about the validity of web analytics in general. Several factors contribute to making web analytics a valuable tool, despite the possibility for false data. First, the vast majority of users, especially those who you are most interested in, will not bother faking or omitting this information from their requests. More than 99% of web users use a major browser that accurately reports all information in requests. Robots may fake information, but how many do is hard to detect, perhaps one or two percent. As there is no way of knowing what the "correct" information is, it is usually valid enough to analyze the information that your users wished you to get from them. Because of the low quantity of falsified data, any analysis that cover data from web logs will have a very low margin of error and can be accepted as near accurate. Finally, whether the metrics you choose to track represent any real-world quantities or not, they do represent measurable quantities. In analyzing trends you can compare values from distinct time periods and produce valuable growth information from that.

Visit Time Issues

Because HTTP requests are distinct, there is no absolute way of determining which request comprises a single visit. In addition, Proxies add another factor by obscuring the source of the requests and making it hard to distinguish different users who may be visiting at the same time.

View Time

For web analytics to estimate how long a visitor was viewing a page, it generally looks at the time between the request to that page and the next one in a visit. However, the requests that make it to the server may not include all the pages viewed. Browser caches and web caches will deliver pages to users that never register on your site. So a user could browse three pages on your site, then return to a previously viewed page or two, then continue to a new one. Between the third and last, there is no request information on your server and the entire time between the requests is counted as view time for the third page. If a user has several browser windows open at once, he could be viewing another site during the time between requests to your site. If you have pages that automatically refresh themselves (because they host advertisements or contain continually updating data) then these will obviously have an average view time of about the refresh rate, which may not correlate to the time a visitor actually viewed the page.

Finally, the last page of a visit is where the user either clicks a link to a new site, types in a new URL or closes the browser. In most cases, you have no record of when she left the site. This means that you cannot determine how long the last page view was. In the case of pages that contain extended information that a user was searching for, this could be a significant amount of time that is never recorded.

Visit Duration

This last point becomes especially important when trying to calculate the length of the entire visit. Because there is no record of when the visitor left the site, visit duration, does not include the time the visitor spent on the last page of the visit.

You can set up a script so that each link that leaves your site goes through a redirector first. This means that you get one last request in your log files as the visitor is leaving. If you install this script then you can track the view time of exit pages and your visit duration will include the entire length of the visit for visitors following links to another site. Some visitors will close their browser or type in a new URL rather than following a link. The only way to track this is to install some JavaScript code on every page of your site that makes a final request to your site before the page changes.

Fortunately, there are a few techniques that can be employed to improve the accuracy of visit tracking.

Cookies

One of the most popular techniques for improving visit metrics is to configure your web server (or site) to manage 'session cookies'. A session cookie is assigned to each visitor who does not already have one. The cookie lasts until the visitor closes his browser. So each cookie is associated with all of his requests for a single session. While each visitor's browser may still cache some of the requests, two different visitors accessing your site through a web cache or proxy server will make distinct requests to your server.

Session keys in URLs

Some web servers and content servers allow you to create session identifiers that are put in the URL of each request. This usually takes the form of a CGI variable, but could sometimes be an extension of the request name. In order for this to work, every link on every page needs to be dynamically changed to include the session ID. Then, as a visitor browses through your site, each request is tagged with the session identifier, making it simple to combine the proper session codes into a single visit.

A major advantage of session identifiers in URLs is that web and browser caches will not cache the item between sessions because the request is distinct. Your server will still not get requests on repeat visits to a given page in the same session that has been cached by the visitor's browser. However, the session identifiers have some disadvantages too. First, they do not exist on the first request of a visit because the file requested did not contain an ID. So using URL-based sessions' keys will not properly identify entry pages of visits. Second, if visitors bookmark a page or publish a link to your site, it could contain a session ID which will confuse the session tracking algorithm.

Client-side Applets

While HTTP protocol is stateless—that is, there is no connection between subsequent requests from a given visitor—it may be possible to have your visitors run some software that does preserve state. For example, you could develop a custom client-side program that interfaces to the data your server provides or you could include a link to a Java applet in each page of your site that collects and returns tracking information about where your visitors are going around your site. With this technique, you can gather details about the pages visitors accessed, even if they are pulled from the browser cache. A custom solution like this could send information back to a server application on your web server and, if logged in a format similar to web logs, can be analyzed as web logs and provide the most accurate information about visitor behavior. Unfortunately, such client-side applets tend to increase the download time of your web pages. In addition, you will always get some users who have turned off Java support in their browsers and won't get your applet. Finally, some savvy customers may be upset about your information collection practice and view it as an invasion of privacy. Installing such a tool could provide deeper insight to customer behavior, but at the loss of some customers.

MOVING BEYOND STANDARD METRICS — CAN USABILITY BE MEASURED WITH WEB ANALYTICS?

Measuring usability by means of web analytics is not as easy as one would perhaps think. Traditional web metrics, to be sure, will not do the job of the number of page views per visit, the bounce rate, the number of visits per visitor, the average visit duration, etc. None of these metrics can tell us anything about navigational problems.

Although it is true that frustrated or confused visitors might end up producing many page views per visit, for example, highly engaged visitors might do the exact same.

So, the question remains: How can we identify usability problems simply by looking at click stream data? Is it possible at all?

A possible way of identifying a frustrated or confused visitor must be based on how often they go back and forth between the same pages. A visitor who runs into a problem, is likely to stop and go back to make sure he or she didn't miss something. This might even happen repeatedly since visitors are likely to double-check before abandoning the site altogether.

Consider the following click stream.

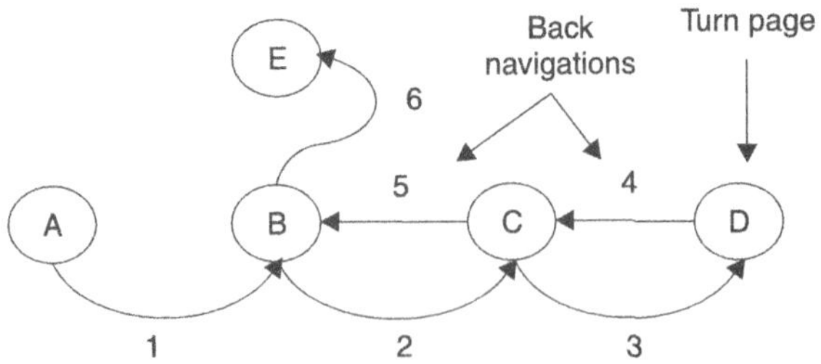

Figure 11.7 Visitor page navigation pattern.

The circles represent pages seen by a single visitor. The arrows indicate the direction of the click stream.

A is the entry page, while B and C are pages that lead to a particular interest point, D. Having looked at D, the visitor decides to go back to C, and further back to B. Finally the visitor makes a new move forward from B to E.

As can be seen from the figure, there are four forward navigations and two back navigations. We say in this case that the Back Navigation Rate is 50% (2 divided by 4). Notice also that D can be seen as a turning point in that the visitor decides to turn around here. We call D a "Turn Page".

When is a High Back Navigation Rate Bad?

Is it good or bad that the Back Navigation Rate is 50%? Well, it depends. You cannot always say it's a bad thing, because sometimes visitors just like to explore links by moving back and forth on the site. This is especially the case on the home page where visitors often explore many different links before selecting a specific page for closer inspection.

Keep it Low for Your Check-out Procedure!

However, imagine now that you are looking exclusively at a check-out procedure or a similar conversion process. In this case you certainly do not want users to go back and forth many times! A check-out procedure, to be sure, is supposed to be linear, not zigzag.

Turn Page Rate

But you can do more to identify problematic back-and-forth movements. Notice that in the click stream presented above D appear as a turn pages. This, however, happens only once. Consider now a case where the visitor produces repeated turn pages.

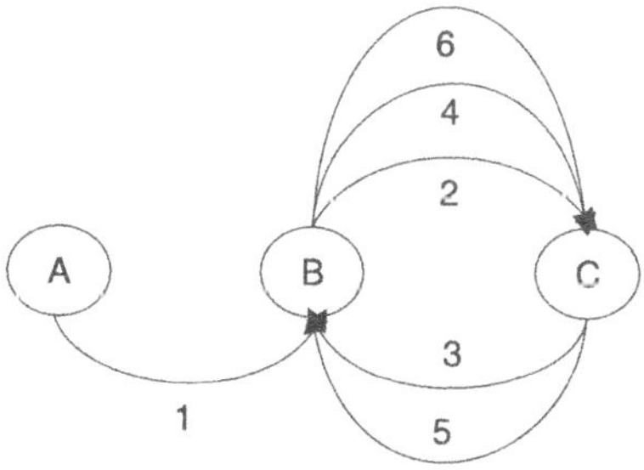

Figure 11.8 Turn page pattern.

In this case B and C are both turn pages, and both of them appear as such two times. We can capture the difference between the former and the latter click stream by a metric say "Turn Page Rate". This rate is calculated as: First, you slice your data so that you only look at turn pages. Then you divide the number of page views by visits. This rate is 1 for D in the former click stream , but 2 for both B and C in the latter.

END POINTS

Designing web analytics dashboards? Dashboards are great because they enable you to set targets, track your progress, and obtain early warnings. This is extremely important if you want to optimize your web activities on a continuous basis.

But how do you build a successful dashboard? How do you ensure relevance and impact? How do you ensure that your dashboard lead to concrete action?

Although there are many ways of building dashboards, it always boils down to the following steps:

1. Target your dashboard
2. Select only the most relevant metrics which are aligned to your business goals
3. Visualize data as much as possible
4. Include benchmarks
5. Explain the results
6. Make the dashboard interactive

Target Your Dashboard

Do you work for a large company with several departments? Are you the responsible for distributing updated reports to many different persons on a monthly basis?

In this case, you should first of all think about your target groups. How can the users of your dashboards be categorized according to their needs? And how can you best build dashboards that serve these different needs?

For example, you could operate with the following groups:

- Web team
- Marketing department
- Sales department
- IT department
- Top management

Each of these groups is likely to demand very different types of dashboards. The top management might want a high-level aggregate view of all web activities. The sales department might want a list of new hot leads. The marketing department might want to measure ROI of their online marketing activities. And so on.

Even if you are only building dashboards for yourself, you should think about the different contexts in which you will use dashboards.

What is the purpose of the specific dashboard you are building? Are you trying to measure the effects of the newsletter? Are you aiming to optimize the internal search field on your website?

The more focused you make your dashboard, the higher relevance and impact it is likely to have. Focus is also the prerequisite for the next step, namely to select the right metrics.

Select Only the Most Relevant Metrics

In case you don't already know, a metric is a measurement which quantifies the success of your web activities. Given that "success" is a subjective thing (it depends on the goal you set yourself), a measurement becomes a metric the moment you decide it to be so.

In principle, all measurements could therefore be turned into metrics. The art, however, is to confine yourself to the most important measurements.

Web analytics includes so many interesting measurements (as is evident from the discussions throughout this chapter) that it is possible to get lost and there could be a whole lot of other metrics which we have not discussed. Let me instead simply say that web analytics measurements divide into the following main groups:

Marketing metrics which measure the effectiveness of search engines, online banner campaigns, e-mails/newsletters and other traffic sources.

Engagement metrics which measure the website's ability to retain visitors, stimulate interest in content and make visitors perform certain actions.

Usability metrics which measure the effectiveness of the website's navigation, including the website's search field.

Conversion metrics which measure the website's ability to convert visitors into customers, leads or prospects.

Loyalty metrics which measure the website's ability to make visitors come back often and with short intervals and to use certain functionality repeatedly.

If you break down each of these main groups, you will get a very long list of potentially interesting measurements. From this long list, you should carefully choose a unique collection for each dashboard target group.

Visualize Data as Much as Possible

Human mind is much better at understanding visual forms than processing raw numbers. If you want your dashboard to communicate clearly and rapidly, you must carefully consider how to apply visualization. In the end visualization can be what makes or breaks your dashboard.

Visualization of data is not simply about choosing the right chart for the right numbers. It is also about using colors appropriately, arranging the information in meaningful ways, putting visual emphasis on important information, using icons for warnings, exploiting space in the most efficient manner, etc.

One of the best books I have read on data visualization for dashboards is "Information Dashboard Design" by Stephen Few. Although his views are sometimes a bit extreme, the underlying principles are no doubt sound.

Include Benchmarks

Metrics are almost useless, if they are not related to standards of good and bad values. In order to make a particular metric stand out as good or bad, you must include benchmarks.

There are several ways of doing so. The simplest type is a static value indicating your goal. For example, such a static value can be displayed in a column graph by a straight horizontal line. In gauges, you can add color ranges, e.g., green, yellow, red—indicating good, medium and bad values.

It is also possible to work with dynamic benchmarks such as a line calculated as X % increase of the value previous year or, even more sophisticated, an error band from a linear regression. Finally, benchmarks can be calculated as average values across content sections, across the company's websites and/or across competing websites.

Explain the Trends

Benchmark is one way of providing your dashboard with "context". Another important way is to include information which explains your main metrics. Ideally, a dashboard should consist of a number of data visualizations which supplement each other.

Although dashboards can rarely offer exhaustive explanations, you should at least try to include the most obvious first step in an in-depth analysis. Let's say you include a line chart showing an upward traffic trend on your website. In this case, it would be interesting to know which traffic source has contributed with most new visitors. This can be done, for example, by adding a bar chart which breaks down the traffic on sources such as direct entries, search engines, link traffic or paid-for campaigns.

Immediately the dashboard viewer will understand not only that the traffic has gone up in the last few weeks, for example, but also why this might be the case. Even if you always need to supplement with in-depth analyses, you should still think in terms of cause and effects when designing your dashboard.

Make the Dashboard Interactive

I believe it is important to distinguish between dashboards and in-depth analysis. A dashboard should enable the viewer to see all of the relevant information on a single screen. In-depth analysis, on the other hand, involves exploring data and searching for answers by applying new filters and looking at data from different angles.

The primary purpose of a dashboard is to monitor, not to analyze. Having said this, however, there is no reason for a dashboard not to support exploratory analysis. The best dashboard applications allow the viewers to move seamlessly from a passive state of monitoring to an active state of analyzing. In doing so the dashboard transforms itself into a powerful analytical application, which enables the viewer not only to see "what" is happening, but also "why".

Here are some interactive features that I consider important to a dashboard that supports analysis:

Global filters: The ability to remove unwanted data from the entire display.

Local filters: The ability to remove unwanted data from a particular chart.

Highlights: The ability to highlight selected segments across all of the views.

From static to trend: The ability to transform a single KPI (e.g., a gauge) into a trend line and vice versa.

More charts: The ability to quickly add or remove a chart to the display.

Dashboards are a powerful way of monitoring websites and distributing information to different target groups. However, they can be extremely difficult to design, because successful designs require deep insight into the needs of the target groups as well as into the field of web analytics.

REFERENCES

Weiss, Sholom; Indurkhya, Nitin; Zhang, Tong and Dameru, Fred. *Text Mining—Predictive Methods for Analyzing Unstructured Information:* Springer, 2005.

Burby, Jason; Atchison, Shane and Sterne, Jim. *Actionable Web Analytics—Using Data to Make Smart Business Decisions:* Sybex, May 2007.

INDEX

F

G

H

I

L

M

N

O

P

Q

R

S

Author's Profile

Soumendra Mohanty is currently a Senior Executive and Global AIMS Lead at Accenture. He also leads the assets and thought leadership initiatives across the technology capabilities at Accenture India Delivery Center. Mr. Mohanty has more than 15 years of experience of working on large Business Intelligence and Analytics programs for several Fortune 500 companies.

He received his masters degree in Computer and Applications from the College of Engineering and Technology, Orissa. Mr. Mohanty is widely regarded as an expert and thought leader. His experience includes information management strategy development, technology roadmap planning, DW/BI systems implementation, analytics solutions, and transforming/mobilizing large outsourcing engagements in the information management area. Mr. Mohanty has authored numerous journal and conference papers in the fields of data management and business intelligence. He has authored the book *A Practical Guide to Data Warehousing Design and Implementation,* published by Tata McGraw Hill. He is a regular speaker at many international conferences such as CII where he is the Keynote Speaker, Informatica World Conference, Business Objects World Conference and Teradata User Conference.

Made in United States
North Haven, CT
04 November 2026

21764886R00225